Of Passionate
Curves and
Desirable
Cadences

Of Passionate Curves and Desirable Cadences

Themes on Waiwai Social Being

George Mentore

University of Nebraska Press

Lincoln and London

Portions of "Grief and Shamanic Breath" have been previously published as "The Glorious Tyranny of Silence and the Resonance of Shamanic Breath," in *In Darkness and Secrecy: The Anthropology of Assault Sorcery and Witchcraft in Amazonia*, edited by Neil L. Whitehead and Robin Wright (Durham: Duke University Press, 2004). Portions of "The Archer and His Bow" have been previously published as "Society, Body and Style: An Archery Contest in an Amerindian Society," in *Games, Sports and Cultures*, edited by Noel Dyck (New York: Berg Publishers, 2000).

Library of Congress
Cataloging-in-Publication Data
Mentore, George P.
Of passionate curves and desirable cadences : themes on Waiwai social being / George Mentore.
p. cm.
Includes bibliographical references and index.
ISBN 0-8032-3175-x (hardcover : alk. paper)
1. Waiwai Indians – Social life and customs.
2. Waiwai Indians – Rites and ceremonies.
3. Waiwai philosophy.   4. Indigenous peoples –
Ecology – Guyana.   5. Guyana – Social life
and customs.   I. Title.
F2380.1.W25M46 2005
2004026289

Set in Janson by Kim Essman.
Designed by A. Shahan.
Printed by Thomson-Shore, Inc.

I dedicate
this book
to Chakana,
Kaywe,
Kimiknu,
and Jenny

Contents

List of Illustrations

Photographs

Figures

Maps

Table

Preface and Acknowledgments

This book has been many years in the making. Perhaps, some would say, too many years. I can certainly attest to the fact that the manuscript has been rewritten in its entirety at least three times—each rewrite the result of a return visit to the Waiwai. Contrary to anticipated criticism, the frustration for me has not been with issues of perfection, writer's block, or constant fieldwork stimulation, but rather with the volatile attainment of a stylistic balance. The challenge has been to arrive at a proper weight of emphasis, a comfort of prose that would reduce the distance between the Waiwai and us while at the same time retaining the necessary discomfort that alerts us to the radical and threatening distance of their otherness. This peculiar concern for balanced, weighted prose has occurred whenever I entered my classroom to teach about the "Waiwai way of life."

As a practicing anthropologist, I have found that most of my "exotic" narratives about Amerindians have gained their particular prevalence immediately after my annual visits to the Waiwai during the summer academic breaks. Upon my return, instead of persuading students to reevaluate critically their intellectual positioning of truth and power in the making of reality, these studied descriptions of mine only served further to extend their confidence in the absolutism and superiority of their world. I usually found at the end of my fifteen-week ethnography courses that for many students anthropology had become yet another, albeit scholarly, means of confirming and justifying their dominant world views. Somewhere in the midst of lecture presentations, classroom quizzes, textbook readings, essay writings, and final examinations, students had lost sight of the Waiwai and other Amerindians and found comfort in an anthropology that thoroughly represented us and our world.

Teaching and my students have quite obviously sensitized me to the problematic of balanced prose. In this book you will witness the result of my various attempts to find the proper weight of emphasis upon the similar and the different, the familiar and the strange, the soothing and the intimidating that exist between the self and the other. Yet, as I hope you will be able to confirm, I think I have also learned a good deal from my experience among the Waiwai that has had nothing at all to do with the symmetry of writing.

We anthropologists have tended to place a great deal of emphasis upon our marginality, brought about formally by the rite of passage called "anthropological fieldwork." In a world different from the one sending us out to do "field research," the individual human experience of being there can never actually be conveyed beyond the phenomenological moment and place of the physical body. Suspending the reality of this fact has been, I believe, an underlying reason for the strong focus upon interpretation in anthropology. The principal skill for producing effective ethnographic narratives continues to be the art of cultural translation. Into mediums conveying the learned and felt experiences of being there, the ethnographer translates the knowledge gained from living outside a familiar world. To be convincing, however, the ethnographer must rely on knowledge produced from both worlds. Matching the best possible descriptive terms from one world with those from the other becomes the specialized craft of the marginalized. Transforming the contents of the isolated private sensorium into objectified sharable knowledge assumes the best possible means for conveying, to the imagination of others, the experience of the field researcher.

One regret I have in not being able to perform this feat of cultural translation to the best of my ability has been the decision not to provide the names of the Waiwai who have had the greatest impact upon my research. I would have liked to name them, each and every one. I would have shared in their joy at seeing their names in print and their stories in *karita* (writing). Not that personal names mean the same to the Waiwai as they do to us or even, indeed, that personal names carry into print the same emotional impact for them as they do for us in our literate world. My disappointment lies rather with the possible negative consequence of actions that could result from matching a name to an actual individual. I also would have very much liked to contribute to the scholarship on Waiwai genealogy by providing traceable names for other researchers. But alas, the greater moral concern to conceal identities from those who might misuse such data in our now more accessible globe has persuaded me to forego this pleasure and duty. In this work all the names of principal Waiwai participants have been altered to pseudonyms.

Many people and many very special relationships have contributed to the tenor, content, and completion of the book. I have never been good with names (remembering them, that is), as for me it has always been the individual and not the name that mattered most. I hope that those whose names I do not mention, but who know how much they have contributed to this final work, will understand my deep appreciation.

In Guyana the late Denis Williams never once stepped out of his creative and intellectual roles as guide and facilitator of my research; he was always the consummate artist and scholar. To this day his widow and longtime confidant, Jennifer Wishart, continues to encourage and support not only my own, but all Guyanese Amerindian scholarship. Retired Major General Joseph Singh, whom I first met as a young officer in the Guyana Defense Force stationed in the hinterlands, not only has a passion for the "Bush" but a true and lasting love for the Waiwai. The painter George Simon, who through the years has moved in and out of an interest for archaeology, nonetheless retains his deep commitment to Guyanese Amerindian lifeways. Over the years various ministers of Amerindian Affairs and other members of the government of Guyana have been indispensable to my research. And to all those people such as Edward and Carol

Gonsalves, Basil Rodrigues, Mr. and Mrs. Magnus Stephen, the late Reverend Dainty, and Alfred Isaacs, who all helped me with the incidental and yet crucial aspects of living in Guyana, I thank you all.

In the United Kingdom I would like to express my gratitude to all my teachers in anthropology: Joanna Overing, whose influence upon my work I am only now beginning fully to comprehend, Ioan Lewis, David McKnight, Jean La Fountain, Maurice Bloch, Julian Pitt-Rivers, A. L. "Bill" Epstein, and David Harrison. For their intangible but useful contributions from outside the academy, I would like to thank Jill and Douglas Tallack.

In the United States all my colleagues from the Department of Anthropology at the University of Virginia have to be recognized, but most particularly those who had a direct affect on the manuscript as it developed. I would like, therefore, to thank Edith Turner, Roy Wagner, and J. Christopher Crocker: Edie for her constant inspiration, Roy for those long, revealing confessionals in the corridors of Brooks Hall, and Chris for his never-ending insights into structuralism. I here also offer a special thanks to my loyal confidants David Sapir and Herbert (Tico) Braun. It would be amiss of me not to mention Peter Roe and Sr. Gaspar Roca, who provided my family and me with an opportunity, when it was dearly needed, to achieve a productive and pleasant period between career moves.

Without my family, not one moment of the long journey into knowledge would have been possible. Jennifer, Kimiknu, Kaywe, and Chakana have been and remain the substantive matter in the regular indeterminacies of my life. Nothing I can say here could pay adequate tribute to them for helping me become who I am.

Finally, to the Waiwai people, I say thank you. I hope this book will serve to reveal and to celebrate not only your contributions to knowledge, but also the very possibility of our all appreciating and enjoying the many different ways of being human in the world.

A Guide to Pronouncing Waiwai Words

The following phonetic symbols have been used to write Waiwai words:

Vowels

/i/   High-front unrounded, sounds like *e* in *sleep*.
/e/   Mid-front unrounded, similar to *a* in *air*.
/ï/   High central unrounded, as in *should*.
/u/   High back rounded, similar to *o* in *moon*.
/o/   Mid-back rounded, similar to *o* in *only*.
/a/   Low front unrounded, similar to *a* in *arm*.

"Tense" Consonants

(following, in part, Robert Hawkins 1998:149)

/t/   Voiceless unaspirated alveolar stop.
/s/   Voiceless alveolar grooved fricative.
/sh[š]/   Voiceless alveopalatal grooved fricative.
/ch[č]/   Voiceless unaspirated alveopalatal affricate.
/n/   Alveolar nasal continuant.
/ñ/   Alveopalatal nasal continuant.
/r/   Alveolar with popped lateral release.
/r̃/   Alveopalatal with popped lateral release.
/y/   High front semivowel.

"Relaxed" Consonants

(following, in part, Robert Hawkins 1998:150)

/k/   Voiceless unaspirated velar stop.
/m/   Bilabial nasal continuant.
/p/   Bilabial voiceless fricative.
/w/   High back semivowel.
/h/   Central unarticulated aspiration.

Prologue

You see before you now a precautious text, once writing, once the images of an individual's experience, once part of the lived world. Tracks of the abstract, prints left behind of experiences from the past, they can, nonetheless, lead to what lies ahead, to that which has left its trace in the imagination. In this text you and I will stalk an intellectual quarry. Through a diversity of experiential terrains, we will follow the curves of a sustained passion and be ourselves perhaps entrapped by the desirable cadences of our quarry. ?

Observe the Observer Observing the Observed

> I looked up and gasped when I saw a dozen burly, naked, filthy, hideous men staring at us down the shafts of their drawn arrows! Immense wads of green tobacco were stuck between their lower teeth and lips making them look even more hideous, and strands of dark-green slime dripped or hung from their noses. (Chagnon 1968:5)

> I found Nuer pride an increasing source of amazement. It is as remarkable as their constant aloofness and reticence. I have already described how Nuer would interrupt my inquiries. I mention here three incidents typical of the cavalier way in which they treated me. On one occasion I asked the way to a certain place and was deliberately deceived. I returned in

chagrin to camp and asked the people why they had told me
the wrong way. . . .

At this same camp, at the end of my stay, when I was sick
and being removed by steamer, I asked the people to carry my
tent and belongings to the river's edge. They refused, and my
servant, a Nuer youth, and I had to do it ourselves. . . .

On one occasion some men gave me information about their
lineages. Next day these same men paid me a visit and one of
them asked me, "What we told you yesterday, did you believe
it?" When I replied that I had believed it they roared with
laughter and called to others to come and share the joke. Then
one of them said, "Listen, what we told you yesterday was all
nonsense." (Evans-Pritchard 1974 [1940]:182–83)

Fully to realise this entirely natural conception of primitive
man, the civilised student must make a great effort, and must
forget for a time all that science from its origin to the present
day has taught of the difference between man and other animals. . . . It is, therefore, most important to realise both how
comparatively small really is the difference between men in a
state of savagery and other animals, and how completely even
such difference as exists escapes the notice of savage men. (Im
Thurn 1967 [1883]:350–51)

A judgment has been passed, surreptitiously carried in the process
of writing. Within literate coherence, moving with its production
of meaning, an implicit verdict of categorical difference has been
pronounced.[1] For those objectified in the above excerpts more than
their mere difference has been decided upon, however; in each case
it becomes difficult for the reader not to be confronted by the im-
puted negativity of their otherness. Yanomami hideousness, Nuer
pride, and Amerindian animality register as the inverse to the writers' valued notions of beauty, humility, and humanness. These latter
traits play at existing in the realm of the banished as unmentioned
but ever present absences of ideal states. Of course literate closure

permits the impression of an immediate focus falling upon the anthropological Other, but at the same time it also provides us with the anthropologist as principal hero, the one with whom we sympathize, the one possessing the enlightened attributes of our civilized virtues. Heroically poised at the sharp end of Yanomami ugliness, Nuer deceit, and Amerindian savagery, the authorial anthropologist converts his apparent vulnerability into an act of moral worth.[2]

Brought about by confronting otherness in its own environment, the anthropologist's necessary exposure to self-insecurities has seemingly to await the aftermath of text in order to regain its esteem. By writing about the events and persons that once exposed his weakness, the anthropologist can reclaim his lost sense of security and, more importantly, share it out among his readers. Writing and reading serve as means to reconstruct the past and the Other, and, in so doing, to defend us (the literate) against the encroachments of time and otherness.[3] Commitment to describing the cultural logic and moral values bolstering different social systems can only but provide grounds for questioning our own modes of support. Nevertheless, the shaped innocence with which we wield the social and cultural bases of literacy helps us to avoid or to reduce the impact of self-reflective critical inquiry. It also permits the judgment of negative difference to be easily passed on to the Other.

Innocent of the play of its own collective social forces—which in exile function as if they were continuous innate entities—but also being obligated to closure around the social and cultural constructiveness of otherness, anthropological literacy often judges the Other's subjectivity as if it was beyond the enclosure of constructiveness. Hence Yanomami ugliness appears less as an effect of their socially enforced "fierceness" and more as the result of their innate individual inferiority. Nuer pride receives scathing criticism not necessarily because it results from an instilled confidence in the political use of personal violence, but because it appears as the sentiment of morally flawed individuals. Amerindian savagery, rather than being explained in the positive terms of "animism's" symbolic processes or cognitive significance, draws instead the dubious merit of demonstrating a religious belief presumably distanced in the origins of evolutionary time. I would argue that such portrayals of difference possess their own determinants; they are not the translucent effects of otherness but rather the consequence of anthropology's authorial function.

Outside, seemingly in the terrain of personal experience or natural tendencies, lives the difference of the Other's subjectivity. And because recognition of its own constructiveness remains innocently absent from anthropology's textual coherence of difference, anthropological literacy also appears as if it were similarly the product of experiential or innate subjectivity. It may seem at first as if this similitude could eradicate the evident difference between the individual as anthropological object and as authorial subject. Yet, in the process of making the experience of the Other an object of textuality, even in passing reference, anthropological literacy articulately registers the difference between itself and its object. It is particularly with the concept of innateness—that is, with the very continuousness of the natural—that the literary act attributes a deficit to the Other's subjectivity.

In the continuous world of the natural, the author's subjectivity has already arrived at a fixed, ongoing point of reality, while that of the Other is denied this reality by being somewhere on its way to this final point. For example, if it were not for their innate lack of concern for facial hygiene or perhaps the deleterious effects on their physiology of induced drugs, maybe the Yanomami could appear as attractive as the image of beauty their author has stored away but uses nonetheless as comparison. Similarly, if it were not for their natural fault of pride, the Nuer might well be blessed with humility. And the Amerindian savage, but for his lack of humanness—would he not be here with us at the absolute point? In a text struggling to reinstate its producer's once dislocated self-esteem, the anthropological Other's subjectivity readily receives the verdict of being negatively different when it recedes from the pivotal point of the author. The author, or more correctly the author's literary act, occupies that space of intermediacy between the anthropological Other and the reader. It is often thought of as central. More significantly, it is frequently considered a privileged position. This is due in part to the technique and the hard-fought-for historical legitimacy of making the Other the object of anthropological knowledge. The anthropological Other cannot "be" without the creative will and literary culture of the author. As such, the Other is made to clear the ground for the central position of the author's positive subjectivity and the judgment of its own negative difference.

Writing helps to create both the author's role and the textual objectivity of the anthropological Other. It gives form to their separate entities by drawing them together in a structural relation. It allows the author to sustain the academic discipline and to perpetuate the significant themes of the literate culture. In writing, the central and privileged subjectivity of the authorial anthropologist and the literate culture's expectancy of an anthropological genre serve to steady the distinctive character of anthropology's discursive techniques.[4] Hence they ultimately assist its character in producing more than "an epistemological attitude" (Sperber 1985:18). Through its interpretative methods and despite its generation of difference, anthropology characteristically attempts to represent the Other from the Other's perspective. But in doing so it nevertheless continues "to mistake the representation of an object for the object itself" (Sperber 1985:20).[5] This "justified crime" (Althusser 1983:14) gives to the Other, as it were, a specific anthropological existence and fixes an authoritative register for the active agency of writing. Identities gain their expressive qualities from the literary act. The kinds of identities formed are the direct result of a literate coherence. In the forming, however, anthropology must be seen as a minor contributor in a much larger project of knowledge control.

Registrations of Existence
Think of it. On or soon after each of our births, we (in Western and Western-influenced societies) immediately become the object of a meticulous textual registering; we become the central account of a coherent record and the official knowledge of a legal document.

rationalizing the & national

"official"

"social fact"

Our "Certificate of Birth," the authorized document recording the registration of our entry into the world, seeks to capture and confirm an intimate emotional moment with cold bureaucratic text. This is no ordinary corralling, no capricious corroboration. Recognized by means of the certificate, the rational classifying arm of the state reaches into the private and familial and claims a fresh ingredient for its own continuance. It does so in its national language. It does so with its own print technology. It does so with very specific notions of time and space. And in the claiming it serves to reaffirm categories of being human, not so much as the product of a state bureaucracy, but rather as the condition of a universal reality. The state, in registering the births of its citizens, sustains its own existence.

The "original" birth book held by the state as well as the certified "copy" of registration have written into themselves a generalized reality of being. Remember that the "true" copy records in the first instance not the event of the birth but rather its registration by the state. The copy gains its veracity from being an officially produced document printed on government paper, by government press, and carrying the same information as recorded in the original birth book. What it copies from the birth book is the registration of an individual's "real" entry into a particular place at a particular time—an individual with a particular name, particular gender, and particular relationship to particular people. The particularities seem essential to the kind of reality assumed to be captured by the text. A biologically specific individual becomes a specific social fact by the writing and by what the writing reinforces. The printed text of the document interrogates and demands information of a kind that augments the specific centralized authority of the state and the "naturalness" of this authority.

My birth certificate has printed on its top and center, in red serif caps, the name of the country in which my entry into this world took place—"British Guiana." In small caps immediately beneath this heading are the words "copy from the register of births in division no . . . district . . . in the county of . . . in the year . . ." In the first of the eleven headed columns below these words is a demand for the sequential number of my entry; mine was the 106th birth registered in that specific year for that specific county in that specific district in that specific division of British Guiana. In the second column, the words "when and where born" attempt to forge the event of my entry both to a definite date taken from a calendrical reckoning of time and to a definite numerically defined residential space inside the given district; here the state's demand is unequivocal. In the third column, with the heading "name if any," it further seeks confirmation of my individual presence. It is not, however, until the eleventh and final column that the request for my name delivers the implication of what it additionally seeks to know and implicitly to achieve.

With the colonial state working, at least ideally, to register individuals identified by certain fundamental Christian forms of morality, in the final column the request for "baptismal names if added after registration of birth and date" serves to imply a kind of reinforcement for persistent religious codifying. The code, when deciphered, should read thus: just as at the core of all authoritative religions there resides a legitimate divinity, so too at the center of all "true" political orders there lives the legitimate authority of the state. Sovereignty and divinity orientate similarly—that is, with a rigid centrality. Their essential character remains the same—naturally central. When this essential centrality begins to influence individuals, it produces prime candidates for membership in the community of citizens. It could be said, therefore, that my baptismal names—or more correctly the request from the center for them—operate like the ritual paraphernalia of an initiate; they serve to identify me as an authentic candidate for a Christianized colonial order. The knowledge concentrated at the center, held by the state in the birth book, aspires to be the original authenticating accoutrements of my identity. This is how the modern state attempts to constitute itself—that is, by possessing knowledge about its individual citizens, by projecting such knowledge as its own ingredient, and by presenting it as if it were the collective membership of the community. Through the text of the certificate, by the registering of information surrounding the event of my birth, the British colonial state seeks to know, possess, and order my individual identity in such a way as to align it with its own essential character.

The centering, which apparently allows for an efficient control of knowledge, permits the copy to mimic the original. The certificate, the copy of the registration of knowledge, gives the impression of resembling the original by its representative centralizing technique. Centralizing imitates the action of irreducibility. What lies at the center can be modified no further; it can be copied and redistributed but can no longer in itself be reduced. Yet in registering the knowledge it seeks, the center and its centering tend to give to knowledge the quality of their own irreducibility. They tend to give to knowledge the quality of absolutism—that is, the character of an irreducible reality. Hence I become, in the registering of my birth, that which the colonial state has become: a known irreducible reality. And note, not only have I—the object of a registering and the product of a copying—been centered to a point of individualized identity complete with recorded Christian names, but I have also been reduced quite carefully to very specific sexual, racial, and national realities.

From the middle and through the fourth column of the certificate, the state demands written verification of my sex. The demand seems motivated by a concern to know and, in the knowing, to control a wild and potentially destructive eroticism. If left outside society to run wild beyond the restriction of its cultural forces (that is, the Empire and Pax Britannica), the natural individual body of the latent colonized citizen may leave the center empty with no substance to reproduce itself. The sexual body must be corralled; it must be centered; it must be reduced to an absolute reality of known productivity. In this case it is gendered to be constructive for the community.

From the center and through the fifth column, the state demands the name, surname, and description of my father. In this column and in a few words, the certificate verifies the conferring of an individualized social identity, the proper reproductive channels of sexuality,

[handwritten margin note, left side top:] reducing the irreducible individual & a little bit confused here

[handwritten margin note, left side bottom:] PRODUCTIVITY controlling sexuality

and the inscribed racial and national categories to which both my father and I should belong.

The registrar's pen scrawls the words "George Mentore, Black, Native of British Guiana." My father and I have the same first name and the same surname. It is understood that the privileging of patriliny provides my name, and the body the name identifies, with their proper filial bonds. The agent of the state works with the notion that the confluence of male and female sexual behavior produced the entry point from which I descend. He dutifully records what are taken to be the results of intercourse, not just the birth of a child, but also the possibility of parenthood and the potential for a new governable individual. A child, by definition of sequence, immediately becomes subject to a higher preceding order. The parent, particularly the father, instantly represents this order and gives shape to its asymmetry. I would argue that the registration of birth and, of course, of parenthood, help not only to reproduce and reinforce this asymmetrical structure, but also to substantiate its irreducible consanguineous naturalness. I would like, in addition, to contend that the same feature of irreducibility giving shape to the parent/child relation carries over to the racial inscription.

British colonial rule considered "racial blood," like filial substance, to be inherently possessed through genetic transmission. Its logic viewed "blue blood," "white blood," "black blood," and "colored blood" to be passed down in succession from parent to child. From the logic of successive transmission, if the state knew the blood of the parent it would know the race of the child. Origins were made to be important. Where individuals came from was made to be important. Known origins allowed for a fixing; they provided the possibility of attaching a permanency to individuals—a seemingly necessary requirement for the continuance of the state. Registering the origin of racial blood empowered the colonial state with knowledge it deemed vital to its existence, and at the same time it objectified the traced origin of a racial identity for the registered individual. In the document the objectified category of race gives to the registered individual an additional mark of distinction. Made a person, given a gender, fixed with a race, the individual can now be correctly classified for community membership. The state can with empirical conviction be convinced of its own existence. It can with censuses, statistics, polls, and other forms of registering verify the constitution of itself as being with a definite population. The certainty of the known content and boundaries of this population hangs on believing in the irreducibility of the distinctive identifying markings of its individuals. Fixtures like the concept of personal names, gender, and race function as the knowledge desired to be known about the individual in order to constitute the political form of the population and to provide the bases for making claims about shared nation-ness.

Being "native" to the subject territories of the British Empire factors in as crucial evidence for establishing the origins of an individual's British-ness. Being native-born to British Guiana logically associates the individual with the colonized land, and, in so doing, stabilizes both in subordinate relations to the Motherland. The "factualness" of birth and the "naturalness" of asymmetry between parent and child duplicate themselves in the relation between nation and national. The irreducible qualities in birth and hierarchy suggest—as with racial blood—where British-ness originates and subsequently travels to with legitimate force. It is these very same qualities that work their way into the mother tongue, giving to it the facility to surge through the "imagined community" (Anderson 1992) of subject nationals. Reading, writing, or speaking in the mother tongue immediately marks the national with the quasi-filial properties of nation-ness; together, they become the ingredients for mutual sharing. In other words the nation can know its own community or can imagine knowing itself through the inscriptive(s) of its language. Revealingly, in its appropriation and use of the concept of nation the state similarly imagines it can know its citizens by the mutual markings of their mother tongue. In fact, in its modernity it appears to depend thoroughly on this knowledge.

By being transfused, so to speak, with British-ness, not necessarily through our ties to each other and not only through our births on

British soil, but also through being subject to the required official mother tongue of Britain, my father and I become known as "Native" to Britain. We are transcribed. We are made to correspond exactly to an authoritative native text and entered into its authoritative central register. Clearly choice is not an issue. The irreducible reality and innateness of nationalism takes away choice. One has to be born somewhere; one has to be born in a language; one must, therefore, be native to some place and language and, thus, have nation-ness. It is very noticeable that the state strategically obtains the power to know and to record and, hence, to control such aspects of identity, it being no coincidence that the content of what it controls is "real naturalness." Indeed, much of what goes on in the registering of birth has to do with insuring the state's power to orchestrate national identity—even to the extent of guaranteeing its ability to confer such identity on individuals not native-born to its territories. I would argue that for this to be functional, evidence of the so-called "real" quality of being native must be known as and projected as "natural." This is why, for me, any naturalization of individuals by the state represents more than an expression of its political power, for it also demonstrates what the nation-state conceives itself to be legitimately concerned with in the management of individuals.

This persistent strategic appeal by the state to what it understands as the known irreducible reality of naturalness clearly displays itself in other authoritative registers. I would argue, for example, that this appeal can also be found in the anthropological register. I should say that, for me, the significance of this lies not in the spectacle of the appeal's earnest request for absolute truth, but in the nonchalant though crucial consistency of its presence in authoritative registers. The suggestion is that this consistency enhances the authoritativeness of the registers. When both the colonial state and its citizens take part in the same plot, albeit in different performances, the effect is a convincing argument for the play on reality. I am not so interested here in whether or not the performances actually reflect reality as I am in the plot's constant claim that they do so. It seems much

Assumptions of belonging

more interesting to me to find out how different registers convince themselves and others that they have achieved their similar ends. I am also interested in when these registers supposedly achieve their objective, because, in my opinion, they do so when their objects independently recognize themselves in the textual record. To put it another way, it is when you can recognize yourself in your own birth certificate or, for example, when you can recognize yourself in an ethnography claiming to be a faithful record of the society and culture into which you were born. I surmise that all this would depend a good deal upon how much one were already convinced by the register's project of faithful reproduction.

Let us take, for instance, *The Negro Family in British Guiana* (Smith 1971 [1956]), a highly respected anthropological attempt to record what could be interpreted as my own positional objectivity. "Positional" in the sense that early ethnographies (such as *The Negro Family in British Guiana*), influenced as they were by Radcliffe-Brownian theories of social systems, considered human beings to be "components or units . . . occupying" a "position in a social structure" (Radcliffe-Brown 1971 [1952]:9–10). First published six years after my birth and five years after its author carried out his initial field research in West Coast Berbice, the ethnography reads like an authority on my early identity. Yet when I engage this text I do not recognize myself nor do I recognize any of the people I now know as Berbician or Guyanese.[6] In other words I am unconvinced by its appeal to and registering of an irreducible natural reality understood in racial, consanguineous, and national terms. Having said this, however, I have often wondered, given the opportunity and the inclination, how I would rewrite the author's rendition of myself so as to be more recognizable by myself. How would I redeem the representation of myself from the anthropological record? Perhaps because the author and I share the same mother tongue, the same Western notion of serial time, and have even been exposed to similar kinds of anthropological training, one could argue that my rewriting or redeeming would not amount to a very different picture of myself than his. But would I still focus on myself or other

Does having same been put in the mentor's position give a right / more of a right / justification to write about other people?

Guyanese as "aspects of the social structure"? Would I consider myself as having belonged to a "lower-class Negro family" (Smith 1971 [1956]:4)? Would I indeed accept the essential racial identity the author writes into my category of being? I know these are hard questions, perhaps unfairly asked and out of context because of the colonial environment in which the author wrote and the anthropological functionalism that heavily influenced his theoretical position. Nevertheless, his own sense of being an "Englishman" (Smith 1971 [1956]:7) and what this would mean in its structural relation to the colonized citizens of British Guiana make me think that his and my registers would be substantially different. My own guilty text would, I hope, possess a different sensibility and relation to the experience of being in the world. It is with such an awareness that I embark on an anthropological writing of the Waiwai.[7]

The Category of Known Amerindian

Like my own certified category of being, that which appertains to the Waiwai has been made coherent by and to the state as an irreducible natural reality. Having been fixed in the criteria of ethnicity, race, and nation-ness, our culturally conceived natural distinctiveness functions to keep the boundaries between and around our categories of identity. In the imagined community of the nation, to be Guyanese is to be a member of an interlocking population comprising six historically distinct "races" and "ethnicities" locally referred to as African/black, East Indian/Coolie, English/white, Portuguese/Potugee, Chinese/Chinee, and Amerindian/Buck (Smith 1962; Drummond 1980; Sanders 1987). In addition, whenever the state objectifies the image of the Amerindian in its discursive forms of national presence, it is with the acquired knowledge that Guyana possesses nine discrete "tribes."

In its official text the state presents the Akawaio, Arawak, Arecuna, Carib, Makushi, Patamona, Waiwai, Wapishana, and Warrau as its national Amerindian presence. Here the known Amerindian amounts to an anatomically determined individual belonging to a biologically fixed racial and ethnic totality. Only such an Amerindian can be recognized by the state and, for example, become eligible for access to its many modern services such as medical treatment, formal schooling, and jobs. While being reassuring to the state and helping to constitute and facilitate its operations, the form of Waiwai identity with which the state works bears very little resemblance to those the Waiwai hold of themselves.

This is not to say that Waiwai identities, in so far as they are a product of Waiwai social and cultural systems, are not the consequence of a literary register or that the role of author does not play as crucial a part in their construction as it does in ours. Indeed, I argue that the Waiwai do have a text of the world—a text that they write upon their bodies, their houses, and their social fabric. They do, in their own way, seek and prepare coherence and, in so doing, objectify otherness. Yet in the quality of their registers, in the very character of their "literary acts," they create a radically different coherence of being from our own. The attempt by the state to make Waiwai differences understandable in its own terms comes into effect as the state seeks greater efficiency in the control of its parts. My attempt to write about them will, I admit, do the same, not necessarily for the sake of efficiency but for a continuity of anthropology. On the other hand, probably because authorship belongs to them and appears to generate techniques of representation specific to their qualitative inscriptions, the Waiwai texts express a subjectivity consistent with their own ideas of reality.

Tracking the Threat of Otherness

My writing seeks the intellectual spoor of what could dramatically be referred to as a menacing alternative logic.[8] It is, in our Western cultural genre, an attempt to track an internal Waiwai consistency to and through its consequences of social being. In this attempt three primary forces have assisted me. The most prominent has been my many years of contact with the people who call themselves Waiwai. The intimacy rather than the duration of this contact has allowed me to adopt certain theoretical stances. Of less significance, but just as strategically effective, has been the relatively copious literature currently available on the Waiwai. Yet possibly because of the level of consciousness I take in regard to my writing on the Waiwai, where my personal experience with the people and the text on them converge and diverge cannot always be clearly discerned. To complicate matters even further, the part played by my own subjectivity—in affecting my writing—precedes my experience with both the literature on and my intimacy with the Waiwai. Quite simply put, I knew about the Waiwai long before I ever read one word on them or met a single individual from their community.

This emphasis on the interwoven relations between my intimacy with the Waiwai, my engagement with the literature on them, and my consciousness of an intervening subjectivity should suggest to you that, for me, ethnographies should not be simply about writing books. Regardless of how much they may yearn for it, authors and their works never achieve autonomy; they are just as heavily influenced by the processes of human existence as any other category and product of society. In my case the informative early years in a rural village on the coast of Guyana, the ever-present tropical forest looming in the background, and the disciplinary techniques of formal colonial schooling have all in their own way contributed to my authorship. It was from the bright, tight living spaces of the village grid lots that I first came to notice and appreciate the dark, aromatic luxuriance of the coastal forests. It was beneath the newspaper-covered walls of a one-room house on stilts that I first heard the stories about befeathered forest peoples. With their hoary tales of contact, the returning "balata bleeders" (rubber collectors) and "pork knockers" (gold diggers) caught my youthful imagination and pitched it to a peak of sustained excitement. Their images stayed with me on my way to the dull shores of England, during my stunned immersion into London's urbanity, through my earnest perusal of musty library books on South American Indians, and, years later, on my first field trip back to Guyana and the Waiwai. The balance between these influencing processes has, I think, ultimately affected my writing. In other words this ethnography serves not only as the end result of tracking an alternative intellectual principle, but also as the cultural imprints of a writer in pursuit of his own desire.

I think that to take the cultural alternatives of others seriously— and not to use them simply for rarefying our own realities—we should willingly allow that which is real for us to be challenged by otherness. Our realities can be safely threatened by the freestanding coherence of others. In allowing these realities to be confronted and embraced by the alternative truths of others, we may come to know ourselves not in ranked realities, not in exalted proximities to truth and knowledge, but in the pooled possibilities of human existence. The desired effect would not necessarily be the thorough overturning of beliefs in our own truths, but the potential redeployment of them around reality's negotiable character.

My life with the Waiwai, my exposure to the written text about them, and my experience with worlds that have seen me as Other have educated me on the negotiability of sustainable truths. We are indeed who we are through sustaining certain realities about the world. But the tremendous collective effort placed in the sustaining should partially expose the likelihood that these realities only remain so in terms of their sustainment. Stalking alternative realities and their techniques of confirmation has remained my principal anthropological goal. In my writing of the Waiwai, I have sought to present not only what may be unavoidably interpreted as an exotic alternative of being human, but also, and more seriously, an audacious and menacing challenge to the endorsement of fixity in our own reality of being. I have found that my encounter with Waiwai society, my experience of anthropological literacy, and my placement in the scheme of occidental culture have in their interwoven ways assisted me in tracking what I can only think of as the intellectual prints of a viable alternative challenge.

Shepariymo

A voiced resonance rather than a visual textuality, a passionate curve rather than a languid line: let me introduce you to a Waiwai literacy of social beauty. It is an appealing knowledge about people. Take care, however, because in the literary imagination, the suspension of reality for the imagined may be so effective that the imagined can actually take the place of the real. In this knowledge about people, it is not people themselves who will be introduced—that is, individual beings in the world—but rather the result of a knowledge about people constituted as the anthropology of social persons. Mine will not be an attempt to fix individuals in text, but an effort to recall and introduce to the literary imagination the social beauty of Waiwai personhood. It begins with the simple, clear curve of a circle reaching out. In the process of making itself, the circle returns to where it began to meet the point from which it started, to be complete, and to be well formed. Depending on your point of view, the circle either will have no inside and no outside or it will make possible the center and the circumference—in other words, the very possibility of a presence.

Outside of Time, Inside the Circle

When first I came to Shepariymo (Big-Dog Village) in September 1978, I had to visit the large, dilapidated thatched house that was home to the Shamawa family. The traditional conical roof leaked in the rain. The hard bare-earth floor dissolved into pools of mud where the raindrops fell. The doorframe leaned slightly toward the central plaza, as if silently gesturing to strangers the correct way to the place of public introductions. The low single opening made all who enter bend, and I felt I was giving homage to an ancient yet proud form of forest domicile. As I entered the spacious gloom of the wide interior and gazed around, my eyes slowly adjusted from the sunlight outside and I was greeted by objects of a highly gendered domesticity.

Inside, tall staves of fresh blood-red wood leaned against the wall, their aromatic odor hovering in the heavy air. The staves had to await such time when they would be carved into the lethal shape of bows. Stalks of arrow reeds, cut and tied in sheaves, reached across from one roof beam to another, harmless now, but they too waited to be dressed for death. Tufts of feathers, still clinging to the skins from which they grew, hung ready to give flight to the arrows. An old ax rested against the wall, its cold face still strong and its edge still sharp. Paddles, some brown with wear and others recently shaved so that they looked stripped and nude, crowded together along the wall. On the floor next to them stood a small clay pot containing the odds and ends of a craftsman's fixings. Larger pots, some of clay, some of tin, blackened by the smoke of many a cooking fire, lay around the ashes and smoldering logs of the hearth. The women's working domain was visibly mapped out by an array of woven baskets, fans, and trays filled with peeled yuca, palm fruit, and fluffy balls of cotton.[1] Even the empty carapace of a large land tortoise improvised as a matron's seat betrayed the feminine realm. Cotton hammocks and one or two dyed sessile hammocks sagged precariously or swung gracefully in open space. From the raised platforms in the back, the deep-throated growls of tethered hunting dogs sent their snarling menace to meet the unfamiliar intruder. The raucous cries of plucked parrots and head-bobbing macaws circled around and up into the dark cone of the roof, announcing the presence of a guest.

Shamawa had built his house at the *mitata* (the main entrance) of the settlement. It is the privilege of the *kayaritomo* (village leader) to do so. As visitors enter the settlement along the narrow path from

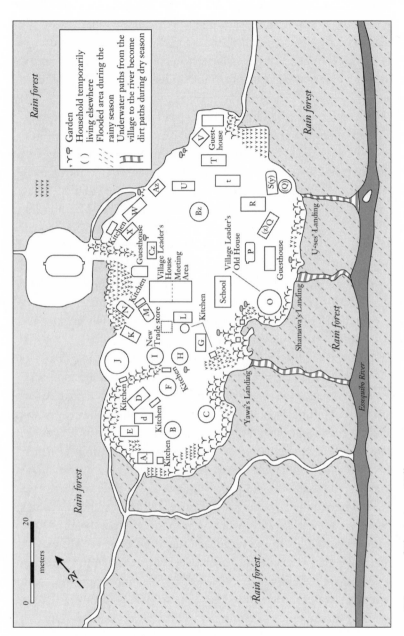

Map 1. Diagram of Shepariymo Village

the river, they must first pass his house. The only problem with this specific location at Shepariymo was that in the rainy season the rising current of the river carried its floodwaters into the house. In the dry season, however, the house stood about 150 yards from the river, at the top of a gradual incline and behind a narrow ribbon of trees.

Passengers disembarking at the river's edge during the dry season encountered a yellow clay embankment high enough to dwarf them. At the canoe berth the embankment was worn through by years of traffic from travelers. It stirred the senses to walk up from the bank of the river, along the path under the canopy of giant trees, and onto the cleared ground of the settlement plaza. The full dramatic affect of alternating terrains could be felt. After floating for so long on water along the corridors of the forest and then walking on land still constrained to a woodland path, the traveler's sense of confinement found release only when it reached the cleared ground (*yamriyakataw*) of the settlement. The houses stood close to the forest and the river, but they faced in toward each other around the open central space of Waiwai public life.

Shamawa lived with his wife Awam, their unmarried daughter Eriwoch, and her baby child, Eus. In the same house resided their three unmarried sons, Aruyowk, Sorewea, and Shoa, and three unmarried daughters Eup, Arym, and Ancipr. From their eyes and facial expressions, every one of the sons and daughters as well as the granddaughter emanated the singular personality of their father.

Shamawa was tall, big boned, and strong. The features of his face were elliptical—his plucked eyebrows and eyelids made his eyes appear bulgy and froglike; his flat nose, broad nostrils, and thick lips were symmetrical and perfect. This perfect symmetry presented to the world an air of slow calm and assured control. He was an impressive man in a community of many impressive individuals. Yet for me, and I believe for many others too, his most imposing trait lay in his frequently confirmed capacity for virtue in substance and in fact. Even the physical symmetry of his features seemed to match the absence of contradiction between his speech and action. No one

I knew or heard of ever found an instance of hypocrisy in the man: he was what he said and what he did, and what he did and what he said conformed to the moral principles of his life. How much of this consistency belonged to the man himself and how much came from his role and experience of being kayaritomo was hard to determine. Certainly, however, such attributes were well suited to the character of leadership that his village constituency sought and found in him.

It was strange, to me, how his image and his name existed in a literature beyond his cultural comprehension. He never gave me the impression that he actually understood or even cared what this literary presence meant. He remembered the Panakurï (Sunfish-people) who visited in his youth and took photographs of him holding a cooked monkey's head (Guppy 1958:83), consoling his brethren at Kanashen (Dowdy 1964:114–15), and crouching beside a fire at Yakayaka (Meggers 1973 [1971]).[2] Their cameras and literary imaginations surely must have seen in him what his constituency saw. From his countenance and in his very bearing, the favorable quality of his personality radiated; it attracted attention and, in an unassuming way, demanded to be noticed. It was a quality we normal and imperfect humans recognize, admire, and envy as something that, even if we wanted to, we could not ourselves achieve. Moral totality was the sum of his character.

His wife, Awam, also confirmed the blend of a personal and public goodness. Generous almost to a fault, her thin, sinewy frame belied the vast volume of physical work she constantly contributed to the community in the role of wife to the village leader. She was like an agitated bird, always moving, always alert to the mood of the community and the frequent requests of its occupants. It was an eerie sight to behold her returning from the farm every morning weighed down, doubled over, and hidden beneath a huge backpack of firewood that seemed to float by its own will toward her house. The gentle hum of voices, the rhythmic grating of yuca, and the clitter-clatter of early morning activities always began first in her house and drifted out toward and among the others until the whole community was fully awake. Never idle, Awam was the successful high energy behind the scenes keeping the civic life of the *ewtoto* (village community) intact and running smoothly.

Shamawa and Awam were a devoted couple; their very devotion to each other appeared like an emotional adhesive keeping the community together. They did what all Waiwai husbands and wives do publicly to state their relation of marriage. They bathed together. They ate together. They went to the farm together. They complemented each other's social existence. Yet they did it all in a style that gave the impression of a transcendence. It may have been that their marriage existed more in the public eye than did any of the others. This distinctiveness was not forced or staged in any way. It was sincere. Preoccupied with maintaining their own connubial contributions to each other, their marriage had no room for false or contrived claims. It was, as it appeared, a constant and binding relationship that allowed the other marital units to coalesce as a village community.

Across the path of the main entrance to the settlement stood the beehive house of Shamawa's and Awam's eldest daughter Emekuch. She lived with her husband, Enkik, and their three small sons, Inat,

[handwritten margin note: marriage – do everything together]

Rayi, and Uewmas. Like her siblings, Emekuch betrayed in her face her father's calm presence, while in her tolerance for hard work, her mother's energy.

Enkik had come from Surinam. He claimed to be from a Trio community there, but identified himself as Chikena—another people from the eastern forest. He was an attractive man, slim, well built, with dark eyes that in an unusual way held your attention almost to the point of embarrassment, forcing you to look away. Regardless of the language you were speaking in, he always gave the impression of understanding and agreeing with every word you said. He was gifted with a sharp wit and always had a joke that could tweak out smiles from even the most sullen of audiences—a prized talent, it seemed to me, for one of the village leader's principal son-in-laws.

Moving in an easterly upriver direction around the central plaza, you would encounter a cluster of three cigar-shaped houses facing inward toward each other at the second major entrance to the settlement. Everyone knew the canoe berth and the path joining the river to the settlement at this location as U-ses' Landing. U-ses was probably the second most important secular figure in the community. He was an *antomanñe* (work leader). Whenever communal work needed to be carried out, upon advice from the village leader, he would walk ceremoniously to the center of the plaza and, in a high falsetto voice, sing out clearly "*onhariiiiii, onhariiiiii, onhariii-iii.*" This call beckoned all able-bodied men to the communal meal, after which U-ses would lead them to the site of work. There he led by example.

A nonstop worker, U-ses would keep at his task until it was finished or the night forced him back into his house. A soft-spoken man of Shereu identity, he presented a somewhat shy and unassuming personality. Yet his knowledge of practical things made him at times overbearing, particularly when you were slacking off at whatever you were supposed to be doing in the collective task. Without a word and with the sheer weight of his dexterous activity, he could shame you into greater effort. To make matters worse, he offered an infectious smile—a courier of compliance to the most indolent of workers.

U-ses was married to Etap, Shamawa's father's sister's daughter. Indeed, her husband and Shamawa called each other *yatho* (brother)—an artifice of the Waiwai system of matrilateral and patrilateral cross-cousin marriage. She was a round-faced woman with a mellow complexion just like her husband's and, like her husband, had radiating lines at the corner of her eyes that made her face smile even when her mouth did not. She loved to smile, but when she did, her lips exposed the vacant space where a tooth should have been. She was a known lover of fun and regularly led the women in the Anaconda Dance on festive occasions. She and U-ses lived with their five unmarried children, Chichem, their eldest son; Iwopar, their second son; and Wra-a, Owimar, and Kocimoro, their daughters. During my first stay in the community, however, she remained subdued because of a lingering scandal.

U-ses and Etap's house stood close to and between two others whose doorways opened onto shared ground at the head of the path leading to the landing. All three houses had their "butt ends" to the central plaza, but because U-ses's house had at its end a second door opening onto the plaza, a sense of isolation was avoided for the cluster. To the east of the path and of U-ses's house lived Awawatak and Anawochek, and to the west lived Emtushen and Apimach.

Awawatak and Emtushen were brothers from Hishkaryena communities further south in Brazil. Emtushen's wife, Apimach, was sister to Akow, who was married to Apuw, U-ses's daughter. Akow, Apuw, and their baby son were visiting from Brazil and were temporarily staying with Awawatak in his house. Meanwhile, Emtushen was hosting his wife's other brother, Aywek, who was also visiting from Brazil with his wife, Awacha, and their two children. It may have been a tight squeeze, because Emtushen had a young son and Awawatak had a daughter and four robust sons of his own. The advantage was, however, that while the guests remained, U-ses carried a substantial labor force from his cluster to the sites of communal village work.

Further to the east of U-ses's cluster, up around the central plaza and more away from the river, lived Akiamon—the cause of Etap's lingering scandal. The community had ostracized him as punishment, ostensibly for his scandalous liaison with the wife of his neighbor and joint work leader. He had once shared the duties of an Antomanñe with U-ses, and like U-ses, he too worked hard. He was a renowned flutist, an attractive man with a charming personality, which made all who basked in its warmth feel relaxed and safe. Everyone wanted to be in his company, and yet, for at least the first six months of my stay in the community, I never saw or heard of his presence. Because of his scandalous behavior, he could not attend or take part in any of the public affairs of the community at least until the next summer clearing of fields. He kept to his own household cluster and skulked in and out of the settlement by way of the side paths and entrances—a sad figure in a community that found joy in each other's company. Yet what was being penalized was not so much his individual right to the companionship of fellow village members as it was his prerogative to speak as a leader.

The duty to speak publicly, to voice directives openly to the community even in an oblique Waiwai fashion, comes with the position of work leader as an indulged privilege. As in many other Amazonian societies, the duty to speak "consists of a celebration, repeated many times, of the norms of traditional life" (Clastres 1989:153–54); it is the celebration of convivial community life itself. What the Shepariymo community sought to punish in Akiamon's adultery was not some sexual sin or individual guilt, but the unauthorized use of leadership to attain an advantage for himself rather than for the community at large. The punishment removed Akiamon's leadership duty to speak, because it was judged that his duty to speak—exercised only in the role of work leader—had unfairly enabled him to acquire his extramarital favors. In its additional daily application of his exile, the punishment also stated very clearly that its very own functioning inhabited the social space of the community.[3]

Akiamon was married to Akuchiruw, Enkik's sister. Like his wife and brother-in-law, Akiamon identified himself as Chikena. He and

Akuchiruw had a baby son and three daughters living with them: Rukupanasu, the eldest, and Iwatariei and Uchimatuk. In a separate, adjacent house lived Apakan, Akuchiruw's old mother. In contributions to and dependence on her daughter's domestic space, Apakan was part of Akiamon's household. Their household formed part of a cluster that also included the house of Uwa and Akach.

Uwa, Apakan's brother, was married to Akach, who identified herself as Aramayena. Their magnificent conical-roof house held a prominent position on a slight rise looking down on the plaza from the northeast. Its front door faced the settlement center, and through it, with playful regularity, would cascade Uwa's and Akach's ebullient sons, Chuma, Rike, and Riama. They were a handful for their parents and their elder sister, Owipat, who could often be seen chasing them from the house in an awkward run, encumbered by her baby sister, Iyakar, wrapped around her hip.

To the east of Akiamon's house and at the extreme eastern end of the settlement, the house of the most recent members nestled beneath the overarching branches of the nearby trees. Utok, his wife, Chmaku, and their three young children were not, as far as I could tell, directly related to anyone else in the community. They had come on a visit from Surinam with a party of Trio men. Utok had been advised not to make the grueling two-month mountainous trip with his wife and children, but he did. On the return journey, Chmaku hurt her foot and could not keep up with the rest of the party. The family was left behind and had no alternative but to turn around and head back to Shepariymo. They barely made it alive. Low on provisions, exhausted, and with the coals of a never-ending fire smoldering in a leaf backpack, they were picked up by passing hunters at the Surinam Landing, about half a day's canoe paddling downriver from the settlement. Shamawa invited them to stay and live with his people, and they did.

To everyone it seemed appropriate for Utok to build his house in that part of the settlement already associated with the southern and eastern "Forest Dwellers" of the community. Utok considered himself to be Tunayena, while his wife, Chmaku, referred to herself as Katuema. Perhaps no bonds of kinship or marriage tied their family to any other Shepariymo resident, but the imagined bonds of a preexisting residential and linguistic natal identity operated as if they were substantiated kinship relations. In relative terms, Utok and Chmaku were much more closely "related" to the people who grew up in the forest to the south and east than they were to those who lived here in the forest and to the north in the savannas.

[margin note: Ex: relation by residential living]

The more "local" people—that is, those who grew up here in the upper reaches of the Essequibo River and in the southern Rupununi savannas—built their houses roughly located to the north, west, and southwest of the settlement plaza. They were the source of an inner core of clusters in the community and gave central form to the way the social relations of the community configured itself. Their houses were like a clutch of eggs resting in a nest, and, in the way they were related, predicted the location for every new abode.

Arumarawan was a longtime resident. His house could be found at the north end, where he lived with his wife, Yenayaw; their bachelor son, Aruchiripin; their beautiful teenage daughters, Eyapen-n and Akasar; and their youngest, the boy Ska-a. Arumarawan was a quietly proud and conservative man—in every fiber of his powerful body, a Mawayena. His skin was always painted. He always had his upper arms and lower legs wrapped with strings of beads. On every occasion that allowed for display, he wore his nose feathers. He walked with feet turned in just like a duck; his broad feet and splayed toes could wear no shoes. He refused to speak any languages but Waiwai and Mawayena. His voice was soft and musical. Every morning he expectantly brought the community into the new day with a repertoire of traditional tunes from his bamboo or bone flute. A virtuoso on either instrument, his talent and knowledge brought spiritual contentment to the community and enhanced its material credentials of human existence. While Arumarawan lived in the settlement, the community knew it possessed a tangible path between the material and spiritual worlds.

Yenayaw was a private woman. Attentive to her husband and children, she cared little for the pretensions of the world outside her

*[handwritten note at bottom: *Mention noting what each individual contributes to the community]*

immediate family. Like Arumarawan, she conveyed a confident air of tradition. When she moved, her substantial frame emitted the sound of jingling bells. Under her floral frock, around her hips, and attached to the sides of her beaded apron, tiny bells and seeds tinkled with every step she took. She was the only Marakayena living in the community, and when she spoke to her children, only they understood what she was saying. Everyone respected her and gave her a clear berth with regards to her intentions.

Living next door to Arumarawan was his son-in-law, Umachar. He could not have been much younger than his father-in-law, yet he was married to the young and beautiful Akuis. Many different stories circulated about how Umachar *manmo* (captured) his bride with help from his father-in-law.[4] In all the stories, however, it is clear that some out-of-the-ordinary reason accounted for the union between these two people who belonged to different age-grades. It was already common knowledge that Umachar had, as a young man, been married to an older woman. He had to have patience. When she died, he married her daughter. The father of his second wife had been Umachar's cohusband while he was polygamously married to the first wife. When his second wife also died, Umachar married Akuis. It is said (mainly by the younger men of the community) that, although initially uninterested in Umachar, Akuis was lured into her romantic affection for him by the magical sound of his flute. Every night while they were courting, Umachar played an aria of love taught to him, it is claimed, by the man who was to become his father-in-law, the master flutist Arumarawan. Hawked-nosed and bowlegged, long hair oiled, combed, and tied in its bamboo tube, Umachar always appeared neat and tidy. He took a particular pride in being seen well dressed in public. It may have been obvious to everyone that his marriage to a beautiful younger woman had placed an extra burden of vanity upon his square shoulders. Three years into their marriage, Umachar and Akuis had two daughters, Orus and Uraet.

In addition to his son-in-law, Arumarawan also had his married son Itup living within his cluster of households. This situation was unusual but not rare. Given the particular circumstances, it was certainly not unexpected. Itup had only recently married Iam-mir, the daughter of Onish and Chiwosom. The couple should have been in bride service and household dependence to Iam-mir's parents. However, Iam-mir's father had died not so long ago, and while her mother, Chiwosom, had remarried and was living on the other side of the settlement with her new husband, Erimink, the marriage was not stable. A practical decision had been taken not to place the added burden of a young marriage upon an already stressed household. So Itup built his new house next to his father's house. It was a major social coup for Arumarawan to have both his married son and his son-in-law living with him as dependents, and it certainly added to his local prestige. His household had drawn to itself, by way of marriage to Umachar, a Waiwai man, and by way of marriage to Iam-mir, a Hishkaryena woman.

Situated between the houses of Itup and Akiamon but behind the house of Uwa was the dark, rectangular thatched house of Shamew and Aruim. I was never quite sure why Shamew built his house at this location or why his house was adjacent to or in the midst of the clusters it intersected. His house was older than Uwa's house, and Itup had only recently become his neighbor. Like Shamawa and Arumarawan, the kindly and jovial Shamew had been one of the earliest settlers to the site, hence the houses around him may have been the accumulative result of shifting residence and rebuilding. In terms of social organization, however, this antecedence does not explain why his neighbors were motivated to build within his vicinity. One strong suggestion concerned his wife Aruim.

The adorable Aruim had once been the wife of Uwipon, who was previously married to Erikayawch, Umachar's mother. Women married to the same man usually consider themselves to be sisters, if they are not already so related. The extension of matrifilial ties between Aruim and Umachar as a result of the sisterhood between Aruim and Erikayawch would have made Aruim not just Umachar's mother's sister but also, more significantly, his classificatory mother (in other words, he would have called her *yeme* "mother," and she would have called him *oparï* "my child").[5] With Aruim now married to Shamew, the logical extension of kinship ties allowed Umachar to regard Shamew as his classificatory father. This relationship would certainly have suited Umachar, for although he and Shamew belonged to the same age-grade, the fact that he could call him father meant that Shamew could consider Arumarawan an affine—preferably a brother-in-law. There were indeed some distant bonds of kinship reckoning, which did allow for this situation. It was, however, more Aruim's ability to call Arumarawan brother that seemed to lay the groundwork of legitimacy for Umachar to claim Akuis as his mother's brother's daughter and, thus, for her to be in the proper connubial category. Perhaps in this regard it is best to think of Shamew and Aruim's house as belonging to Arumarawan's household cluster. Shamew and Aruim lived with their two sons, eleven-year-old Ramem and four-year-old Sayama.

In anticipation (and maybe even in shrewd and subtle persuasion) of his son Aruyowk's future marriage, Shamawa had built a small but "modern" house on the high ground next to Umachar's abode. It was a rectangular, thatched-roof house resting on short tree-trunk blocks, with steps that led into a single room, floored and walled with wooden slats. It was this kind of house that the missionaries built for themselves when they first came to the Waiwai region in 1949.[6] No missionaries were around now, but the effect of their ideas upon Waiwai domestic architecture, particularly for the younger members of the community, was clearly evident.[7] The only other encroaching architectural style came from the wattle-and-daub adobes for which the savanna-dwelling Wapishana were famous. These two styles seemed to be the trend for the future; however, they required much more work in their initial stages of construction than was the case for the traditional completely thatched style of houses. The heavy boards for the slat houses, for example, had to be cut and hauled from the forest, sometimes for great distances. Although easy to obtain by digging up the earth near to the settlement, the clay for the adobe walls required fetching large quantities of water from the river in order to attain the mud mixture. These houses were generally thought to be much easier to keep clean, much warmer at night, and much drier during the rainy season. Aruyowk's slat house did indeed possess all these qualities, but it also boasted prized views of the plaza and of the main path into and out of the settlement. In addition the principal trail to the largest settlement farm went right by its front door. Throughout the first time I was resident in the community, Aruyowk was away among the Wapishana working in the South Rupununi savanna; consequently, his empty house—offered to me by Shamawa—became my temporary home.

In our mutual understanding of the offer, it became evident—through the ways in which house location related to statements about residential obligations—that our social ties had to operate along some acceptable parameters governed by filial or affinal relations.[8] These were at first ambiguous, taking their leads from what the Waiwai could interpret about who I was and what I was doing among them. Initially, because they saw me constantly writing and even possibly because of my clumsy and noisy way of moving through the forest, they all called me *pocha* (grandfather). In addition I was masculine and alone. In other words I was a man without a wife—meaning that I had no control of or access to a local farm. Alone and masculine, I had no way of maintaining myself without a wife and the cultivated produce from a farm. This situation meant that I had to be dependent upon a resident household that did have access to a farm or that I had to attain a wife in order to claim such access. One role of village leadership is to act as short-term host for visitors and, in this capacity, Shamawa did allow me to refer to him as an affine. Male strangers seem better placed in this category, because it allows—at least on the surface level of formal etiquette—the married women of the village to refer to visiting men as their "brothers." I did indeed refer to Shamawa as *o-poimo* (my brother-in-law), while Awam and I called each other *ñoño* (brother) and *achi* (sister) respectively. It was not until many years later that the relationship between Shamawa and me changed to one in which we behaved to each other in a proper filial manner.

Upaek, T-tawore, and their year-old son, Utech, were my neighbors. They were a young and, when compared to the other village members, a "modern" family. They had appropriately built a slat house on tall stilts. They wore either ready-made clothes obtained from hinterland trade stores or clothes made from shop-sold materials. The principal family harbinger of these "outside" traits was T-tawore, who grew-up and went to school in Karadinawa—the southern most Wapishana settlement in the Rupununi.

T-tawore spoke Wapishana and Guyanese Creole English. As in the case of most Wapishana young women, while attending a state-administered hinterland school she had felt and experienced the weak effects of a precarious modernity. Though not extreme when compared to schooling in the urban and even rural areas of Guyana, this exposure was, nonetheless, sufficient for transforming her into a "modern" citizen and, in the eyes of many young Waiwai men, was regarded as somewhat appealing. A Wapishana wife meant easier access to things Guyanese. A Wapishana wife would know about the strange foods of Creole culture and perhaps even know how to prepare and cook such dishes. She might even know how to decipher the accentuated Creole ways of behaving. For a young and ambitious Waiwai man, having such knowledge in advance could mean the difference between conveying a proud confidence and feeling the sting of shame from the oftentimes-harsh critique of Guyanese modernity. Even without such knowledge, however, a Wapishana wife brought an understanding of savanna life—a longtime talked about but little experienced world for most young Waiwai.

Upaek was the son of Shamew and Aruim. Although his mother claimed Mawayena and his father Waiwai ancestry, the fact that he grew up and lived in a Waiwai community meant to him and to others that he was first and foremost Waiwai. As suggested by his successful marriage to T-tawore, he was, nevertheless, very attracted to non-Waiwai and nonforest ways of being. Thus it was in him that I first encountered the epitome of that strange contrast between the modern and the traditional among the Waiwai.

It was in Upaek that I first began to comprehend the fallacy of the modern Western boast about its dominant acculturating effects. In him, in his curiosity and encompassing will, I witnessed the Waiwai rebuttal of the unconscious yet prevalent arrogance of our crusading Westernization, which saw only the righteous (or deleterious) effects of its own presence in others. While blinded to the fact that the so-called dominated and acculturated forest peoples had used us—without any notion of "culture as property"—to attain their own ends, we arrogantly continued to believe and act as if the (theoretical and imagined) evolutionary forces of change had propelled us further and with qualitatively greater benefits (and disadvantages) than they had the Waiwai. Even in the fullness of its impact—where all its character becomes the curious center of a forest people's scrutiny—Westernization remained the object of a discernible Waiwai frame of understanding. What I observed in the living, breathing immediacy of Upaek was that stroke of social and political genius whereby Waiwai culture had, without vainglory, quietly extended its supple edges to incorporate some of the intricacies of Western otherness. Being Waiwai remained, after all, a vibrant lived statement, where many other Amerindian cultural proclamations had long turned into the throttled gasps of an exhausted people.

Upaek represented, to me, the sublime testimony of a tenacious Waiwai will filled with a deep-layered sylvan historicism.[9] He was in his very name the living embodiment of such a claim. The Waiwai custom of recycling the memory of the dead by giving to living kindred the name of a deceased relative had allowed him to possess his deceased mother's father's father's name. Even the tried and tested Waiwai skills of archery were still his in vast and usable amounts. The favored Waiwai bodily comportment, which conveyed a patient and calm demeanor, expressed in him the confidence of a people who knew well the dangerous power of spoken words. Yet both he and his wife were two of the very few people in the community who spoke Guyanese Creole English. Unlike his wife, however, Upaek actively sought to improve his Guyanese by learning how to read and write in English. I often found him with his nose between the pages of a small green-covered dictionary—a rare sight, not only because very little printed text existed in the community, but also because the level of literacy was low among the young and was achieved only by a very few motivated elders. It was, in addition, a primarily biblical literacy confined within a missionary-inscribed Waiwai text.

During the entire twenty or more years of UFM (Unevangelized Fields Mission) missionary activity among the Essequibo Waiwai—that is, from their first establishment of a field station at the abandoned settlement of Erepoimo in 1950 and later at Kanashen (Evans and Meggers 1955; Guppy 1958; Yde 1965; Dagon 1967), no English—Guyanese Creole or North American—was ever taught or encouraged among the Waiwai. Since the departure of the missionaries, the Guyanese government has attempted—through one notable individual—to install its national brand of schooling in the area. This is said to have first occurred at Kanashen in 1972. From Shepariymo the children had to paddle canoes and walk for about an hour in order to attend the school at Kanashen. There is a horseshoe bend in the river a little downstream from Shepariymo that, during the dry season, permits travelers to dock their canoe at one end, walk across the peninsula to the other side, and from there take another canoe the short distance to the Kanashen landing. When I arrived in the community, the school was not in operation. The headmaster and the school's only qualified teacher, Nisden Uwpa (a Wapishana from the southern Rupununi settlement of Aishalton), had taken sick leave and returned to the savannas. No one came to replace him or substitute for him, and no school ever functioned in the community while I was present. As regards secular and religious literacy, some effects of exposure to schooling had taken hold, but not to the extent of transforming Waiwai culture out of all recognition.

In direct relevance to the form and guiding logic of Shepariymo residential space, secular and religious literacy had not yet molded or privileged in the Waiwai conscience any collective cultural statements on individualism leading to ideas about an essential, unique, and autonomous subjectivity. No legitimating link between the divine identity of the Christian God and the secular authority of the modern state had been established by any promotion of an individual subjectivity in literacy. The "text" and the "author"—the divine biblical word and God, the law and the state—had not crystallized as autonomous entities pointing to each other, reinforcing each other, and thus legitimating the projection of an authentic self. A world saturated with text, preceding authors, and textually obedient subjects was not yet the world of the Waiwai. Schooling had begun to lay the groundwork for the development of such a world but as yet had not seen any substantial results for its efforts. Waiwai houses did not, for example, reflect spaces determined by concerns for the modern rationalization of the individual. There were no rooms for specific individual uses: no bedroom, no dining room, no utility room, no bathroom, and while the introduction of a separate kitchen was an aspect of some Wapishana-influenced households, there were no separate rooms for cooking in any of the Waiwai homes. A few houses had doors, but none of these had names or numbers on them. There were no streets to be named. There were no geometrically determined spaces that could become the object of a meticulous legal document, nor any written law that could uphold the right to individual property. All in all only a Waiwai culture of immediacy, perhaps best understood as an "oral here-and-now of living," made itself prominently available to itself as an authority. In this world it was difficult for any distant form of rigid centrality to track down and claim obedience from an individual, for here the body was not yet defined in terms of an autonomous selfhood.

Not even what could be regarded as the most Westernized members of the community, like Retawp and Ketmar, who lived with their six children behind the house of Upaek and T-tawore, could be fruitfully approached from the autonomous paradigm. Retawp and Ketmar were Wapishana from the settlement of Karadinawa. They had moved down out of the savannas to settle with the Waiwai and were able quite legitimately to do so because their daughter Netcha was married to Anawach, the classificatory brother of Awam, the village leader's wife. Nevertheless, if they had not also been husband and wife, even being affines to the most prominent household in the settlement would not have been enough for them to become members of the community. If they had been single, neither Retawp nor

Ketmar could have lived in the settlement as recognized members. That is, neither of them could have built a house, had usufruct to a farm, and lived in the settlement as a single member. Neither one of them could nor would have even wanted to live on his or her own as an independent entity; widowed, divorced, or single people live in the households of their closest kinsfolk. There is no place in Waiwai village membership for the category of the autonomous individual.

A certain level of Wapishana individualism did exist for Retawp and Ketmar. As far as house location was concerned, this influence manifested itself by their not living close—at least in terms of a Waiwai appreciation of spatial distance—to their daughter's house. Being savanna people, they were far more comfortable in the wide-open landscape of the Rupununi plains than in the forested confines of the Guiana Shield. Coming from an ambulatory rather than a riverine culture, they were principally hikers, not rowers. Their culture operated with a dual residence pattern in which, at certain times of the year, individual family households would fuse and live together at long-established settlements in the savanna and at other times would fission and move to isolated homes at the edge of the forest where their farms were located. The established settlements had dwellings built well apart from each other with neighbors not even in shouting distance. Hence living at Shepariymo on the other side of the settlement plaza, not more than a hundred yards from where their daughter lived, was not an issue for Retawp and Ketmar. For the Waiwai, however, the fact that no spatial logic and hence no socially determined moral standard seemed to govern why they had situated their house in its current location marked Retawp and Ketmar as different. They were full members of the community, but their Wapishana difference could not be reconciled as easily as the differences of other non-Waiwai village members who, despite their differences, were still forest peoples similar in many more ways to the Waiwai. Like the other Wapishana living in the settlement, Retawp and Ketmar betrayed a host of cultural differences that kept them more distinct from other villager members. Perhaps the strongest of these pertained to their preference not to seek out or contribute to the collective village work that was a constant feature of Waiwai village life. They preferred to work much more on their own with assistance from their immediate household relatives. It seemed to me that this kind of disposition allowed them to be much more susceptible to the interpretation that they were influenced by Western individualism. Nevertheless, not even a collaborative Wapishana and Western notion of individualism could in residential situ overturn the Waiwai categorization of village membership.

Waiwai village membership functioned in such a way as to allow members to leave their houses and farms for prolonged periods and not lose their residence status. This was the case for Chichem and Atmik, whom I did not get to know personally because, for the entire time of my stay, they were living on the Rio Mapuera in Brazil. The area around their vacated house was kept clean and their farms were well tended by close family members. No one entered their house or used their belongings or harvested from their farms. The residence status of an absent village member becomes void only when the absent member household has built another house and cut another farm at another settlement location. Only when this has been confirmed by eyewitness account will other village members strip the house of its reusable parts and harvest the crops from its related farms. It was my distinct impression that the Shepariymo community was waiting patiently for news about the nonreturn of Chichem and Atmik. The possibility of this outcome was signalled by what the community already knew about the personal history and the quality of connubial circumstances and forces linking Chichem to Shepariymo. Chichem had obtained his membership to Shepariymo by way of his marriage to Atmik. This relationship seemed to be the only firm social bond binding him to the community. In the knowledge and understanding of the community, the moral forces of his particular marital relationship did not appear to be as strong as those binding him to kindred and other social circumstances in his Hishkaryena community on the Mapuera.

Atmik was the daughter of Arumaw, the widow of Epemap, who had also been polygamously married to Shawu, the mother of

Akaway. Both widows now lived with Akaway in his deceased father's very large conical house. Akaway was married to Nisu, and they had a year-old daughter named Riakwo. Thus the recently married Atmik had her house built right next door to her brother and the women she called mother. With their marriage and its residential proximity, Atmik and Chichem declared their correct obligations to the Akaway household. From the principle of uxorilocal postmarital residence (in which the new husband moves from his natal household to live close to his wife's natal household), Chichem became directly obligated to the Akaway household. This took its most empirical form when some of the products from any masculine-defined work went from Chichem to the Akaway household. In Waiwai deliberations, living close together facilitates the subtle personal negotiations required to instill reciprocity between households. The social demand for the products of individual labor seems to contend most starkly at the level of household interaction. The demand from the household to which an individual belongs vigorously contends with the demand from other closely related households. In the case of uxorilocal residence, most of the products from the individual labor of the dependent brother-in-law or son-in-law end up outside his own household and inside the household of his wife's kindred. This applies also to the products of labor from the dependent in-law's wife. In this particular instance, Atmik continued to assist her overly demanding elderly mothers as well as maintaining her own household chores. In addition, with two widowed mothers as well as a wife and child to support, the demand for masculine contributions of labor to the Akaway household appeared to all in the community to be proportionally high. This would not have been such a critical issue, however, if Akaway had not been so disadvantaged by his small physical stature.

He was a tiny man: smaller, by at least a foot, than any other adult in the community. His small physique made it almost impossible for him to pull a man's bow and let fly the arrow that would bring down the game demanded as the proper masculine contribution to the household. His fingers were short, his eyes furtive, and his demeanor, though confident, nevertheless showed an inability to take on the posturing that is generally accepted as a sign of Waiwai masculinity. It was very tempting for me to interpret from this that what I saw in Akaway the individual was Akaway himself—unencumbered by the cultural representations of Waiwai personhood. It had seemed to me like an opportunity for liberty—that is, for him to be freed from the constraints of Waiwai social expectations—for after all, did not the very limitations of his body release him from any anticipated social fulfillment? My bias soon faded, however, for even with his short body and seemingly deficient attributes of manhood, Akaway the individual still operated within a Waiwai cultural paradigm of masculinity. This remained so even while the very paradigmatic masculinity itself presented his manhood as limited in its scope. He certainly was the butt of many jokes that made fun of ideas about the small, the soft, and the weak. It did not appear to me that these jokes were malicious or mean, for in many instances Akaway himself took part in their recitation and even joined in the laughter. It seemed evident that there were many levels of social acceptability and that Akaway could not be firmly placed in any particular category of deviance. Nevertheless, within the main Waiwai category to which his bodily attributes came to be represented, he could not actually stimulate enough collective sentiment to command respect. Particularly in light of the circumstances and specific history of his household relations, no respect was given.

The fact remained that everyone understood why Chichem did not fulfill his obligations of bride service to the Akaway household for very long. Akaway could not sustain enough influence in his role as brother-in-law to keep Chichem in a residentially dependent relationship. This "weakness" also made it very difficult for anyone else in the community to activate any influence he or she may have had over Chichem. The way his household was formally related to the community could be traced through Akaway. While the widows Arumaw and Shawu did have a strong matrifilial hold over Atmik, sentiments aside, in terms of material sustenance this hold only produced more of the same products the women of the household could already provide. Akaway's household needed and wanted Chichem but had very little influence over him compared to those drawing him back to his Hishkaryena community on the Mapuera.

On the southeast side of Akaway's house lived Iwap and Amish-amish. They were a charming old couple whose combined depth of knowledge and experience seemed to provide them with the con-fidence to be always ready with smiles and laughter. It was a dis-arming assuredness, for everyone acquiesced to the enchantment of his and her affectionate faces. Perhaps the charm and its deep fortitude stemmed from the fact that they were both crippled and had been so for a very long time. Iwap walked with a pronounced limp. With every step he took, his upper body came down in an ungainly manner upon his crooked right leg. Once while he was living on the Mapuera, when he was sleeping overnight in a tempo-rary shelter on the river, a tree had fallen on him, damaging some of the disks in his back. As for Amishamish, she had suffered from polio. Both her legs flopped uselessly under her. She moved about with the aid of two ancient crutches, which must have been supplied to her through the missionaries. After many years of transporting herself by using her arms, the muscles of her shoulders, in contrast to those of her legs, were hard and lean. Iwap and Amishamish were very special people, and to this their physical disabilities bore wit-ness. Common community knowledge explained the cause of their disabilities as based on shamanic vengeance. Everyone knew about the strong shamanic abilities of Iwap. They knew he possessed the skills to attract and direct spiritual powers. They also knew that one outcome of these practiced skills could be a counterattack from spiritual forces directed by opposing shamans. Nothing is coinci-dental in Waiwai interpretation. Iwap and Amishamish possessed a depth of knowledge and experience, and because of this, they were both physically crippled—obviously the victims of harmful intent from dark shamans outside. They shared the burden of their phys-ical misfortune with the community, however, particularly with the household most attached to their residential cluster.

Amishamish and Atmik called each other sister, because their mothers (Kria and Shawu respectively) were daughters of the same Mawayena woman (Nrie). Amishamish called Arumarawan brother, because her father (Uruwarush) and Arumarawan's father (Akaway) called each other brother.[10] Amishamish's only daughter, Hyawa, was married to Ponu, one of Arumarawan's sons: in other words, Hyawa was married to her mother's brother's son. Ponu lived uxorilocally to Iwap and Amishamish. Although the two households occupied two adjacent but separate dwellings, they shared one hearth. This sharing of the same fireplace stated clearly the special quality of the relations between the two households. The mother and daughter doted on each other. Their excessive fondness could simply have been the result of Amishamish's incapacities and Hyawa's understanding of what the correct behavior should be for a daughter with a crippled mother. Contrary to the behavior expected of a son-in-law in bride service, however, Ponu did not express the usual signs of his role—that is, of begrudging patience and assertive composure. The first, patience, would derive from having to wait for the birth of the first child, which would release the new husband and his household from the formal bonds of service to his wife's household. The second, composure, would come from the knowledge that even in his current subordinate role, the new husband had at least moved out of the unenviable position of *karipamšam* (young bachelor) and was on his way to becoming *porintomo* (a member of the "Big-Man" social category). Yet Ponu did not present himself in any of these expected or familiar ways. This could have been because he knew that the disabilities of his wife's parents would require him to be permanently tied to their household, and so he resigned himself to the situation. But it could also have been that he had acquired a certain amount of satisfaction from the community esteem he received for the way in which he accepted the situation. The moral gain seemed to outweigh the disadvantages. Either way, the young couple devoted themselves to the elderly pair, and in such a fashion as to suggest that their households were not two separate units but a single joint household of their residential cluster.

A strategically cultivated row of banana plants separated the houses of Ponu, Iwap, Akaway, and Chichem from the group of dwellings situated furthest away from the central plaza. The row started indistinctly behind Iwap's house, went up past the back of Akaway's substantial building, and turned away from the central plaza before coming back down and around to the front of the settlement behind Shamawa's house. Cowering by the towering closure of forest trees immediately behind them, the banana plants stood in the clearing almost completely surrounding the houses situated within their confines. The placement of the banana plants was no accident; it followed a similar practice found in Waiwai cultivated fields, where each farm plot within a field was distinguished from its neighbor by a distinct crop planted along its boundaries. Indeed, as one looked back around the settlement, one could see the strategy of planting certain easily recognizable plants in places where the intent was to demarcate domestic space. This was not a statement about privacy or even about ownership, but a kind of "reminder" or "prompter" for all occupants of the settlement as to where the boundaries of domestic space began and ended. These "plant prompters" often marked the point where certain protocol of behavior began and ended. And they certainly assisted in defining the differences between the cleared, unoccupied space of the plaza and the residential spaces on its periphery. They also seemed to suggest an attempt by certain settlement members to state a kind of marginality.

The people who lived in the banana-plant enclave had access to the central plaza through cleared ground that went by Ponu's house. A path at this location led off down to the river to what everyone called Yawa's Landing. Another path at the southwest end led into the forest and along the embankment for two or three hundred yards before ending at a further downriver landing. The enclave consisted of six households drawn to each other by a complicated series of kinship relations and marriage alliances. Senior men and women headed four of the six households. Only one of the four could seriously claim, however, to be a stable and developed household capable of being identified as a main focus for a residential cluster.

Yawa and Utumat lived with their seven children in a classic rectangular Amazonian house.[11] Utumat had initially been married to Iwap, but because Iwap at the time already possessed two other wives (one of which was Utumat's mother, Uyawet), and because Yawa had no wife and sought one, they all came to an amicable arrangement whereby Utumat left Iwap to become the wife of Yawa. She was a quiet woman whom I did not get to know very well, not only because she resided in that part of the settlement furthest away from the plaza but also because she had no time for company. Her dependent children, all boys barring the last, certainly kept her occupied. A constant round of food preparation, especially yuca reaping, peeling, grating, squeezing, sifting, and baking, largely confined her to domestic chores. Her eldest dependent son, Amakayan, must have been about seventeen years old and was an excellent hunter. His and his father's successful forays into the forest for meat also kept Utumat working on the preparation of food. In this way and many others, Yawa was a diligent husband and father. He too shunned company and had little use for frivolous conversation. In his case this might have had something to do with the congenital deformity of his right hand, which only boasted the stumps of a thumb and two fingers. This did not impede the normal activities of his life, but he did seem overly conscious of his star-shaped hand.

Three dwellings stood very near to the house of Yawa and Utumat. One belonged to Yawa's widowed mother, Chape, whom everyone considered to be a member of her son's household although she lived in a separate house. Another dwelling belonged to Isokikor, the recently married son of Yawa and Utumat. Isokikor had married one of Shamawa's daughters, Ika-aror. Perhaps because Shamawa already had two dependent sons-in-law living close to him and because Yawa's household remained large and in greater need of assistance, Isokikor and Ika-aror built their house in the Yawa cluster. Their virilocal choice appeared to be better suited to Isokikor than to Ika-aror, since the former did little to change the circumstances of his natal household interactions, while Ika-aror kept the grassy path between her mother's house and her own well trodden. The other dwelling belonged to Anya-am, Ihar, and their one-year-old son, Muno. Ihar was the flighty-eyed daughter of Utumat. Many said that Utumat had conceived Ihar while still married to Iwap, and indeed, if it had not been for Iwap's efforts, the many sons Yawa begat with Utumat would have left him without any son-in-law for a very long time. As it turned out, Anya-am lived in uxorilocal residence to Yawa, the man married to his wife's mother, whom his wife called father and whom he referred to as *tam* or *tamchi* (father-in-law).

Anya-am's mother, Chiwosom, also lived in the banana-plant enclave. Brought to Shepariymo by her current husband, Erimink, she had come not long previously from Kašmiyawkï (Electric-Eel Village)—another Waiwai settlement on the Rio Anawa in Brazil. Her household was a troubled one. It possessed a turbulent social history, which, by community knowledge, could be traced to the sequential deaths of individuals once married to Chiwosom. She had been married to a Hishkaryena man named Onish whose sister (Anawochek) was married to Awawatak, Chiwosom's brother. Chiwosom and Onish had three children, Anya-am, Iam-mir, and Ichipow. As I mentioned above, Iam-mir lived with her husband, Itup, in Arumarawan's household cluster. When Onish died, Chiwosom married a Katawina man (named Awayerak) whose sister (Uchiwo-os) was the mother of Epimach, the wife of Chiwosom's other brother, Emtushen, who currently lived on the other side of the settlement in U-ses's household cluster. With her second husband, Chiwosom had two sons, I-ioay and Ichamap, both of whom (with their brother Ichipow) lived with their mother. Unfortunately for Chiwosom, her second husband also died. In the opinion of the community, these deaths and the subsequent breakdown of the households of the deceased had very logical causes, all of which led to Chiwosom.

Erimink possessed all the signs of a man aspiring to Waiwai grandeur. He was the son of "Waiwai" Weychar, one of the very first Wapishana to marry and live in the Waiwai community. His mother, Ika-ar (also known as Ika-amer), conceived him and his sister, Wsae, with "Waiwai" Weychar.[12] Both parents were now dead, but Erimink and Wsae retained their ability to speak fluent Wapishana and Waiwai. Wsae in fact married the Wapishana man Nryhe; they lived with their three daughters and son (and visiting husband's brother's son) in the house closest to the path leading into the forest on the extreme southwest side of the banana-plant enclave. As I mentioned above, Wsae's and Nryhe's eldest daughter, T-tawore, married Upaek and—from a more Wapishana appreciation of residential space—felt no pressure to have her house built right next to her mother's in the enclave. Nonetheless, Wsae and Nryhe lived uxorilocally to Erimink. Because their mother, Ika-ar, had at one time been married to Yawa's father (Umiku) and Chape had called Ika-ar sister, Erimink and Wsae referred to Yawa as brother and called old Chape mother. Through these latter relationships Erimink carefully linked himself to the very influential social network surrounding Chape's brother, Arumarawan. It should also be noted that his father, "Waiwai" Weychar, had at one time been married to the Parukoto woman Marukacha, who was sister to Niawa (also known as Iamwir), the husband of Yaypi, the mother of Awak, to whom Shamawa was once married. Erimink and Shamawa belonged to the same age-grade, grew up together, and referred to each other as brothers. They were longtime competitors in many political struggles. Numerous times Erimink had attempted and failed to form a community of his own at an independent settlement. The recent death of his Wapishana wife, Mary, unequivocally stalled his aspirations to leadership. He had living with him five dependent children from this marriage. His eldest daughter, Nisu, had been, to all political intents and purposes, lost to him in her marriage to the ignoble Akaway. Yet Erimink persisted with the grand plan to reinstate his ambitions—not an unreasonable intent considering that, in this society, any senior age-grade individual without a spouse soon turns into a social and economic parasite dependent not only upon resident kindred but also upon community-wide sentiment. If single parents do not quickly acquire a spouse, they either become a dependent of the very same household they once headed—resulting in the loss of their hard-earned status and esteem—or they become reliant upon a diminishing community altruism that fades because of collective household parsimony. Erimink's ambition far outreached a reasonable intent, however, for his plan required not just remarriage, but rather an attempt to remarry into the extremely influential and dense network of kindred to which Chiwosom belonged.

Chiwosom was the sister of Ewasheshe, the one-time leader of Yočo (Bone Village). The Yočo settlement had been briefly established slightly upriver from Shepariymo when, in February 1976, the entire community left overnight on the weeklong journey to the Rio Anawa. This move marked the final exodus of the once huge agglomeration of settlements on the upper Essequibo River. Plans for the first main move began in 1973 after (what in Waiwai lore has become) Ewka's famous dream or vision about returning to the Rio Mapuera. If a position of "Paramount Chief" could be seriously determined for the Waiwai (and it cannot), then Ewka would have been its individual occupant. For many years he had been the leader of the Yakayaka (Banana Village) community. During the 1960s, possibly at the peak of missionary activity in the area, Ewka endured as many as five settlements—with approximately 528 people—located in very close proximity to Yakayaka (Dagon 1967). Almost immediately after his dream, Ewka instigated preparations for cultivating farms at the Mapuera site, and two years later, in August 1975, he and some members from the agglomeration of villages in and around Yakayaka left for the new settlement called Shepurïtopon (Howler Monkey Rock Village). Another set of members under the leadership of Yakota, Ewka's brother, followed the same process, but they cleared land and cultivated fields on the Anawa, at the Kašmiyawkï (Electric-Eel Village) settlement. During this period Ewasheshe and his community resided at Tïtkomïtu (Brazil-Nut Village), one of the settlements close to Yakayaka. He and most of his community were mainly Hishkaryena from the Rio Nhamunda region in Brazil. Overlapping affinal ties and obligations to many members in the agglomerated villages initially kept Ewasheshe in Guyana. A little after Ewka and Yakota left, Ewasheshe did move his community from Tïtkomïtu to Yočo, but seven months later—allegedly after a disagreement with the then resident district officer over the right to use certain traditional plant products in catching fish near the Kanashen settlement—the Yočo community left for Anawa. The abruptness of the move must have disconcerted the Shepariymo residents, but no one more so than Erimink, whose scheme for obtaining a new wife in Chiwosom now had him traveling to Anawa to claim his bride.

When Erimink finally managed to persuade Chiwosom to return with him to Shepariymo, their marriage never did quite settle into a smooth working enterprise. Certainly in its relevance to furthering Erimink's political aspirations, the marriage never fulfilled its expectations. In its constituted immediacy, the marriage brought eight dependent children into a single household. All these children had to be fed and cared for within the auspices of the marriage and its household, but Erimink's personal anxieties about Chiwosom's reputation for killing her husbands kept him from bringing home the game he caught in order for her to cook. From Chiwosom's point of view, however, this lack of compliance to the cardinal rule for fulfilling the role of a husband and father had her regularly complaining to her coresident brothers and to Shamawa. To make matters worse, her compromised situation forced her to encroach upon the reciprocal flow of social products from her son Anya-am's household—products that should have been moving between the households of Anya-am and his father-in-law, Yawa. When all was said and done, any political aspirations Erimink entertained stalled when his marriage could not produce a smooth-running household. No one beyond his most immediately influenced kindred and affines would have followed him to a new settlement as its community leader. Without the unencumbered avenues of social and economic exchanges brought about by marriage and its affinal alliances, few people had any confidence in the prospect of Erimink's leadership. Without the proper exchanges between husband and wife, a household could not be maintained and, therefore, no relations between

KILLING

households could be successfully drawn together to build a settlement community. In addition, in classic Amazonian fashion, no such community could be maintained over time without a leader who possessed the subtle powers of persuasion (Kracke 1978; Thomas 1982; Clastres 1989).

Erimink was anything but subtle. Indeed he possessed a celebrated reputation for using direct physical force. His brutal killing of two women and three children routinely appeared as the episode most indicative of the Waiwai genre of cruel-death tales.[13] His violent history and "wrongs" (or "ugliness") were certainly not tolerated, but unlike our modern Western intolerance for homicide, Waiwai collective opinion did not associate murder exclusively with a deep-seated and irreducible individual human evil.[14]

In Waiwai society individuals who kill do not do so by themselves; they may be the source of violence but not the final cause of death. Important factors such as the circumstances leading up to the "scene of the wrongdoing" and the "time of death" require certain opportunistic alignments to take place for there to be a killer, a victim, and a homicide. No one dies accidentally in Waiwai society. Death always implicates human intent, but it also immediately identifies spiritual causality. No amount of direct physical action can bring about death without the active compliance of spiritual forces. The community of Shepariymo tolerated Erimink the murderer because the ability to succeed in killing does not depend upon human violence inside an individual but rather upon the whim of outside spiritual forces. The Waiwai seek, nonetheless, to control all potential physical violence with the social force of convivial residential living.

A kind of force vibrates from the Waiwai moral ground of kinship relations. The full impact of this force brings itself into active effect from the face-to-face interactions of coresidence. Living together, in ways that allow for the resonance of proper social relations, gives village society an overall moral right to command the individual bodies of its members. It justifies this role not only by claiming to create internal village conviviality but also by claiming that, with the very act of coresidence, it jettisons all dangers to the community out into the active bodies of distant peoples and their settlement spaces. Successfully living together also confirms the existence and legitimacy of a greater, more transcendent spiritual authority, one that while being both within and beyond human presence, nevertheless gives its sanction to conviviality and the ways this has been achieved. The Waiwai refer to the relations under which living happily together resonates as being *poyino* (of common filial substance). The kinship relation most indicative of poyino is *epeka* (the relationship of uterine relatives). Together, poyino and epeka specify the desired ideal community ties of the *ewto* (village settlement, "place-where-people-live"). It is the womblike character of the settlement, intercommunicating through the epeka that acts on a very necessary internal difference the Waiwai call *wošin* (the relationship of affinal relatives). Epeka and wošin are the primary complementary yet oppositional entities of village community life. The ideal function of Waiwai coresidence appears to be the subordinating of the inherent dangers of the affine to the safety of uterine substance and the balancing of the two. It almost seems as if the settlement—like a traditional communal house with its symbolism of the womb—constrains the individual bodies of its residents to comply with the moral forces of convivial sociality. Hence an adorning of their bodies with the amicability of collective village life could control even the violence of Erimink and Chiwosom.

Such objectives of containment also continued with the only other household I have not so far mentioned, one located in the banana-plant enclave. Puyen, Itokmir (also known as Ikmirkmir), and their many dogs lived in a dark, conical-shaped house southeast of Erimink and Yawa. The house was set off a little from the others, not enough to state that its occupants lived apart from everyone else, but just enough to suggest that its location signaled something odd about the couple. The community loved Puyen and Itokmir; a clear sense of such affection emanated toward them from almost everyone. At first I thought this might have been due to pity. So much of Waiwai social philosophy revolves around marriage and the process of becoming a parent that it seems almost like living a truncated life not to be a father or mother. Puyen and Itokmir belonged to their respective gendered senior age-grade, but they were without children in their home. They appeared to fill this void with the breeding and caring of dogs. The long-held Waiwai reputation for trading in hunting dogs applied to many other Shepariymo inhabitants, but Puyen and Itokmir had cornered the market with the sheer number of dogs they owned.[15] No one could approach their house without being announced by the tonitruous growls and barking of their pack. The more highly valued dogs were tied up on raised platforms all around the inside of the house. The couple named, regularly bathed, and painted them. These dogs could well have been "surrogate children." No such "children" could, however, transform the household of Puyen and Itokmir into a hub of an acceptable household cluster; such "children" had no means of transforming their natal household into the focal point of other dependent households. They could not bring the kind of "beauty" that human sons and daughters brought to their parents.

Puyen called Iwap *apa* (father). He called Utumat achi (sister) because she was his mother's sister's daughter. His mother, Hmota, had not only been married to Iwap but also to Imoyay, the father of Etap (U-ses's wife). Puyen, therefore, also called Etap sister. He called both Yawa and U-ses *poimo* (brother-in-law). Hence, because they considered each other brothers, Yawa, Erimink, and even U-ses fell on the affinal side of relations to Puyen, and he referred to them as wošin (affinal relative). Itokmir's mother's sister's daughter was Amishamish (Iwap's current wife), whom Itokmir called sister. Itokmir's mother's sister's husband's brother's daughter was old Chape (Amishamish's father's brother's daughter) and Yawa's mother. Itokmir referred to Chape and Yawa as epeka (uterine relative). Puyen and Itokmir were both intimately linked to the households around them in the enclave, but they were not affiliated in a clear-cut residential sense to any cluster of these households. As in the case of every village resident, their calling and referring to other members of the settlement by kinship and marriage terms of address drew them into multiple and dense networks of community-wide relations.

These relations made experiential sense at the level of face-to-face intravillage living. They functioned to attract and bind the individual bodies of members into the empirical reality of the settlement. As a selection of distinct households, the settlement only made sense to its inhabitants in the ways in which each household interlinked with others to produce the collective community of the village. In the kinship and marriage terms exchanged, each individual body and household carried the social means and justification for composing the specific form and organizational character of the community. They comprised at one and the same time both the means and the actuality of convivial village society. When composed at the extreme of its capacity, the village community exhibited the classic Amazonian traits of a political and economic autonomy. It also contained an aesthetic that purposefully turned back upon itself to reproduce an appeal for societal continuity.

Like the other members of Shepariymo, Puyen and Itokmir adorned themselves with the beauty of residential conviviality. Even though they could not establish a household cluster of their own or affiliate themselves to others without undermining the prestige of their senior age-grade status, nevertheless, they implemented who they understood themselves to be through a network of face-to-face relations. Only in these relations did they appear to experience proper social being. Like all other community members, they achieved social beauty and appeal by first seeking and sustaining a life as epeka and wošin. They wore these categories of relations inside and upon their bodies in such a fashion that whenever and wherever they went, the settlement went with them. In the intellectual space of Waiwai collective knowledge, the community to which individuals belong moves with them like an ambulatory communal house.[16] Being literate in the social history of the community means knowing how to read the intellectual garments of village identity. In Waiwai social epistemology, to know the face or body of an individual Waiwai is to possess the knowledge about which community

that individual belongs to and, in addition, the particular relationship one might have with that individual. Conversely, to know the
community to which the individual belongs is to possess already the
knowledge of who the individual is and how one might be related
to that individual. One is in the category of either epeka or wošin to
others. Being able to act out in the lived spaces of settlement life the
expected roles shaped by these categories provides the fulfillment of
individual social being and the collective continuity of society itself.
Being epeka or wošin identifies an individual with a known community. This is beauty at the personal level, for it brings the individual
into the social symmetry of the community. At the collective level, it
is the felt joy of an aesthetic that comes from experiencing the very
continuousness of society. Both the aesthetic and the residential
expression of the continuousness require, however, the completion
of a circle.

We could have entered the circle of houses around the central
plaza at any point in introducing the community of Shepariymo.
The movement from one house to the other would have brought us
back to where we had begun. Yet the main entrance to the settlement onto the cleared ground of the plaza opens beside the house
of Shamawa, the village leader. And like the direction in which the
bowls of beverage move from hand to hand around the communal
circle of drinkers, it seemed appropriate to introduce the individual
households by beginning with the house of the village leader and
moving from there in an easterly to a northerly, then a westerly, and
finally a southerly direction around the settlement. In Waiwai ideas

the circle—with its *tamnoñim* (roundness), its *řořo* (center), its *ĕčïwo*
(periphery), its *yawï* (inside) and *yumkay* (outside)—expresses the
perfectibility of domestic space and timelessness. Through actually
forming a circle with the body or with the physical structures of
a dwelling, a creative energy seems to become available to participants. No single body or household can generate the vitality of
the circle on its own. The circle demands cooperation and interdependence. It brings community into viable existence and sustains
it within a spatial circuit. Like the womb, it acts to define a center

with a "boundedness" and an inside with an "outsidedness." The one always implies the other. The one cannot be without the other. Producing community life in the form of this aesthetic requires the perceived symmetry of tamnoñim. With this in mind, in order to complete the circle and the particular organizational accent of Shepariymo, I have yet to mention two more households.

Anawach, Netcha, and their two-year old, Ominai, lived in a relatively small rectangular house between the houses of Ponu and Shamawa. The house fronted onto the central plaza but also backed onto the banana enclave. This conformed to the compromise expected from Anawach's relations to other community members. As I mentioned above, Retawp (Anawach's Wapishana father-in-law) lived on the high ground to the northwest. Strictly speaking, Retawp had not implemented the Waiwai postmarital residence preference for uxorilocality. Hence we find Anawach living close to Ponu, whom he considered an epeka (their fathers called each other brother). He referred to Iwap and Amishamish as well as Puyen and Itokmir as wošin (his father, Yaymuchi, called Amishamish and Itokmir sister). Anawach also referred to Yawa as wošin, because his father called old Chape (Yawa's mother) sister. His father currently lived with the Mapuera Waiwai and, while in terms of settlement location Anawach resided virilocally, it seemed rather obvious to everyone that because his wife, Netcha, had no kindred over the Serra Acarai in Brazil, he was in essence correctly residing close to his wife's kinsfolk. He certainly possessed a good balance of epeka and wošin to sustain him socially. Indeed, even with his relative youth and fledgling household, his representative wošin relation to Shamawa carried considerable local prestige. Shamawa happened to be on the receiving side of the wošin relationship with Anawach, because he had taken Awam as his wife—a woman Anawach called sister (the daughter of his father's mother's sister's son Ayk). Yet Anawach gained little else from his brother-in-law relation with Shamawa, not because of his youth but because of his neighbor and epeka Ipamar.

On the edge of the plaza, in the house in front of the houses of Ponu and Puyen, lived Ipamar, Iknukim, and their two children,

Rona and Unitak. Ipamar was brother to Ponu and son of Arumarawan and Yenayaw. A barrel-chested man with powerful, mus-
cular arms and legs, he held the reputation for being the finest hunter
of big game in the community. He too displayed the conservatism
of his parents. But for his khaki short pants, he always dressed in
traditional garb: long hair oiled and in a bamboo tube, feathered
earplugs, beads, and armbands. In collective village hunts, he was always *poturu* (out front). Like Ponu, he referred to Anawach as epeka.
His wife, Iknukim, was the daughter of Awak, a Mawayena woman
whom both Shamawa and his father (Emachek) were married to at
the same time. Depending on the moment and the circumstances,
Iknukim could be heard calling Shamawa either father or brother. A
vivacious woman with a strong personality, Iknukim continually exhibited a social presence equally strong as her husband's. In terms of
support to the village leadership and community morale, they were
indispensable. By being epeka to Anawach and by taking Iknukim as
his wife, Ipamar had in effect canceled out any debt Shamawa had
incurred in taking a sister from Anawach and his pool of epeka. In
fact, the dependent wošin side of the relationship fell upon Ipamar.

The social dependencies and moral obligations of kinship and
marriage held the circuit of Shepariymo household relations in
place, but the particular accent or dominant resonance that they
manifested depended upon the marital hub of a single household.
The weight of the community circle hung primarily upon the moral
character and strength of relations exhibited inside and intersected
outside through the household of Shamawa and Awam. The very
making of Shepariymo was associated with Shamawa and Awam.
The physical site of the village had been initially cleared for use as a
field through Shamawa's initiative and subsequently developed into
a fully fledged settlement. When in 1971 Shamawa decided he had
taken enough of the discomfort due to the overcrowding of people
living in and around Yakayaka, he and those households closely related to his own moved to the current Shepariymo location. As the
initiator of the site and the move, and with the success of having
others follow him to the new settlement, it was understood by those

example of the locales

around him that he would be given the opportunity to *mïtonho* (keep together) the circle of households comprising the community. The success of this lay in Shamawa's ability to maintain the smooth workings of his own marriage and household. It was substantiated—at least for political purposes—by the ways in which relations between his household and those within his cluster operated.

Here Shamawa's relations with his daughter Emekuch and his son-in-law Enkik were strategically significant. If the moral obligations of epeka and wošin could be properly maintained between these two households, then those extending out from the household of Enkik and Emekuch (to Enkik's mother's brother Uwa, and to Enkik's sister Akuchiruw—married to Akiamon), they would maintain the important Chikena side of the community and settlement. Equally significant were the wošin relations (of father's sister's daughter and mother's brother's son) exchanged between Shamawa and Etap (U-ses's wife), which helped to keep the Shereu, Katuema, and Hishkaryena side of the community linked in as part of the circle. The relations extending out from the household of Etap and U-ses interlocked with the other households by way of their own epeka and wošin relations—specifically as sibling groups linked to each other by a series of marriages. Shamawa considered himself as coming from the Parukoto, because both his father and his mother grew up in communities of these people at the headwaters of the Mapuera.[17] Awam, however, referred to herself as coming from the Mawayena, because her parents grew up in communities of these people who lived next to the Parukoto a little downriver on the Mapuera. The marriage of their other daughter, Ika-aror, to Isokikor continued the forging of these two peoples, but—more immediately significant—it drew in and further linked the household of Yawa and Utumat (Isokikor's parents) as well as the household of Anya-am and Ihar (Isokikor's brother-in-law and sister) and, of course, all those other households linked to the latter by epeka and wošin relations. It should be kept in mind that Ika-aror was mother's brother's daughter and father's sister's daughter to Isokikor. In respect to the marriage between Anya-am's sister Iam-mir and Itup (Arumarawan's son), this union overlaid and reinforced the already existing relations between the Shamawa and Arumarawan households. Indeed, Awam and Arumarawan referred to each other as epeka (because Awam's father was mother's sister's son to Arumarawan). When we include the high status relations of senior age-grade household heads with the accumulated strategic relations of epeka and wošin, we could conclude that the household of Shamawa and Awam possessed the heaviest weight from the most influential relations in the community.

The mïtonho capabilities of their household—that is, those acting upon the primary relations of epeka and wošin, allowed the other households and clusters of households to be configured as the particular settlement circle of Shepariymo. Because of the extent and strength of the crosscutting and extended epeka and wošin relations aligned to the household of Shamawa, Shepariymo identified Shamawa as its kayaritomo. The ability to draw and hold the social relations of kinship and affinity together create and sustain the community circle and, in doing so, provide for the means to identify leadership and the burden of its responsibilities. These modes and relations are not, however, restricted only to the functioning and identifying of leadership. They are the very substance of what it means to become a social being in Waiwai society and exist for proper appropriation by all individuals.

It can be reasonably argued that without the effective force of and access to the relationships subsumed within epeka and wošin no Waiwai settlement or village community can come into social reality. The circle of individuals and households depends upon these conceptual and objectified categories in order for the residential life of the community to be acted out. The beauty of the circle expresses itself by manifesting the symmetry of its parts in the whole. Its intellectual and practical balance cannot be approached, however, without first establishing the difference and opposition between the principles of the epeka and wošin. Once maintained as mutually exclusive, it then becomes the work of the aesthetic—appealing to symmetry—to mïtonho the irreconcilable but complementary parts. When they make up the constitutive Waiwai truth of the meaningful whole—for example, as poyino—in community life, access to these categories appears almost like the very rights and obligations of the social person. No one can be a member of this society without being in an epeka or wošin relation with others. Certainly, in this regard epeka and wošin could theoretically be referred to as jural entities. They constitute, as aspects of social personhood, not only the individual but also the community and the settlement.

Conceptual Ideals of Time and Space

The analytical usefulness of the "House Society" concept may well place the Waiwai only in "the very weakest end of the spectrum that house societies constitute" (Rivière 1995:203). In the strictly formalist sense, recognizing the ideas that produce House Societies demands identifying "a corporate body holding an estate made up of both material and immaterial wealth, which perpetuates itself through the transmission of its name, its goods, and its titles down a real or imaginary line, considered legitimate as long as this continuity can express itself in the language of kinship or of affinity and, most often, of both" (Lévi-Strauss 1982:174).

In the case of traditional Guiana Amerindian societies, it may be difficult to hold to the view of the village community as a "corporate body" with jural rights because, "while these ideas provide the conceptual basis for societal continuity, they do not give rise to discrete social units" (Rivière 1995:202). It could, nonetheless, be argued that the only relevant discrete social units for these Guiana societies exist solely within their "invisible" conceptual world. This would be the case not because "in Guiana . . . settlements are merely transitory evidence of a continuous and real although invisible world" (Riviére 1995:202), but because traditional Guiana societies consider the real and invisible world as eternal—that is, *outside of time* itself. Hence the eternal cannot be found, for example, in the immortal, where continuous time more often functions and, indeed, becomes subject to discontinuities. In this respect—that is, in terms of being real, invisible, and outside of time—the Waiwai ideas about epeka and wošin can be considered enduring discrete social entities in their epistemology. For like the enduring entities that constitute the sun, gold, rock, and mountains—but unlike the mortality of the body and the impermanence of the village settlement—epeka and wošin compose the poyino (of common filial substance) as the a-temporal ideal of the circular House. Access to these entities does entitle the individual and the settlement to social personhood. Thus the concept of durability remains crucial, but, in Waiwai ideology at least, this seems best dealt with not from an understanding of "the house as a grouping [which] endures through time" (Carsten and Hugh-Jones 1995:7) or of transmitted properties that "concertina time" (Lea 1992:130) but rather from an understanding of a durability that exists outside of time. In the formalist view, this conclusion may indeed put the Waiwai at the "weak end" of the House Society paradigm, but what can be learned from the volume of scholarship on lowland South American societies tells us that the Amerindian conceptual world appears stronger and far more enduring than its physical counterpart.

In the Waiwai case, as the merely transitory representation of "putting, so to speak, 'two in one'" (Lévi-Strauss 1982:184)—for example, epeka and wošin in poyino—the instance of Shepariymo physically articulates the concept of poyino as the House. "The house accomplishes a sort of inside-out topological reversal, it replaces an internal duality with an external unity" (Lévi-Strauss 1982:184). I do not think a reversal necessarily takes place, nor do I think that the external unity of poyino as the House replaces the internal duality of epeka and wošin. At the level of the transitory physical structures of both the natal house and the community settlement, however, where epeka (in filiation) and wošin (in marriage) couple to produce the poyino ideal, the eternal conceptual reality of the House does function to encompass. If this can be considered an external unity, then it is one made in the aesthetic image of the circle—a circle needing to retain the differences it encompasses. These differences do not disappear; they merely become contained, the circle containing them as a duality in order to sustain itself. In this Waiwai sense, the circular House exists outside the temporal and spatial reality of Shepariymo. It existed both before and after the people and the site gave Shepariymo its transitory physical presence in the world. Perhaps the more empirically inclined may say one always needs the physical world to verify presence. One could state, therefore, that the people who lived before and after Shepariymo and the settlements they built before and after it are the only factual evidence of a Waiwai concept of the circular House Society. Yet even such evidence must rely upon conceptual ideals, in the case of Waiwai ideology not preceding ideals held before or in time in any antecedent sense, but ideals outside of time fixed in what could be successfully interpreted for them as spiritual and cosmological spaces.

The Eternal Conceptual Circle
Shepariymo did disappear in 1986. The forest undergrowth crept and crawled its way around the abandoned standing structures and recarpeted the central plaza. Thorns and razor grass populated the gaps between the saplings that had sprung up where people and dwellings once were. The site again belonged to the forest. The people of Shepariymo moved (about a half-day's paddling) downstream to start a new settlement called Akotopono or Akomïtu (Mortar Village). In relocating they became the Akotopono community.

There were many reasons for the move. One certainly appeared to be the desire to be where representatives of the Guyanese state could have easier access to the community. Guyana claims 83,000 square miles of territory (85 percent forest, 10.5 percent savannas), with over 90 percent of its current population, 705,156 (1999 estimate), living on the narrow northern coastal plain. The Waiwai who live on the Essequibo River in the extreme southern regions of the country have little contact with central Guyanese society. They officially occupy about 4,450 square miles of Guyanese territory.[18] In 1978 there were approximately 127 to 143 individuals concentrated in the single village of Shepariymo. When they moved to Akotopono, the population had grown (in 1998 it had risen to 230 people). They have "beneficial" occupancy of some 2,050 square miles in an "enclosed district" of approximately 2,400 square miles (Guyana Government 1969:208).

Akotopono sits on an ancient Taruma site upon the left bank, at a bend in the river that allows for a perfect view of any approach from either side. In the dry season wide, flat rocks appear in the river, convenient for the washing and drying of hammocks and plants. Behind the settlement and the narrow belt of forest surrounding it stretches an unusual but small savanna called Gunns Strip. Here light aircrafts can land in the dry season. During the early period of missionary work in the region, Gunns Strip had been the principal point of entry for the North Americans.

At that time the settlement was identified with the leadership of Umachar. When it once again became a lived space for the Shepariymo community, Shamawa held on to his leadership position. This indeed was one reason why the community could move as a complete village without dividing. Unfortunately Awam died and Shamawa could no longer act as kayaritomo. The community kept together, however, initially with the leadership of Upaek and later with that of A-awp (Shamawa's brother, who married one of Arumarawan's daughters).

In the summer of 2000 the Akotopono community again disappeared, this time due to the heavy rains and flooding that literally washed the settlement away. Today the Akotopono community is the Masakïnaru (Mosquito Village) community. The new site can be found a few bends up river from Akotopono and has overland access to Gunns Strip. Immediate and long-term pragmatic concerns may well explain the cause of every settlement move. Yet if one were to follow the pattern of village settlement movement up and down the Essequibo, even before Shepariymo, I think one would find the same cycle of occupation occurring over and over again.

Part of any account of the movement of a people considered by many to be "semi-nomadic horticulturists" (Fock 1963; Yde 1965) would have to be informed at some point by factors from their subsistence way of life. Even at the time of my first visit—though they did not make up any measured sum of Waiwai daily or annual life—subsistence farming and hunting were major aspects of a Wai-wai pattern of existence. At the time money had very little use in their economy. The Waiwai did certainly appreciate and desire the industrially manufactured sugar and salt produced outside their society. While these, like other outside-produced commodities, were difficult to purchase because of problems in gaining access to money, the main difficulty arose from problems in getting commodities supplied to them from the various outside sources. They could and did barter hunting dogs, parrots, and grater boards to neighboring peoples (such as the Wapishana in the Rupununi savannas and the Trio in southern Surinam), and, with the money they received for these trade goods, they would try to purchase such outside-produced products as fishhooks, fishing line, gun powder, soap, clothes, sugar, and salt. But this kind of bartering and purchasing required special journeys lasting from two to eight weeks. Such trading has been going on for a long time, arguably even before Amerindian contact with representatives of European societies. The hardships involved, however, have not diminished. In acquiring outside or Western-produced commodities, certain already-held Waiwai gains have to be forgone, and in many instances these simply do not warrant the loss. Perhaps at the core of the issue lies a specific Waiwai way of understanding the relationship between the socially produced product and the producer. This is not a society, for example, that configures an autonomy of the productive self extending to a justification for an essential relationship between the self and the purchased product. Here buying a product does not give the purchaser an absolute sense of ownership over the product. In addition, property does not have the kinds of moral and jural authority that could be rarefied as the object of a rigid political scrutiny. The material and technical aspects of subsistence life obtainable through access to land are not necessarily determined by a control that can be owned as a property. In Waiwai ideas, even the crops they grow remain subject to the "timeless-circle" of the House, an eternal factor with the capacity to force movement along a circular path that is beyond human control.

Farm soils can only sustain cultivation of the Waiwai staple crop of yuca for a limited period. Yuca has about a nine-month maturity rate. To obviate restrictions upon continuous demand and offset the gradual loss of production due to the high rate of soil leaching, the Waiwai always plant intermittently and harvest from fields planted in the previous years. They plant new fields every year. When they clear the forest for a field in August, plant it in October, and reap from it in June of the following year, they continue to reap from the same field (if they replant there) at a reduced rate for three to four years. They also augment their surrounding settlement fields with auxiliary river farms located usually not more than a day's paddling away from the main settlement. It is these auxiliary river farms that become the potential sites for future settlements (and conversely, are the old settlement sites that become auxiliary river farms). Many sites, like those of Akotopono and Masakïnaru, have been resettled more than once. They may even retain the same name (as in the case of Akotopono), with the story of how the site came by its name being passed on from generation to generation. Shepariymo, for instance, came by its name because when the residents first moved in they heard the howling of a very large dog coming from the direction of the nearby lagoon. Nevertheless, in the end even these ingenious strategies of agriculture and nomenclature, for what could be interpreted as a combined bodily and intellectual marking of places, become subject to the uniform motion of the inert circle. Ultimately, for the Waiwai, the eternal energies of the circular House move entities along and around in a perpetual motion of recapitulating stages.

In each case, from Shepariymo to Akotopono and from Akotopono to Masakïnaru, the eternal conceptual circle guides the form and structure of the village settlement. Communities and their settlements appear and disappear; the foliage of the forest parts, and we see people claiming their right to a part of and as a force in the making of the circular House Society. The foliage closes, but only to be reopened again in another theater, with another circular stage of performers and spectators. They all adhere to the blueprint of an eternal architectural landscape. It is a conceptual grid allowing them to appropriate and withstand the constant changes in their society. For example, the single communal-house settlement with its households and household clusters has been transformed into the single "agglomerated" (Rivière 1970) settlement, drawing into one central village community what, in the past, would have been a string of single communal-house communities and settlements stretched out along the river. The eternal circle of the communal house now forms the circle of houses comprising the agglomerated settlement. Also, in the fundamental Waiwai aesthetic of circular encompassment, the House has allowed for the incorporation of other peoples into the community. If one were to be informed by a discourse of biology, it would be quite reasonable to assume that "there are no people who call themselves Wai Wai alive at this time; the last member of the group who called themselves by this name died 20 years ago or more" (Robert Hawkins 1998:25). Here the principle of encompassment has succeeded to such an extent that those judging it from other criteria such as those of biology have not been able to give encompassment the capacity to preserve Waiwai identity. The various peoples who refer to themselves as being born or raised in communities identified as Aramayena, Chikena, Hishkaryena, Marakayena, Mawayena, Parukoto, Shereu, Tunayena, and Wapishana and who all now live in Waiwai communities do call themselves Waiwai. The circular society of the House permits them to do so. They remain persuaded by the precedent of those individual Waiwai who invited them to live with them. The corporeal mortality of these individuals may no longer exist, but the eternal spiritual and cosmological forces that vitalized them certainly do, and they allow for a continuance. In the immediacy of residence, they make and remake being Waiwai. The transformative power of the circle recapitulates being Waiwai in and upon the individual bodies of those living in the ewto (village settlement) and ewtoto (village community).

[handwritten marginalia, left margin: identity about about residential living]

[handwritten note at bottom: understand this theme but when/where did he bring in the womb?]

From the Sutured Wound of Being

Adorning the Body, Knowing the World

Even without the supposed ritual requirement of "torture" or imposition of "pain," "the body mediates the acquisition of a knowledge"
(Clastres 1989:180). It is an acquired knowledge about society constituting and sustaining itself in, on, and through the corporeal being
of the individual (Douglas 1971; Foucault 1979; Gell 1996). At the
same time, however, it is also knowledge about human subjectivity
attaining its consciousness by means of this very same corporeality (Scarry 1985; Scheper-Hughes 1991; Merleau-Ponty 1992). In
other words knowledge of the lived world is experienced through
the body, while knowing the lived body is dialectically experienced
through the self (Gadow 1980). The lived body, as an acting and
vulnerable subjectivity in the world, mediates between society and
the self. In this relation it is the greater distinction between the world
and the body, rather than that between the self and the body, that
society seeks to reduce by inscribing itself upon and in the body
as an adornment and as a memory. It seems the "primary unity"
(Gadow 1980:174) of the lived body—that is, between the self and
the body—helps to produce the very vulnerability of the body in
the world, where the unifying immediacy of self and body radically
contrasts with the lack of immediacy between society and the body.
Indeed, in order to constitute and sustain its own existence, society
has repeatedly to evoke its presence by way of somatic realties; a
bodily understanding (Bourdieu 1990) or knowledge becomes an

imperative requirement for social existence. Written on the body, felt in pain, made desirable by and fulfilled in the self, the obtained juridical knowledge of the body is about social belonging. To become a social person, the individual must submit to society (Fortes 1973; Harris 1989; La Fontaine 1989); the body has at least to respond with an appearance of adhering to social determinants (Marx 1976b [1859]).[1] The individual unified with society—to the degree in which the self is assumed to be in unity with the body—appears to be a major societal concern. Of course society can never be quite certain of subjectivities' commitment, but in the habitus of bodily techniques, it appears to achieve some level of reassurance (Mauss 1973; Bourdieu 1990). In the body and hence in the lived world, with the collective compliance of individuals as social persons, society confirms its presence. Tracking this social presence from the impressions made by the body in Waiwai society has been one of my principal concerns.

How do the Waiwai achieve the ideal secondary unity between the individual and society? What are the characteristic features of this unity? Where does it present itself in order to become known? When if at all is it challenged? And why does it take the forms and meanings it manifests in their world? The trails to some of these answers meander through a representational and interpretative landscape where "savage," "inferior," "mythic," "divine," "filiated," "affinal," "mutable," and "adorned" bodies present themselves as cultural landmarks. Indeed, the Waiwai body offers itself as both the terrain upon which the imprints of cultural meanings can be traced and as the very monument of such inscriptions. On the Waiwai body—that is, principally through the cultural artifacts of its adornment—we can see the knowledge about social belonging produced, displayed, and achieved. It is a knowledge that allows the individual to be positioned in relationships determined fundamentally by categories of gender and kinship. To know the meanings of these categories requires their objectification in historically ordered forms—the culturally specific metonymy, so to speak, of gender and kinship. In attaining the unity between individual and society, however, the categories of gender and kinship have to be more than simply the objectified knowledge of social forms; they also have to be metaphors of being. In other words they have to be persistent social realities as well as subjective experiences. Their imperatives appear to be necessary here because while the body of the individual dies, the social category of the person lives on. As individual subjectivities expire, collective concepts and beliefs about being—for example, a man, a woman, a wife, a husband, a brother, a sister—remain in the world in other individual agents of society. Thus does the overall motive of an anthropological pursuit become the tracing and interpreting of Waiwai concepts and beliefs about the social person—the describing and explaining of representations of the secondary unity between the individual and society.

In our "modern" world of international tribunals and aspirations for universal human rights, it would appear to be a very risky business to deal with notions of a culturally determined selfhood. To expose any relation between culture and the self could run the risk of exposing the role power plays in producing the relation and, perhaps, the necessary dependence between culture and selfhood. In revelations of this kind, the risk may more often lie in undermining the moral aspirations of the dominant cultural views about subjectivity. Perhaps unwarranted, but nonetheless logical, is the tendency for truths about subjectivity to lose their credibility because of suggestions that they may have been made by humankind rather than by some essential and autonomous factor outside or beyond human causality. In the realms of natural justice and individual liberty, for example, it would be difficult to argue for a historically and culturally produced self that did not recognize these essential factors and allowed them to be its moral judge and desire. Yet in many ways, this may well be just what much of the literature on the anthropology of the self has been intimating if not actually stating outright.

In the cultural differences that anthropology presents, it is often difficult not to give to these differences the very possibility of an alternative perceiving and hence of a dealt-with understanding of a culturally specific selfhood. It is foolish, if not academically naïve, to deny subjectivity to others. Yet in the recognition of the self, the care of the self, and the development and fulfillment of the self, are these other kinds of selfhood that anthropology frequently represents in other cultures not just different versions of the same Universal Self? No, I think not—certainly not, if this universal selfhood happens to be the one produced from our historical and cultural understandings. The inference seems to be that the different cultural implements, processes, and even goals that societies apply in the production of themselves from individuals differ precisely because societies engage culturally specific notions of the self. The two-way relationship between self and society would, of course, necessitate an applicable consciousness of the social world providing for the self. Arguably much of the work of culture deals with this dialectical factor of the individual and collective consciousness between self and society. That it goes about this differently for different societies seems to suggest that while subjectivity may well be a universal factor, the Universal Self is not. Thus a singular intrigue of Waiwai subjectivity must be the determining of when and how Waiwai culture configures and shapes the self and, conversely, when and how Waiwai subjectivity provides for the influencing function of culture. Surely this must be crucial for interpretation, if for no other reason than that it allows us not to jump to conclusions about Waiwai statements and actions that may appear at first glance to be similar to those produced by our own historical and cultural understandings. Nowhere is this more of an issue than in regard to bodily adornment, where the meanings given to the body and its adorning address some of the most interesting questions and answers raised about the self and society.

"You look like and behave like a woman, so you must be a woman on the inside, right?" "You look like and behave like a black man, so you have to be black on the inside, right?" "You look like and behave like a child; you must be a child on the inside, right?" "You look beautiful, so you must be beautiful on the inside, right?" Perhaps too simplistic a way of putting it, but we should keep in mind that we are speaking here about an imaginary body, one already possessed by the signifying logic of symbolic representations. As an object of the human imagination, the body becomes something altogether different from its "physical" being (Merleau-Ponty 1992). In our current Western understandings of the self or the "modern soul," the gendered body, the racial body, the infantile body, and the perfectible body all seemingly reflect the idea of subjectivity in the very corporeality of the body. It could be argued that this allows the Western capitalist body-rituals to more easily repossess the self on behalf of their individual participants (Gell 1996; Cavallaro and Warwick 1998). By helping to create the idea of the body possessed—that is, as an owned object in a world where levels of felt alienation, domination, and invisibility appear very high—the rituals of the repossession of the body are simultaneously rituals of the repossession of the self. Ideologically, the repossessing of body and soul is tantamount to the achievement of a liberty. Presumably no longer owned by the moral confinements of others, the liberated self and body can find fulfillment for its own individualism. The gaps between desires and their satisfaction can, at least temporarily, be sutured with the felt completion of individual being. Satisfying the desires of a femininity, a racial identity, being a child, and/or being beautiful completes, but it also confirms as well as achieves a kind of justice and freedom. In this kind of social democracy, it almost amounts to an individual right to be gendered and racialized, to have a childhood, and to be beautiful. The sutured wound of being—that is, the coming together of the body and the modern soul—completes the person as an ideally unique individual; it is the very felt experience of being alive. In this kind of ideological tradition, not only is there no life or, indeed, no death without the body, but there is also no consciousness, no self-awareness without the body.

Within our "modern" ideas of pain and death, "each only happens because of the body" (Scarry 1985:31). Hence when the body experiences pain and death, it is because sentience and life are reduced to the body. For us it seems the sentient and living self is the body. But how useful is it to extend this view to others? For example, "that pain is so frequently used as a symbolic substitute for death in the initia-

no hierarchy in difference for WaiWai
b white ppl have pointed hole like sunfish
b black ppl have skin like monkey
& no biomedical ritual term

tion rites of many tribes is surely attributable to an intuitive human recognition that pain is the equivalent in felt-experience of what is unfeelable in death" (Scarry 1985:31). Does this "intuitive human recognition" get produced because of the same inherent qualities of a uniquely autonomous self and body? Does it also mean that if these tribal individuals could feel death, that death for them would be like pain? Difficult questions, but it should be noted that because intense physical pain is a state without "referential content" (Scarry 1985:5) and, indeed, "the reality of physical pain is [inaccessible] to anyone not immediately experiencing it" (Scarry 1985:29), we have to return to culture and its representations of such phenomena. Because death and pain supposedly destroy the content of consciousness for the inaccessible subjectivity immediately experiencing them, the entire project of "remaking the world" (after death and pain) involves constructing objectified realities out of immaterial feelings. In the Western imagination, this kind of presencing of being may be the most indefatigable role the body has to perform.

From tattoos, piercings, and plastic surgery to the auctioned dresses of a dead British princess, the anxious body strives to confirm its presence. Even though "identities may be forged . . . out of a conscious and critical act of self-dispossession" (Cavallaro and Warwick 1998:205), such identities, nevertheless, assume and work with notions of an authentic selfhood, the status of which is acquired from culture and society. The tricky business of knowing that one possesses a distinctive self and body and yet still having to present such knowledge with an absent self and body seems to be the assigned duties of our adorned coverings. For example, the acclaimed carnality of the body "transmuted into dress as a substitute flesh . . . do[es] not shroud the supposedly natural body, but rather its absence" (Cavallaro and Warwick 1998:155). As an assemblage point for the embodied self, the wearing of clothes seeks to bring into presence that which it covers. Even the developed muscles of the nude—rather than naked (Clark 1964 [1956])—body-builder attempt to bring into presence a gendered perfectibility that simultaneously states—in its "dressed" absenting of what it builds on—the precariousness of its essentialist claims (Dutton 1995; Balsamo 1997). As with clothes and developed muscles, so too with tattooing, for "in terms of the basic body-image of the subject, tattooing produces a paradoxical double skin" (Gell 1996:38). Integral and indivisible, the tattooed skin "draws attention to nakedness . . . and what tattooing reveals, beyond the revelation of nudity itself, is an inside that comes from the outside . . . the exteriorization of the interior" (Gell 1996:38). One should keep in mind at all times the conscious fiction or artificiality of wearing clothes, muscles, and tattoos, because in each case the culture of fashion, body-building, and tattooing merely reinforces further our notions of what is "real" and "natural" about the embodied self. In addition the Western concept of a real and natural individuality does not disappear under the multiple attempts by society to categorize and distribute such ideas as the constituted evidence of its own presence. Indeed it remains the fundamental message of our Western tradition to be constantly preoccupied with the precariousness of our essentialist notions about the embodied self, which, if it were indeed real and natural in its features of an authentic presence, would not need the constant preoccupation of culture. What, however, about Waiwai subjectivity and embodiment? When and how does cultural adornment configure and shape Waiwai self and body? When and how does Waiwai subjectivity and embodiment provide for the influencing function of culture in adornment?

Savage and Inferior Bodies

If establishing origins does indeed impress, it surely would be arresting for students of Guyanese history to be informed that contrary to many English and German authoritative registers, the claim to first European contact with the Waiwai and their neighbors was made not by Sir Robert Schomburgk, but rather by a nonliterate Jewish Dutchman named Gerrit Jacobs (Bos 1985). It appears that between 1718 and 1720—some 117 years before Schomburgk's more celebrated meeting with the Guiana peoples—Jacobs, a trader with and slaver of Amerindians, chanced upon the "Atorai," "Trio,"

"Tunayena," and "Waiwai" in the region above the Rupununi and the Corentyne rivers (Ijzerman 1911; De Goeje 1943). Jacobs traveled twice to the diverse peoples in the south.[2] On the first journey, his memory served as the only parchment for recording his encounters. On the second journey, Salomon Sanders accompanied him; Sanders was an expert on precious metals who certainly could read and write. Sanders's tasks were to chronicle the events of the journey and to investigate Jacobs's report about a mountain of gold and silver located in the upper Corentyne area. The governor of Surinam had commissioned his assignment. No mines of wealth were found, but we can garner from his journal invaluable images of the Waiwai living on flat, fertile land extending into forested mountains, the trees of which were fashioned by them into canoes. Sanders's text suggests an agricultural people keenly aware of the value of good soil and land (Yde 1959, 1960, 1965; Dagon 1967; Hills 1968); an advance riverine culture cognizant of the advantages of dugout canoes (Roth 1929:x; Fock 1963:9; Yde 1965:238–43). Yet, quite apart from what it may intimate about the Waiwai and their neighbors, the text also reveals that these forest peoples had fervently aroused both the curiosity and the cupidity of the European.

The journal and the second journey had been initially inspired by Jacobs's oral account of having seen a golden disk of an Amerindian's nasal pendant. It was this facial adornment, purposefully drawing attention to the body of its wearer, that led to Jacobs's anticipation of affluence and the governor's sponsored quest for auric wealth. Inscribed with its own culturally specific meanings yet still communicatively broad enough to impress itself (not without some irony, of course) upon the imagination of the European, the adorned body of the Amerindian found itself the stimulant to a strange and avaricious desire. A desire that, incongruous to Waiwai expectations, ignored the calculated human qualities behind the object of its craving. A desire that foregrounded material wealth while keeping in the background the human face of an adorned alterity. A desire that appeared comfortable with attributing ignorance to an alternative rationality that encouraged the wearing rather than the selling of gold. In con-

[handwritten margin notes:]
pretty old children on their breasts, very close to mother

bodily contact intimacy

size of apron = status symbol - womanhood, motherhood

girls wear smaller ones (not to do w/ covering parts)

[left margin handwritten notes:]
a genre for you?

families bathe together never alone

bathe A LOT, sometimes a day

different understanding of dirt, filth

cooperative understanding of hygiene

young boys bathe together

families bathe @ different times, wait for each other

* scary things in water

spicuous discordance to its offered stimulant, this rather rapacious but selective appetite invigorated the interpretative forms of most, if not all, the early descriptive accounts of Amerindian presence in the Guianas.

When he first met the Waiwai in 1837, Schomburgk remarked, with his rather nineteenth-century Prussian sensibility, that they were "filthily dirty in their habits" (1931 [1841]:171). His reference, it may be assumed, was to their black and red painted bodies. About their Parukoto neighbors, however, he says:

> The men are stout and well made; the forehead high, nose slightly arched, and features regular: their heads are adorned with caps made from the feathers of the breast of the eagle, the crest of the egret, the macaw, and the parrot. (Robert Schomburgk 1931 [1841]:170)

The nearby Mawayena were distinguished by other exotic traits:

> Their head was compressed laterally, and their facial expression, on account of the lustrous eyes, brighter. They wore their

hair tied up into a long tail carried in a 10 to 12 inch sort of cone made of palm-leaves from which a number of strings with the most variegated feather-attachments fell dependent. (Richard Schomburgk 1922 [1848]:376)

On his second 1840 journey into the Guiana hinterland, he met the "Pianoghotto," who, it can be assumed, were the same as or a group related to the Parukoto. He says of these people that:

In their costume they quite resemble the [Mawayena]: indeed so much care had been spent on the pig-tail that it would have done credit to the most fashionable Parisian hairdresser. The body was not decorated in lines, but with the exception of the face, was painted red from chin to toe. The men wore plenty of beads around the loins and shoulders and . . . below the knees cotton strings from which a number of tassels were dependent. (Richard Schomburgk 1922 [1848]:383)

Here, in one of the more famous early descriptive texts about the peoples living in the vicinity of the headwaters of the Guiana Shield, we have the images of cultural distinction that subsequent writers to the region made a point of highlighting and elaborating upon (Barrington Brown 1876; Roth 1929; DeFreitas 1944; Yde 1965; Farabee 1967 [1924]; Meggers 1973 [1971], to name but a few). The descriptions and interpretations of Amerindian body adornment and alteration varied over the decades, but always an inference persisted—an inference that ultimately fixed these accounts with a coherent singularity.

A confirming eminence of modernity surged through the literature. It secured itself with descriptions of the Amerindian body set apart by association to inferiority. It used the expression of the Amerindian body, with its cultural markers of difference, to interpret a lowliness in its presence. By situating Amerindian difference in the category of inferiority, modernity claimed for itself a singular superiority. It was in this way, it could be argued, that the applied theoretical techniques of an evolutionism came to perform perhaps their most effective work.

Evolutionary theories functioned, I would like to argue, to inform the modern writers' interpretative procedures and to preserve their assumptions about difference and hierarchy. They pulled concepts together and pushed them apart to produce meaningful assumptions, all the while allowing readers to believe they perceived in the Amerindian body a reassuring association with the fishes, fowls, and fauna of the forest.[3] Amerindians were likened to objects in and of a primitive landscape. They could indeed be credited with having human culture—and with it, be distinct—but it was a cultural distinctiveness that—in utilizing what the writers interpreted as the artifacts of a hostile, unforgiving, and insalubrious tropical forest—made the bearers appear closer to a distant evolutionary point of origin in savage nature.[4] In the category of "savage" other, the objectified Amerindian body was used to orientate and ground the modernity of a "civilized" readership; both diachronically and synchronically, modernity existed in an evolved present, apart from and above an uncivilized primitive world.

Schomburgk, for example, presented the Amerindian as part of an unexplored wilderness, to be "discovered" and "documented" as validation of British territorial boundaries in South America. The Amerindians' wild substantive presence (or rather, the recorded knowledge of such presence within a national rhetoric of state claims to newly acquired sovereign properties) provided the justification for their wardship. The unknown became knowable in very particular ways. Being discovered as savages and being classified as such brought Amerindians immediately under the paternalistic, rational, and generalized protection of the colonizing state. Hence, unbeknownst to them, not only was their status as "minors" officially inaugurated, but also, like the very land they occupied, their savage bodies became the subject properties of a higher, civilizing order.

William Curtis Farabee, the intrepid North American ethnologist, "collected" Amerindian culture for the Pennsylvania Museum.[5] As can be gleaned from his comment that "the Waiwais decorate

their bodies with color and ornaments without special significance"
(1967 [1924]:166), his text does not display a willingness to attribute
to the Waiwai any reasoned response to their adorning activities.
To do so—in the coherent theoretical schemata of his time—would
have been tantamount to indicating that at least the basic ingredients
for representing the political hold of the state upon its citizens were
already formed within the body of the Amerindian. This would have
placed the modern polity, which he represented, in the explicitly
contradictory position of denying full membership to those clearly
entitled to it under its very own criteria—thus setting in disarray the
justifying evolutionary schema that gave shape to judgments about
difference. Conspicuously, however, the capacity for independent
human reasoning was denied to the Amerindian. Without this essential requirement, the law of the modern state could not function
successfully within or upon the Amerindian; hence, membership in
the community of the civilized could not be offered to the savage.
How indeed could the "triple alliance . . . between the law, writing,
and the body" (Clastres 1989:179) become interactive within the uncivilized other if the intellectual capabilities for its inducement were
not already firmly set in place? Apparently lacking any indigenous
interpretative heuristics, body painting and ornamentation provided
ample evidence of the lowly outside status of Amerindian otherness.
Collecting the "bric-a-brac" of such strange and savage cultures
merely placed the supposition of savageness and strangeness into
the confirmable condition of an inferior exteriority.

Walter Edmund Roth, a British civil servant and enthusiastic part-
time ethnologist, was, like Farabee, an avid collector of Amerindian
ornamental curios and exotic knowledge. His explanation for Waiwai personal apparel amounted to considering it "holiday attire"
or "decorations common to times of merrymaking" (1929:ix). Yet
despite himself and the blinkers of his own cultural prejudices, one
cannot help but notice the strange and wonderful contradictions
this colonial magistrate brings before us in regard to the signifying complexities of tropical clothing. One might take, for example, his own rather insightful decision not to wear hobnailed boots

on his 1925 expedition to the southern Guiana forest, but instead to carry a dozen pairs of "india-rubber" soled shoes.[6] Then one might observe his loathing for the Wapishana Amerindians of the Rupununi savanna, who, influenced by their earnings from the rubber trade, "neglected" their "provision fields" and "squandered" their "wages . . . mostly in clothes" (Roth 1929:viii).[7] Their "verminous" bodies lacked the application of soap; they were plastered with imported perfumes and brilliantine and plied with intoxicating amounts of alcohol; they consequently appeared as a "demoralized" people to the visiting justice of the peace. On the other hand, "the Waiwai are a delightful and charming set of people—clean, industrious, and happy . . . at present they are moral, and during the whole of my month's stay among them, I saw no drinking" (Roth 1929:x). Roth explained this difference between the moral and the immoral Amerindian, the uncorrupted and corrupted savage, in terms of the relative "distance of their native haunts from centers of civilization" (1929:x). Although he spoke of the British colony as being "out-of-the-way," he nevertheless understood and worked with the notion that its named administrative centers were the locales of civilized society. While the influences of civilization could not, however, corrupt him—because, as an administrator of the law, he already embodied the austere eminence of rationality—they certainly took their toll on the prelogical, premodern, and peripheral Amerindians.[8] Located on the outside, in the wilderness, before modernity, and presumably without rational thought for guidance, savages succumbed to the susceptibility of their debilitating inferiority.

One can see in these collectors' discoveries and documentations fervent yet technically surreptitious attempts not only to know and to possess but also to demarcate and to contain and, in so doing, to control the perceived wild inferiority of savages and their primitive world. Yet fully to comprehend this view, one would also have to consider the ponderous fiction that coexisted with the idea of inferiority. Savages may have been deemed low in human status, but they were not without their own coercive effects. If they were thought, indeed, to be limited by their so-called lowliness, they were, nonetheless, capable of emitting an assertive force. With such an understanding of the inferior, control can mean many things, but most of all it can mean the capability of reducing any possible threat or challenge to the eminence of modernity. Certainly the modern masters put the notion of the inferior savage to their own uses, either, as I am arguing, to substantiate their dominant position at the end of an evolutionary scale and/or to verify the greater efficiency of their own techniques for capturing and administering truth. At the same time, their intellectual quarantining inadvertently worked to control the obvious creative forces of the inferior savage. It clearly developed as a workable means for cordoning off the legitimacies of Amerindian realities. Meanwhile, beguiled by the technical precision and rigor of their own interpretative processes, the early travelers-cum-writers, in constructing their intellectual enclosure around the inferior savage, successfully closed out the alternative yet equally fastidious expositional processes of the Amerindian.

Even the professional Danish anthropologist Jens Yde gives us the impression of being too preoccupied with salvaging culture to conceive of an adorned Waiwai body informed by its own theoretical principles. Yde and his compatriot Niels Fock divided between them the task of studying the Waiwai, with the former concentrating on material culture and the latter on religion and society. From their 1960s monographs, we gain the impression that here were career academics seriously engaged in recording and classifying, for scientific prosperity, what they understood to be the quickly vanishing traits and beliefs of traditional Waiwai life. Yde's detailed descriptions and illustrations of Waiwai material artifacts sought, however, to give empirical conformation to his theory of "culture areas" arrived at by identifying, classing, and comparing regional items. His theory ultimately crosshatched the indigenous and foreign origins of cultural traits. Although he periodically appealed to some of his own and Fock's anthropological explanations for Waiwai behavior, these did not figure much beyond the social forces of development and survival. In fact when dealing with body adornment, Yde carries us no further than did Farabee. If we compare what he says about body painting, for example—"the complicated patterns on the face . . . are also purely decorative. No particular meaning is attached to them" (1965:216)—his and Farabee's comments arrive at essentially the same conclusion. In other words we receive the impression of culture devoid of its inner native logic. In such expositions, cultural practices cannot be attributed to their self-determined principles, because the patterns of indigenous reasoning remain quarantined behind the detailed descriptions of human action and its material products.

Relying heavily upon the causal determinants of biological need, environmental condition, and adaptive strategy, the archaeologist Betty Meggers also placed the Waiwai within a recognizable culture area. For her, Waiwai body adornment was not clothing per se, but a "cultural response to [a] biological fact" (1973:98)—that is, the fact of having to adapt to the "terra firma" environment of Amazonia. Her point is that in "the humid heat of the Amazon basin" clothing covering the body "retards heat loss and consequently hinders normal physiological processes" (1973:98). In the grand scheme of evolutionary procedure, covering the body with inappropriate garments was not a successful strategy for survival. On the other hand, to choose the feathers, seeds, and bark of the immediate environment was the necessary constraint for locking a cultural group in its most functionally successful stage of development. Thus in the end, according to Meggers, it was both the "availability" of and the subsequent "adaptation" to regionally specific materials that determined the kind of artifacts worn by the Waiwai, the cultural area to which they belonged, and the level of cultural development they could achieve. If culture possessed an inner logic, it was housed in its functional adaptability to ecology. Being so neatly quarantined, however, reduced Amerindian reasoning to the successful functioning of its culture, a culture having merely to maintain itself in the ranked stages below modernity.

Where, then, should we begin in any serious attempt to discharge Waiwai interpretations from the intellectual confinements of an inferiority? Surely we must first assume that a general coherence runs *clothing interpretation by early Europeans as an example of how we always assume they're so dumb BUT maybe there is a reason that we just don't see*

throughout their statements as it does through ours; that certain consistent principles hold their ideas together in order for them to be meaningful. Surely, as social beings, the Waiwai would also be subject to the controlling forces of an authoritative registering—a registering capable of capturing the kinds of reality assumed to be conveyable. Surely, in producing social beings, this registering—be it on the body or on the page—should not be weighed down by an inferiority. If all human individuals, to be social beings, must be drawn into and sustained within society—let us say, by the cultural techniques of society—then the issue should not be about why the cultural technique of registering the body expresses an inferiority. Let us say, indeed with another kind of guilt, that as a registering, Amerindian body adornment should at least be released from the confinement of signifying a lowly exterior savagery.

guilt - the bias that's always there

To the Mutability of Embodiment

Mythic Bodies and Divine Coherence

Let us in a mischievous manner begin with Waiwai mythic registers. Not necessarily because myths can show us how Amerindian thought "expresses itself by means of a heterogeneous repertoire" (Lévi-Strauss 1974:17), a repertoire with a nevertheless extensive limit, but rather because, as a repository of human thought, as an extensive limit, myths can serve as the sites of introduction to collective representations of social being. The suggestive tease, however, lies in offering the Waiwai mythic register on their own social presence as the narrative competitor with other non-Waiwai commentaries, only to withdraw such an offer as any kind of contender for the absolute last word on their identity. I consider the shared posited Waiwai beliefs and values on human existence already to sit as maxims within the Waiwai collective consciousness; they need no other consensus for validity. Amerindians, after all, did not need the Europeans to "discover" them to become aware of their own collective existence. In the shared impact of being human within Waiwai society, whose logic nevertheless cannot be reduced to individual experience, bodily presence represents itself within the confines of specific communicative codes. Waiwai mythic registering resonates with these codes for the body and its presence.

Let us focus specifically on perhaps the most common Waiwai mythic register for the presencing of the body: the myth of Mawari. Again, we do this not necessarily because it can lead us to different "modes of consciousness" (Hill 1988) about the mythological and/or historical past, but rather because it exemplifies a coherent interpretative technique or a "shared experiential and interpretive framework" (Hill 1988:2).[1]

I should add that my concern is not with the theoretical issue of pitting ideology against reality or false consciousness against material truth. Such an approach often carries the opinion that any anthropological interest in the consistency of social phenomenon reveals an outdated and false model of society as static form. The advocacy of such an approach is usually for dynamic change brought about by individuals empowered with cultural agency. My hesitation in following such an approach and adopting its opinion stems from my having interpreted this advocacy by some anthropologists as being yet another surreptitious attempt to write the presence of their own culture directly into the fabric of radically different social systems. Justified or not, such attempts recurrently and subliminally detract attention away from the internal logic and intellectual potency of the other's statements. It seems to me that this anxiety about the eminence of modernity—that is, about its possible exclusion from the mythic and/or historical consciousness of other societies, propagates both its interest in cultural change and its placing of agency in the individual other. I am not seeking here to contest the validity of a non-Amerindian presence in Amerindian myth or history. I am merely attempting to highlight and abandon our frequent interpretative tendencies for including our influence (negative or positive) upon Amerindians, for locating our presence over and above their presence, and for intimating, with duplicity, that these result not from the initially stated contingencies of constructed agendas but from some autonomous universal ordering.[2]

The basic components of the Mawari myth were frequently recited to me throughout my residence among the Waiwai. They were not always complete. Sometimes they came in partial response to an inquisitive child. At other times they came in full-blown elaboration of an ancestral knowledge. Yet they always signaled themselves as the basic elements for recognizing the myth itself. In fact the indefatiga-

[handwritten marginal notes:] Isn't it possible that in trying to hard not to do truly you are missing the connections or even what is truly similar/really?

ble features of the myth are so tenacious that not even the Christian missionary's censored translation for the anthropologist Niels Fock could eradicate them and prevent them from being perceived (Fock 1963:38–42).[3]

My collection of myths came principally from the recitals by Iwap, Uwa, and Arumarawan, old men of the Shepariymo community. It was clear to me, however, from those particular moments when these men faltered in the telling and their wives chimed in from the background with the correct prompts, that certain elderly women also possessed mythic knowledge. They may not have had the appropriate status to stage and speak whole myths in public, but they knew the essential components well enough, and, as wives, were legitimately placed to provide their husbands with the proper lines whenever a lapse occurred in the men's memory. Aside from this rather significant qualification, however, it was generally understood that myth telling provided the opportunities for observing and displaying *takusom* (special knowledge), a quality identified with accomplished individuals who in this case belonged to the age-grade category of *pocha-komo* (old men or grandfathers). The special myth-telling knowledge of the three men was exemplified by their individual oratorical abilities, which included their capacity to remember, recite, and blend essential narrative features of a myth. Yet without their social status of respected old age, the content of this special knowledge could not be convincingly conveyed or given recognition. At the same time not all elderly men possessed special knowledge, nor were they all credited with possessing special myth-telling knowledge merely because of their age-grade status. It was certainly expected that the category pocha could carry the quality of takusom, but it was not always confirmed in every single individual—thus giving greater credence to the meaning of possessing special knowledge.

With myth recitals, individual talent and elderly personhood exemplify takusom and allow for the possession and distribution of the fundamental ingredients of memorial narratives to audiences.[4] Providing the myth teller with his means of expressing special knowl-

[handwritten margin notes: myths belong to specific age grade to tell but everyone still knows them / is this not a kind of hierarchy?]

edge are the rich and distinct linguistic techniques of Waiwai storytelling. For example, all performances of myth contain the use of the term *shakñe* to establish the period of mythic time. It connotes distant time, presumably a temporarily recaptured distant past. This only works effectively, however, when the demeanor of the actors and the atmosphere of the setting in the myth purposefully convey the impression of shakñe. Thus, when extravagant and overly temperate actions are juxtaposed to each other in a narrative, they can serve to demonstrate the specific qualities and kinds of behavior representative of mythic time. Hence mythic actors and mythic landscapes relate to each other in the procedure of tracing mythological temporality. Needless to say, because of the plentiful pronouncements of the perpetuity of myth, the question as to whether mythic time is only about the past should be discounted. After all, in myth, is not the metatheme as much about the present in the past as it is about the past in the present?

Waiwai myth tellers also make liberal use of the term *kekñe* as a way of indicating, in verbal manner, the formal and public goals of mythic speech. In this regard, the myth tellers also fill their speech with many series of particles (Robert Hawkins 1962). For example they use descriptive particles such as *rha*, which identifies distinctiveness, or *komo*, which specifies plurality. They use particles that suggest the value or manner of their accounts such as *wa* (common knowledge) or *ma* (questioning). They use particles that signal subjective reactions such as *okre* (pleasure) or *okyo* (surprise). And they use idiophonic particles exclusive to storytelling, which work to indicate single events lacking mode, tense, voice, or person. In addition, and perhaps more importantly, the frequent use of particles and the term *kekñe* function to provide the discernible poetic cadence of mythic speech. They appear, at least in this respect, to control procedurally the rhythmic beat and pitch of the myth teller's voice. Together with cadence, they assist in producing the genre of mythic speech. As sound clues to the recognition of this particular oratorical style, however, they also prepare the Waiwai imagination for the reception of mythic bodies.

What can be learned from the representations of mythic bodies in the basic narrative components of myth? Because it claims canonical ownership of the trace to bodies seemingly outside or before Waiwai culture, the Mawari myth provides a particularly significant response to this question. Many different layers of meaning can clearly be obtained from the mythic register, but by concentrating on that pertaining to the representation of the body, a specific double marking may be seen to prevail. The image of the body in Waiwai mythology expresses itself both as mythic courier and as the very message it conveys. Somatic representations fold back upon themselves in recited form and offer up embodied states as the very movement of mythic story lines. They hold plots together and provide convincing drama through the interrelated actions of embodied states. Yet the most persistent attribute of their embodiment appears in converse to what we may understand as the concrete, settled formulation of the body image. Rather than as the incarnate action of a realized fixity, the body image in Waiwai mythology functions much more meaningfully as the negotiable mutability of embodiment.

Waiwai mythological characters move in and around a world where the body can and does change from one form to another as well as from one condition to another. The body of a woman, for example, can take on the attributes of a tortoise, a jaguar, or an anaconda. A school of piranha can even inhabit the body. The body of a man can appear without sexual organs and later on reappear with an overburdened penis. The body can be at one moment filled with excessive hungers and at another emptied or cleansed of its ravenous desires. The body can be gendered with or without its sex. It can have appetites with or without their satisfaction. It can be naked with copious human hair and yet clothed in the colored plumage of birds. It can at one point be greedy or murderous and at another generous or caring. In other words the body image in myth exhibits an exclusive quality of mutability: a seemingly peculiar changeableness featured as a convincing attribute of mythological time and space. Such mutability becomes possible—it could be argued from Waiwai ideas—only because the divine powers of *ekati* (spiritual vitality) have the ability to act upon and release the individual characteristic of the body from its fixed form or condition.

The mutableness of the mythic body possesses its influential credibility precisely because there is an investiture of belief in the effective presence of divine powers. In Waiwai beliefs the mutableness of the mythic body sustains its credibility by being the sublime effect of a durable and ubiquitously divine force traditionally referred to as Kwarokiyim (Great Spirit / Father of Macaws). Invisible yet present in all five layers of the universe, Kwarokiyim nevertheless presides in and from the three-tier realm of *kapu* (sky or heavens)—its principal home and state of purest energy. Its predominant attribute of ethereal movement—that is, of being able to propel its cosmic impulses throughout the universe, has helped to substantiate the belief in its divine ability to enter, settle in, and mutate individuated corporeality. Particularly in myth, where the projectile effect of divine force displays its being in the mutated body, the corporeal claims of individuated fixity regularly succumb and exhibit the transformative force of the distant yet immediate power of Kwarokiyim. It is by being unable to resist the impact and entry of the transformative force of divinity that the corporeal individual can, for example, become jaguar or tortoise and even be capable of communicating with other creatures such as otters and anacondas. Thus the resulting mutability of the body serves to demonstrate not only the vulnerability of the somatic individual and the effective force of the divine, but also (and not without some strain of the paradox), the very determined coherence of divine power. It unsettles. It divides. It creates new forms and new conditions. Nevertheless, the coherence of divine power continues to maintain itself as a resolute concatenation. I would like, in fact, to argue that this divine coherence—manifesting itself repeatedly in the mutability of the body—is a major metamessage of Waiwai myth.

Through the specific technique of body-image repetition—that is, by repeating the image of mutable embodiment, myth subtextually carries the missive about the singular coherence of divinity, particularly of its being able to expand upon itself in harmonious completeness. Divine coherence—as consistent logic repeatedly targeting the mythic body—transforms embodiment with separations, oppositions, and momentary unifications. In this way it recapitulates a subliminal recognition of itself, one that passes through to the social world of Waiwai existence. It becomes, in fact, a principal Waiwai notion of ideal social being. Its very paradox of causing division and change as well as exemplifying the character of harmony and durability actually provides social relations with their critical working contradictions. Appropriated and identified particularly with the authority of masculinity, it becomes an imperative object of men's desire. In this, even when acting as the creative source of feminized forms, it ends up reinforcing and legitimizing the social and political position of masculinity. When interpreted in its negative form, it is often the essential source of an individual or collective destruction. When it is interpreted in its positive form, it is often the rejuvenating approbation of society. Whichever way it turns, whichever location it occupies, whichever articulation it adopts, divine coherence represents a dynamic and paradoxical presence. It is arguably able to do so in myth by making the mutable body the actual effect of its power.

Epeka, Wošin, and the Mutable Womb

In Waiwai ideas about identity, physical ambience and the passage of time have a conforming influence on individuals. The Waiwai say that living with other people in a particular settlement for a goodly period of time will make an individual not only smell like but also look like the people he or she lives with. This is because space and time encourage the necessary exchanges of substances between bodies that allow collective community life to exist. Shared food, fluids, talk, and ideas all help in the daily production of community life and the very quality and features of individual being. All shared substances carry elements of ekatï. From a Waiwai point of view, the supple circuits and metrical rhythms of daily exchange actually assist in stabilizing the volatile spiritual vitalities that constitute the life-sustaining force of the body. They appear, however, to keep the range of this stability within the immediate space and temporal movement of the village community. Such perspectives on residential space, time, and social being all seem to emerge and revolve around the concept of uterine incorporation.

Poyino refers in Waiwai to the relationship that defines common kinship substance. It references the bond most representative of Waiwai social harmony. Within the notion of poyino, however, a structurally subordinate relationship exists: one that from its greater social value and more frequent impositions appears superordinate. *Epeka* (the relationship of uterine relatives) carries the specific meaning of siblingship. It operates as the definitive Waiwai concept of common substance and social harmony. Together, poyino and epeka specify the desired ideal community ties of the ewto (village settlement).[5]

Very much like and indeed thought of as constituting the character of divinity with its completeness in the vaulted womb of the heavens, related individuals from the same mother share similar characteristics by being the products of the same woman's womb. The *yinasisiru* (womb of woman) and kapu ("womb" of the world) become influencing natal spaces for creating the ideal bonds of social harmony. Thus, coming from and living in the same place suggest the criteria for establishing proper ways of being human in the world. To be a proper human person, an individual must be a member of a village community living together as if they were poyino and/or epeka. To disrupt such bonds, to stretch or break them with residential fission or conflict, can put not only the harmonious relationship but also the society—as village—in a dangerous state of mutability. Here the wošin (affinal relative) is the perceived disruptive element.

Possibly because *mansiya* (marriage) entails—at least for the incipient husband—a uxorilocal movement out of the familiar into the strange (Lévi-Strauss 1972; Terence Turner 1979; Overing Kaplan 1984), wošin conveys the notion of stressed relations. Encouraged particularly by the husband's encounter with his new and unfamiliar connubial relations as well as with his incurred responsibilities of, for example, bride service, the wošin relationship directly disturbs

[handwritten margin notes:]
Poyino + Epeka = community

doubting aspect to being human

→ why affine has agency?

not what he would posit how—idea of uterine incorporation
↳ nonincorporate
singularity
↓
doubting
↓
communal

FEELING of uterine concorporateness
↳ feel that member of group
(other group pl = enemies)

where do divine prey into this? ↳ see myths

the calm harmony of common substance. In doing so, however, it is contributing, by the necessity of an imperative process, to the occupancy of the spouse's new social identity. The wošin seemingly and necessarily assists in the incipient spouse's movement toward full social personhood. In this regard it appears as a crucial aspect not just of being married but also of becoming an adult. In the act of disturbing the relations of common natal substance, it is the source of an anxious change in identity. Thus at the moment of marriage and in the motion of postmarital residence, wošin has causal affect upon the incipient spouse. It unsettles from established natal ties and introduces new forms of connubial consciousness. It provides even more committed affinal relations. To leave the known familial space of natality to become *chuwya* (husband), or even to accommodate a daughter's husband or sister's husband in order to become tamchi (wife's father) or *chacha* (wife's mother) or poimo (wife's brother / wife's sister) respectively, is an anxious imperative action toward full personhood. Departure from the familiar and arrival in the strange places a good deal of pressure on the wošin relationship and, consequently, gives to it the reputation of being tension filled. Yet, at least in the gendered ideology of Waiwai society, the wošin movement and its reputation for being tense derive just as much from the role femininity plays in the construction of social space as from the changing characteristics of social status.

Muliebrity acts in specific Waiwai ways as the object of ideological appropriation. The condition of being woman serves, for example, to make the womb a critical site for negotiating identity. With regard to building the ideal natal bonds of social harmony as well as the reputation of wošin, it plays the decisive role of an axis about which these states of being rotate. For example, Waiwai femininity moves the contrasting states of social harmony and disruption around the idea of the womb as container.[6] It gives impetus to the womb as the credential of a secure shelter: a retentive chamber, itself contained by the body of woman as yeme (mother). Indeed the process of substantiating the mortal existence of human life begins with the body of woman. Yet the vitality for this existence has first to enter

the body in order to set the growth of the embryonic substance in motion.

This vitality originates from the divine and, as it becomes the life force of the new human, is called *ekati̇̈*. Understood to be part of the spiritual coherence of divinity, ekati̇̈ initiates a pregnancy by extending some of its vitalities into the woman's body. These vitalities can enter through any of the main orifices of her body. The impetus of the entry seems, however, to be always initiated by means of an already substantiated form of masculinity. Human or animal forms of substantiated masculinity can be the source of the impetus for the ekati̇̈'s entering the woman's womb. The human or animal masculine source can and does contribute part of its own identity to the incipient *rikomo* (child). For example, the explanation given to me by Yenayaw (Arumarawan's wife) for her son Aruchiripin's epileptic seizures—graphically displayed by his spontaneous and regular collapsing to and writhing on the ground—was that the ekati̇̈ of a caterpillar she had seen had entered her body just before she became *tarpkem* (pregnant). Once it has set the process of gestation in motion, however, the force of divine masculine vitalities has to combine with the feminine substance of the womb to produce the fetus and assist in the successful birth of the infant. Together, divine coherence and uterine substance work to give mortal life to the child and, at the same time, to bring into social action the experience of parenthood.

As uterine product, the child assists in the social making of the father and mother. Certainly the full significance of the process of human birth in Waiwai ideas is just as much about the making of parenthood as it is about the making of the child (Rivière 1974; Menget 1979; Rival 1998a). It may even be argued that the very process of procreation ultimately acts to suppress the anxious tensions of the wošin, particularly those between husband and wife. Waiwai marriages are extremely stable, with many partnerships lasting the lifetime of the spouses. Separation or divorce rarely occurs, but when it does, the grounds for annulment usually hinge upon the persistent inability of one or the other of the partners to fulfill their customary

[handwritten in right margin: divine substance + male entrance + female = book]

[handwritten at top left: BIRTH]

role as provider. Generally marriages are long lasting and duly end up becoming, in their relatively unthreatening familiarity, very much like the relations of the epeka. Yet the actual process of becoming parents initiates the change of quality in relations between husband and wife, as well as the quality of those extended jural relations between the husband and his wife's father and/or brother. One might consider in the latter case, for example, that the formal practices of bride service abruptly cease for the husband two to three moons before the birth of the child and, in some cases, cease to continue in any form after the child can walk. In any event the official conclusion of bride service begins with the forming of the nuclear household of the new parents, a coveted stage often marked by the parents' claim of access to an independent farm plot of their own. Nevertheless, such claims, such social developments, and such shifts in tension all appear to depend upon the movement of relations between being a spouse and becoming a parent. Indeed, when the pregnancy occurs, it does seem as if the connubial relation between husband and wife determines the establishment of the child's social parentage.[7]

The womb is, however, not only a place into which the vitalities of life must enter, but also the site from which they must depart in order for human life to resonate. To reverberate socially as *mimiru* (son) or *yimsiru* (daughter) and to bring parenthood into cultural oscillation, the human content of the womb has to give up its interior security for the external space of earthly residence. In the mundane world outside the womb, however, the poyino and epeka seek immediately to replace the womb's protective services. They repeat the containing function of the womb to effect the calm, defensive harmony of natality. Yet, like the mother's womb, they too must release the individual contained. As they do so, at the juncture marked by postmarital residence, the feminine image of the womb's passive tendencies turns aggressive.

Particularly from the viewpoint of male residential movement, vaginal assertiveness becomes identified with the wošin relationship. Together, they act to implement upon the new husband not just sexual but social and economic incapacities. Thus, at least in the initial "tension" (?)

unfamiliar and insecure stages of connubial relations, the body of woman—now not as mother but as *pichi* (wife)—endows a negative attribute to the wošin. In the social space of marriage, femininity performs the task of inserting a tension into affinal relations, but even this achievement has to be curtailed nonetheless.

Waiwai social philosophy privileges community harmony and strives continuously to implement, over those of the wošin, the principles indicative of poyino and epeka. In other words Waiwai moral values prefer not the negative but the positive side of femininity and hence seek to use the latter's calm and secure containment to reduce the tension of affinal relations. The affinal relation cannot itself be removed; the affine is an integral part of social life. But affinal tensions can be confined, and Waiwai moral values proceed to do just that by placing them under the constant scrutiny of the harmonious relations of uterine kinship. Under the vaulted womb of ewtoto (village community), contained inside the ideal of natal substance, affinal and marital tensions succumb to the privileged influence of a collective harmony. In the later stages of a couple's marriage, for example, where children have been born to the union and the relative independence of the household has been achieved, the spousal relationship seems to take on an almost siblinglike appearance.[8] Now providing the natal security for another cycle of offspring and possessing the common bond that gives parental character to the village, the spousal relationship ideally repeats the earlier uterine ties produced by gestation and birth. The strangeness of the connubial relationship should have long passed and the affinal tensions been progressively relieved. Familiarity and calm make the later stages of the marital relation almost an analogue of earlier cross-sex siblingship. Thus, turned to the good work of appeasement, kinship relations and morality resonate as the privileged ordering of the world. In this collective containment of affinal and marital relations, as well as in the representation of social harmony, kinship morality successfully confirms the existence and justification of Kwarokiyim.

Divinity's harmonious completeness or perfectibility is understood to be the causal force in the movement of the womb—that is, the actual source of gestation and birth. By logical extension the impetus of this same divine vitality carries over into the relations of human society. In the same way that it influences the fetus to swell the belly of a pregnant woman, so too does it influence and enrich social relations. It is good, "*kirewani*," say the Waiwai, to live in a village filled with kindred—familiar, friendly faces with ide-, ally nothing but the altruistic intentions of uterine feelings. Hence Kwarokiyim exemplifies the coherent movement of an essential perfectibility that creates harmony, disturbs it, and recreates it while all the time remaining in and of itself a highly desirable entity. In this regard, even while taking on the form and features of femininity, the harmonious completeness of Kwarokiyim remains longed for by masculinity and identified with masculine empowerment. Perfect and desirable, particularly as seen in the befeathered bodies of adorned men, it is the manifest object of masculine aspirations. Yet a masculinity that behaves in feminine ways suggests if not a recognized envy of womanhood then at least a recognized power in the condition of being woman, even when such power can be attributed to divine sources. Arguably any mimesis of womanhood by masculinity may not necessarily be indicative of deep-seated womb envy (Eisler 1921; Dundes 1962), but it could certainly be expressive of a longing for and an opportunity to identify with an empowered presence. The obvious presumption of masculinity as the divine—explicitly referred to as the Father of Macaws—does seek to copy and, in so doing, appropriate the original creativity of birth from woman. It also noticeably affects this possibility through an additional identification with birds.

It can be briefly mentioned here that the attempt in mythic and ritual codes to associate men with birds carries all the other known features of the association with it, ranging from the ability to fly to the celebrated attribute of cloacal birth (that is, giving birth through the common excretory cavity).[9] In Waiwai knowledge men's bodies do not possess the physical chamber or accoutrements for human birth. Nevertheless, demonstrated by the relations ideologically drawn between men and birds, the very same vitality that gives the body of woman its ability to produce kindred does give to masculinity the capacity for cosmic reproduction. Waiwai masculinity claims a closer alignment to the divine by being physically identified with the body of birds. Like women, birds give birth to their young through a lower cavity of their body. Like birds, men at least possess a lower bodily cavity. Kwarokiyim can, as in the process of birthing, move its essence from one heavenly layer to another through the cosmic cavities of the universe. It possesses a single conduit through which the cosmogonic egg can be laid. If woman can by the substances of her body give birth to humans, then Kwarokiyim can through divine spirituality give birth to worlds. The womb of woman—her attached uterus—is dependent, being contained in her body and never able to leave its location, while the womb of Kwarokiyim—its cosmic egg—is independent and can leave its location in order to give birth. Indeed the creative process of both belongs to the divine, but the vaginal birth by woman and the cloacal birth by Kwarokiyim differentiate the two—a difference seemingly picked up by Waiwai masculine ideology both to mark an essential difference between men and women and to draw attention to a similarity between masculinity and the divine.

It is arguably just these kinds of strategies of aligning and identifying masculinity with the spiritual forces of creation that ultimately help to keep the Waiwai social emphasis on male power. They certainly do aid in the drawing of distinctions between what anthropology may call Waiwai "spiritual patrifiliation" and "uterine matrifiliation." Yet because of the primary discursive location of the womb (in any cultural statements about birth), such ideas continue to turn the ideological focus toward the theme of community as uterine relations. In the Waiwai scheme, uterine kindred are themselves the products of a creativity that can be attributed to both men and women and still be privileged to the former by the higher authority of a cosmic masculine gestation. In the Mawari creation myth these ideas become proclaimed truths, not merely through the process of mythic codes, but also in the cultural tradition of giving to masculine subjectivity the mutable agency of divine coherence.

Jaguar :: Anaconda :: Tortoise

THE MAWARI MYTH: EPISODE I

The Jaguar-people had killed Tortoise Woman
and old Jaguar Woman had adopted
the orphaned sons, Mawari and Washi.

The old woman nurtured the boys
to the threshold of manhood
then placed them in ritual isolation
for three cycles of the seasons.

When they stepped forth from
under the large clay pot,
the boys were tall with copious
facial and bodily hair,
but very little hair on their heads.

They were without sexual organs.
They wore no loin cloth and
possessed no body ornament.
They were, however, ravenous for meat.

The brothers gained knowledge
of weapons from Jaguar Woman and
learned of forest plants from Little Bird.
Each brother immediately grew an enormous penis
and desired sexual pleasure.

masculinity

Satisfaction had to wait, however,
on guidance from Otter.
Having suffered copulation through the eye
by the brothers,
Otter protested to Mawari,
suggesting he should instead
fish for an Anaconda wife from the river.

rape

Mawari did so, and after cleansing her
vagina of piranha and finally achieving correct
and safe sex with her,
Uhh...
produced the children from whose incestuous union
came the Waiwai people.

It has already been argued that Waiwai masculine ideology configures femininity as the cause of a man's most stressed residential
move and, in consequence, has even identified it in general with
the negativity of social disruption. From this ideal, the belief system
HARMONY
generates the presumption that the most desirable of all harmonious
relationships is that between same-sex siblings. Thus at one extreme
the cross-gender relation of husband and wife expresses, at least in
its initial stages, the disruption of relationships implicit in wošin,
while at the other extreme, particularly with epeka siblings of the
same gender, siblinghood signifies the social harmony of the poyino.
From the privileged masculine position, however, the bias holds that
the most perfect sibling tie is the yatho or ñoño (fraternal bond).
Thus does the concept of the "community of brothers" become a
dominant ideological way in which society is imagined. In its uterine theme, in its coherence of repeated similitude, and in its form
man=divine
of masculinity, *yatho-komo* (brotherhood) appears godlike. It is ac-
female=
cordingly as fraternal kindred that the appropriated epeka extends
disruptive
into the categorization of Waiwai masculinity, where it functions
both to determine an aspect of manhood's essential character and to
link that essentiality to the character of society. Wošin on the other
hand remains predominantly identified with the negative aspects of
womanhood and with the disruptive features of social existence.

Not surprisingly, therefore, the concepts of wošin and epeka recur
constantly in Waiwai myths. In myth they draw individual bodies together and give them the capacity to be judged as moral or immoral
beings. They actually make myth and society logical, for without
wošin and epeka no narrative can be known and no social relations
can be formed. Like the coherence of divinity itself, they are an
ever-present and nonnegotiable reality, existing, one could say, even

before myth and society. Hence the obvious contradiction in myths that tell about the world before culture began—for such myths can only project a presocial world from an imagination already framed by specific cultural knowledge.

In the Mawari creation myth, for example, to give meaningful substance to wošin and epeka is already to comprehend and value the affinal relation between the Kamara-yena (Jaguar-people) and Wayam Wosï (Tortoise Woman) as well as the maternal bond between Tortoise Woman and her sons. Such intellectual exchange on marriage and filiation in myths provides an awareness of the "real wrong"—or rather, the "real ugliness"—in the killing of Tortoise Woman by the Jaguar-people; it also provides an additional appreciation of the full sorrow of the motherless siblings. The brothers are recipients of a sympathy that can only be given by those who recognize and feel moved by their tragic misfortune. They have, through uterine substance, been given an identity, one they cannot fully and with integrity live out as sons of a dead mother; nevertheless, they still possess the comfort of their fraternal relation. A recurrent mythic theme epitomized here in its perfect form as yathokomo, the concept of epeka represents the imperative familiarity, safety, and goodness of kindred relations—all qualities in contrast to those of the wošin—qualities that the mutable body in myth seeks to problematize and enhance in order for these relations to be considered effects of moral truths.

By the means of shared somatic symbols in the mythic discourse on epeka and wošin, Waiwai moral governance emerges and persists at the levels of individual consciousness and collective social realties. It appears to be able to do so by setting the very limits of legitimacy to masculinity, by arranging the differences of gender identities against each other in opposition and in complementarity, and by aligning the attributes of gender to the proper order of the world. None of these features can become known, however, without the presence of bodily forms.

In the myth Jaguar Woman's adoption of Mawari and Washi seeks in essence to mimic, but cannot in actuality replace, the maternal bond of motherhood. Being such an essential and irrevocable feature of identity formation, epeka cannot be imagined as not having a causal affect on the social development even of the culture heroes. Hence the murderer (by implication) of the brothers' mother takes on the role and responsibilities of motherhood, guiding the orphaned boys to masculine maturity. Yet, possibly because of the obvious parody, her actions appear as cynically poor replicas of the maternal obligation. From the beginning the myth portrays Jaguar Woman's own kinsmen as the killers of Tortoise Woman; the Jaguar-people correctly appear ruled, at least in part, by their carnivorous appetites. Though they are instinctive predators personifying premeditated murder, their wošin character is nonetheless balanced by the pacifying moral obligations of epeka displayed, even in poor mimicry, by Jaguar Woman. Indeed Jaguar Woman and Tortoise Woman purposely stand in direct opposition to each other, but only after accomplishing the mythic work of signaling the similarity of their motherhood and the crucial place of matrifilial ties. As mothers, real and fictive, Tortoise Woman provides and Jaguar Woman continues the kinship position that allows the brothers to possess and maintain their uterine relations. Here the gender of motherhood assists in producing the distinctive similarities of their roles. Nevertheless, the marked difference between the species remains an important factor, one that functions to generate the particular ideological interpretations for the ultimate skepticism and contrast between the parenting of the two females. In Waiwai ideas the slow, herbivorous tortoise signifies the pacification attributed to the epeka. They also strongly suggest that the fast, carnivorous *kamara* (jaguar) signifies the predatory affine who, from the point of view of epeka, quickly consumes kinsmen through the obligations of marriage. With the character of the tortoise, and certainly until the event of her death, the representation of motherhood and its consequent matrifilial ties stay unproblematic. With the jaguar, however, the parody of both motherhood and filiation problematizes and presents Jaguar Woman as a potentially ambiguous character. Quite simply put, Jaguar Woman represents the ambiguity of having the

metaphor

complementary yet opposing aspects of spiritual patrifiliation and uterine matrifiliation in a single category of person. The mother's womb with its incorporating spiritual and uterine substances is also the site of affinal being.[10]

In Waiwai society, eligible persons marry their *o-wayamnu* (literally, "my-tortoise," the poignancy of which is not lost in myth by calling the mother of the heroes Tortoise Woman). In anthropological parlance, *wayamnu* can be referred to as an indirect address term for the "potential spouse," which includes both unrelated opposite-sex persons and genealogically related opposite-sex cross-cousins.[11] From a theoretical point of view, this aspect of Waiwai kinship terminology appears to prescribe bilateral cross-cousin marriage while, at the same time, suggesting preference for marriage with the mother's brother's daughter / father's sister's son, the contention being that the structural presence of possible marriage to the sister's daughter / mother's brother suggests the preferential ideal. In marrying the sister's daughter / mother's brother, ego confirms mother's mother and father's sister as conterminously occupying the category position of chacha. In other words, in the Waiwai kinship system the logic in chacha of FZ = MM results from the structural possibility of marriage to the sister's daughter / mother's brother. This sustains the equations of ZD = MBD and MB = FZS (Lave 1966; Rivière 1966a, 1966b, 1969a; Lévi-Strauss 1969 [1949]). In the other sequence—that is, of marriage to the father's sister's daughter / mother's brother's son, where FZD = MBD and FZS = MBS, the systemic logic repeats mother's brother's daughter / father's sister's son as a potential spouse. A recurring statement in both sequences, therefore, the potential spouse category of mother's brother's daughter / father's sister's son has itself situated at the center of Waiwai marriage preferences. It subordinates the other alternatives to its prevalence and limits the pool of relatives from which marital unions can be formed. By tracing ties to the known close categories of relatives, the connubial relation of wayamnu can be found. Necessary ambiguities occur, however, in the relatives who have to sustain both sides of the opposing epeka and wošin relations. This is particularly the case with chacha.

In Waiwai chacha can mean "old woman," "grandmother," and/or "father's sister." When she plays her part in mythology, chacha often operates with the specific meanings and identities of mother's mother and father's sister. It is as such, in the image of the jaguar, that she presents for social scrutiny and contemplation the anxious ambiguity of connubial prescription. She carries, for example, the recognized significance of "close relative capable of changing into a relative-by-marriage." Generally, however, she represents "woman beyond the age of reproduction and sexual attraction," innocuous and unthreatening. Specifically, though, she is "mother of mother" / "mother of father" radiating congeniality through her daughter / son to her grandchildren. But she is also father's sister and, hence, a potential wife's or husband's mother. As the mother-in-law, her character is more aloof and stern. In their totality, the parts she plays convey an inherent contradiction and the prospect of tension. The notable occasion when she carries the contrast between epeka and wošin to its extreme is that of sister's daughter / mother's brother marriage, where wife's mother also happens to be ego's sister. It is these opposing and ambiguous qualities of chacha that the myth attempts to convey in the character of Jaguar Woman. The tension between epeka and wošin is not, however, restricted to the body of woman in myth. *need to learn to define terms*

Between Mawari and Washi, epeka prevails as yatho-komo. In fact the heroes' spiritual and supernatural qualities appear directly connected to their fraternal relations. Because of the fact of the sibling ties between the heroes, the events of the creation account show the mutable but durable continuity of divinity as well as the relations between this continuity and the constant primacy of epeka. Having the mythological heroes related as uterine brothers endows divinity with a quality it shares with humans, but at the same time the relationship permits divinity to imbue humanity with some of its own attributes. The preeminence of epeka derives in part from this divine connection. By contrast the subordinate identity of wošin struggles fitfully with its discontinuous and disruptive impermanence, attributed more to human failings. Affinity, after all, draws to itself the connotation of relatives entangled in the controversies of formalized sexuality and reproduction. Yet out of affinity comes filialness, a prominent condition within epeka. As the system implies, filialness—the product of sex ideally accommodated by marriage—is the living embodiment of a parent's mortality, for it signals the pending demise of the father's and the mother's bodies. In Waiwai ideas, the presence of a son and/or a daughter proclaims to the world that the parents (two affines) have "eaten" each other sexually. The consumed parts, now contributing to the life of the child, ultimately devitalize the bodies of the parents. But, as I have mentioned, filialness also signifies the fact of being able to produce more individual members and the continuance of society itself. Here filiation can be considered the product of a kind of sacrifice, a consequence of a giving to society on the part of the parent, whereby the gift of the parental body to society provides for the continuance of social life. In this context filiation and human society rise to be associated with continuity and divine durability. Thus, while filial relations arising from sex, marriage, and birth signal discontinuity and the mortal condition of impermanence, they can also, when arising from the gift by parents to society, exemplify continuity and durability.

With their weighted roles and responsibilities of being proper sons and daughters, mothers and fathers, the two sides of filiation repeat—although dully—the constant contrasts between epeka and wošin. The same occurs in siblinghood, but here the repetition reverberates rather clearly, with the contrasts rebounding off each other when they declare the category opposition between brother and sister. Within epeka, when the contrast is set in terms of gender, the sibling relations of ñoño (brother) and achi (sister) weakly repeat the features of sex found heightened in wošin. With brother and sister, as in general with individuals who call each other epeka and as with individuals of the same gender, the negative reciprocity of sexual exchanges between such categories of persons acts as the fundamental moral logic and force for the strong prohibition against incest.[12] Sexual relations between individuals in these categories can never be gifts that initiate reciprocity; in Waiwai

logic, this would be like eating one's own body, eating one's kindred, or eating—instead of sharing—the meat one kills. Between
siblings, particularly between siblings of the same gender, sexual
exchanges are on the hyper-forbidden side of human interaction
precisely because they drastically close rather than open the circuit
of prestations between individuals. Same-gender sibling relations do
not have the degree of productive difference required for generating
the necessary debt or hunger for further prestations; their similitude
successfully eliminates any of the objectified differences necessary
for initiating prestations beyond themselves. Same-gender sibling
exchanges are thus similar to divine prestations—that is, they generate gifts that can never be repaid. In this regard such altruistic
exchanges can be said to produce the pure gift and—particularly
in the same-gender sibling relations of the divine brothers, Mawari
and Washi—to come from the most pure of kindred relations. In
the masculine bodies of the tortoise brothers and in the fact of
their brotherhood, epeka triumphs. Yet wošin still competes. When
depicted by the bodies of the *okoimo* (anaconda) and kamara, for
example, it adopts the specific character role of tamchi and poimo.

Mawari and Washi gain their wives from the anaconda in its
aquatic world. Yet it should be noted that the brothers have no
desire for women before such need is indirectly introduced to them
through their initiation to manhood by the jaguar. The brothers receive their manhood and male sexual desire from their jaguar wošin,
but only after the correlation has been drawn between hunting and
masculinity. The brothers hunger first not for sex but for meat.
Corresponding to Waiwai cultural ideas about the generative social
influence of residence, it is the presumed effects of living among
the feline carnivores that encourage the brothers' initial inclina-
tions; to live among kindred is to share in kindred substance. In this
case the impulse for meat is transmitted bodily as the contagion of
desire. The jaguar's carnivorous character passes to the brothers.
The conscious desire for meat and the gained knowledge of manhood, with their pleasant and unpleasant consequences, are set in
contrast to the presumed human loss of living in the divine world,

a loss equated with the misplacement of peaceful innocence and the absence of adult responsibilities. The knowledge of manhood becomes meaningfully associated first with desiring meat and, thus, with hunting—the correlative action for fulfilling the desire—and second with desiring sex and its corollaries, in Waiwai ideas, of access to orifices and the achievement of orgasm, ideally within the institution of marriage. Manhood and hunting, meat and sex exist in mythical epistemology both to explain and to justify the categorical actions of men and the essential conditions of masculinity. One might consider, however, the particular direction from which the known qualities of mortal masculinity derive.

From both the jaguar and the anaconda—the tropes sharing the symbolic reference of the in-law—manhood becomes aware of itself as hunter, meat eater, and sexual being. In direct contrast to the divine masculine feature of pacification portrayed in the yatho-komo of the sons of Tortoise Woman, mortal masculinity receives its primary identity of predator and the object of its sexual desire through the affinal relations of the Jaguar-people and the Anaconda-people. Indeed, in Waiwai logic manhood can only provide full status to an individual by actually activating the wošin relations of father-in-law and brother-in-law, thereby releasing the position of chuwya for social occupancy. Here in the myth, the ideas about mortal masculinity and affinity are constructed in the equivalence between the jaguar and the anaconda—an equivalence convincingly affirmed by predation and sexuality as indomitable features. In their distinct yet interchangeable categories, the powerful feline and the giant constrictor serve to achieve the equivalence by having their two categories repeatedly drawn into the same intellectual field. Thus do the predacious and erotic characteristics not only become synonymous with, or metonymic of, the jaguar and the anaconda respectively, but they also (by what has been called the mechanism of "paradigmatic association" [Leach 1976:15]) carry over into other beings that, in the Waiwai cultural context, assert similar attributes. It is, however, not simply an issue of transposing the characteristics of the feline and reptilian carnivores to humans. The more complicated assertion

[handwritten marginalia: "source of manhood" and "marriage required for manhood"]

is the attributing of the characteristics of predation and aggressive sexuality to specific human relations and roles.

It is, for example, the specific antagonistic quality given to "feeding off of kindred" that the predation of the jaguar and the eroticism of the anaconda carry over to the social relations between in-laws. From the depletion of natal kindred to the consumption of sperm by the wife's vagina (to make more kindred), the controlled enmity or suppressed hostility of affinal relations corresponds to the image of predation. In addition, like other lowland South American peoples (Viveiros de Castro 1992; Descola 1996b), the Waiwai conceptualize and act on the relationship between the hunter and his prey as if it was in and of itself determined by affinity. Indeed, to be masculine, the hunter and the husband must be in a relationship of meat exchange with both human and animal affines. From meat exchanges to wošin relations and mortal masculine identity, the degree of uneven reciprocity existing between partners suggests not only a mere giving and taking, but also an indebtedness—one seemingly absent from the relations of brotherhood and divine masculinity.

Mawari and Washi—on the receiving end of the in-law relationship with the Anaconda-people—acquire knowledge about being "proper" men. After acquiring their desire for meat and their inclination for hunting from the jaguar, and after some trial and error, the brothers gain additional knowledge about their masculinity by accepting women and body adornments from the anaconda. When they learn about proper sexual intercourse and proper bodily adornment, their bodies take on the correct appetites and regalia of manhood. In other words through reciprocal affinal relations and an attending somatic consciousness, their individual bodies receive their proper social and cultural identities. By being the beneficiaries of someone else's knowledge, however, their bodies have gained at the cost of another's loss. Such receiving bodies, in Waiwai terms, are considered highly aggressive and indicative of predation. Yet instead of being portrayed as the aggressive victimizers, the receiving bodies of the brothers are depicted as the victims of aggression. In fact the brothers' bodily aggression is purposely displaced onto their in-laws. The wošin, not the epeka, is endowed with the attribute of predation. The epeka, not the wošin, is prey to the avaricious hunger of the meat eater. It appears that the debt incurred by the brothers—from receiving their humanizing knowledge—outweighs the loss of such knowledge by their givers. The imposition of subordination, resulting from receiving and displaying their proper identity, weighs heavily upon the brothers. Until such time as they can make an equivalent return to their father-in-law and brother-in-law, what they give in the meantime in terms of obedience and obligatory connubial duties cannot be repaid. In this sense of instilled perpetual returns, the myth uses the image of predation to invert Mawari and Washi as the victims of in-law prestations. When looked at carefully, however, none of the myth's subtle applications of analogic relations between predator and wošin, prey and epeka, giver and receiver can in fact operate effectively as intellectual material without first having to rely upon the body as symbol of shared experience and knowledge.

Consistently serving to convey myths' most elaborate statements, the body functions as the principal subliminal topic of narrative negotiation. It appears at the base of a logic that draws wife exchange and masculine adornment together to give meaning to Waiwai notions of manhood. It is indeed the basis upon which gender differences are built and given cultural meaning. In fact without the body not even the circuits of kinship relations and social status can begin to find their ideological expression; Waiwai men could not, for example, maneuver among themselves for positions of authority and prestige without the confirming somatic similarities and differences that the body offers to their understanding of kinship and gender. Being epeka and/or wošin has, for example, its masculine and feminine specificities, as brotherhood and sisterhood—while retaining their shared uterine generality—become experienced and known differently precisely because of bodily attributes. The body, or perhaps more accurately the perception of the body's form and outer covering, comes to serve as the irreducible means for the expression of human knowledge—in this specific Waiwai case, of knowledge about gender and kinship in a world where these forms of knowing take on the fundamental role of communicating to society the individual's particular commitment. Society generally needs such commitments from the individual in order to persist; it cannot be sure of itself in collective terms without this sense of bodily and—by supposed implication—moral devotion from the individual. This is how society, as it is known, passes on in time and in the world. By its relative cultural presence through the individual, one society can continue in its specific distinctiveness from another society that similarly manifests itself through its own individual members. Waiwai society, for example, using its particular cultural knowledge about gender and kinship, takes hold of its members' bodies to unite its collective self with their individual subjectivities. Thus when one of its members admits to having parents and uterine kindred, identifies them as epeka, and expresses certain forms of moral obligations to them as epeka, that member not only produces cultural statements about social relations and locations, but also produces distinct commitments that reassure society of its closure on the alienating distance between the individual and society. Such then are some of the most significant forms of cultural knowledge about society in the narratives of Waiwai myth and, most emphatically, in the adornment of the Waiwai body.

The Fish-Egg Apron and the Body of Woman

THE MAWARI MYTH: EPISODE II

When Mawari was fishing for his wife
he hooked from the river certain
cultural artifacts associated with women.
One of these was a *keweyu*, a woman's apron.

The keweyu was not, however,
made of seed beads, but of fish eggs.

These must have perished, as did the beautiful bands,
tubes, cotton, and feather adornments
that were later given
to the Waiwai by the Anaconda-people.

(margin notes, left side:) apron → symbol of social identity

apron=symbol of feminine fertility

Mawari pulls the identifiable accoutrements of womanhood up from the river. One such item, the keweyu (apron), the myth describes correctly—yet ironically—as made not of seed beads but of fish eggs. Quintessentially feminine, the apron properly has its mythical source in the aquatic symbolic field where the ideas of terrestrial waters and earthly fertility structurally relate and align to the domesticity of marriage as well as to womanhood. The full intellectual force of the apron's dynamic symbolism centers, however, on its association with the egg and the egg's literal capacity for birth. Traditionally made and worn by Waiwai women not only as a cultural statement of their adult feminine status but also as a graphic display of their legitimate right to fertility, the beaded apron, tied around a woman's hip, approximates a certain kind of somatic reality or knowledge objectified on the surface of the skin for all to see and confirm.[13] In conceptual terms the woman's dependent uterus has multiplied itself, manifold as the strung-together "eggs" of the independent beaded apron. The apron becomes, in other words, an embellished outer and collective statement about an inner and individual capability of feminine fertility. Yet there is more here than just a reference to the relation between ideas about indigenous physiology and female apparel, for the apron has the additional facility of capturing and representing the principal status and character of womanhood.

The established cultural and intellectual links for drawing similarities between beads, eggs, and uterus permit the apron to assert its relations to certain social roles for women, particularly those of wife and mother. In this regard the apron functions as a highly readable metaphorical expression of womanhood. Apron, wife, and motherhood are drawn and hold fast to each other while confirming their veracity by their links to eggs and uterine fertility. The apron appears to reinforce the logic held within the meanings of the social roles, and at the same time, by actually being worn, extends the power of such logic over the body. In this way it helps to fit the socially significant roles of womanhood to the female body—that is, in being worn it actually assists in bringing the female body into sight in its rather distinctive social ways. Intriguingly, while it may indeed hide those parts and qualities of a woman's body understood to be both erotic and fertile—and in the hiding seek to control such examples of femininity—the apron just as smartly presents these somatic features with a presence that only a garment of its kind can make possible.

[handwritten margin note: presence of absence drawing attention]

The adorned presence of the apron tells of the hidden body parts, their qualities, and their associated links to producing a wife and a mother. It is a visual and public presence about the potential and actuality of the female body, but it is also a presence with a meta-narrative, one that tells about the cultural constraint of the body by society. This metanarrative about the sexuality and fertility of the woman's body under control obliquely yet specifically references the societal power to make wives and mothers from the very bodies of women. In both kinds of narrations, however, the adorning apron obviously contrives to have its message known; its message must become the constitutive knowledge of what is understood as the significant Waiwai categories of being woman—a knowledge about feminine social being that can be not only perceived but also felt by those who actually wear the apron.

The full intuitive confirmation of such knowledge, perceived and felt, does not depend solely upon recognizing and acting with the similarities drawn intellectually between beaded apron, eggs, and uterus. Here the signs of femininity, conveyed by the apron and turned into the metaphors of social reality, evoke and help to sustain the similarity of differences between the bodies of woman, man, and child. The signaled femininity suggests that when a Waiwai woman becomes aware of her sexuality, she presumably becomes aware of her body's erotic potency or barrenness, its vibrant effect or waning influence, its capacity for libidinous pleasure or pain. In each of its forms of somatic sexual consciousness, the body of woman depends on relations drawn to other bodies and their various categories of social representations.

While experiencing the specific erotics of womanhood as a wife, for example, a woman may not only corroborate the effect in herself of the giving of her body or the giving of the products of her body's efforts to the presence of her husband's social being, but she may also bring the social reality of her husband's body into verifiable existence. A man is able, in other words, to substantiate his manhood as a husband through the conjugal relations his wife brings to their relationship. In an analogous structural manner, a son and/or daughter can claim or substantiate his and/or her own uterine existence through the knowledge of their birth from a woman's womb and the moral and emotional bond to a mother's body. Through relations to gendered and age-defined bodies, a woman can gain and offer experiential knowledge of her motherhood.

Thus does her body, as mother, come to know the swell of its growing fetus, the pain of giving birth, the leak of its lactating breasts, the constant weight on its hip from an infant in a sling, and the restrictions—during the child's early infancy—on eating certain kinds of food. Here somatic knowledge interprets as the similarity of differences between being wife and mother, and yet the body not only serves to register the perception and emotions of these particular categories of being woman, it also functions to make known the moral ground upon which these and other Waiwai social relations must be built.

Bodily knowledge carries and broadcasts Waiwai morality. In doing so—very often at the level of implicit understandings—it permits behavior to be judged and negotiated. Certainly, what can be known about the individual in various social roles and relationships fully depends upon the capacity of the body (both as subject and as object) to be descriptive. Waiwai descriptions of womanhood, for example, as wife or mother (and the relations these roles have with husband and child in order to make wife or mother meaningful) point to the fact that not only does knowledge about the body of woman precede social understanding, but also such knowledge directly contributes to understandings of what constitutes a *kirewani wosi*—a "good" woman.

An individual described by the wearing of an apron expresses an embodiment understood to be woman, a womanhood understood to be embodied while being both provocatively concealed and proclaimed by the apron. Included in such descriptions would be the potential of the body to achieve vaginal sex and birth—potentials unlikely to be actualized without direct engagement with the bodies of man and child respectively. Here the obvious somatic similitude of the social differences contributes directly to the moral ground upon which the body of woman gains its architecture of meaning. A wife, for example, gives and receives sex from her husband and, in the process, brings about the proper physical knowledge of her marital relationship—a knowledge of physical intimacy that will further help her body to produce a child and inaugurate her role as mother. Sexual exchanges acquire their most socially contained and positive values (apart, perhaps, from the instance of the wayamnu category) when their particular expressive bodily forms take on legitimacies within the categories of wife and husband. In this way they help to establish what makes a "good" wife out of a woman's body and a "good" husband out of a man's body. While a woman expects sex from her husband, she in turn fulfills her moral role in the connubial relationship when her feminine sexuality meets and receives her husband's masculinity through the acts of sexual intercourse and childbirth. Interestingly enough, in a similar structural fashion what can be said about sex and birth can also be said about food.

A wife expects, for example, to receive raw meat from her husband in order to clean, cook, and redistribute it for consumption. As a moral expression of her relationship to him, she (or better still, the understood role she plays in the category of wife) demands and expects hunted meat from the husband. She considers herself a proper woman and wife whenever she performs the tasks of cleaning and cooking the meat her husband has given her. The moral value of meat provider or hunter placed on the husband contributes to making a "good" wife out of a woman. Of course, under all these same criteria a woman or man can become a better or worse wife or husband. The main point—that is, the one generally understood in Waiwai epistemology—is that the criteria for making and confirming social and moral persons have their foundations in the descriptive terrain of knowledge about the body.

As Mawari leans forward and retrieves the bodily adornment of woman from the river, the myth verifies in him the active agency and empowered subjectivity of a gendered social being. Through the narrative actions of his body, the myth gives voice to an instrumental and privileged masculine selfhood. It tells its audience about the durable powers of divinity and divinity's seemingly logical affinity to manhood. It proclaims in Mawari's gesture of fishing the apron from the river that hunting for meat and seeking for a wife are analogous acts: thus does his body address the issues of marriage and the desire to become a husband and father through the masculine act of predation. And yet, even in giving to manhood a certain kind of bodily privilege, the myth nevertheless has to set masculinity off against femininity. For without the one the other cannot be known, cannot indeed become the object of desire that fulfills and completes the gap of an unfinished social personhood.

His is a hard body attuned to the rigors of hunting in the rugged and foreign terrain of the forest, a body caught up in the representation of divine and masculine existence. His body, as the agent of discovery and knowledge, fishes from the river the quintessential apparel of womanhood. It is in this act of seeking "to catch" food and sex that the masculine body discovers and understands for the first time the very object of its desires. Her body by contrast is soft, being more accustomed to the domestic chores of household and village life—a body mortally measured to the work of human birth and culinary routines. Close are the intellectual associations between her body and the apron. Made with the soft, glutinous eggs of fish, the mythic apron, like her body, expresses the contrast and the ultimate irony of the interdependence between the bodies of men and women. Here the apron represents the body of woman and qualities of womanhood apparently "caught" by the masculine effort. Her body is what is discovered and known. The products of her labor and the erotics of her sex are obtained with one swoop of masculine agency. In the apron her body conveys to womanhood its specific qualities of a mortal perishability as well as a mutual fulfillment to the contrasting and incomplete genders. Only this contrast of femininity and the consciousness it delivers to the masculine body actually bring the roles of husband and fatherhood to Mawari's anxiously sought after social identity.

Unlike the divine masculine form of birth, the mortal feminine form depicted by the mythic fish-egg apron produces life that must inevitably perish. Clearly different when compared to the durability of divine masculine existence, feminine birth nonetheless displays a fulsome adorning of life in the apron that, even in its fading, remains attractive, desirable, and fulfilling. Indeed, it succeeds in enticing Mawari to keep on fishing for his "true" woman, the one that will complete him as a man. In other words, by inverting the role of the hunter who becomes captivated by that which he hunts, the mythic apron and its significances continue the theme of the complementarity between contrasting genders.

In shape the apron mimics the body line of a woman, curving from the waist down along the hips to the upper thigh. Made traditionally from the hard *karakra* seeds (but now more often of traded glass beads), the horizontal rows of strung seeds, framed with cotton weave and tassels, hang with heavy seduction. When worn in conventional style, the apron adorns the front of the hips while the buttocks remain uncovered. With satisfaction, the lower front entrance to a woman's body receives the cultural embellishment of an erotic confinement—a statement not only of some beauty but also of power. The garment pulls in the gaze of its observer. It draws the viewer into a visual encounter. When locked into the exchange, the track of communication between apron and observer seduces the gaze to be convinced by the now heightened presence of the concealed vagina. The seductive way in which the repeated rows of strung seeds hang, appearing to cling just barely to the curves of the hip and thighs; the articulated flexibility, permitting the graceful partnership between body and garment; and the suggestive cotton fringes, providing that sense of provocative boundary—they all work to beguile the gaze into accepting the messages that the feminine body sends by way of the apron. There is beauty and persuasive power in the body of woman—a body, indeed, subjected to forces providing legitimate references for the completion of masculinity, and yet, a body with power of its own to make itself attractive as the source of fulfillment of manhood. With the apron womanhood confirms itself and cues manhood for full personhood. In its epistemological form, the mythic fish-egg apron symbolically connects human sexuality and fertility not merely to the obvious lower frontal part of a woman's body but, more subtly, to the erotics of her body and to the desirable social categories of wife and motherhood—categories absolutely essential for the realization of being a husband and a father. Here the concept of the beaded apron with all it can intellectually generate affirms itself as representative of a shared and collective knowledge about the body.

The Body's Outer Designs and Inner Wisdom

THE MAWARI MYTH: EPISODE III

Seeking a wife in return, the Anaconda-people had come
to the village of the Waiwai as visiting in-laws.
They were tricked from receiving a wife
but left in the roof of the communal house
the gift of their own body adornments.

Before this time the Waiwai wore inferior plain body
adornments.
It was the visit of the Anaconda-people and the memory of
their beauty
which encouraged the art of body decoration.

The gift of women and the idea of bead and feather adornment
originated from downstream in the aquatic village of the
anaconda.
Indeed it was the blood of the anaconda Petarï
that gave mortal life and plumage to the birds.

In the origin myth about male ceremonial costumes, the Ana-conda-people, dressed in their finest attire, visit the village of their Waiwai in-laws. Seeking wives in return for the women they had already given to the Waiwai, the Anaconda men encounter instead a naïve ineptitude from their in-laws and leave the village empty-handed. Before departing, however, the Anaconda men place the gift of their own body adornments in the roof of their in-laws' com-munal house. Prior to this visit the Waiwai wore plain and inferior adornments. The Waiwai cherish the attractive gifts of armbands, hair tubes, cotton tassels, and feathered adornments left by their guests. In a similar narrative style to that of the fish-egg apron, however, immediately after the departure of the Anaconda-people, the splendid artifacts of ceremonial vestures fade.

Why are the mythical Waiwai such inept hosts? The intuitive declarative statement of the myth suggests it is because they lack an eye-catching and exuberant bodily covering. In Waiwai ways of thinking, a strong correlation exists between possessed knowledge and bodily adornments. Before the endowment of beautiful clothes from their Anaconda in-laws, therefore, the Waiwai are without proper or highly valued cultural knowledge—hence their social in-eptitude in not returning the gift of wives to their visiting in-laws. Their plain and inferior garments explain their social and moral deficiencies. The Anaconda-people, on the other hand, know how to behave, know how to be proper beings, and, indeed, exemplify such knowing in the splendor of their attire.

What then lies behind the gift that fades, the gift of knowledge, which—after being generously given—lacks luster and disappears? It seems that long after the splendid clothes have faded, what re-mains and certainly appears significant is the Waiwai's vivid collec-tive memory of the Anaconda-people's sartorial beauty. The images of a material but temporary beauty remain as memory—a memory manifested as visual knowledge. The internalized yet shared visual knowledge of and even desire for the aesthetically pleasing bodies of their in-laws is the true gift received. Once they have accepted the unrefusable gift of beauty, the Waiwai want to be like their Anaconda in-laws. What is beautiful and indeed irresistible about the bodies of the Anaconda-people is not the freely given outer designs of their adorned presence, but the internal wisdom that the temporary outer designs encase and help to verify. This irresistible beauty of a verified wisdom actually corroborates the very existence of Kwarokiyim for the Waiwai; indeed, such wisdom can be said to constitute the declarative beauty in the harmonious perfectibility of the Divine. The Waiwai want to be like their Anaconda in-laws not merely in what the latter wear and how they wear it but rather in the splendid divine ways in which they understand and move in the world. Beyond the correlation between body adornment and knowledge, there exists this most significant fact—that is, that the retained visual image, not just the object presented to the gaze, actually becomes the substance of the wisdom that initiates the growth of social and moral understandings. Waiwai visual memory repeats the designs of bodily adornment and makes them representative of a contained internal wisdom.

Perhaps because social and moral understandings are so crucial to the forming of human identity, the question of their permanency becomes an important intellectual issue for Waiwai philosophy. Clearly, any threat of impermanence to the constituted elements of identity would have immense ramifications for societal continuity. The query, at least in the myth, seems to concern this very quality of the impermanence of knowledge. An inclination toward this arises and persists in the way myth problematizes the representation of knowledge.

Their own amorphous character can threaten social and moral understandings—hence the attempt to give such understandings a design or a patterned arrangement with communicative capabilities. With the application of decorative designs, the inherent liquidity of knowledge becomes formally adhesive. Indeed, it may even be suggested that the actual mention of fading artifacts is in itself a decorative design of myth attempting not only to copy, but also, in the copying, to solidify and harness the ephemeral essence of knowledge. And yet the outer designs of the body and the internal wisdom they solidify remain vulnerable; this is because as soon as they are communicated and copied as visual memory, their liquidity once again returns. Knowledge can never remain inert. Every attempt to make it so—that is, in the perpetual conservational reservoir of its creative designs—inevitably results in its weakening and gradual transformation. It seems the curious incidents in the myths of artifacts fading after being received as gifts seek to address this peculiar quality and essential vulnerability of knowledge. As the formalization of decorative designs in visual memory, knowledge betrays both the attempt and the failure to command its inherent liquidity. This presence of a deep-seated skepticism in Waiwai intellectual ruminations exposes, perhaps somewhat bashfully, their ideological belief in the futility of any kind of power over knowledge. For this reason, however, it remains instructive to witness the specific narrative ways in which the myth portrays the origin of body adornment as the creative activity of the Anaconda-people.

Waiwai visual knowledge of bodily attire is stimulated by the flow of productive creativity from the Anaconda-people's aquatic village. Consistent with ideas about the liquidity of knowledge, the Anaconda-people's watery home is the initial site of social understanding. In another, more subtle reference—from the myth about the origin of birds' plumage—the blood of the anaconda Petarï instills mortal life and color to the birds for the first time. Here the myths successfully repeat and convey the information that sartorial knowledge has its source in the anaconda—that is, in its aquatic realm and in the blood of its body. The myths also repeat the message that all sartorial knowledge and the social and moral understandings they contain depend on visual imaginary.

The mythic message sets in place the actual relations between the vividly displayed objects of bodily adornment and the visually capable imagination. The relations' instrumental ability to process the distribution of visual knowledge between object and imagination logically follows as the possibility of a shared memory displayed on the surface of Waiwai bodies. The principal mythic message to hold on to, however, is not the one which repeats where such knowledge originates, but the one which echoes that such knowledge becomes shared memory whenever it acquires and opens up the possibility of being internally received as a visual image—a seen knowledge needing once again to make itself objectified as cultural fact in the world. From interpretations of this kind, body adornment can be said to represent both a personal commemorative knowledge and a collective cultural knowledge while, at the same time, being dependent upon the principal factor of visibility.

In the episodes of the origin myths, where both the jaguar and the anaconda portray aggressive predatory and sexual desires, the specific sensory code of sight operates to express the totality of equivalences between the feline and the reptile. The sight code formed by invisibility and visibility transfers the meaning of events in one episode to another; it carries with it the specific isomorphic message of a consuming visual knowledge. Epeka becomes, for example, the target of an immoral feline attack from the in-law when its invisibility is betrayed and the Tortoise Woman's hiding place, under an upturned clay pot, is uncovered. The chacha Jaguar Woman initially hides Tortoise Woman under the clay pot. The same chacha in the same myth also hides the perfect epeka, that is, the brotherhood of the origin twins, Mawari and Washi. This time, however, invisibility succeeds, for the brothers survive in the village of their Jaguar in-laws to leave the large clay pot as adult men. In the other episode the imposition of the visit from the Anaconda-people is actually brought on by the disobedience of a young woman who, having been told by her chacha not to look at the middle of the river, does so. The chacha again hides the woman under a clay pot, where she remains invisible to the hungry and ardent sight of the Anaconda-people. There are attempts to betray her presence, both by the smell of her menstruating body and by the customary food of fish eaten by secluded menstruating women. These all fail, with the Anaconda-people departing and leaving behind the splendor of their adornments for the Waiwai to see. Invisibility also operates in the mutable bodies of some of the mythic actors. Indeed, before the chacha hides her, Tortoise Woman changes into a "real" tortoise. Throughout the myth, Mawari and Washi escape death and the violence of their in-laws by changing into different animals. The fish that seeks to betray the hidden young woman to the Anaconda-people is a transformed Anaconda man who is stamped to death while attempting to leave the hiding place with his precious information. Being invisible and becoming visible in another form, while fraught with the contradictions of safety and danger, life and death, nevertheless operate as codes of meaning for the importance of sight and the visual imagination. They redolently express, it seems to me, the general significance of seeing, the eye, and the possible privileged place they have in the formation of Waiwai knowledge.

This intimacy of relations between knowledge and visual memory can be glimpsed in the episode where Mawari and Washi have sexual intercourse with the otter. Best known as the favored assistant to the *yaskomo* (shaman) and the *maywin* (spiritual helper) to many Waiwai fishermen, the *wayawaya* (larger fin-tailed otter [*sarara*: smaller fin-tailed otter]) turns up as pivotal character in many myths. Like all such helpers, the otter is often addressed in kinship terms or referred to as *yoku* (pet). As kinship terms can denote and pets connote close family ties, the sexual act with the otter seems tantamount to incest (or indeed, of homosexuality when one regards the relation as fraternal). In Waiwai ideas such a flagrant act of immorality can only have been carried out by someone outside the compelling grasp of society and, hence, by someone lacking in the proper forms of knowledge. It is, however, the way in which the heroes perform sex with the otter that confirms and compounds this fact—indeed, the brothers render coitus with the animal in the orifice of its eye. It might be considered that one of the otter's distinctive features is its large, round eyes and that as helper to the shaman, the otter often has to guide its human kinsman along the sacred paths by using its superior sense of vision. Its eyes and its eyes' distinct ability to see in a way no normal human eyes can see convey the meaning of an enhanced visual wisdom. In other words the otter has great shamanic qualities precisely because of the knowledge gained through its increased ocular powers.

In the myth the otter's great wisdom interlocks with and has an effect on the great moral ignorance of the heroic brothers. Immediately after their act of indecent sex with the otter, the brothers discover how to bring their desire under control and, thereafter, know how to have correct sexual intercourse with women. Their initial immoral act, however, is not merely a case of an indiscriminate and technical ignorance about proper sex. As far as the Waiwai meta-understanding of myth is concerned, the brothers' indecent act is itself indicative of what happens if the logic of societal norms does not claim its role in the close governance of individual desire. Certainly, in the narrative sequence the brothers' desire for sex already sits in place, but the intellectual awareness of whom sex should be with and how it should be carried out in order to conform to the correct kind of sex does not. Such knowledge cannot be irreducible to ideas of sexuality. In Waiwai collective thought, all knowledge of internal human emotions should ideally be subject to social control; in this case, individual sexual desire and satisfaction must be understood, ordered, and distributed out into society where they can become the very substance of society itself. In this regard correctly displaying such knowledge in action with the body as well as on the body with adornments confirms the pedagogical process and the effect of social power. The dispensational wisdom of the otter's eyes provides the guidance toward these manifested truths.

In the pragmatic demand from society, the brothers' mistake in having sex in the eye of the otter appears logical—that is, they make the correct mistake. The brothers recognize that orifices allow them entrance into the body, that their penises are intended for an orifice, and that there exists an orifice through which their penises can enter for sexual satisfaction, conception, and birth. Where sexual gratification and the generation of human birth are concerned, the brothers enter by the wrong orifice. But in terms of the acquisition of intellectual rather than sentient knowledge as well as the manifestation of such knowledge as visual memory, they enter by the correct and proper orifice. Such knowledge, here governed by societal concerns, primarily associates with masculine bodies; it is constituted as an internal visual memory that the bodies of men, like the bodies of the Anaconda men, represent for further collective consumption. In this instance body adornments represent the confirmation of society's hold upon the individual, not only on the individual body but also on the individual self. The commitment of subjectivity to society by means of its bodily representations confirms, at least in part, the secondary immediacy of the lived body—that is, the unity that exists between society and the individual.

Here opens our particular point of departure from myth to body adornment. Framed by the act of sex with the otter and reframed by the inverse act of sex through the eye, the double entendre presents knowledge and visual memory for assessment. The structural contrast and parallelism drawn between the lower ventral orifice of the body and the upper frontal orifice of the face bring together acknowledged somatic signifiers. Such structural ordering may occur not only because of the human body's assumed anatomical symmetry, but also because in Waiwai theory the eyes and the vagina have recognizable functions that allow them to become the principal signifiers for the concepts of sight and birth. Further, as extensions of these concepts, the "language" of body adornment expresses Waiwai belief about visual memory and knowledge. More accurately, the simple syllogism infers that because visual memory relates to knowledge and body adornment relates to visual memory, the prepositional statement should be that Waiwai body adornment specifically relates to the expression of knowledge.

visual memory ← body adornment
↓
knowledge ←

And Toward the Body Encompassed

Adorning Embodied Subjectivities

A traditional Waiwai girl would have adorned herself with the white beaded *keweyu* apron and *apomi* (armband) beads after her first menses and ritual initiation into the age-grade of *amas-komo*. Tied around her waist, the sexually seductive beaded apron announced both the erotics and the fertility of her womanhood. Wrapped around her upper arms, the long string of white beads impressed an attained and controlled young adulthood upon her body. The cultural grasp of her body by society through the adornments made these attributes visible for all to see. They must be seen in this manner, for they bore witness to the triumph of society over the individual. She had become a woman physically, but she had also been made into one culturally and, as such, displayed her individual submission to the social power of the collective. The Amasï girl succumbed to being a young adult Waiwai woman and, from within this social category that others before her and now still occupied, she prepared herself for the expectant rewards of marriage and motherhood as well as the elevated status they would bring to her and to the category itself. On her body for all to see, her submission flourished as a vivid and constant public event of womanhood. In this regard her keweyu and apomi served as visible statements and confirmations of her body's commitment to the particular demands of Waiwai adulthood. Yet the submission and its visible expression came at some expense; they came from ritually confining her body from sight in silent and solitary seclusion—a process that awakened a necessary vulnerability.

For as many as two moons an initiate girl had to be confined to the small space of a miniature windowless and doorless leaf hut (Fock 1963:154–57; Morton 1979, 1983–84; Sullivan 1988:323–24). Her head was shaved. She could not speak (except in whispers to her attending mother). She could never look up to the sky. She had to restrict her diet to light, liquefied barely life-sustaining foods. And she certainly had to abstain from sexual intercourse. In other words she had to remain invisible not just from others but also from herself. In the confines of the make-believe womb, her invisibility reduced her body to an absence both from the world and from her former selves. Nevertheless, what was actually happening to her in terms of the ritual was plainly visible to all. For like the swollen belly of a pregnant woman, the little leaf hut loudly broadcasted the event and process of her confined body. It was as if the first bleeding of her body began the circumstance of her dying and the procedure of her burial—actions that the ritual of confinement continued precisely in order to remake her as a woman.

This ritual of social death and rebirth had the purpose of terminating her childhood while creating and protecting her new body. It sought to protect her body from the social opprobrium of ugliness—a woman unable to be desired as a wife and unable to be objectified as a mother. To provide her body with beauty—that is, to construct her womanhood in the pleasing, honorable images of wife and mother, the ritual particularly targeted the major upper and lower openings of her body. It placed, for example, a heightened vigilance upon what entered and what left her mouth, her eyes, and her vagina. It seemed as if the overall immediate effects of her sexual abstinence and dietary restrictions would keep her cervix in place and in good order, make sure her skin was smooth and of good color, and prepare her body in general for a career of vigor and obedience. Perhaps more than at any other social time, in this period of ritual liminality the body and society achieved their most intense levels of immediacy and maybe even their greatest distance from the self. For in the confines of the hut, the Amasï-to-be intimately experienced the vulnerability of her body; a vulnerability that, once realized, desperately sought for the security prescribed for it in the social domains of marriage and motherhood—the very same security objectified and expressed in the bodily encompassment by the keweyu and apomi.

To produce the full and coherent meanings belonging to womanhood, however, the actual grammar of a bodily adornment had to bring the particular vocabulary of the beaded apron and the armbands together. On their own the armbands merely confer to the body the meaning of an adult status, a status difficulty to bring into actuality in Waiwai society without the added distinction of gender. To move in social terms along the desired pathways and into the security of legitimate identities requires the addition of a gendered status. The beaded armbands, together with the beaded apron, convey both the adulthood and the sexual status of woman. As a complete statement upon the body, they present a highly visible "text" of womanhood; a "text" constantly presenting itself to be "read"; indeed, a "text" that in its complementary role serves to draw the attention specifically of masculinity. In helping to confirm the legitimacy of the path followed in ritual toward the making of womanhood—a path clearly chartered in myth—the beaded armbands and apron secure adult femininity in the cultural literacy of the community. Redolent with the similarities of adulthood in woman and man, the armbands must be structurally coupled with the apron to confirm the unique distinctiveness of woman and, thus, its particular differences from masculinity.

A traditional Waiwai boy would have adorned himself with the *miiso* (bamboo hair tube) and apomi beads after he began to show the physical signs of an adolescent masculinity and passed through ritual initiation into the age-grade of *karipamšam-komo*. His wrapped and encased hair exhibited an energized and controlled masculine sexuality. His beaded armbands conferred and confirmed the heightened adult status of his sexuality. In wearing these adornments his body in effect signaled the commitment of its signifying virility and strength to society. The work of initiation gives legitimacy to this commitment and to the demands society has upon the body. Attributes like courage, discipline, and strength—which initiation instill and test—must be aspects of the individual masculine body and, through the body, aspects that help to sustain society. The initiation process and its ritual accoutrements spell out these features and aims.

To my knowledge the Waiwai no longer practice the ant-biting initiation ritual for young men. It remains, nevertheless, a well-remembered part of many of the older men's life history. Indeed, it seemed to me that it had taken on the intellectual proportions of a historical yardstick by which current-day youth could be compared and judged lacking. The general impression was conceded that young men today were not as brave, obedient, or strong as the karipamšam-komo of yesteryear. While this deficiency, in any conversation where it was the topic, could be traced to many aspects of being young in current-day Waiwai society, it often came down to the fact that no one now passed through the ant-biting ritual. I have to say that this deficiency reputation was a concern even for the young men themselves, whom I often saw taking the opportunity to perform specific feats of endurance that tested their threshold of pain. Interestingly enough, when compared to the initiation ritual for girls, the ant-biting ceremony for a boy becoming a karipamšam—though very physically intense—was nevertheless not as elaborate or as prolonged. It simply began with the weaving of reeds for two *yukiupon* (ant belts). Between each space along a row of overlapping strands on both reed belts, an angry ant was held in place by the weave. In the plaza, in full view of everyone, a belt of ants was tied around both of the boy's legs just below the knees. There he had to stand without moving, without crying out, without showing any signs of discomfort, until he either said "*Ñisha-taka*" ("Enough" or "I have had enough") or collapsed from the pain of the constant stinging by the ants. When he recovered, he was entitled to wear a mïiso and apomi.

As with the initiation of the girl, the ant-biting ritual took hold of and transformed only one body at a time: there were and still are no formal "rites of passage" in Waiwai society for groups of people. The individual had to undergo the ordeal alone. The affects of the ritual sought to undermine, not build, the possibility of an alternative community in the liminal domain and moment. The body of the initiant had to succumb to a powerful sense of vulnerability in order to accept the offer of the only possible community available to it after liminality—that of Waiwai society. If one of the metaphors of liminality is death, then what the body did in this ritual space and time was to die alone. The silence and stillness the boy had to maintain in order to become a man mimicked death. Yet this was a kind of living death, where the virtues of courage, discipline, and strength got infused into the body and remade it into manhood. The burning stings from the bites of the ants injected an excruciating heat through the skin and into the body.

The Waiwai consider the experiencing of this heat to be the epitome of what the full vigor of life should feel like. It is like a kind of solar energy inside the body. It administers strength to the recipient, the kind of strength needed in the community to sustain it. It is the kind of strength that allows the body to endure running for miles in the forest to catch fleeing game; the kind of strength that allows the body to endure the discomfort of a swarm of biting insects while clearing the forest for new fields; the kind of strength that allows the body of a young man to endure days of paddling a dugout canoe upstream against strong currents. It may even be argued that from the Waiwai point of view such strength is also the felt experience of divine coherence, because like the life-giving vitality of ekatï that enters the body of the newborn baby, the heat from the ant bites ultimately originates from Kwarokiyim. With the ant-biting initiation producing these kinds of bodily experience and knowledge, an inner subjective manifestation of an adult masculinity becomes conscious and waits only to be displayed as an externally adorned "textuality."

While being the social locations for the end of childhood, the age-grades of both amas-komo and karipamšam-komo also contain the very poignant experience of an ever-imminent completion.

The point of all Waiwai social biographies is to attain marriage and parenthood. In fact being karipamšam and amasï are merely social stages for the impending fulfillment of adult identity actually achieved in the higher age-grades of *porintomo-komo* (married men with children) and *anačwan-komo* (married women with children). A necessary stage for the propulsion to full personhood, the status of young adult has first to claim and proclaim its achieved distance from childhood and its pending arrival at full adulthood. What may have been confusing in the ambiguity of the changing body, the visibility and meanings of the armbands make clear. It does not appear to be enough for young Waiwai adulthood just to experience its intellectual abstraction in the world by the practice of specific roles and obligations. Young adulthood looks for the more constant and empirical properties of the armbands. In the first place the armbands signal the lost of childhood, but in the second, they inscribe the anxiously remade person as young adult. Armbands remain on the upper arms of Waiwai adults throughout their lives. The deep impressions they make upon the skin and muscles of the arms can be interpreted as evidence of the on-going relation society has with the body, and perhaps even of its own collective anxiety about needing to fill the gap between itself and the body—indeed, of actually continuing to exist as a social fact.

The armbands and the hair tube are the undeviating body adornments of men's adult masculine status, while for women, armbands and the apron carry the visual message of their adult feminine status. For both men and women, therefore, armbands make reference to the achieved adulthood of their bodies; meanwhile, the hair tube and the apron primarily refer to the gender differences of their bodies. I say primarily, because, depending on their size and embellishment, the hair tube and apron can and do also refer to age-grade status and all that it infers. A long, plain tube can completely contain the short queue of a young man and a short, decorated tube can reveal the long queue of an adult man. It should be noted, however, in the particular example of the long, plain tube, that it is not so much that the tube hides a part of the body, but rather that it reveals that

hair

the body has something to hide—in this instance, the prematurity of youth. For the older man, the tube gregariously displays the fact that it can barely contain the girth and length of its wearer's hair. The large, heavy bead apron of an adult woman and the small, lighter apron of a young woman help to contrast the difference not only in body growth between older and younger women, but also in the social status such body growth signifies. On the body of a Waiwai *toto* (human individual), therefore, the difference between a *rikomo kïru* (boy child) and a *rikomo wosï* (girl child) would not be heavily marked. The difference, however, between rikomo and karipamšam would indeed be marked by the absence or adorned presence of a hair tube, while the difference between rikomo and amasï would be marked by the absence or adorned presence of an apron. The relative size of the hair tube signifies that a man belongs to the karipamšam-komo age-grade or to one or another of the senior age-grades—that is, porintomo-komo or pocha-komo. The same applies to the size of the apron a woman wears; a small apron signifies that she belongs to the junior age-grade of amas-komo and a large apron signifies she belongs to the senior age-grade of either anačwan-komo or chacha-komo.

Thus can be found in these formal combinations of dress and status some of the answers to when and how the partnership between the corporeal and the sartorial acts to assist society in its fundamental project of maintaining itself. Working most effectively through the sanctions of ritual initiation, Waiwai society permits adornments to invest their properties of cultural credence to the body. Yet we should not forget that the individual body also conveys a good deal of its somatic credibility to adornments. And for this reason, I must reintroduce the Waiwai idea that this somatic credibility does not only pertain to the bodies of humans.

Becoming Birds

As if to corroborate as fact the suspicion that ritual carefully follows the course charted by myth, when Waiwai men want to be seen at their most impressive, they become birds. On special ceremonial occasions, men place decorated bark bands over their arm beads that support the fan-shaped *aporaka*. Made from the red tail feathers of the *kwaro* (macaw), the aporaka juts up four feet into the air from the bands on each arm. In addition huge bulbs of black curassow feathers dangle as tassels from the armbands. In Waiwai the word *aporï* refers both to arm and to wing. The emphasis on the arms and the concentration of the larger feathers at this part of the body is an attempt to embellish the crucial difference between men and women and the similarities between men and birds. Other forms of upper-body feather wear also heighten the suggestion that men connote the avian world and women do not.

Some men pierce their nasal septum and lower lip, through which they place, respectively, *kewnaruyaka* (two pinion feathers) and *tašiproku* (tassels) made from the breast feathers of the red macaw. Some own the brilliant orange diadem *aroko*, the feathers of which are taken from the rare mountain bird *peu* (cock of the rock). Every man, however, can and does cover his well-oiled head with a liberal amount of white feather down plucked from the breast of *yayïmo* (harpy eagle). In addition every adult male has to have the feathered bamboo hair tube of mïiso encasing his trussed pigtail. Both men and women comb their hair forward, from the crown of the head to just above the eyes, where they cut the bangs into a fringe. They allow the hair to grow long at the back, but the women coil their hair into a bun that sits behind the head, while the men tie their hair into a queue that hangs behind the back. For normal everyday garb, the men encase the queue inside a plain bamboo tube or a personal bamboo flute. On very special occasions they put the end of the queue into a more elaborate beaded tube that has, attached to its end, a bulb of *powiši* (black curassow) feathers with yellow and white breast feathers of the *yakwe* (large toucan) upon its crown. A glorious sight to behold, a Waiwai man decked out in full traditional sartorial regalia effuses an impression of fowl and flight, distancing himself from the dowdy attire of women.

Both men and women wear the *waru*, a necklace of red (and sometimes white) beads. Men and women also wear the *šakapa*, the chest bandoliers, but the men use strands of red cotton string and the women use strings of opaque seeds. A woman's ceremonial *katami*, a corsetlike bead-and-feather truss worn on the lower back, could claim a close second place to the apron as the most distinctive garment of female attire. Men wear the *kamisa*, a red cotton cloth, around their loins. A proud hunter may add his *kamarapičo*, his jaguar-skin belt, but on a more regular basis his kamisa would be held up only with a *ekonparači*, a loin string with small, rectangular bead-and-feather tassels hanging on each side of the hip. Both men and women may wear the *emehta*, a bead bracelet, but the women wear one on each wrist while the men wear one only on the right wrist. On their left wrist the men tie the *amčnenču*, a bark bracelet. All Waiwai, male and female, young and old, wear the *wašpa*, the blue-and-white band of beads tied just below the knee. Some also wear the *wašpuruam*, a bark ankle band. Apart from the kamisa, apomi, and mïiso, the wearing of all other artifacts of male body adornment depends a good deal upon the whim and panache of the individual. The overall effect, nevertheless, is one in which men appear more resplendent than women, with their splendor shining ideologically as the confirming radiance of birds and the divine coherence empowering such brilliance.

If the body adornments mentioned so far mark and emphasize a certain kind of difference within society, then the artifact of attire most suggestive of social homogeneity may be the *panatarï* (earplugs). The word *panatarï* comes from *panatu* (ear). Immediately after a child is born, its ears are *natpe* (pierced) and kept open literally to receive the panatarï. Because the eyes of a newborn baby cannot as yet behold the brilliance of the world, its ears are pierced so as to allow them "to see" sounds. In other words the head is culturally "opened up" to permit knowledge its rightful place in the construction of the incipient person. All Waiwai throughout their lives wear an earplug of one kind or another. From a mere sliver of wood to the elaborate ear discs that carry the *ešeyatu* (throat) beads, an ear adornment always can be found "opening up" the earlobes of a Waiwai. Earplugs are reflective discs surrounded by a ray of tiny bright feathers set in a wad of *maani* (black adhesive latex). The latex also secures the decorated earplug to a splinter of wood that is put into the earlobe. To keep the plugs from falling out, a string is attached to the rear tip of each splinter; the ends of the strings are then tied to each other behind the neck. On special occasions the white beads of ešeyatu are worn affixed to the earplugs at the back of the ear. For men, the ešeyatu hangs as one piece from ear to ear under the chin. For women, it falls as two separate pieces onto each breast, with the feathered ends covering the nipples. What the panatari do visually is to give the impression that the face possesses another pair of eyes, orbs that peer unblinkingly from the head. What they also do most emphatically, with the help of the ešeyatu, the diadem, the feathered bangs, and the hair combed forward from the crown of the head to the eyes, is to draw attention to the front of the head.

Feathers in the Face

The Waiwai linguistically indicate the significant parts of the body with the terminal noun syllable /ri/. *Yehta-ri* refers to the foot, *iwaho-ri* to the calf, *osotmu-ri* to the knee, *wehtu-ri* to the belly, *ponu-ri* to the navel, *yimka-ri* to the back, *eretu-ri* to the liver, *mota-ri* to the shoulder, *apo-ri* to the arm, *amo-ri* to the hand, and *yuhtupu-ri* to the head. The Waiwai also linguistically subdivide the head with /ri/ terminal phonemes. They call the neck *yupumu-ri*, the chin *iyowya-ri*, the tongue *yunu-ri*, the tooth *iyow-ri*, the mouth *yemta-ri*, the cheek *peta-ri*, the nose *ewna-ri*, the ear *pana-ri*, and the eye *ew-ri*. It seems that linguistic indicators have been given visual congruence with body adornment.

Significantly, this has been accomplished by the particular aesthetic image of radiant encirclement. For the head it is the diadem; for the neck, the necklace; for the arm, the armband; for the belly, the loin string and belt; and for the legs, the knee bands. The theme of radiant encirclement continues all over the surface of the conventional Waiwai body: on the chest with the bandoleers; on the wrist, the knee, and the ankle with the bands, beads, and bark. It could be argued from these clues that one of the principal messages conveyed focuses on the notions of bodily constraint and control, and, in addition, that this tempering conspicuously concentrates on the particular zones of the upper body. The way adornment places emphasis on the encirclement of the body, particularly from the waist upward, certainly suggests an attribute of significant importance to the upper regions of the Waiwai body.

Adornment themes of bodily openings and encirclement recur most prominently at the head. The waru circles the neck, the ešeyatu encompasses the face, and the dazzling aroko crowns the ceremonial head. A woman curls her hair into a bun, while a man trusses his queue with *krewetu* (sisal grass) string and puts it in a mïiso. With the pierced alterations of the ears, nose, and lower lips, the head becomes a very culturally distinct part of the Waiwai human anatomy. Of all the cultural statements made by the adornments of the head, however, perhaps those articulated by feathers placed in the perforated orifices of the face carry the most significant meanings.

Hair figures obtrusively as a force controlled. Both men and women encourage head hair to grow to great length, only to control it by cultural artifact and design. The Waiwai do not, however, encourage the growth of body hair; a good deal of the day spent relaxing involves the nonchalant epilation of body hair. They particularly discourage the growth of facial hair. A Waiwai face must be kept clean of hair—even to the removal of eyebrows and eyelashes. The human face should be clear and bright like the sky in the upper firmament. Its eyes, like the sun, should emanate a glow that lights up the front of the head. The eyes, orbs of vision in the head, must be kept clear and bright, unobscured by the dark hairs surrounding them. The Waiwai word for hair, *yepoči*, is the same as that for feather. Thus, it can be said that while they systematically remove human facial hairs, they just as methodically replace them with the "hairs" of birds. But the color and relocation of this embellishment are not arbitrary, for while they remove the dark hair from around the eyes and face, they replace them with bright feathers set in the ear, the nose, and the lower lip. In other words the energy of hair, represented here by its rapid growth, comes under cultural control by being removed and intellectually improved upon with feathers.

In their specificity as entrances, the orifices of the head engage Waiwai sensibilities. In this regard, one could say, they acquire structural significance from being in opposition to the lower orifices of the genital region. Waiwai concern about what enters the body at the top and what leaves it from the bottom preoccupies their aesthetic of being. This concern expresses itself objectively in their managed adornment of facial orifices. The result is a distinctive structural patterning to facial perforations, the form of which appears consistent with vital sensory points. A statement about sensory perception does, indeed, find assertion in the symbolic gesture. Its inference hints at an "opening up" and, in so doing, at an amplifying of the ability to hear by piercing the earlobe, an enhancing of the faculty of smell by piercing the nasal septum, and a strengthening of the skill of speech by piercing the lower lip. In other words the different sensory powers are being symbolically enhanced by a theme on open orifices, yet these open orifices are themselves expressive of the one facial opening not marked by actual perforation—the eye. In Waiwai ideas the eye and seeing have been given esteemed powers of sensory perception.

If the final /rï/ syllable of the Waiwai words for the parts of the face indicates a composite category, then in the penultimate syllable the vowels /u/ and /a/ group the facial parts into two separate sets. The first set use /murï, nurï, turï/ and the second use /yarï, tarï, narï/. In other words the structuring of these phonemic and syllabic sequences place the neck, the tongue, and the throat into the first set and the chin, the mouth, the cheek, the ear, and the nose into the second set. The /a/ vowel set has a further subset marked by the consonant of the penultimate syllable—for example, *yem[t]arï, pe[t]arï, pa[n]arï, ew[n]arï*. Thus, in the subset a close phonological association occurs between yemtarï (mouth) and petarï (cheek) on the one hand, and panarï (ear) and ewnarï (nose) on the other. The one anomaly in these sets pertains to the word for eye—*ewrï*. It is the only two-syllable word in this /rï/ composite category, and while being related closely to *ewnarï* (nose), it does not fall into either the /u/ or /a/ vowel sets; ewrï functions as a separate member.

This phonological structuring of the words for facial parts suggests a similar cognitive ordering for which the primary dialectic is one between seeing and eating. Here I wish to concentrate only on the former, but to discuss the one without the other does create certain limitations. To appreciate the full affect of the meaningful dialectic, both attributes must be kept in mind even while I am discussing just the one. If the eyes dominantly represent the sensory receptors of the face, then it must be understood that the dominant feature symbolizing the act of consumption is the throat (and of course, by association, the tongue and the neck). The verbs *esetakaši* (to hunt), *esereme* (to have a meal), and *esehsa* (to breathe) derive from the noun *ešeturï* (throat). In Waiwai thought and action a very strong correlation exists between hunting, eating, and death by spiritual "blowing." The location and the function of the throat help to establish these relations. While the location and function of the throat connote the downward passage of food into the belly, the eye denotes a sensory transition of knowledge into the extensive interior of the body.

In Waiwai the orifice of the mouth claims an intellectual space as a cavity that deals with the production of vocal sound. The verb stem, *mtapo* (to talk), comes from the noun *yemtarï* (mouth). Such vocal actions as *emčapu* (to yawn) and *emkotu* (to grunt) also derive from this source. But the similarity between *ewre* (to laugh) and ewrï (eye) and the dissimilarity between the former and yemtarï (mouth) is striking. This interesting distinction, one indeed supported by Waiwai custom, suggests that they may perceive laughter as a thing they do with the eyes and not with the mouth. Actually, this works very closely with their views about the dangers of an open mouth. The hazardous qualities of the mouth—in contrast, for example, to the benign orifice of the eyes—may explain why this opening does not figure prominently as a metaphor for the other orifices of the face. As I have mentioned, a strong phonological resemblance does occur between the verb *to talk* and the noun for *mouth*, between the verb stem allomorphs *eni/enw* (to see) and *ewri/eri* (eye), but, interestingly, no such coupling occurs between *enče/eče* (to hear) and *panari* (ear) or between *sunuk* (to smell) and *ewnari* (nose). By their relation as orifices, their upper location propinquity, their similar benign character, and their phonological closeness, the ear and the nose, with their functions of hearing and smelling, can be thought of as another form of seeing. In addition (and as it may well be linguistic coincidence, I do not want to place too much weight on this point), the /nari/ occurring only in the ear and nose syllabic sequences also form the structure of the word *anari*, which means "another," "one more," "in addition to," or "a counterpart to." In this sense and because of the bifurcation of meaning between consumption and vocal sound, even the mouth in its latter connotation can be thought of as "another" eye with the capacity to "see."

If food constitutes one of the proper major objects that pass through the mouth, down the throat, and into the body, then knowledge may be its counterpart passing through the eyes, the ears, the nose, and the lips into the body. The act of knowing or to know can be spoken of as *htino*, coming from the word *yu[hti]puri* (head). Thus, when one speaks of knowing something, one says "*Wihtinoyasi*" (I know it) or, in contradistinction, "*Yihtinopirawasi*" (I don't know it). The general implication is that what one knows or does not know can be determined by its place inside or outside of the body respectively and that the entry of such knowledge properly takes place by way of admission into the body through the head. The head and its orifices act as the means by which the visible ideas of knowledge pass into the body. When a Waiwai says he smells smoke, for example, he does not have to confirm this by looking for visible signs of a fire; the visual idea of fire has already been substantiated by his sense of smell, which has carried an image of smoke into his body. The same applies to sound, for often the corroboration for the kind of animal that lurks unseen in the forest comes from the mental image conjured up by its call or those of other animals near it. The Waiwai say that their capacity to mimic animal sounds and to speak different languages derives from the ability to visualize sound. They come to know the song of the toucan and the words of language by memorizing the sounds—in other words, by keeping a visual image of a particular tune or utterance in the body. Hence, in Waiwai ideas mental imagery can be assumed to operate as a constitutive form of knowledge.

Like dreams, retained visions of sound and smell become internalized forms of actual perception. By its passage through the head and into the body, such knowledge of the outer world develops as a value for personal empowerment. In Waiwai culture the accumulation and clarity of interior visions creates a verifying sense of social prestige. For example, it is certainly not an arbitrary desire of Waiwai young men to want to increase their mental images by "seeing" different things, different places, and different peoples. The increment of their visions adds to their social being and may even be interpreted as the action by which their social status can be generated—only people with properly constituted knowledge hold the positions of responsibility in society. In this way, however, the knowledge that men come to possess constitutes a set different from that appropriated by women.

One very noticeable facet of Waiwai culture is that women are not just more associated with the domestic space of the settlement; they appear more constrained by it than men. I do not mean by this that the constraint should be understood only in negative terms—at least not from the kinds of results it produces in the form and meaning of identity. Certainly, from a Waiwai point of view (and from my own perspective of a theory of power that does not merely focus upon possession of force but rather on its instrumental application), a greater or lesser level of constraint produces the very positive identities of gender differences.[1] The constraint from domestic space can be thought of as being extended by the very women on whom the force has its effect. Thus the actions and perspectives of women in their daily life remain restricted to the domestic routines that keep them within the confines of the settlement and its nearby farms. What they perceive and know of the actual world comes primarily from this domain. In contrast the experiences of men comprise both the domains of settlement and forest. Here the imperative of knowledge constituting gender differences seemingly returns legitimacy to the differences. A man should have knowledge of the wider world and a woman must be cognizant of the details of settlement domesticity in order that they both become proper social persons. That one set of knowledge gains greater authority has in part to do with the native belief concerning the greater amount to be perceived in the domain outside the village. More than this, however, there exists a conviction within the collective ideology about gender that men's knowledge is stronger—that is, more vivid, more bright than the knowledge possessed by women. This comparison of the strength of vision applies similarly to knowledge found among men, where greater or lesser authority depends a good deal upon the degree of vividness a man can use with respect to knowledge.

Among men, the intellectual positioning of the differentiation of their authority appears most strikingly where the sources of lay and shamanic knowledge contrast. It is believed that what the ordinary man knows comprises more than what women, young people, and children know but much less than what a shaman knows. Of course this privileged positioning has something to do with the kind of knowledge a shaman acquires, but even so, one should note how the acquisition of shamanic wisdom demands a certain facility that only the vividness of knowledge can achieve.

When traveling in search of a client's lost ekatï, a shaman's visionary journeys depend crucially upon his clear "sight" and knowledge of the mystical paths. A patient's life or well-being relies upon the shamanic ability to retrieve and replace the detached spiritual vitality. The shaman knows the paths because he has memorized them; they are mapped in his body. Thus, at his initiation and while curing, he sees and travels the mystical pathways. The image of these paths, however, must not only be known but also illuminated, for to be lost on such a journey is the equivalent of death. Seeing requires light, and on shamanic journeys clarity or obscurity of vision can literally mean the difference between life and death. The enhanced powers of mental imagery imply an intense vividness of vision the like of which only the shaman possesses. At the same time, however, these enhanced powers gain their elevated authority only in the shamanic role. This may be due to the fact that such facility insures human safety in the potentially hazardous terrain of the mystical. The mystical landscape is said to have many dangers, and, for willingly jeopardizing his own existence in the course of securing someone else's, the trade-off for the shaman is a higher social status for what he knows and how he knows it. In the latter case, how he knows it is in part due to the legitimacies given to his acquisition of the means of spiritual knowledge.

The technical capacity to impede external stimuli while concentrating on internal imagery allows for an intensity of spiritual perception. This practical skill of mental imagery cultivation in shamanism (Noll 1985) assists the memory, which, in turn, helps to sustain a clarity of vision. Acquiring such means of knowing for the purpose of successful spiritual travel imparts social authority to shamanism. It is an authoritative means of knowing, because—at least at one level of interpretation—shamanic cultivation and control of mental imagery actually produce the ranked differences between the lay knowledge of the material world and the religious knowledge of the spiritual world. The fundamental contrast between these bodies of knowledge lies not so much in their divergent realms as in the techniques of their acquisition. Of course none of this works without an understanding of the body as having an interior that can be entered from the outside.

Everyone in Waiwai society has the potential to become a social person—a potential that society makes available in order to maximize its own perpetuity. The Waiwai enact this knowledge immediately after birth with the piercing of the ears of the newborn baby. They culturally open up the head and allow knowledge its rightful place. Just as society institutionally prescribes the domains of knowledge, so too does it inscribe the appropriation of the different sets of knowledge that constitute the content of the person. Displaying the consequence of acquired knowledge with graphic inscription upon the body seems to be one function of body adornment. In

Waiwai ideas the bright colored feathers on the head and in the facial perforations represent the light and flight of knowledge into the body. In this capacity feathers are statements about knowledge; they are external images of the intellectual human condition. On the surface of the face they draw attention to and illuminate the points of entry. In the process they also force the eye to note the status of the socially modified person. Particularly for adult men, the striking posture of feathers draws attention to the face as the entry point and the body as the receptacle of knowledge. The dispositive statement is a grand one and reinforcing one, for it proclaims men's knowledge as "stronger" than the knowledge of women, young people, and children. And because women, young people, and children are believed to have different and "weaker" sets of knowledge, they do not wear the elaborate feather costumes. Thus in the collective ideology of Waiwai society, the legitimating posture of greater wisdom reserves itself only for the category of men—a category of masculinity empowered by beliefs about bodies filled with vivid visual knowledge.

Seeing and knowing have a copresence in the Waiwai cultural configuring of subjectivity. Such a configuration of the self can be attributed in part to an imperative congruity given to the eye and to the knowable experience of life. In traditional Waiwai understanding, the individual body as a whole is thought to possess ekatï. In addition, however, the human eye possesses a distinct spiritual substance called *ewrï ekatï* (spiritual vitality of the eye). In other words the eye has the attribute of an energy source all its own, separate from that which gives vitality to the whole body at the chest. This vitality brightens the eye and, with its radiance, confirms the presence of life itself. In fact, the word *ewrï* (eye) is the same as that for birth. The meaning of the two words has its correspondence in the sense of an energized human embodiment. At death, when permanently detached from its physical body, the spiritual vitality of the chest remains on the earthly plain, while the spiritual vitality of the eye rises to take up occupancy between the earth and the first stratum (Maratu-yena: Guan-people) of kapu (the celestial spiritual world). Let me say immediately that I have not found any suggestion in

Waiwai ideas that the individual personality of the self and/or body continues after physical death. There does not seem to be any traditional belief in an immortal soul that lives on after death as the remnants of a unique individual personality. The spiritual vitalities, which once gave life to the individual body, merely return to their original source within an undifferentiated divine coherence. From a Waiwai point of view, it could be argued that to experience and be conscious of experiencing selfhood the individual body has personally to "see" in a variety of sensory forms, and that the constituted experience of physical being is this virtuosity of seeing. As a kind of knowledge, "seeing" does require experiencing the subjective body and its embodied subjectivities. In regards to the latter, however, it is not a case of rarefying or giving objective priority to an authentic ego; rather, like the paradoxical double skin with its inside and outside, it is a case of the exterior suggesting itself as the very source of the internal. To be human in Waiwai belief, an individual must be "seen"—he or she must be the intellectual experience of an imagery known by others. Giving sight to those physiologically visionless sensory features of the face, the Waiwai cultural production of knowledge outwardly marks itself. An individual must not only accumulate knowledge to be human, but must also be subject to that accumulation and be seen by others as the adorned object of their vision. Perhaps the Waiwai term best suited for explaining this aesthetic of being is *mewrï*.

The Design of Vitality

I once spent many hours talking to Iwap about what to me had been the puzzling Waiwai distinction between *ukuknon* and mewrï. He was knowledgeable about these things, and I had wanted simply to find out why almost every Waiwai material artifact had a painted design upon it. Not just the human body but even dogs were painted daily with different, very intricate geometric designs. They call all such designs mewrï. In addition mewrï refers to rock engravings and is even used as the verb *mewrito* (to read). Iwap carefully explained that *rowa-kuknon* (earth[-reckoning!] = map), *nuni-kuknon* (moon[-reckoning!] = calendar), *kamo-kuknon* (sun[-reckoning!] = clock), and even the ukuknon of a photograph were not mewrï. This was particularly confusing to me, as he further insisted that while *wenato* (footprint) could be a ukuknon and the traced outline of a hand could also be ukuknon, a *yamoto* (handprint or fingerprint) could not be so defined. It was difficult to know what to make of this at first, and even in retrospect it appears that a certain degree of ambiguity has to be part of the interpretation. This is so, I think, because of the Waiwai attempt to deal with the intellectual placement of new incoming Western goods that they highly value but that, nevertheless, come from cultural contexts driven by different rationales. Needless to say their very attempt to handle the incorporation allows us to view the conceptual logic working within and on behalf of their traditional knowledge. The one sound way I had of approaching the whole issue came from an anthropological theory of communication.

We could, for example, talk about the distinction between uku-knon and mewrï as being similar to that drawn between metonymy and metaphor—that is, between sign and symbol. We could then begin by saying (following Leach 1976, but see also Sapir and Crocker 1977) that communicative events, with their message-bearing entities, convey information in some very basic defining ways. The message-bearing entities of communicative events can, for example, be defined either as an index or a signal (Leach 1976:21). The index message-bearing entities can further subdivide into a signum and a natural index (the latter possessing the properties of metonymy). Symbol and sign belong to the same signum category of message-bearing entities, but while a "*signum* is a *sign* when there is an intrinsic prior relationship between A and B because they belong to the same cultural context" (Leach 1976:14), a "*signum* is a *symbol* when A stands for B and there is *no* intrinsic prior relationship between A and B, that is to say A and B belong to different cultural contexts" (Leach 1976:14). The basic thesis seems to be that while signs have "wholly fixed conventional denotation," symbols have "separately-defined denotation" (Leach 1976:13). Could it then be that the Waiwai notion of ukuknon corresponds to the message-bearing entities of the sign signum, while the notion of mewrï corresponds to that of the symbol signum?

It could indeed be argued that because, for the Waiwai, movement across the distinctive features of their landscape and movement of the sun and moon across the sky belong to the same cultural context of a measurable reckoning, maps, clocks, and calendars can be readily appropriated as signs for what they depict. It would not, for example, be difficult to insist on an intrinsic prior relationship of a metonymic kind between the position and movement of the sun in the sky and the position and movement of the hands of a clock. Yet what about the relationship between a photograph and the photographed, or that between the footprint and the foot, or that between the traced hand and the hand itself? In what sense would this relationship be possessed of a message-bearing entity that was intrinsically prior or wholly fixed and conventionally denotational? Could the conveyed information be similar to that of the measurable reckoning communicated in the other examples of ukuknon? Perhaps each photograph, footprint, and traced hand possesses qualities transferred from that which they represent as sign—qualities understood to be of a measurable reckoning. What does appear unequivocal, however, is that whatever these relationships help to convey, they are similar enough to have their message placed in the category of ukuknon yet different enough for their message not to be placed in the category of mewrï.

Between the fingerprint, rock engravings, painted body designs, and what they all represent, an asserted similarity has been imposed. In their categorization as mewrï, they appear to function as symbols rather than as signs. For example, in the case of a painted design of a frog on the human face or on a material artifact, the design decorates with no intrinsic prior relationship of similarity between it and the face or artifact. In other words, the frog design is not a sign of the human face or the material artifact. It could, however, possess an asserted similarity whereby the meaning of the frog design carries over to the face or material artifact. In this instance the design and that which it decorates can symbolize the carried-over meaning. The difference between mewrï and ukuknon would rest, therefore, on this ability of the former to act as a symbol and the latter to act as a sign. For the Waiwai, however, the fingerprint, the rock engraving, and the painted body design are mewrï, because they are images of a transferred vitality. The object receiving the vitality gains mewrï as an added outer presence. And perhaps, from this presence, the cogent metamessage of the difference between ukuknon and mewrï could be that the spiritual vitality transferred cannot in any reasonable way be subjected to a measurable reckoning.

It is also rather revealing that [m]ewrï and ewrï have a linguistic congruence, particularly when one considers that the asserted similarity between birth and eye—conveyed in the word ewrï—references the concepts of life and knowledge. As one tries to understand the importance of Waiwai adornment, this link between birth/eye and life/knowledge reveals an important facet about mewrï as a transferred vital image. Here the life-giving and knowledge-giving vitalities transferable with birth and eye infer, with mewrï, a similar relation between life, knowledge, and adornments. An added reinforcement of life and knowledge seems to be implied with the mewrï of adornments.

One might consider, for example, the case in which an *asoku* (a particular sequence of wavy black lines drawn on the red painted background of a clay pot) mimics a *wewe mewrï* (outer designs of trees). No Waiwai would consider a pot to be complete without its transferred vital image of a painted design. The image is like its adorned skin, covering the clay body of the pot. While it may indeed be a copy of the adorned skin of a tree, the fact of its transference by its designer supplements the image—that is, the asoku adds to the pot the addition of its designer's own vitality. Again, I would like to reiterate that this is not the supplement from an autonomous and authentic individual subjectivity producing unique creative designs, but rather the supplement from a repertoire of divinely influenced ideas. In the particular example of the painted pot, the spiritual vitality of the wewe mewrï, giving life and knowableness to the tree, transfers to the asoku, giving life and knowableness to the pot. The actual mimicking or mirroring of the design records the transfer. What the individual human "transferer" contributes to the transfer is the actual component of individual human agency, which, if repeated often enough, allows the particular design to become associated with that individual. Only from the act of repetition and the subsequent association of the repeated act with the individual can it be said that a potter always puts the signature of his or her personal design upon the potter's works. Now indeed, from this premise it is possible to say that to see the pot and to recognize the design is to know the maker of the pot. In the logic of this argument, the associated mewrï reciprocally allows the pot to be completed and its "transferer" to be known as its particular potter. Like the spiritual coherence of the divine, mewrï brings both pot and potter into knowable existence. As with pottery and all other manufacturing activities in Waiwai material culture, so too with the adorned body, the exterior suggests itself as the very source of the internal. The adorned Waiwai body displays its capacity to be filled with the vividness of visual knowledge—indeed, to experience subjectivity as mewrï.

The lines on the crusty bark of a tree, the pattern on the smooth scales of a fish, the spots on the soft fur of a jaguar all infer the outer presence of an inner being. In addition, to see/know surface designs is to echo the internal presence of spiritual vitality. In this regard mewrï operates as a culminating fact of life and knowledge. To take in and retain in the body the patterned designs of the external world is to be vitalized by the knowledge of that world. The volition to display this knowledge by reproducing it on the outside of the body places the producer at the epicenter of the known world. When the reproduction of knowledge and the self takes place upon the body, the producer sets his or her being within an observable and attainable social context. In other words the producer gives back to the external world the transferred covering that once belonged to the world. And there, certainly not without some degree of moral trust, it exhibits itself for further social consumption. The distinctions drawn between the external and internal designs of entities suggest that the daily adorned body seeks—with its variable designs from an identical repertoire of divinely influenced ideas—to establish itself as an entity with inner and outer knowledge. Like the outer surface of all objects, the skin must have an outer design, and, like the inner subjectivities of these objects, human subjectivity must be embodied with its outer design. To alter daily the outer appearance of the body is to be daily cognizant of and contemporaneous with the idea of one's humanity and the humanity of others. From an anthropological perspective, it is interesting to observe how this represented form of bodily experience strategically functions to legitimize the particular Waiwai rendition of human difference. Interestingly enough, while masculine humanity vibrantly exhibits its greater vividness of wisdom in society, it also legitimizes its position as a privileged internal knowledge in all social bodies.

Similar to other lowland South American societies, Waiwai society highly values the objective to establish a balance between oppositional tendencies. Being associated with the process of reconciliation accrues social worth. In seeking not only to represent but also to control the knowledge of the lived world, the mewrï of body adornment attempts to reconcile the contradictions of the known world. It is, however, the mewrï of men that depicts the most vivid vitalities and greater strength of control. That is, the adornments of masculinity reflect a "brighter" vitality and "stronger" knowledge on more "controlled" bodies. By achieving this aesthetic of harmony—this beauty of balance to the body adorned—masculinity succeeds in attracting greater acclaim for men. From their constant forays into the forest, men successfully accumulate vast amounts and vividness of knowledge pertaining to the wider world, and, on their adorned bodies, they proceed to depict their control of this knowledge in graphic splendor. This balanced blending of the greater forces of masculinity displays and at the same time justifies the prominence of masculine power. While body adornment marks the social difference of gender, it also works to establish rightful ranking. Thus, by engendering and appropriating equilibrium between the knowledge of the lived world and the experience of masculine subjectivity, the social category of masculinity claims to be more representative of society. Theoretically, however, this would also mean that men were the objects of a greater influence from society. In other words, between the masculine body and society, the distinction of a difference has been reduced. The play of negotiable knowledge and power has become the reconciled property of individual manhood and its social categorization, but some would say at the expense of a possible exuberant distancing between the body and society.

The ideological hoop that Waiwai society enables masculinity to curve around the characterization of social relations assists men in reconciling the contradictions of their own social being. It provides masculinity with the very means for modeling the perception of its own social existence. It also allows the indulgence of becoming preoccupied with the cultural reproduction that situates and privileges knowledge as masculine. Constructing the conceptual curvature of masculinity, differentiating its image of personhood from others within and outside of society, and establishing the custody of the most prestigious knowledge with manhood has permitted the bodies of men to occupy the dominant intellectual spaces and the dominant intellectual spaces to occupy the bodies of men. As I have discussed, this is perhaps no more the case than in regard to the prevailing Waiwai ideas about kinship, where the links between siblinghood, godhood, and manhood facilitate the bridging of concepts for a moral perfectibility established in the notion of the community of brothers. Experienced in the circular coherence of divinity that is mirrored not only in the residential curvature of the village settlement but also in the encompassment of the adorned body, Waiwai masculinity resolves the competing images of itself. In the divine brilliance of Kwarokiyim, transferred to and controlled on the individual village and human body, all contradictions ideologically disappear. Yet theoretically they never disappear for long, nor do they ever disappear completely. There is always this remainder, because power—in its very exercise—exposes its own vulnerability in order to keep on working so as to maintain itself. In other words, for the intellectual curvature of Waiwai masculinity to manifest its particular form, a partnership with power, a power exercised in the very manifestation of the masculine, is required. Power cannot live outside of its cultural renderings. In this specific case it grips hard the individual body and intellect of those maneuvering within the Waiwai rendition of the masculine.

Clearly, body adornment does not register any naïve concept of a lowly exterior savagery from inside Waiwai ideas. Contrary to earlier opinions, the decorated Waiwai body does possess "special significance," which may indeed include the personal joy dressing up for festivals produces but also, more informatively, signifies the critical position the adorned individual occupies in relation to fundamental social and cultural categories. In addition, while not necessarily arguing against the thesis of a hidden determinant in the relation between ecology and physiology, so many implicated social and cultural elements factor into why the body is adorned in the way it is and with the particular items used that these factors simply outweigh the cultural-adaptation thesis. Some may even argue that far from the culture of adornment's being responsive to the biology of the body, it is in fact the biological that responds to the cultural. That is, any knowledge about the body, to be knowledge at all, must be represented by culture—even that knowledge that can be called the "biology of the body" has to be culturally rendered. Knowledge does not exist in any understandable terrain outside of human culture.[2] The very object of knowledge may indeed be in the world, but this can only become known as the content of an epistemology through culture (Wagner 1981; Rorty 1989; Geertz 1993). Hence in this emphatic sense, by actually being the epistemological property of culture itself, biology clearly responds to culture rather than the other way around. The Waiwai do not respond to the changing physiology of the child's body with ritual ceremony and adornments because they apply some inferior or deviant form of biological understanding to the body. The physical transformations of the child's body at birth and adolescence can be seen and interpreted by all in the constituted knowledge about the vigorous effects of ekatï within the body. In fact the breaking out of the culturally understood physical substances of the infant's and adolescent's body into the social world activates the corresponding cultural responses of ritual ceremony and adornment. In other words, Waiwai cultural knowledge about the body generates further cultural responses to control the effluent energies. In a fashion similar to the way it is used in the architectonics of the village settlement, the Waiwai theory about the divine aesthetic of the circle permits encompassment—as the vigor of spiritual vitality—at various stages of bodily change and at particular points of the body.

In seeking to discharge Waiwai interpretations from the intellectual confinement of an inferiority, I have sought to argue that the divine aesthetic of the circle operates as a consistent heuristic principle holding the logic of Waiwai ideas together. In order for their ideas to move with meaningful inference toward the production of social knowledge, the general model of an encompassing aesthetic must function. In this regard, I suggest that individuals subject themselves to the controlling forces of this authoritative registering because only divine encompassment captures the kinds of reality assumed to be conveyable knowledge. For the Waiwai, the lived world is alive because of the transformative mutable power of divine spirituality. With the themes of bodily orifices and adornments as well as with their particular association with sight and birth, the encompassing aesthetic repeatedly registers the ability of the divine not only to move into and out of various entities but also to control such entities as the constituted content of knowledge. This certainly seems to be the case in myth and ritual, where collective representations focus on these specific ideas. For instance the concept of uterine incorporation materializes at the center of an emerging and revolving epistemology about residential space, time, and social being. Even in the substantive world outside of myth and ritual, however, the original vitality of the divine manifests itself as the ekatï sustaining human life. Indeed, the prolonged absence of ekatï from its corporal host explains the sickness the body suffers, while the permanent absence of ekatï explains the death the body experiences. Meaningful human life has to be processed within an understanding of spiritual vitality. The circular orbs of the eyes do not just serve as metaphors of an incumbent mechanics for "seeing/knowing"—they are the very curvature of divine coherence and spiritual energies. It is these energies that give full meaning to the processes of differentiation and complementarity among living entities.

The Hidden Hazard of Generosity

The Gift from Poniko-yim

We heard *shepurï*, the howler monkey. His aged cough cracked the canopy in prelude to an immense aria. Then, like a hollow wind, his prolonged plea took up air and surged in one single breath through the trees. In tones of primordial delight, his monstrous voice, his terrifying roar, obliterated our self-aggrandized esteem. We looked up and saw him. His red-brown beard and heavy-shouldered quizzical frame peered down upon our limp, whispering tones as we passed on the forest floor beneath. In rampant rage, in a raucous riot, reveling at the sight of our human insignificance, his cantata of conceit filled the warm midday air. At any other time some of us in his audience might have broken off from the passing line and cut short the esoteric insult, but today all in our party of well-armed hunters were intent on much more prolific game.

Earlier, as the veil of morning mist rose above the village, Utok had rushed onto the central plaza. At dawn he and Uwa had gone out in search of *kwanamari*, the fruit of the *turu* or *patawa* tree. *Onhari*, the communal meal, had already been called for the men working on rethatching a roof. Disturbing the circle of men eating, Utok hastily informed them that he and Uwa had sighted a large herd of *poniko* (white-lipped peccary) deep in the forest.[1] Uwa had remained in the forest to keep track of the herd. Work on the house was canceled. The men quickly mustered themselves together and, with Utok in the lead, we left the village in single file.

Almost every man in the village was in attendance. Enkik, who had been out hunting toucans, and Ipamar, who had been fishing, were immediately sent for and soon caught up with our party. Uwa's ten-year-old son, Chuma, managed to persuade his elders that he should join them. I looked around and counted only four men absent. There were twenty-three of us in the hunting party. Four carried shotguns, while the rest were armed with bows and metal pointed arrows. Seven men brought along their best hog-hunting dogs.

We met Uwa in a dim glen. Thin beams of sunlight filtered between the trees. Through them pollen could be seen floating slowly down onto the dank carpet of leaves. Into an eerie stillness enhanced by legions of cicadas, a nearby toucan released its sharp, repetitive three-note call. No one in our party said a word. No one had any need to speak. We had all assembled like this many times before. Uwa pointed to the tracks where he had last seen the herd. A few of the older men hummed in agreement. Before moving on to follow the tracks, Shamawa motioned to us to gather around him. We all bowed our heads as he led us in prayer.

Listening to this Christian ritual in the depths of an ancient forest, I thought its form out of place, abrupt, and overly ornate for the occasion. Yet I had to remind myself that Shamawa was not only village leader and chief church elder but also informally a shaman with a very special long-standing relationship with *poniko-pen* (the collective spirit of the peccary). The stories of his extraordinary exploits with poniko-pen were many, and they all helped to reaffirm the social and political prestige the community bestowed upon him. One favorite recurring tale told of how Shamawa, on returning one day from his farm in his canoe, completely unarmed, unexpectedly received the *kwak r̃esï* (gift) of over twenty peccaries from Poniko-yim (the Spiritual Father or Leader of Peccaries). The great white-bearded leader of the herd led his "people" directly in front of Shamawa's canoe. With paddle in hand, Shamawa proceeded to club as many of the hogs as he could. When he arrived at the village that day, to the amazement of the community, his canoe was piled high with meat from Poniko-yim. The extraordinary event only further convinced everyone that Shamawa clearly possessed close and privileged spiritual relations with the divine.

Agitated dogs mulled about between our legs. Our bent muscles rolled taut as we leaned upon long bows. Our solemn congregation prayed for a repeat of the gift from Poniko-yim. Then we all took to the trail in inspired pursuit.

The mass of hogs clearly marked the trail for some distance as they indiscriminately trampled through the undergrowth. They were nomads of the forest. They feared nothing. Their "village" traveled with them, and every night they snuggled around and on top of each other to form a heap of heaving, snorting slumberers. In the morning they moved on foraging for food. Even the dauntless solitary jaguar would not confront an entire herd but would wait on a low branch to pounce upon an unlucky laggard. In their relations with humans, poniko would periodically offer their bodies as gifts in exchange for tribute. No hunter would raise his weapon against the gray-bearded boar at the head of the troop, for he was the personification of Poniko-yim, and to kill him would forever cause the gift of hog meat to be denied to humans. In return for this respect to their leader, the herd has even been known to trot into the center of a Waiwai village plaza to sacrifice a few of its company to the clubs and knives of women and children. Now, on the trail, the porcine spirit invited only the men to collect their gift of meat.

We broke from our file formation and fanned out into a line. For some unaccountable reason we lost the trail, found it, lost it again, and regained it finally after separating into small groups. A thick, musky odor became stronger as we closed in on the strange rattling of teeth and clattering of hoofs. Our wide circle of hunters quietly began to tighten. The cordon divided into groups of four to five men who, when the attack began, would hunt together. My group consisted of five men, four of whom belonged to the karipamšam-komo (young men age-grade). Before we could actually see the herd, two shots boomed out from the other side of the circle. Then pandemonium broke out in a chaotic response.

A deafening cacophony of screaming hogs and men reverberated around us. Our group sprang toward the frenzied din. A scattered fragment of the herd angrily emerged and descended upon us with flaying teeth. In unison we raised our arrows and guns and let loose a barrage of missiles. The sounds of slaughter resounded throughout the forest. Hogs fell, rose, and ran drunkenly for a few steps, finally to fall in expired breath. Young ones, shoulder to shoulder, wove panic-stricken through the confusion as their larger parents were brought down. Routed, the remaining herd tore into the foliage in a mad rush. Now was the time for the trained dogs to be brought into action.

This stage of the hunt the Waiwai call *shepari yawtowari*. After the herd dispersed in the first flurry of the attack, the dogs, which until this moment had been on their leashes, were sent off after them. They caught up with the herd or a part of it; the hogs stopped, turned, and confronted the dogs. In their defiance the hogs made a peculiar barking sound that signaled to the approaching hunters that they had halted and stood facing the dogs in bellicose array. Retreating to a safe distance, the dogs began to howl. When the hunters arrived on the scene they approached hidden from the dogs and their quarry, for if the dogs detected the presence of their masters they would move toward them, further disturbing the already nervous herd. From their concealment the hunters made their kill.

At the end of the chase, each hunter collected the hog he had killed. The distance from the scene of the kill to the village was far, so we gutted the hogs; a large ungutted peccary can weigh between twenty-five and forty kilos, making the journey home a backbreaking chore. If a hunter kills more than one hog, he may submerge one in a nearby stream to conceal it from predators and return for it later, or he may ask a companion who has not made a kill to carry it for him. We made backpacks on the spot from the leaves of the *lu* palm and the inner bark of the *sarai* tree.

Arriving back at the village, each man went to his house, where his wife and the other female members of his household immediately prepared to clean the hogs. With boiling water and sharp knives, the women scraped off the wiry hair. When they had finished, their husbands cut up the animal for distributing and cooking. By late afternoon the women had their pots boiling and everyone was getting ready for the evening revelry.

As the night's shroud gathered around the village, a great feast was in progress. The men congregated at the meetinghouse, adorned with white feather down sprinkled on oily heads, long tail feathers of macaw protruding from nostrils, and faces painted in delicate designs. The women, with hair tied up and florid dresses brilliant under the Tilley lamp, murmured and tittered gaily. There was praying, singing, and much merriment. Far into the night the villagers sampled the fruits of the hunt. They recited tales about the events of the day and similar hog hunts of the past. The Waiwai once again had taken many "children" from Poniko-yim. In the distance, like a hollow wind in the night, we could hear the surging, long-winded lament of shepurï, the howler monkey.

The Gift Distributed

We had killed fourteen hogs during the hunt: three were brought down by guns, one by a dog, and the rest by arrows. Four men, Umachar, Shamew, U-ses, and Enkik, killed by means of *shepari yawtowari* (literal meaning unknown, but general meaning is "to hunt with dogs"). Only twelve of the twenty-three hunters present had actually killed hogs: Yawa, Amakayan, Isokikor, Shamew, U-ses, Awawatak, Arumarawan, Umachar, Enkik, Aruyowk, Utok, and myself. Isokikor and Arumarawan had shot two hogs each.

As far as could be ascertained, every household present in the village at the time of the hunt—barring those of Ponu (H) and Iwap (I)—received meat from the 14 hogs (letters refer to households as depicted in map 1 and table 1).[2] The households headed by Anawach (G), Chichem (K), Retawp (N), Akow (Y), Aywek (Z), and Itup (AZ) were absent from the village for various reasons. These absent households constituted 13 adults and 10 children. Including the households headed by Ponu and Iwap—which numbered 4 adults and 2 children—a total of 29 individuals from a fluctuating village population of 143 people went without meat from this peccary hunt. Comprising 20 individual households, the remaining 114 village occupants who consumed the 14 hogs consisted of 58 adults and 56 children.

Eight of the 12 successful hunters retained their catch for cleaning and cutting up in their own households (see fig. 1). Yawa kept his kill and his son Amakayan's kill, while U-ses, Shamew, Utok, Awawatak, Arumarawan, and Aruyowk also kept their kills for cleaning and cutting up. From the 7 households and 8 hogs killed by these men, 7 other households received portions of cleaned meat for their own use.

Yawa (D) gave cleaned and cut meat to Akaway (J) and Nryhe (A) "because," he said, "they are my neighbors." In fact Yawa had distant kinship ties with both men, which, if he had chosen to, he could have brought into effect to explain the reason for his gift of meat to them. For example, Nryhe was daughter's husband's father's sister's husband to Yawa, which is equivalent to brother (DHFZH = B), and Akaway (a relation a little more complicated by the disparity between their age-grade ranking and kinship designation) was mother's mother's sister's husband's son to Yawa, which is the equivalent to mother's brother (MMZHS = MB). In this particular instance Yawa wanted to emphasize the propinquity of neighborly relations—that is, relations determined by what he considered to be his social commitment to people living close to him. Nryhe and his son Tapkus both attended the hunt, but neither of them was successful. Akaway did not attend the hunt.

Following the same reasoning as Yawa, U-ses (R) gave cleaned and cut meat to the brothers Emtushen (Q) and Awawatak (S), who actually lived in his cluster of households. Through the marriage of U-ses's daughter Apuw (absent at the time with household Y) to Emtushen's wife's brother Akow, there existed the classificatory father/son relationship between U-ses and the brothers (for example, to Emtushen, DHZH = S, and to Awawatak, DHZHB = S). When questioned about why he had given meat to the brothers, however, U-ses chose to emphasize his close residential ties with Emtushen and Awawatak. Both brothers were at the hunt, but Emtushen was unsuccessful, and while Awawatak's dog managed to kill an infant hog, it was considered so small and insignificant that U-ses insisted on offering him more meat.

Shamew (U) gave cleaned and cut meat to his son Upaek (M) and to his son's wife's father, Nryhe (A). Upaek was not at the hunt. Arumarawan (W), who had killed 2 hogs, shared the larger one with his daughter's husband, Umachar (X), giving him some in its cleaned and cut-up form while keeping the rest for his own household use. He gave the smaller hog, complete and uncleaned, to Puyen (C), his FBDS = ZS (potential DH). Utok (V) shared his hog, in its cleaned and cut-up form, with Akiamon (T). When asked why he had done so, he responded by claiming that Akiamon was his friend, even though it was possible that he could have said it was because they were neighbors, as they lived so close to each other, or that they were brothers, as both exchanged fictive sibling relations with each other.

Four heads of households unsuccessful in the hunt received 6 whole hogs, uncleaned and uncut, from 5 successful hunters. The 5 successful hunters who gave these hogs were not themselves members of the 4 receiving households (that is, except in the case of Amakayan and Aruyowk, who did give whole hogs to their respective heads of household). As mentioned above, Arumarawan gave 1 hog to Puyen. Umachar, who had killed his hog by means of shepari yawtowari using Ipamar's dog, gave his hog to Ipamar (L), his wife's brother. Isokikor (F), who had killed 2 hogs, gave 1 to Anya-am (E), his sister's husband, and the other to Shamawa, his wife's father. It should be mentioned that after Anya-am cleaned and cut up the hog he received, he gave some of the meat to his stepfather, Erimink. Enkik (P) gave the hog he shot to his father-in-law Shamawa. The hog I killed was also given to Shamawa.[3]

In total Shamawa received 4 whole hogs: 1 from me, 1 from his son Aruyowk, 1 from his son-in-law Enkik, and 1 from his other son-in-law Isokikor. Shamawa returned 1 whole hog to Enkik. After cleaning and cutting it up, Enkik gave half of the hog to Uwa (Bz), who was one of the first to spot the herd but was unsuccessful in the hunt. After cleaning and cutting up the rest of the hogs given to him, Shamawa gave meat to Isokikor and myself.

Game caught by a "living-in" dependent relative automatically belongs to the head of the household. The only exception to this would be when the hunter has killed using a dog or a weapon belonging to an individual living in another household. In such a case the game goes to the person whose dog or weapon assisted in the kill. In this particular peccary hunt, only Umachar fitted this category. As I have already mentioned, Umachar had killed using Ipamar's dog. One should keep in mind (as an interesting side note to the principle), however, that Aruyowk killed his hog with his father's gun. Did the hog go to his father because his father was the head of his household or because he had used his father's gun? Indeed, did Umachar give his hog to Ipamar because he was in an interhousehold dependent relationship to Ipamar as his brother-in-law or because he had used Ipamar's dog? It seems that if the commitment to give a hog is tied to an obligation of kinship or marriage, an even greater reason for giving and receiving the gift exists.

Although a level of reality does exist where friendly and neighborly relations hold a form of independent meaning for the Waiwai, such meaning will nevertheless always derive its reference from the dominant collective notions about kinship and marriage. There can be only one way to live as proper people—that is, in poyino—in relationships that act as if they were driven by the axiom of common filial substance. The moral outcome of convivial sociality forms into poyino by the very fact of the natal-like constraints of communal village residence. Friendship and neighborliness—like the connubial bonds in the later years of marriage—result from subordinating the inherent dangers of human relationships to the familiar forces of uterine morality. Even the necessary wošin relative, in many ways, has to submit to being like but not quite like epeka. Ultimately, at ideally every level, the notions about poyino should define the character of all village social relations. And the peccary hunt helps to bring about the circumstances by which the defining characteristics of poyino can formally saturate the expression of collective village life.

In that almost magical and spontaneous moment when the unpredictable free-ranging herd of peccaries saunters into the orbit of the villagers' world, the very quality of residential relations opens up and becomes attentive to the possible flow of gifts. The excitement everyone feels and shows when the cry of "poniko" is first heard does not stem merely from the known drama each peccary hunt produces, nor even from the prospect of being satiated by the profuse amount of meat generated by the hunt. The principal thrill comes from anticipating the infusion of joy that the gregarious porcine vitality will instill by being the gift that extends and fills, with a massive surging expression of poyino, the routinized relations of the village. Knowing that the great artiodactyl herd of the rain forest has deemed it propitious to visit the vicinity sets into motion all the possible strands of overlapping relationships that will be agitated and allowed to flow with exchanges from the overabundance of meat. The immediacy and sheer number of meat exchanges push all the inevitable and mundane consequences of daily life into the background. The flow of gifts permeates the social space of convivial satisfaction. That which is common, that which is shared, that which reveals the truth of poyino can be observed and experienced in the wide distribution and consumption of poniko meat. Of course none of this could possibly take place without well-established differences—that is, without the well-held beliefs about the otherness of wošin.

Of the eighteen total exchanges that occurred *between* heads of households, twelve (66.7 percent) could be considered examples of wošin-based meat transfers: Arumarawan to Umachar = WF/DH; Arumarawan to Puyen = MB/ZS (fictive); Umachar to Ipamar = ZH/WB; Enkik to Uwa = ZS/MB; Enkik to Shamawa = DH/WF; Shamawa to Enkik = WF/DH; Čoči (author) to Shamawa = WB/ZH (fictive); Shamawa to Čoči = ZH/WB (fictive); Isokikor to Shamawa = DH/WF; Shamawa to Isokikor = WF/DH; Isokikor to Anya-am = WB/ZH; Shamew to Nryhe = DHF/SWF. There were only two (11.1 percent) very obvious cases of meat transfers between epeka from different households (that is, with the exclusion of the intrahousehold whole-hog exchanges of Amakayan to Yawa and Aruyowk to Shamawa); these were the f/s and s/f exchanges of Shamew to Upaek and Anya-am to Erimink respectively. There were four other possible epeka-based exchanges—for example, f/s from U-ses to Emtushen, f/s from U-ses to Awawatak, b/b from Yawa to Nryhe, and b/b from Utok to Akiamon—but these, in addition to the possible affinal exchange of mb/zs between Yawa and Akaway, have been designated as neighbor and friendship transfers instead. Even if all the very obvious and possible filial-based transfers were tallied up, they would still only constitute 33.3 percent of the total exchanges of meat. On this occasion and from these parameters, the wošin-defined exchanges of hog meat clearly predominated.

Here then, it could be argued, is an instance of the necessary differentiation between the categories of wošin and epeka that bring the making of poyino into motion. The moral ground upon which the ewtoto believes it is built can here be seen to be achieved as well as activated by the actual exchanges of meat between wošin. The kirewani in the individual exchanges is interpreted as the "goodness" of poyino. The good hunter, the good husband, the good wife, and the good in-law become so by the infusion of poyino, stimulated in this particular case by the killing, exchanging, and eating of poniko. Indeed, by their being the outcome of a spontaneous communal hunt, the prestations and counterprestations between wošin provide the basis upon which an ideological theory of coexistence can be actualized.

In addition to the series of wošin and epeka exchanges from which the majority of the village population received meat for their individual household consumption, the onhari hosted by the village leader, with offerings of cooked meat from each attending household, also provided both a channel for collective village consumption and a statement about community coexistence.

Onhari and the Household

Any occasion for the communal consumption of food is called onhari. It is an almost daily ritual of collective village meals held most often in the village leader's house. It can also be held in the house of a head of household hosting a communal work event, particularly if the end product of the communal work appears to benefit only those of the hosting household. A good example would be the case when a man, having built a canoe for the use of his own household members, needs assistance in hauling the canoe from the forest to the river. The canoe builder would inform the village leader of his need for assistance. He and the male members of his household or cluster of households would go out hunting for meat for the occasion. The women of the household(s) would prepare and cook the hunted meat and yuca bread for the meal. Onhari would then be called, and the attending men would first eat and then go to the site from which the canoe would be hauled. If the work takes all day, the men would return for a closing meal at the house of their host. At communal meals for collective work of this kind—that is, for tasks designated as the work of men—only men attend the meal.

When the communal meal is for collective work that includes men and women, both men and women would attend the meal. On the occasion of joint communal meals, men and women would eat separately, the men forming one circle and the women another, with the food and drink being passed in an anticlockwise direction around the circles. It would be fair to say that onhari is most often called for men only, and at such times women will not even approach the circle of men. Whenever onhari is called as the result of a peccary hunt, however, the village leader always acts as the host and everyone attends the meal. In other words, on the occasion of a communal meal and through the position of the village leader, the village community consumes the cooked meat of a spontaneous communal hunt and in doing so exemplifies the principle of poyino. Indeed, with political leadership and onhari the very principle of poyino becomes a substantive fact. Being together, eating and drinking together beyond households and clusters of households as an open expression of shared village life, exemplifies the fundamental character of ideal human relations. One should take note, however, that even with such ideals, difference is maintained: the circle of men and the circle of women never publicly eat as one.

For Shepariymo, Shamawa and his wife, Awam, together constituted the principal individuals occupying the position and role of political leader.[4] Not that the Waiwai would say Awam was kayaritomo. Only Shamawa was said to be village leader, but what this actually meant in Waiwai collective understanding pragmatically included Awam. It was understood, if not openly stated, that without a wife no man could ever become a village leader, and it was the customary practice for a village leader to relinquish his duties if his wife died. Apart from accomplishing the culinary duties required in bringing meat and yuca together for a communal meal, the social facts of marriage also permitted the necessary difference of affinity to crosshatch as the political relations of the village.

Without wanting to reduce the political to the purely functional criterion of "maintaining order," I would say it is rather evident that competency in the political field often does get judged in terms of mediating disputes. Being well placed in the network of village relations offers leadership a legitimate means of maintaining harmony outside the immediate influences of kinship ties found within the household. This placement frequently allows the ranked differences of affinal relations to perform the work of maintaining order—particularly those affinal relations created by the so-called giving and receiving of wives through marriages. With their sanctioned influence over married daughters living uxorilocally, fathers and mothers can have customary control over individuals in households other than their own. "Pure affinity" (in other words, total strangeness between residents) only occurs on the margins of the conceptual core of filial and affinal relations constituting the political field of village leadership (Rivière 1984:74). This is where leadership would be at its weakest—indeed, where village fission would be more likely to take place. As a consequence of this reality for maintaining collective village harmony, any communal meal hosted by the village leader goes a long way in expressing the extensive reach of village leadership and preserving the "fiction" of poyino.

Beyond the households and on the plain of crosshatched village relations, onhari serves as a major social, political, and economic feature. Yet clearly it is able to do so only in structural opposition to the more private meals of the individual households. The social and political terrains of the communal village meal and the individual household meal both depend upon specific tracks of transactions that bring them into meaningful oppositional reality.

For the particular case of the peccary hunt, a number of complicated exchanges of hog meat preceded the two final destinations of consumption in the individual households and the collective village. All the exchanges activated relations primarily *between* households—relations dominant and dormant, filially and affinally defined. One way of placing these exchanges in an order would be simply to trace the hogs from the hunt to the meal. To do so accurately, we would have to follow each hog through three main stages of transformation—that is, from whole hog, cleaned cut portions, to cooked meat. Each transformation stage reveals clues about the direction of interpersonal exchanges. These stages become particularly significant because, deeply implicated in the symbolism of a hog's particular state during transformation and at the time of exchange, are statements about the quality of relations existing between human recipients.

Hog Meat and the Successful Hunter

The exchange of *woto* (raw uncleaned meat) implies a relationship characterized by formal duty. The exchange of *tuyonho* (raw meat, particularly portions cut and cleaned) suggests a relationship of a less formal character. *Nïye* (cooked meat and cooked food generally) indicates a relationship of a more relaxed quality between exchange partners. These meat-defined exchanges do not function within a strict juridical principle; they merely operate as a general guide for identifying and interpreting the supposed quality of relationships at the time of transaction. Households acquiring hogs in their raw, unclean state would do so more often from personal kills or from in-laws (fundamentally ZH, WB, WF, DH). Meat received for cooking after it is cleaned and cut up comes from a neighbor, friend, epeka, or wošin. Cooked meat is either consumed within the household among the nuclear family or at a communal meal by the corporate village. Clearly, from any spontaneous communal hunt, the number of possible exchanges of meat in a village of twenty households can be considerable. In addition, the exchanges can alter their overall pattern on every occasion a hunt takes place, only depending on who does or does not succeed in the hunt and on the particular obligations and commitments of the successful hunters to their neighbors, kinsmen, and community at large. The actual types of exchanges, however, remain limited.

In theory, at the level of whole-hog exchanges (that is, of raw uncleaned meat) between humans, only four possible permutations can take place. As I mentioned above, from a spontaneous communal hunt, whole hogs caught by a hunter go to his own household for cleaning and cutting up *except* on occasions when the hunter has killed using a dog or weapon of another (in which event the game goes to the person whose dog or weapon assisted in the kill). If the hunt has been poor and there is a known scarcity of meat, a hog may go to the village leader. If a head of household unsuccessful in the hunt is affinally related to the successful hunter, the hog goes to his household for cleaning and cutting up. The processes of cleaning and cutting up pertain only to those households in possession of whole hogs.

A hunter kills and brings home the game, while the female members of his or another household clean the game. If the successful hunter retains the hog for cleaning in his household, he cuts up and subsequently distributes the meat himself. If he gives the hog away (in the above cases) and the female members of the receiving household clean it, the male head of the receiving household cuts up and distributes the meat. After the hog has been cleaned and cut up, the household head sends a message to the successful hunter (the recognized original human producer) inquiring whether or not his household wishes to have some of the meat and, if so, which portion. Once a hog has been cleaned and cut up by a household, this represents that particular household's ownership of the meat. In other words, it is the actions of cutting up and subsequent distribution that denote ownership of whole hogs killed in a spontaneous communal hunt.

As can be discovered from the examples of the peccary hunt, a recipient of portions of cleaned raw meat can be a neighbor, friend, epeka, or wošin. Givers of cleaned raw meat do not have to be successful hunters, nor do their receivers have to be attending members of the hunt. Givers of cleaned raw meat are cleaners and cutters of a hog, while receivers are unsuccessful hunters, nonattendant at the hunt, or just not in possession of a hog. Received cleaned raw meat is for immediate cooking. Intriguingly, portions of cleaned raw meat do not go to the village leadership for the purpose of onhari. If the village leader receives cleaned raw meat from another household, he and his wife assume it is for their own household's personal consumption. Only whole hogs or cooked meat go to the village leader as contribution to the communal meal.

At the level of the whole-hog exchanges, the interesting fact arises that the village leader and the wošin assimilate similar structural positions as receivers. Both relationships tend to have a rather formalized character (in the sense of being subjected to known customary practices of behavior) that is imparted to the manner of the exchanges. Nevertheless, in a situation of scarcity the village leader always receives priority over the in-law. The difference between the village leader's, as opposed to the wošin's, receiving of a hog from a successful hunter at this stage of meat exchange is that the former accepts the hog as a kwak řesï for distribution to the entire village. If, on the other hand, the village leader receives a whole hog from his in-law as an *esimtaka* (that is, as part of that affine's obligatory duty to him), he has the options of retaining the hog for consumption within his own household, distributing portions of it to other households directly, or offering it to the corporate body at a communal meal. To reiterate, in his capacity as political leader the village leader receives only cooked or uncleaned raw meat for communal meals. More often, as a recipient in-law, he receives uncleaned raw meat, which he can dispose of, with discretion, in whatever direction seems appropriate at the time. All food for communal consumption has to go to the village leader for distribution. The position of leadership exists at the center of all joint village activities and, because the major activity of corporate village life is onhari, a spontaneous communal hunt strongly assists leadership in expressing and maintaining its almost irreplaceable centrality in the wide network of exchanges that bring about the realization of a collective village poyino. None of this, of course, can be actualized without the successful hunter.

In times of scarcity, whenever a communal meal is held, the occasion generally pays tribute to the successful hunter. This would never be a case of deliberately focusing on a particular individual hunter. Almost all Waiwai cultural procedures avoid direct and intense public honoring of individuals. Indeed, being placed alone in the isolating scrutiny of the public gaze is excruciating for most Waiwai. Thus, in the collective congenial space of onhari, the guests merely speak indirectly about the celebrated hunter. They may talk in general terms about other hunts that unfolded in a way similar to that of this most recent hunt. They may even pay oblique tribute to the successful hunter by jokingly disparaging aspects of his immediate accomplishments such as, for example, the small size of the animal he has killed, or how the animal initially outwitted him, or how it may have inflicted or caused the infliction of some harm upon him. As a general statement, one could argue that the mere fact of convening in effect celebrates the successful hunter. No doubt a scarcity of meat may encourage an attitude of greater appreciation of the hunter. It would certainly be reasonable to suggest that the communal meal in and of itself helps to convey hunter appreciation regardless of scarcity or the number of contributing hunters. Public esteem for the hunter in onhari is not merely about his skills in the hunt, however; it is even more about the auspicious outcome of his gift to the village community. In other words it is more about the favorable results of a moral power that influences the hunter to give and the community to receive the produce of the hunter's efforts. The moral confirmation of the gift unambiguously exists in the meal. It is here—particularly in the distributive space of onhari and with the village leader but also in individual household meals and with the wošin—that the successful hunter confers his virtue to the village, submitting it to a rigorous cultural appreciation.

With the spontaneous communal hunt and its generated events of meals in individual households and onhari, the force of Waiwai culture does not necessarily seek (as might be analytically expected) the achievement of an ideological focus on production. Here the cultural processes do not overly emphasize the success of the hunter in killing game. What cultural power does achieve, particularly with the processes of meat cleaning and cutting, is an accentuating and valuing of the moral imperatives to give and to receive.

The Waiwai political economy of the hunt ideologically concentrates not so much on the production as upon the distribution and consumption of meat. The hunter's moral responsibility to give, rather than his moral responsibility to kill, sustains the greater cultural esteem. That is not to say that there does not exist a whole series of imperatives to encourage the hunter to hunt, but, in regards to that which attracts primary significance for Waiwai ideals, it is the exchange rather than the initial production of the gift that stands out. Both the capacity for individual generosity and the obligation to accept contain high moral value. And, within the context of the hunt, they do so by being strategically placed at points of greatest significance for the Waiwai. From the processes of cleaning and cutting, the gift of meat exercises the power to induce the effect of poyino, which extends circularly as the very veracity of Waiwai morality. To give and receive the kwak ɾesï of tuyonho verifies a highly valued knowledge of the correct way to live as a village community. The kwak ɾesï of tuyonho becomes linked to the system of political leadership and the politics of the household by way of the meal, and in each case the function of the communal meal and of the individual household meal perpetuates the veracity of the relations between meat and poyino. It seems to me that the theoretical significance of this conclusion rests in where one places the emphasis in the definition of power.[5]

The Gift Cooked and Eaten

Part of the answer as to why and how the ideological framing and emphasis upon meat and filiation operate must include Waiwai ideas about the character of relations between all social persons—in this specific case, even those substantive social relations existing between categories of humans and animals. Some of the more current and influential literature on Amazonian societies has once again highlighted the particular propensity of Amerindians to extend to animals many of the characteristic features of human social identity (Descola 1992, 1996a, 1996b; Stephen Hugh-Jones 1996; Viveiros de Castro 1998). The presupposition, in this literature, is that for Amazonian societies, continuity prevails between the differences of human and nonhuman beings. For analytical purposes the continuity can be classified according to two intellectual processes historically identified by anthropology as totemism and animism (Descola 1992).[6] Totemic systems "exploit the differential relations between natural species to confer a conceptual order on society" (Descola 1992:114), while animic systems "use the elementary categories structuring social life to organize, in conceptual terms, the relations between human beings and natural species" (Descola 1992:114). In anthropological determination, therefore, animic systems permit Amazonian peoples to "treat plants and animals . . . as proper persons" (Descola 1992:114). Animism here functions "as a mode of identification . . . specified by at least three dominant types of relation: predation, reciprocity and protection" (Descola 1996a:94). Perhaps the most instructive relation for an understanding of Waiwai ideas would be reciprocity, in which the animic system inverts predation to define exchange relations particularly in terms of indebtedness.

The animal persons, who become the meat the Waiwai eat, place a moral obligation upon the Waiwai not only to reciprocate as they would with human persons but also to do so in the specific role of dependent receiver. The compunction to reciprocate in the subordinate role stems, in the first place, from the very act of destruction that killing produces. What the hunter destroys by killing the animal for food are the immediate possibilities resulting from the social relationships the animal possessed with those of its kind. In the case of the Waiwai it is the destruction of the highly esteemed relations of poyino between the dead animal and its living relatives that disturbs them the most and that produces talk and action indicative of (but not quite the same as) having a "bad conscience" (Stephen Hugh-Jones 1996). If having a bad conscience is interpreted as internal knowledge and feelings of remorse that lead to recognizing not only selfish desire but also "guilt" and "sin," it would be difficult for me to apply this to the Waiwai case. Indeed, the "feeling of guilt" (Descola 1996b:130) for orphaning the "children" of the "parents" they have killed may arguably be manifested, for example, in the practice of sometimes bringing home the young animals and keeping them as pets. I would like here merely to suggest, however, that such "adoption" not only indicates some concern for the taking of animal life and an "ambivalence towards eating meat" (Stephen Hugh-Jones 1996), it also reveals the character of relations the Waiwai assume they replace when they offer continued social ties to the orphaned animal. As surrogate parents, the Waiwai admit to killing the parent(s) of the pet animal but in addition they clearly state the kind of relationship they think they are replacing. Needless to say, they do not seek to "become" the actual parents of the pet animal; they fully comprehend that their surrogate relations can never return the originally destroyed relationship. But for this very reason, the hunter-cum-killer of the pet's parent(s) will always be indebted not only to the orphan but also to the other entire animal "relatives" of the deceased beast. In the social politics of Waiwai hunting—specifically, with the spontaneous communal hunt—it is the social personhood of the peccary and the asymmetrical relations formed between peccary and hunter that articulate perhaps the most conspicuous ideological reinforcement of communal village life and its particular ways of being the very means to political power.

Of all the hunted animals, only the white-lipped peccary can exclusively implicate a spontaneous communal hunting group. Among the four distinct types of Waiwai hunting groups—that is, the spontaneous communal hunting group, the arranged communal hunting group, the joint household hunting group, and the individual household hunting group—only the first directly involves the gregarious white-lipped peccary. An arranged communal hunting group can only be formed by the authority of the village leader and solely for the purpose of providing meat for communal meals at a collective village work session or a major community festival. Unlike a spontaneous communal hunting group, an arranged communal hunting group can deliberately segment into small units and hunt any game it comes across as the group encounters it. (The one exception to this occurs when an arranged communal hunt has been organized for the collective harvesting of fish, where men, women, and children gather as a group at a prearranged location on the river. In such a case and to some extent, spontaneous communal hunts and arranged communal hunts may appear analytically similar to each other.) A joint household hunting group draws its members from a limited number of different households, where the primary objective of each hunter is to hunt any and all game specifically for his own household consumption. An individual household hunting group is composed of hunters who belong to the same household and who hunt any and all game only for their own household needs. Each type of hunting group seeks to involve the violent relations between the hunter and the hunted as the immediate objective of its formation. Yet in this predacious context, only the spontaneous communal hunting group can be identified as being directly dependent, for the cause of its formation, upon a single species of hunted animal.[7]

The way in which the white-lipped peccary galvanizes the individual hunter to form one large group of hunters suggests impulsive force on the part of the animal. Waiwai cultural interpretation translates this as a deliberate act of *kwak r̃esï makï* (gift giving), one that pulls hunters into company with each other and entwines them in relations with the animal. Success in the hunt—that is, direct receipt of the gift of woto from poniko-pen—means the death of a peccary and the destruction of a highly valued poyino relation within the herd. The debt incurred and its obligation—for the successful hunter to be subordinate to the creditor—resemble the characteristic social conditions for a wošin who has received someone else's sister or daughter in marriage. In this sense the gift received seems more like esimtaka—that is, an object of exchange filled with the obligatory duties that the receiver now owes the giver. Once a gift has been received, one could argue, it is no longer a gift; it no longer carries the meaning of *no* reciprocity or *no* counterprestation that it once did in its initial state when it was being given. Conscious acceptance of that which is given as a gift transforms the gift into a debt (Lévi-Strauss 1972; Mauss 1990 [1950]; Derrida 1992). A successful hunter of a spontaneous communal hunting group clearly perceives the almost sacrificial act of giving that the herd of peccary performs in presenting itself for slaughter. This, I argue, is because Waiwai culture presupposes the relation of poyino among the members of a peccary herd. With the white-lipped peccaries' characteristic gesture of "donating" their kinsfolk to the violence of the hunters by wandering into their path, the interpretation produces an understanding that a highly esteemed relationship is being given up that, when accepted, can no longer be a gift.[8] In Waiwai ideas while the slaughtered body appears as a gift for the peccary, for the hunter it is the incurring of a debt and the imposed site for the rendering of a moral duty. In this particular case of the spontaneous communal hunt, the predatory act of hunting has indeed been inverted to define exchange relations in terms of moral indebtedness. This occurs by extending to the white-lipped peccary the principles of social personhood extant in human society as well as by the act and meaning of exchange. With the extension, however, the Waiwai cultural understanding of reciprocity reveals recognition of the idea that, intentionally or unintentionally, humans can bring hostilities down upon themselves by their own actions.

As in the act of sacrifice and the conscious recognition of all gifts, Waiwai culture configures that the force of the peccary's generosity initiates the violence of the hunter. In other words the act of giving exercises a power. The giving in this case becomes a power when the violence of the hunter knowingly transforms the gift into meat received.[9] The cause of the hunter's violence has its source not in the hunter but in his victim. Perhaps in this sense and this sense only—that is, when and where the receiver rather than the giver emits the death blow—the gift of meat from the peccary may appear more like the suicidal desire for death at someone else's hand than like the blood sacrifice of a sacrificial victim. Nevertheless, from the Waiwai perspective of their relations with the peccary, the slaughtered body contains the evidence of the hunter's action and the reason for his bad conscience, both caused by the personal and intimate generosity of the peccary. As the causal site for the hunter's violence as well as the proof and explanation for his act, the slaughtered body of the peccary admits a whole new attribute and changes from being generous and peaceful to being avaricious and aggressive.

In death the body of the peccary sets off a series of human reactions the ideological interpretations of which may be explained in terms of the now rapacious attitude of the peccary. Once again, to corroborate, this certainly is a result of human social attributes being extended to the animal, in this particular case identified in terms of the moral principles of vengeance—the expected Waiwai behavior by close family members for all deaths of kinsfolk. In other words the Waiwai expect the extreme reciprocal demand by Poniko-yim to be the sickness or death of a Waiwai. Indeed, at least one of the explanations I heard for the wide distribution and consumption of meat from a spontaneous communal hunt was that they serve an apotropaic function—that is, that the human exchanging and eating of meat deliberately seek to avert the harmful intent of vengeance from Poniko-yim. The Waiwai say that the complex weaving pattern of the giving and taking and the eating of meat after a poniko hunt is like the complicated weave in the little basket a threatened traveler places in the path of an approaching jaguar. They say that because of the intellectual curiosity of the jaguar, it will stop and seek to unravel the puzzle of the basket rather than attacking its prey. Meanwhile, the jaguar's intended human victim should have made well his escape. This seemingly incidental shift in identifying the rapacious side of the peccary with the jaguar conforms to much of what has already been argued in the literature about the negative reciprocity these two animals symbolize in the myths of the region (Lévi-Strauss 1970; Reichel-Dolmatoff 1997). Of course the absence of reciprocity occurs between the rapacious animals and their equally rapacious human counterparts, who behave more like rivals than allies.

In this representative mode, negative reciprocity and predation serve to indicate—perhaps for the purpose of human contemplation (Lévi-Strauss 1970, 1972, 1973)—the character of those social conditions existing when an affine has received a spouse and has yet to repay. Hence, between Poniko-yim and the Waiwai there exists, one could say, an ongoing relationship seemingly characteristic of wošin relations. Such an understanding begins, nonetheless, by first having to identify the features of poyino operating among poniko-pen. As I have suggested (by what some in anthropology would call the Waiwai "animic system"), the white-lipped peccary herd has many of the social qualities pertaining to a village community of other people, and one of those primary qualities that the system imputes to the herd is its distinct oppositional duality of identity. In one mode, that of poyino, the peccary herd behaves generously and peacefully. In another mode, that of wošin, it behaves avariciously and aggressively. These modes toward an oppositional duality (which often allow the peccary to operate in myth as a symbolic intermediary) intriguingly assist Waiwai thought upon such sublime topics as the quality of collective life and the character of individual death. Toward a wide spectrum of ideas that include the sensual gastronomic and erotics of marriage, the joy and sadness of paregal and hierarchical relations, and even the calamity of the parents' ever-impending death after their child's birth, the modalities of the peccary herd's dual identity provide an ordering for the very content of human thought. It is a mode of ordering that allows for the circuit of contemplative ideas about the human condition understood to be dependent upon the specific oppositional duality of the corporeal body.

As the principal venue for coordinating procedures of Waiwai thinking and feelings, the body has been sighted by Waiwai society as a central problematic and, as such, understands one aspect of itself as being capable of violent aggression and another as being the very object of violence. In such conceptual and experiential frames, the problematized body has to deal with the intellectual and sensual configuring of itself in the mode of the jaguar, which kills and eats peccary persons, but it also has to deal with the simultaneous configuring of itself in the mode of the peccary person. In the latter mode it must confront the inevitable violence of its own death and bodily transubstantiation.

The Waiwai understand death as the terminal transubstantiation of the body, where the transformative process of the dying body assimilates a process similar to that of meat as it is being eaten. Devourment is the idiom of death. This is in part the reason why the logical structures between *esetakaši* (hunting), *esereme* (eating), and *esehsa* (breathing) have their roots in *ešeturï* (the throat). In order for it to die, a body should be the object of a hunt and the target of a hunter. In all Waiwai interpretations of death, the body becomes a *wayšapin* (corpse) by being successfully hunted. If a corpse is the successful outcome of a hunt, then it should also be the object of a meal. In other words the raw uncleaned meat (woto) of the hunt must be transformed into the cooked food (ñïye) of the meal. Here the culinary act attempts to clarify the murky ambiguity between the body that eats and the body that is eaten.

When served as food, cooked meat passes into the mouth, down the throat, and into the stomach of the living body. There in the stomach, gastric processes—understood by the Waiwai as another kind of "heating"—once again transform the food and pass it out of the body as waste. Upon taking in the smell of his or her own or someone else's fart or shit, the Waiwai immediately exclaim "*¡kicha wehtko!*" and spit to the ground to expel the smell. *Wehtko* is their word for fart and shit—and I have to admit, I was the butt of many jokes early on in my learning of their language when I used to mispronounce the word for fire, *wehto*, as wehtko. The two words register a categorical difference, but they also phonetically mark a strong conceptual similarity. Between the heating processes of fire and the stomach, a meaningful correlation is attained. The smell from the gastric heating of food and the smell from bodily waste corroborate the transformative processes within the stomach. The heat of a fire turns raw meat into a kind of plant food that is often good to eat, while the heat of a living body—that is, of its stomach—transforms the food into a kind of plant waste that is not good for human consumption. (Much of the logic for this kind of thought can be found in the Waiwai myth about the first yuca plant, which I discuss in a later chapter, "When the Cicadas First Sing.") The heat of fire and the heat of the stomach determine the kind of plant matter meat gets transformed into and whether or not it is suitable for further human consumption. But in this cultural procedure, because each heating process can simulate a structural equivalence as well as a structural opposition to the other, the two can also set the issue about the vicious contrasting dualism of identity into an anxious swirl.

In various frames of Waiwai thought, different kinds—but not all kinds—of heat appear as forms of eating. For example, the heat of the crematorium and the heat of the stomach transform meat into plantlike matter by a process of devouring. Both heating processes "eat," but one cremates and the other excretes. Both transform meat into inedible matter. One should consider, however, that the heat of the crematorium and the heat of cooking both use fire, but only the latter transforms meat into food. Hence fire can produce edible and inedible matter. Indeed, when cooking game and when cremating a corpse, the heating process does subject both bodies to the heat of fire, but Waiwai ideas regard only the cooked game as suitable food for human consumption. It seems that when ideas about the heat of fire relate to cooking game, they do not do so in the idiom of de-vourment. Only when the heat of fire is also the heat of cremation is it understood as the heat of the stomach, and all heat of the stomach transforms meat into inedible matter. Only the transformative heat of the stomach is idiomatic of devourment. This is in part due to the difference the Waiwai culinary system places upon the corporeality of animals and that of humans, but it is also due to the structural equivalence of devourment drawn between the transformative heat of the stomach, which excretes, and that of fire, which cremates.

No doubt the overall cultural procedure does indicate distinctive differences between the dead body of an animal person and that of a human person. And doubtless this overall indicative procedure gains assistance from recognizing certain similarities between the corpse of the cremated and the body of the cremator. But where would these similarities be most significantly experienced and/or thought about? Where we find no distinctive differences drawn between the corporeality of animal and human, and where we can find the animic principle of continuity strongly prevailing, both bodies become the property of a contemplative and experiential process concerning the transformative heat that eats. Thus do the structural equivalences between the cremated and the devoured body fit the Waiwai into the regional paradigms that reinforce the intellectual and experiential association between death and cannibalism (Overing 1986; Viveiros de Castro 1992; Taylor 1996; Clastres 1998).

Here transformative cannibalistic heat translates as the producer of a negative reciprocity. It should be remembered that only the creative cooking heat of fire turns meat into proper food for meals; the destructive cannibalistic heat of the stomach produces inedible matter—that is, no food and no meals, in other words, negative reciprocity. There can be no joy or sociality from the products of cannibalistic heat. Only cooked food becomes the context of meals and, therefore, represents the efficacious power to produce positive exchanges. This, one could argue, is why the political so avidly seeks out and appropriates the power of meals; in their capacity for positive exchange, meals actually come to represent the shared joy and sociality of filiation. To appreciate this fully, we would have to see the white-lipped peccary as representing the quintessential Waiwai meat food as well as occupying the position of affinal relations with the Waiwai. We would have to conclude (as I am suggesting Waiwai ideology does) that to be in the category of affine is to be in the category of proper food. At an instrumental level, the creative heat of the fire that cooks the body of the affine makes it possible to eat the meat of the in-law. At a cognitive level, it is the relative strangeness of the affine that makes it possible to place it in the position where affinity can be cooked. But an interesting yet consistent thing happens to consumed affinity that highlights the structural equivalence drawn between the two types of cannibalistic heat. As I have mentioned, the cannibalistic heat of cremation eats only the body of a poyino—an incorrect source of food for proper social beings. Interestingly enough, the cannibalistic heat of the stomach as it consumes the meat of the wošin transforms its affinal matter into a category equivalent to that of the poyino transformed by cremation. To put it another way, just as marital relations turn into filial-like relations after the birth of children and the intimacy of living together, the consumed wošin relation transforms into poyino and, like cremated and excreted matter, can no longer be the source of further exchange. Hence, while continuing to be the desired experience of what it means to live in shared communion with other village members, poyino can, nevertheless, only be "actualized" (or, to use the Waiwai metaphor, properly "cooked" as food for meals) by the transformation of the wošin. In cultural reality the efficacious power of productive and positive reciprocity belongs to the affinal relations of marriage. Even though poyino remains highly desired, the nonproductive and negative reciprocity of filial relations actually continues to be the intellectual property of a terminal category—that is, incest and the end of society.[10] Ultimately, it may even be concluded, having village leadership functionally bond to the gratifying of a terminal category may be one of the grand schemes of Amerindian political philosophy.

The gift of life and happiness offered by the peccary and wošin, yet accepted by the Waiwai as the debt of meat and marriage, helps to formulate the problematic facts of a bodily existence. For the individual to know and experience the joy and comfort of a gratified bodily appetite, the individual must know and expect death. For the individual to know and experience the joy and comfort of living within the familiar circle of poyino, the individual must know and expect the strange otherness and indebtedness of the wošin. Such thinking and feeling provides for the body what I interpret to be the full significance of the anthropological conclusion that in

Amerindian philosophy "the social state in itself entails mortality" (Overing 1986:90). For the individual to be a proper social person, filled with moral virtue, the individual must confront and accept a seemingly inevitable subordination to society and an impending bodily annihilation. The logic appears to be that if it were not for the facts of death and society, the individual human body would happily live forever (Lévi-Strauss 1970; Overing 1986). Without bodily hunger there would be no need to satisfy the appetites—no need for food and sex, no need for hunting and courting. Like eternal spiritual vitalities, corporeal existence would be perpetual; the corporeal body and its spiritual vitalities would not separate and occupy different permanent domains as the achieved outcome of lethal attacks upon the body and upon esteemed social relations. But in Waiwai reality as well as Waiwai ideology, the body needs meat and marriage and must, therefore, live with the contradictions of having to kill and be killed, to cook and be cooked, to eat and be eaten—indeed, to be a social person susceptible to giving and dominating as well as to receiving and being subordinate. Birth and death belong to the body. To have any form of control over human mortality and over its very own existence, society has to have control of the body. In this regard sex and violence couple as a primary focus for social control. Yet even though both aspects coexist in a tangle of expressive statements, in Waiwai cultural ideas it is violence—particularly in its principal representative form of the hunt—that appears preeminent.

A good deal certainly can be said about the bodily appetites of sex suggested by the relations between meat and marriage, particularly in the context of the quintessential meat of the peccary and its role as the affinal food. Such suggestive erotics could be presented within the Waiwai metaphor of lyrical seduction that does work with ideas about hunting, courting, eating, sexual intercourse, vomiting, ejaculation, the "grand death" of postmortem decomposition, and the "small death" of postorgasmic flaccidity. But because Waiwai ideology concerns itself preeminently with the bodily hunger for meat and its gratification through the process of hunting and cooking, the analysis has instead concentrated on the violence of the transformative heat of the body. It is this violence in the hunt that brings about the meal. This is how the meal gains representative power. It is indeed why the political process of Waiwai society discerns and seeks out the context of the meal in order to gain access to the resources of power. In the overall scheme of the system, however, the power of violence cannot be centrally accumulated in the political, because in the end the violent hunger of the body's transformative heat produces only the terminal category of a negative reciprocity.

The meals of onhari and the individual household represent the nonnegotiable products of a proper social existence. They lead, for example, to the completed sacred circle of the village and the full flow of familiar filial substance—that is, to poyino as the ideal achievement of residential life. Without collective village meals and individual household meals, neither the private nor the public aspect of village life can be meaningfully viable. Clearly, meals do not just provide for the physical sustenance of individual members; they also provide the means for allowing the politics of kinship to stay alive in their legitimate forms. They permit, for example, the particular moral obligations of kindred to find pleasing expression in the producing, preparing, and consuming of food. Perhaps more than any other activity, eating together from the same pot confirms certain beliefs and satisfies certain desires about being a proper person in Waiwai society. The simple political and social function of meals keeps the order of beliefs and desires in place. In addition the same order that conspires politically to keep the meal of the individual household in its private domain also conspires to bring some of its attributes out of the private and into the public realm of onhari. For instance, collective meals meaningfully leave to the domestic such behavior as men and women eating together in the same circle, but by ritually prescribing that everyone should eat out of the same pot, they mimic the domestic meals' essential ethos of an unguarded conviviality. In other words the public domain uses some of the social familiarity of the private to make the collective politically safe. Assisted in its administrative role by the network of overlapping relations of kinship and marriage, political leadership draws upon the meanings and events of public meals to express itself formally. In those obvious moments during onhari when the boundaries of the individual households have temporarily disappeared, political leadership and collective village life tactically identify with each other and establish their formal reality. Yet in what could be considered the legitimizing process of village leadership, public meals doubly protect the social collectivity. Because public meals provide leadership with access to the village collective and because poyino is the expressive ideal of mealtime conviviality, political leadership cannot in and of itself reach out and profit from or amass coercive power through the manifesting of community. In a defining Waiwai style, it could be argued, society surreptitiously lures leadership into the circled trap of poyino. Leadership certainly builds and manifests village community upon the social relations of kinship and marriage, but as a centralizing force it cannot appropriate such community and relations in order to negotiate a further, more extensive political field for itself. This, to reiterate, is because beyond themselves, the formal ideal community and relations of poyino have no negotiable products.

Poyino configures the dead-end achievement of a continuous sacred circle. It is (despite its contrary proclamations in various aspects of Waiwai culture) a continuous violent "eating" of kindred, tantamount to incest. Like incest, it is a kind of cannibalism, which—if openly acknowledged—would be the true culprit for precipitating the end of society. Perhaps not surprisingly, therefore, in its relation to wošin it adopts a rather tense and paradoxical position. Revealingly, in the same way that Waiwai cultural logic transfers the cause of violence from the hunter to the hunted, it also transfers the cannibalistic impulse from poyino to wošin. Just as the slaughtered body contains the evidence of the hunter's action and the reason for his bad conscience, the wošin similarly contains the evidence of poyino action and bad conscience. Even the source of poyino action and bad conscience may be attributed to the same force—that is, to the personal and intimate generosity of the wošin. Thus at the moments of its desire and achievement, poyino registers a contradiction, for without marriage and the in-law it cannot correctly take form. One should consider that it is exchange with wošin that produces positive reciprocity. It is the death of wošin that sustains mortality. It is the cooking/eating of wošin that ultimately helps to clarify relations of poyino. All in all, to be properly filial necessarily implicates affinity. Yet the very object of desire that wošin permits conceals the fact of its negative reciprocity. Wošin has nothing to hide and nothing to lose. It is the obvious other side (may even be the subconsciously denied or transformed inside) of poyino. On the other hand poyino conceals the hazard of a knowledge that can reveal its very own shortcomings. Significantly and in no more understated yet dramatic form, it conceals that devastating knowledge about an ever-imminent extinguishing of a divine spiritual presence from the confines of the human body.

The life force of the human body, ekatï, originates as part of the spiritual coherence of divinity, but it initiates and sustains all forms of life. It is the actual heat of the vigorous body, speculated as the felt experience and confirmed knowledge of divine coherence. Its radiance as the vitality of the eye similarly corroborates the spiritual and physical presence of life and divinity. Even the evidential growing body of a child reinforces belief in the vital effects of ekatï. As a corporeal aesthetic, the spiritual design of ekatï fills the lived body and permits itself to be shared. Indeed, Waiwai belief suggests that this sharing of similarly channeled spiritual substance causes the remarkable physical resemblances between individuals born from the same womb—that is, resemblances that result in the relationship of epeka. The same logic extends to the accumulation of repetitive somatic contact and exchanges between individuals who have lived in the same village, the accumulative result being the physical familiarity of poyino. Through corporeal bodies in the collective exchanges of community-wide relations, spiritual vitality circuits and weighs down individuals in the mortal reality of social life. In its bodily manifestations, therefore, spiritual vitality produces experiential time and space, mortal and social aesthetics made calculable by death. Dying assists the movement of spiritual vitalness, because without the terminal exhaustion of the body there would be no need for life's rejuvenescence; life would be continuous. It would also, of course, be nonnegotiable—that is, life would be without calculable transference. Therefore, in cultural reality mortal and social life depends upon the discontinuities of death and reciprocity—the giving and taking of the body. Spiritual vitality, death, and the body coexist as the source and explanation of human society.

Society needs the body. The experience of mortality needs the body. When death comes, it comes to the body in society. During the process, however, death does not merely extinguish the life of the body; it expels the bodily presence of divine spirituality. In Waiwai understanding it is not the destructive outcome of the body but the body's loss of divine vitality that is thought to be devastating. By logical extension the loss of divine vitality from the body also means at least the partial breaking apart of collective society. Both the body and society lose the full appreciation of divine coherence. In other words death takes away the experience of an undifferentiated spirituality. In its bodily and social modes, spiritual vitality expresses a divine coherence captured in the representative character of poyino. The very safety of familiarity, conveyed in the relations of poyino, derives from an understanding of the integrative capacity of spiritual vitality. Where spiritual vitality integrates, the body and society differentiate.[11] The integrative form and safe familiarity of poyino conceals, however, the ultimate consequence of a designed security achieved by means of terminal relations. Within relations lacking difference, within relations fully appreciative of divine coherence, poyino hides the destiny of divine loss. It cannot, however, deny the body. Poyino cannot ignore mortality. It cannot perpetually sustain spiritual vitality. Death, like the avaricious affine, will ultimately unravel the puzzle of filial integrality. It will in the end destroy the storage of filial relations. The severe irony remains, nonetheless, that similar to the generous affine, death can also allow mortal life and filial affection to be the effect of the transformative heat of fire and can nourish the living body in society. The spiritual vitality that gives divine coherence to society must live in the differentiated bodies that share its vitalities. Without death and the wošin, spiritual vitality and poyino cannot manifest themselves as the principal integrative force and form of body and society. In the destructive and at the same time constructive relations between the Waiwai and the white-lipped peccary, we have, I think, an illustrative instance of this impinging paradox.

Grief and Shamanic Breath

Death of Little Eagle

From the other side of the village, from the tight cluster of houses
near the river, a tremulous wave of heartfelt grief kept repeating
itself. Trembling sounds of sadness engorged the damp air and con-
gested the empty spaces between the dwellings. They lifted me
up from my hammock. They carried me across the plaza. They
placed me down unnoticed in among the mourners. All around the
wayšapin (corpse) of Yaymuchi (Little Eagle), the quivering lament
seethed like a stormy sea.

Agitated, coiled, and writhing, they were packed into the small
dark house. They were grief stricken, and they sought to console
themselves and each other with an intimacy of contact and a unison
of sorrow. Their faces blurred into the dim background. Their dole-
ful forms congealed into a dense, seemingly protective circle around
the immediate family of Yaymuchi and his corpse. They were not
individuals; they were a chorus of pain. They came to contribute
their simultaneous emotions and to offer their collective support.
All of them expressed and presumably felt the immediate hurt. Perhaps the hurt first opened each individually to the inexpressible, but
in the collective it closed upon this chorus of lament. The wailing
became a social event for the dead, for the family of the dead, and
for all those wishing to express sorrow. It was the proper thing to do.
More accurately, it was the sound of the proper thing to do—that

sorrow together

one being in pain

is, the thing felt but inexpressible as a feeling. The wailing sought to give sound if not to tears then perhaps to the feeling of pain.[1]

"*Okyo!*"
"I am shocked!"
"*Okyo oyatho!*"
"I am shocked, my brother!"
"*Achi wa mehče?*"
"What has happened to you?"
"*Kokoñero 'Ke-tiřame,' keñke hara.*"
"Last night you said, 'I will return.'"
"*Okrisha!*"
"You lied!"
"*Me-tiřame-si hara, pïra.*"
"You will never return."
"*Okyo!*"
"I am shocked!"
"*Okyo!*"
"I am shocked!"
"*Oyatho wayhi.*"
"My brother has died."

The object of sorrow sagged in its hammock. Its weight pushed tight against the knotted strings. Arms akimbo, legs platted, it seemed asleep. It seemed to contradict its self. At any moment it would rise. Just wait, you will see; he will sit up, throw his legs out of the hammock, and stretch like a fowl cock in the morning. How could it be otherwise? Only a few days ago we saw him do the same thing, as he had done every morning before. Let us wait, but as we wait, let us encourage his spirit. Let us make a noise his spirit can detect. Let us alert his spiritual absence to where we are—here, near to his body. He has only been asleep for a little while; his spirit cannot be far. Let us welcome it with tears. Let us show the sorrow we felt when he had departed and while he had been away; the sorrow we did not at that time express but now desperately want all to see and hear. Meanwhile, as the dense circle of the chorus wails around the rim, at the center let the close female relatives of Yaymuchi tend to his body.

Under the hammock and the body, a fire glowed. Only the immediate surfaces of the area below and around the body received its light. Only the body in the hammock was supposed to feel the heat. The eldest daughter of Yaymuchi cupped warm water with her hands from a bowl on the ground and libated the corpse. In unconscious rhythm with her own wiping and wailing, she poured the libament on to its chest and rubbed it into its skin. She rubbed some into its hands and then its feet. Huddled in a pitiful heap by the head of the corpse was the wife of Yaymuchi. From her bent, willowy arm a craggy hand and outstretched fingers continuously and hopefully caressed her husband. An almost unbearably painful thing to see, and with each caress the chorus seemed to fall into a deeper, more unrequited passion.

For a moment a darker space appeared at the rim. A barely perceptible falter in the chorus, and Shamawa and Awam entered. As the wailing continued, I could hear someone whisper to Shamawa the narrative of Yaymuchi's demise. Awam suddenly cried out and threw herself down by the feet of the corpse. Yaymuchi was her (classificatory) father (FMZS). Shamawa bent his head and prayed. Someone came forward and began to spread the embers of the fire flat under the corpse. All the while Anawach, the son of Yaymuchi, stood shaking with grief. Netcha, his wife, had her arms wrapped around him as if to keep him from the indignity of throwing himself upon the corpse. Slowly, encumbered, Anawach made it to his father's side, where he took up and held his left wrist. Periodically, one of the men in the rim would step forward to console Anawach or personally show respect to the deceased. Ponu put his arms around Anawach and quietly laid his head upon his shoulder. Itup came and stood on the other side of the corpse, where he took up and tenderly held its right wrist. In this way the scene of grief played itself out through the night, but at dawn the spirit still had not returned.

There had been a good deal of discussion about what to do with the cadaver.[2] Some wanted to bury (*totoutato*) it in a "modern" fashion and some wanted to cremate (*totoukopïto yathitopu*) it in the "traditional" manner. In the end they arrived at a compromise in which the body would be buried inside Yaymuchi's house and the house burned down after the funeral.

The men gathered in the house to dig the pit and build the coffin. Yaymuchi's body had been wrapped in a large red cloth with white spots. I believed it must have been what he had used as his blanket. The body lay on a plank, the ends of which rested on some short benches. At the head, on the remaining space of the plank, rested an old brown suitcase. On top of the suitcase was a white rice sack, tied and half-filled with different but unrecognizable bulging objects. The suitcase and the sack were to be buried with the body. The cardinal position of the body remained what it was when Yaymuchi fell in his hammock. His feet pointed to the nadir and his head to the zenith of the sun. Indeed, in line beside the places where his hammock had been tied and where the plank now rested, his pit had been dug. When the men had completed their tasks, they lifted the body and placed it in the coffin. They then lowered the coffin into the ground. Before covering the coffin with the dug-up clumps of yellow clay, U-ses brought Anawach to the edge of the pit. Anawach was still weeping. Ashen-faced, unshaven, his head draped with a large towel, he appeared incapable of thought and action. U-ses mumbled a prayer and the men covered the coffin. Very simply, and perhaps unceremoniously, the funeral passed away.

No longer a young man (maybe in his early fifties), Yaymuchi had belonged to the age-grade of active and respected married men (porintomo-komo). Even though he had been visiting from his home settlement on the Rio Mapuera, he had spent many years of his youth on the Essequibo and had a number of friends and relatives still living in the area. Quite recently, however, he had returned from a brief stay with one of his sons, who lived among the Trio in Surinam. Even in these, his "twilight years," he still loved to travel like young men do as part of their growing knowledge of the world. In fact Shamawa had once counseled him on his "wandering ways," warning him of their dangers. But Yaymuchi ignored him, believing him to be only interested in swelling the ranks of his own village community. He may have been correct nonetheless, because the Essequibo community had particularly cherished him for his knowledge and ability in the building of traditional Waiwai houses. He was most admired, however, for his calm leadership in communal work. Perhaps it was after all this last attribute of his—being able to lead by example, inspired by an indomitable will to complete any task he began—that ultimately contributed to his death.

He had climbed for his arrow, lodged high in a palm tree after missing its target of howler-monkey meat. In retrieving the arrow he passed through a plague of caterpillars whose poisonous hairs brushed against his skin. For three days afterward he bled from his nose and chest, gasping for air through his swollen throat. In pain, he made it all the way back from the hunt to the village. Signaling to his son and other companions not to assist or follow him, he left the canoe, walked up the embankment to his house, and collapsed dead in his hammock. His death had been sudden and unexpected. It inevitably broached a question that all in the village now wanted answered: Who had used deadly spiritual violence to kill Yaymuchi?

Yaskomo: The "Catcher" of Spiritual Vitalities

In Waiwai collective ideas about human fatality, all death results from the intentional implementation of spiritual violence. Waiwai interpretation assumes that even though human practitioners cannot strictly own spiritual forces, they work, nonetheless, through their human host and require the moral will of humans to initiate their technical functioning. The corporeal body of a victim dies because its ekatï, its life-giving spiritual vitalities, have been permanently removed by mystical missiles deliberately set in motion by the malicious intent of human breath. The victim's body suffers its loss of life from the aggressive actions of an individual killer's chanted words, propelled into the wind by puffs of breath. Given through some stolen particle of the intended victim's body (such as fingernails or clipped hair) or through some intimate object of its recent contact (a morsel of food or a favorite fire fan), the ekatï of the quarry are stalked by *erem*—silent predatory words. Gained from the mystical vocabulary of helping spirits, the deadly words either directly force the ekatï of the intended victim out of its corporeal host or further influence some other means to achieve the eviction. Temporary separation of the victim's ekatï causes illness; permanent separation results in death. What occurs is a desperate struggle of breath against breath, vitalities vibrating against vitalities. If the grappling vitalities collapse into each other, becoming one with eternity beyond the targeted body, the victim dies. Being ejected and unable to return to the corporeal body of their host, the spiritual vitalities settle with their original collective source in kapu—the stratified celestial realms of the cosmos. Here, ideally after death, the distinctive parts of an individual's vitalities reside. The ekatï of the human eye, for example, takes up occupancy between the earth and the first stratum with the Maratu-yena (Guan-people) of the celestial realm. The ekatï of the human chest, if not placated by the vengeance of kinsmen, will angrily roam the earthly stratum in solitary phantom form. It is, therefore, the conspicuous corpse that immediately arouses the speculation of the village community.

Because in Waiwai society everyone can claim access to the death-dealing force of spiritual violence, the specific individual identity of the killer is initially very difficult to ascertain.[3] Both through contract or personal use and in its accessible form of erem, the constant availability of spiritual violence directly contributes to the specific killer's anonymity. As in the case of Yaymuchi's death, open access to and availability of spiritual violence evokes the inevitable question, "Who done it?" And yet, because the Waiwai consider *tono*—the ballistics of deadly breath—to be an exclusive part of shamanic knowledge, the profile of the killer is already known. Once implemented and having achieved its result of death, spiritual violence resonates as the repetition of deadly words chanted only by a yaskomo, the "catcher" of spiritual vitalities.

The Waiwai word *yaskomo* comes from the verb *yasi* (to catch or to hold) and from the collective particle *komo*. It has been suggested that yasi "means magical power, supernatural gift and medicine man" (Fock 1963:75, n.10). One should consider, nonetheless, that when referring to snared prey, the most commonly used verb is *nasiya*. The impression I obtained was that nasiya not only referred to the action of successfully capturing game but also to the distinct substantive corporeality of the meat caught. Whenever speaking specifically about the snaring or catching of spiritual vitalities, however, the Waiwai used the word *yasi* more often. In its shamanic context, yasi carries the meaning of a heightened spiritual association with the divine precisely because of the greater familiarity the ekati of the shaman has with divine domains and entities. Divine familiarity and its consequence of yasi identify the shaman more with the spiritual than with the material world. Revealingly, the other category of person in Waiwai society to be designated with the collective particle of komo is that of child, referred to as rikomo.

shaman closer in relation to divine

Waiwai culture provides the understanding that children are not yet fully *toto* (human). That is, in the aspect of their vitalities, children are, like shamans, more of spirit than of matter. The child and the shaman belong as it were to dual communities—the ethereal and the material. In the cases of both the child (particularly the baby or infant) and the shaman, however, the hold upon them seems greater from the community of spirit than from the community of matter. Their bodies are the tenuous materials for the animation of spiritual vitalities that have stronger bonds with their divine sources. The movement of infantine and shamanic vitalities between communities can be dangerous to the more sedentary vitalities occupying the bodies of adults in the material domain. In the case of a newly born child, for example, the members closely related to each other as husband and wife and as new parents to the baby in the material social world have to be vigilant about what enters and leaves their bodies. For instance, as they still contain the residue of spiritual potency, heavy foods such as meat and cassava bread could, if consumed by the parents, attract the volatile vitalities of the baby

not fully human!
spirit > human

[margin note: babies dangerous b/c closer to spirit world]

and in the process "catch" the vitalities of the parents and return them to the world of spirit. As part of what anthropology understands as the couvade (Rivière 1974; Menget 1979; Rival 1998a), Waiwai restrictions on certain foods during the early period of an infant's life function to protect adult vitalities and to assist them in the social construction of parenthood that comes out of the spousal category. As part of Waiwai understanding, these food restrictions are practiced precisely because of the collective perceptions about and beliefs in the volatile vitalities of the rikomo and yaskomo. In their familiarity with both worlds and their ability to move into and out of the body as well as between the social communities of humans and spirits, the spiritual vitalities of the child and the shaman repeat as the resonance of a divine power capable of ensnaring life itself.

[margin note: constantly reminded of human mortality]

Both rikomo and yaskomo conceptually signal to the living the fundamental message of human mortality. The birth of a child pushes the categories of husband and wife along the identity trail to take on the role of parents. In becoming a parent, a Waiwai individual sees in ever-closer proximity the dark horizon of personal death. Every son and daughter weaned from the coherent source of divine power confirms and brings closer that moment of contact with the dark shaman. Death and the dark shaman are "knotted" together at the end of the trail and at the end of the day.

[margin note: if life not ticking time then why this constant reminder of mortality associated w/ age grade?]

In Waiwai *kamo-yemi-topo-iša* refers to twilight and the coming of night. It conveys the idea (in free translation) that "the final loop in tying up the sun has been made." The end result of the movement of the sun through the day is the knot of night on the western horizon. Sunlight and mortality always face west; they are like the dawn, *kamo-yepataka-topo-iša*, "coming directly from the east, facing and moving toward the night." At midday, *kamara-kataw* ("when the jaguar is in between"), from where death begins its move into the night, the sun stares fixedly like the eye of a jaguar upon its prey. In Waiwai ideas, just as a jaguar would stalk, kill, and eat its prey and as a hunter would catch and tie up his game, the dark shaman hunts and kills his victim like the night tying up the day. It is a catching and tying up done with the fatal rhythms of shamanic breath.

[margin note: "catching and tying up"]

With the whispered syllables of lethal breath, an approach has been made. A movement has occurred both within the material world from day to night and from life to death, and between the material and the spiritual worlds from ewto to kapu. The movement of words has a rhythm. The resonance emanating from the chest of the shaman has a cadence, the metrical movement of which reveals not only the location of the shaman but also, in its effect of death, the community of its victim. After the corpse—by dying—exposes the lethal effect of shamanic breath, the relatives of the deceased immediately respond with the unmistakable mournful sounds of grief.[4] Waiwai ritual wailing is the counterpoint to the silent, predatory words of erem and, in its response to the resonance of the dark shaman, repeats the social solidarity of the community in which the deceased lived. It also seeks to place the dark shaman firmly outside the village community, where lethal shamanic rhythms can more reassuringly be identified with other village communities. Like laughter and the shared expression of joy, mournful wailing and its meaning of sadness help to reveal Waiwai ideas about social solidarity. In this regard it is very much in concordance with their traditional ceremonial dialogue *oho-karï* (Fock 1963:216), which was performed after every death.

The Waiwai *oho* (ceremonial dialogue) occurs in various social contexts that cause this single genre to give the impression of producing functionally distinct formal dialogues. The previous ethnographic record states that there was oho for marriage contracts, trade, communal work, festival invitations, and the public display of grief (Fock 1963:216–19).[5] In its traditional structured form, oho involved only two participants seated on low stools facing each other not more than a few feet apart. It was invariably an exchange of dialogue between men, particularly senior men who were not "ashamed" to speak in public and possessed "a deep chest of words" they could use. Women did participate but normally only with a man. The "oho-opener" (Fock 1963:216) or "lead speaker" (Urban 1991) began the dialogue with a single line of speech that ended in a rise of pitch. The lead speaker would continue with these speech

lines until he was ready to pause, whereupon the speech line ended
in a noticeable fall of pitch. At this point the respondent countered
with an affirmative "oho." The declarative speech lines of the lead
speaker and the affirmative counter of the respondent comprised a
"form-defined cycle" (Urban 1991:127) of dialogue. With the participants alternating as lead speaker and respondent, the dialogue
cycles would continue until one of the participants ran out of or
had "emptied" his chest of words. The overall chanting effect of the
cycles sounded more like song than talk, yet their semantic content
and "form-defined dialogicality" (Urban 1991:127) conveyed to the
audience—by "indexical and iconic" (Urban 1991:123) modes (such
as, for instance, the back-channel responses of "oho")—a parody or
caricature of normal everyday discourse.[6]

Specifically with the death-oho or "oho of lament," a resident
close relative of the deceased must cautiously interrogate at least one
representative of every household in the village. Until those present
have performed the public lament for the dead, everyone beyond
the resident close relatives of the deceased is a murder suspect. Particularly beyond the household cluster of the deceased, everyone
becomes a potentially hostile stranger—a dark shaman waiting to
attack the remaining and related spiritual vitalities of the deceased's
relatives.[7] The accumulated exchanges of vitalities between members of household clusters make it extremely dangerous for the living
when one of their own dies. Tiny particles of vitalities belonging to
those with whom the deceased lived get caught, tied up, and carried away along with the dead individual's vitalities. Their capture
may make their owners *karipera* (sick) and may even be interpreted
as causing the *ñerewa* (pain) of the grief felt by the living for the
recent dead. What the close relatives of the dead want most from
those outside their household cluster and those within their village
community is reassurance of amicable intentions toward their being. In other words they want to be reassured of no further loss
of vitalities to themselves from the departure of resident members
and, concomitantly, from the hostilities of dark shamanism. Thus,
in regards to the form-defined dialogicality of the death-oho, the

go back to normality

participants appear to evoke a public display of normal everyday discourse for the good reason of wanting to resume the regular flow of amicable relations—or at least, in the mimicry, of wanting to suggest that the flow of normal conversation implies the resumption of normal relations. Often, however, the actual semantic content of the oho does not cite the normal and the everyday (see Fock 1963:302–12). Yet where the declarative lines of the relative of the deceased mostly question, the affirmations of his partner are filled with the entreaties of friendliness. What remains most instructive is that the form-defined dialogicality of the death-oho forces the semantic content to conform to a formula—albeit an exaggeration of normal discourse. As such, the formula can successfully serve the function of mediating "in situations that are likely to give rise to conflict" (Rivière 1971:306). The social boundaries at which hostilities could begin within the village community apparently occur between the conjugal household clusters, where the everyday exchanges of spiritual vitalities seem less reciprocal and hence more vulnerable. Thus with the death-oho, it could be concluded, the icon of normal discourse in ceremonial dialogue seeks to jettison the dark shaman beyond the boundaries of the village community.

purpose of death oho

As the counterpoint to erem, the death-oho resonates as the formal opportunity to deny any accusations of personal ill will and to affirm conviviality. What is interrogated and displayed in the discourses of lament is not so much the "guilt or innocence" but the emotional calm and good will of every village member and the demonstrative sociability of the community. It seems the ideological Waiwai focus settles upon a dual concern for the quality of human mortality and the knowledge of human character, with its capacity for violence. Knowing about the emotional disposition of those with whom one lives appears to be of crucial interest. Locating where bad intentions reside and making sure—when they erupt—to deter them from accessing violence become the required aspects of social harmony. When this fails, however, and even without knowing the murderer's identity, knowledge about hostile intentions remains the leading evidence toward exposing the killer.

killing only ok when its for food
↳ revenge killing?

The Waiwai configure violence in the same intellectual frame as eating. In their view the ultimate rational conclusion for all killing has to be that it is for food. As I have previously suggested, this notion contains social—albeit ambivalent—approval when the object of violence carefully confines itself to vegetable and animal life (Stephen Hugh-Jones 1996; Viveiros de Castro 1998). In the case of homicide, however, the interpretation of killing in order to eat the victim does not alter significantly, but the question of legitimacy makes the victim's death more problematic. To kill another human being illegitimately is likened to the actions of the solitary antisocial jaguar devouring its prey: the murderer kills and eats the body of the victim without cooking it and without sharing it; the decomposing body disappears like food into the carnivore's mouth.

legitimate killing

rev.

In converse, to kill legitimately—that is, to hunt or to feud in honorable vengeance—is to behave as a proper social being governed by the moral obligations of society, wherein cooking and sharing of the victim's body locate the hunter and the warrior firmly inside the community. A successful hunter will not only make sure the animal he has killed is transformed into cooked meat before it is consumed but also goes to some lengths (even after collective hunts and communal meals) to make sure he never eats the meat of an animal he himself has killed. Likewise, the avenger of a dead relative will, after the cremation or burial of the deceased, take the remaining bones, place them in a hollow bamboo, and "recook" them. If the bamboo bursts in the heat of the fire, the murderer will die. While an illegitimate act of violence tends, therefore, to locate the murderer outside of society and, in fact, makes him or her the target of a legitimate use of violence, legitimate violence succeeds in reaffirming the hunter and the warrior inside society as beings of esteem and prestige. Nevertheless, in both cases it is hostile human intentionality that remains the initial source of violence, while the spiritual force it stimulates is the actual cause of death. The cannibalism of illegitimate violence always resonates in erem. Lethal mystical words, like projectiles from the mouth, can bring about the

human hostile intention → spiritual force → death

death of another human, and death, in Waiwai ideas, can only be initiated by ill will for the explicit purpose of illicit consumption.

Only those people motivated by their own ill will actually make use of deadly spiritual force. In such cases public knowledge and recall of the existing character of relations between community members provide the resident community of the deceased with the identities of possible suspects. In addition public perception of past events and of bodies capable of igniting emotions leading to violence also helps to establish the identity of the wrongdoer. The shared and unofficial obligations of the living to the recently murdered victim begin with having to locate and assemble the evidence of the active presence of individual human malice. Such evidence can be achieved with relative ease, because the range of expectant emotions assumed to be felt by people with ill intent is generally known to result from specific observable actions. The actions producing the felt emotions, which tend to lead to and govern a matching set of responses, actually expose the presence of the bad intent that activates and uses violence. Recalling and perceiving, for example, that so-and-so had been on the retreating side of a dispute allows observers to assume that the retreating individual had felt some *riwo* (anger) or *kiči* (frustration or emotional turbulence) and became possessed with *kičičito* (ill will or, more correctly, "to be dangerous") enough to seek retribution against his or her opponent. The subsequent sickness or death of the offending disputant who caused the anger confirms both the bad intentions of the shamed person and the actual effect of the angry person's violent retribution. Taken together, felt emotions of human malice and spiritual violence cause sickness and death, but they also provide the very clues to answering the question as to the identity of the individual contributing to the ailment or fatality.

In Waiwai moral philosophy, everyone should exercise the social responsibility to guard against wrongly arousing his or her own destructive desires. The general availability of violence as a weapon and the link between ill will and the actual use of violence seemingly compel collective social harmony to depend upon the individual's

can it ever be fault of person decid for angenny or generating ill will from someone else?

emotional calm and bodily discipline. Here where violence can only be accessed through human intent and practice, it is, in an analytical sense, the result of an articulation between the attribute of individual human will and the resources of spiritual energy. In this sense violence is inalienable to the individual, because only the individual can transform its force into the product of destruction. Yet in being irreducible to the individual, violence is, in its potential, the culminating sum of a culturally built identity. The individual, in becoming a social person, consciously ascribes to the body and the spiritual vitalities an acquired knowledge of ownership over the potential use of violence—a knowledge actually constituting the movement of personhood.

Graphically expressed on the adorned body with traditional signs of adulthood and gender but also more substantively in the achievement of marriage and the making of children, the emotional base for the will to violence becomes a known property, subject to customary displays of control by the individual. Being able to exhibit constraint over the emotional base to violence expresses both an individual's commitment to society and the effective means toward collective social harmony. It could be said that in such cases Waiwai culture has indirectly persuaded individuals to perform the fundamental task of managing social turmoil on behalf of society. Here the onus of control does not rest in any rigid centralized institution of governing, but in the supple, overlapping multifaceted realms of personhood and household clusters. In these social domains—that is, through actual personhood and residence, the individual retains legitimate access to the use of violence. In other words the individual uses the moral constraints in kinship and marriage to police human intentionality and to secure harmonious residential fellowship. It is, however, precisely because morality becomes meaningful only within these domains that the constant availability of violence keeps individual control and collective harmony vigilant.

The social and cultural requirement of living together offers the opportunity for expressing, monitoring, and managing the amicable relations of collective social life. Without the fact of residence with others, the need for emotional calm, the potential for violence, and the ideal of community fellowship could not find their current form and meaning. For the effect of residence to best perform its tasks, however, the patterned ties of kinship and the institution of marriage must also be active, for they are the very means through which affection can be shared and violence denied. The dominant moral obligations to love rather than hate and to be kind rather than hurtful toward those related to you and toward those with whom you live have to be in constant practice. Yet each individual's capacity for affection is counterpoised by the known potential for violence from the dark shaman. Indeed, as I have mentioned, the very occurrences of sickness and death confirm the deliberate implementation of spiritual violence and the presence of the dark shaman. Whenever sickness or death occurs, the veracities of violence and the dark shaman acknowledge themselves from within the collective substance of social knowledge and, at the same time, reaffirm the open character of their accessibility. While it is, on the one hand, the access to and availability of violence that directly contribute to the murderer's anonymity and indirectly produce the inevitable demand for suspects, it is, on the other hand, the murderous ill will of somatic emotions that exposes itself to the community of the deceased as the incriminating evidence of wrongdoing and as the definitive means of confirming the identity of the murderer.

In the collective opinion of the community, Yaymuchi died because he had incurred the ill will of an individual unable or unwilling to control his or her emotions; the fine virtues of a cultural constraint could not restrain the inherent violence of a bodily passion. As far as the members of the village were concerned, this was due in part to Yaymuchi's unnecessary absences from the protective feelings of his family and friends living in their community. That is, his recent visit to the Trio village, where he was a stranger and an obvious target for feelings of animosity, contributed to his death. Strangers have no grounds for feeling affection toward other strangers, and, with this lack, fall into the category of potential murderers. In the understanding of his grieving friends and relatives, therefore, Yaymuchi's

assailant lived in another village—a malignant shamanic force outside the immediate constraints of residential filial and affinal moral
obligations. Thus contrasting with the amicable immediacy of residential relations, it can be argued that, among the Waiwai, death and
the dark shaman serve to keep secure the ideological constraint of
a supple political segmentarity. In these ideas violence and shamanism can never be transformed into a rigid repetition of segments;
they cannot, for example, be concentrated as a dominant theocratic
center.

Resonance, Spiritual Vitality, and the Dark Shaman

Let us not return, however, to the now well-turned issues of the
Amerindian society against the state and their definitions of political power (Overing 1983–84; Rivière 1983–84; Clastres 1989,
1994; Santos-Granero 1993).[8] Let us in particular stay away from
the whole evolutionary question of whether or not Amerindian peoples have any prior knowledge of the state or possess any individual
desire for its accumulated power of "rigid segmentarity" (Deleuze
and Guattari 1987; Gil 1998).[9] Let us instead first assume that "there
is no opposition between the central and the segmentary" (Deleuze
and Guattari 1987:210), for surely "there are already just as many
power centers in primitive societies; or, if one prefers, there are still
just as many in state societies" (Deleuze and Guattari 1987:211).
The issue then becomes one of tracking the resonances that operate
within and between centers.

We can trace the resonances of power, in the case of state societies, from a single dominant point of accumulation to their various
vibrating segments. Made rigid by being appropriated as echoing
and reechoing redundancies, resonating sequences can be heard as
the accumulated discourses about, for example, social and economic
classes, racial and gendered oppositions. These repeating and rebounding sequences resonate at the primary center as if they were
the benevolently cared for truths of segments. Every resonance of
the state thus sounds like the echo and not the source of a percussion
of parts.

In the case of the so-called stateless societies of Amerindians, we can trace the resonances of power from their various supple segments back to their localized independent sequences. Here the resonators of power remain dependent upon particular specificities within their own local domains; the various fragments of their universe cannot be made redundant at a single point of intersection. The resonators of Amerindian power can and do indeed illuminate by their vibrations the "lines between all the points or spirits" (Deleuze and Guattari 1987:211), but this power expresses no stiffness; it is pliant, always susceptible to the countervailing resonance of other centers (and perhaps, rather than be heard, is felt).

When feeling, for example, for the vibrations of shamanic power in lowland South American societies, we do not encounter any accumulated resonance at a single dominant point—that is, we do not find any high priest or paramount chief. Like the layered fragments of the Amerindian universe, the segments of shamanic power repeat the vibrations attributed only to their specific spirit. Each segment emits its own sequence of spiritual power. In this way—that is, as the resonator of a segmentary power or as "the sutured wound of a silence"—the shaman can be known through the source of an oscillatory current. Yet in order to reinforce or prolong its vibrations, the percussive movement of shamanic currents has to rely upon the adjacent segments occupied and oscillated by other shamans. In other words the currents from other spiritual resonators assist shamanic source sequences in their vibrant production and yet keep them within their own segments. An interesting feature of these "forces from the outside" is the interpretation of their oscillatory current as negative shamanic resonance. In this regard—that is, as a negative spiritual resonator—the sutured wound of an ominous silence congeals as the knowledge construed about dark shamans. In contrast to the more familiar and positive resonances of the "Light Shaman" (Wilbert 1972; Eliade 1989) heard within their therapeutic and apotropaic spaces, it is instead, I would argue, the strange and negative vibrations of the "Dark Shaman" that reveal the most about the supple segments of Amerindian societies. I would like to pro-

[handwritten margin notes: "dark shuman that brings about segmentation"]

pose that, instead of the healing and protective forces of the light shaman, it is rather the deadly and destructive forces of the dark shaman—particularly in the role of spiritual hunter/warrior—that operate to sustain the suppleness of segments in Amerindian societies.

A distinctive vitality of being has been attributed to the shaman; it has been recorded as possessing the ability to transcend the corporal body of its host (Roe 1982; Crocker 1985; Sullivan 1988; Eliade 1989; Reichel-Dolmatoff 1997). In what anthropology understands as the dream or trance state, the substantive vitality of shamanic being is said to move from the somatic space of the body or the structural space of shamanic practices into alternative domains (Furst 1972; Lévi-Strauss 1972; Harner 1973; Rouget 1985; Basso 1992). The factual evidence of the body remains, sustaining its dreaming or ecstasy in the material substance of the body recognized by all in the local community—"that's so-and-so dreaming in his hammock or swooning in ecstasy." The transcendent vitality, interacting with other beings in the dream or cosmological world, is not hindered by the limitations of a corporeality. Its knowledge of cosmological beings and landscapes empowers it or gives to it the capacity to interact or move effectively within such domains. When it heals as the transcendence of the light shaman, it does so by searching, finding, and successfully returning the dislodged vitality to the body of the patient. When it causes affliction and death as the transcendence of the dark shaman, it does so by the very same abilities and knowledge but with the resulting dislodgment or permanent loss of the patient's body. Thus do the harmful and deadly conclusions of the dark shaman's resonance repeat on the other side of an inverted complementarity. They fit with the positive form of shamanic effects; they resonate off of health, well-being, and life. In both instances, however, it is the body that acts as the convincing signifier.

Much of the literature suggests that the individual bodies of shamans and those of their patients or victims have little if any choice in the matter of being occupied or vacated by their vitalities (Lévi-Strauss 1972; Crocker 1985). The eternal mystic source of vitalities radiates a power that can give life to and take it from in-dividual bodies. Presumably because of the more frequent, distant, and traumatic separations of the shamanic body from its vitalities during dream or trance, the social category of the shaman receives and sustains an ambiguity of dependency and pity from society. The community depends upon the peculiar placement the mystic vitalities maintain in the body of the shaman. It is, however, also perturbed by the hold these vitalities have upon the shaman, for they can send the shamanic body into "seizures of small deaths," where momentarily the local community can no longer communicate with its privileged member. It would be fair to say that while the effect of shamanic power depends upon its working through the body, the individual shamanic body places no direct claim on such an effect. In Amerindian societies this power belongs (if this is even the right word) not to vulnerable human beings but to eternal spiritual entities. Shamanic bodies merely conduct the current of spiritual power into the world. When they kill as the bodies of dark shamans, however, spiritual vitalities frequently take on the deadly resonance of the predator.

The sick are healed and the healthy are afflicted; either way the body becomes the target of a consuming shamanic resonance. The "mystic human causation of affliction" (Crocker 1985:21) needs the body. The body is the site for the vibrating of health and life, sick-ness and death. The body is the space for the shamanic apparatus of resonance. In this space, even within the time of the body, life and death rebound as the resonance of shamanism. As the space of death and the end of the body, the corpse vibrates the dirge and repeats the lethal passage of the dark shaman. The corpse gives presence to death and, as "the object of a collective representation" (Hertz 1960:28), floats as the dominant signifier of the dark shaman in lowland South American societies. It is the effect of a surplus of power. In this regard all death means murder, all murder the malicious work of the dark shaman. Here the dark shaman sutures, with consumptive spiritual vitalities, the cut between the signifying corpse and its signified meaning of death. In the shape and character of the predatory shaman, spiritual malevolence hunts down the body of its prey. It eats the vitality of its victim. Separated from and unable to reclaim its vitality, the body of the victim dies. The corpse, the death, and the dark shaman fuse into a single dreadful scar. Together they resonate the oscillatory trace of a healed wound; they indicate the former condition of a rupture. In other words the very fact of the vulnerable wound of human mortality is known and has meaning in the predatory work of the dark shaman. At the level of anthropological interpretation, this can explain why—even though the corpse may still be speaking with shaky voice or staring in quiet pain—the "decomposition" (Descola 1996b:365) of the social person often precedes the dying body. Hence the obsequies are more for the social person than for the individual body. What the living body does is allow spiritual vitalities to permit the person to invigorate social relations and society itself. But as the object of the dark shaman's predation, as the effect of a surplus power, the corpse and death provide society with the means to restore and retain social personhood even as the individual rots away.

As hunter or warrior, the dark shaman occupies that predatory space between the social and the political. The dark shaman resides in the nightly crevices between every segmentary center of Amerindian society and, as such, actively functions against any possibility of a concentrated political power. No repetition of segments can coagulate to form a single rigid center capable of appropriating in the political the shamanic power to kill. The death-dealing arrows of the dark, bewitching shaman keep the social segments supple, never allowing them to accumulate at one point as the surplus of a single entity. Death comes to everyone. It comes on the dark horizon of the west, propelled by the bewitching shaman. The redistribution of any surplus power placed into healing by the light-curing shaman is, therefore, the energy effect of the dark shaman's complementariness.[10] The surplus can only be forced into its distributive mode by the hostile act of the dark shaman, who causes the "little deaths" of sickness as well as death itself to appear in the first place.[11] Without the violence of the dark shaman, there is every reason to believe that the surplus power of the light shaman could transform itself into a rigid segmentarity within the political domain. Without the dark shaman's ability to initiate death, the shamanic power of life—streaming from the east like the blazing light of the sun—could dominate, as the political, all the supple segmentarities of transcendent presence.

Musings on the Quiet

What for us could be the relevance of tracing the threat from Wai-wai shamanism? The question has, at least for me, one intriguing response. When carefully and critically positioned, the tracing to the shamanic can help us evacuate an unwarranted skepticism of the quiet.

The very desire to have a voice, the longing to speak and to be heard, to have words represented in the world as the expression of a selfhood—these seem crucial to our Western traditions of being. To us silence has indeed become a terror. It not only can give form to the singularity of a selfhood and the substance of a desire, but also—perhaps more profoundly—can threaten to deny presence altogether. Thus neither the silence of the monastery nor that of the isolation cell can compare to the dread of being without presence. Some have suggested that such silent sites of contemplation actually contribute to the presencing of subjectivity (Foucault 1979:143; Scarry 1985:22; Clastres 1989:185). By becoming the quiet places for the pondering of an imperfection or delinquency of the self, these phrontisteries not only corroborate presence but also obliquely confirm the perfectibility of the divine and the morality of the state (Foucault 1979; Niebuhr 1999). Yet one might imagine a being without the presence of voice—not necessarily a being without language, but worse, a being who, with a language, did not use it to empower individual identity. This supposed absence of an empowered presence could indeed be our deep-seated horror of and, dare we say it, need for the "savage."

We can, for example, ascertain such an inclination in the consistent preoccupation of Pierre Clastres with the issue of silence.

"This was what made the Atchei savages: their savagery was formed of silence; it was a distressing sign of their last freedom, and I too wanted to deprive them of it" (1998:97). In his *Chronicle of the Guayaki Indians*, Clastres purposely gives intentionality to Guayaki silence (1998:17); it is the very substance of a "health" and "freedom" (1998:96, 97); and it even metamorphoses into the social "invisibility" of a third gender (1998:293). Again in Clastres's more famous *Society Against the State* and in probably his most brilliant essay, "Of Torture in Primitive Societies," the central concept of the marked body as memory can only begin to resonate with full meaning when silence expresses a "courage" (1989:184) and "consent" (1989:185). This preoccupation with silence does not captivate only Clastres, for in much more subterranean styles, other authors have pursued the topic of Amerindian silence. For example in two very sophisticated examples the intellect and imagination of Amerindian subjectivity take on a "thing-like" cultural presence (Urban 1996:xiii, 65, 71, 173) and a "metaphysics of sociality" (Overing and Passes 2000:12), but only, it seems, from our shared understanding of a possible uncommunicative silence on the part of the subject.

The contrasts made possible by the gap between the civilized and the savage, the modern and the traditional, the state and society are surely of our own making. I would argue that they appear as part of our modern anxieties about being incomplete, of not actually being able to sustain the experience of a completed subjectivity—at least, not one that could be experienced outside of death itself. The incomplete self offers, for example, an explanation of the market forces propelled by inexhaustible desires and inevitable shortfalls in supply. As modern consumers we can never be satisfied. Nothing can fulfill us, for as soon as we have filled that gaping space of want another hole appears, and another need takes the place of that which was consumed (Brydon 1998; Cavallaro and Warwick 1998). Experienced partly through the structure of the signifying orifices of the body, the embodied self understands its presence as a signified incompleteness (Lacan 1977; Anzieu 1989; Douglas 1996; Gell 1996). This incomplete self acts as the emotional and perhaps even as the innovative engine of our culture. The cut between the signifier and the world signified can never be sutured, yet this wound constantly demands to be healed—that is, we force language and the world not just to be symbolic but to be literal as well. The factual reality of the desire for completion; for whole selves; for full citizenry; for the vote; for an education; for a car, a house, and a bank account all implicate the gap from which the Other appears. There betwixt the centers of power—often as uncivilized, primitive, and without the state—the savage Other struggles in meaningful resonance to bring the modern soul into full presence.

One might be skeptical of this opinion but should consider, nonetheless, some of the reasons why, when turning against what we consider to be the vulnerable bodies of women, we continue to call Islamic male honor or African patrilineage "terrorism" or "brutality." In the mainstream of our culture, these signs of barbarism are the obvious result of cultures without justice, without democracy, and without statehood's representation of the treasured autonomous self. They exemplify the denial of access to the individual. They pertain to evidence of what happens when the individual does not become conscious of a selfhood that it should possess and actively seek to make present in the world. To gain access to the individual in these cultures, the state often has to negotiate with segments such as the clan, the family, or perhaps even motherhood. For the modern state such negotiations appear irrational and inefficient, undermining its authority, perhaps even its very existence. But in the much more controllable category of nation-ness, the state possesses a greater capability of receiving loyalty and obedience from the autonomous self. Why? Because in the imagined community of the nation, the consciousness of each autonomous selfhood can achieve the reserved supplementary identity of being modern, of being cared for as a modern soul, of receiving the promise of full presence (Foucault 1979; Todorov 1987; Anderson 1992). Thus do we need the savage to confirm our arrival in the moral space and time of modernity.[12]

One might consider the modern notion that every individual possesses the potential for violence—a force capable of rising up from the deep recesses of an unguarded domain to become the orchestrated property of war (Deleuze and Guattari 1987). Every society recognizes this potential of the individual and, in its own particular way, seeks to conscript this forever-imminent force into its service. Whenever it works on behalf of institutional forms, the violence of the body usually becomes something other than simply a negative force (Leach 1977; Riches 1986). Certainly it can disrupt such forms, but it can also reinstate them and bring about the known boundaries of social roles and political community. When disruptive and negative, the terrorism and brutality of bodily violence reveal the warrior savage. In this guise the savage confirms our civilized presence. Could this perhaps be why most of us can reel off the names of modern-day serial killers but cannot remember even a single name of one of their victims? Our fascination with the killer savage provides the evidential field in which to confirm the actual potency of bodily violence transported from the gaps to the center. On the other hand our horror of the killer savage also assures us of our anxious moral presence at the center. For us (or at least for those of us believing in the ideals of bourgeois modernity), our moral presence seeks to be represented by the state with its appropriation of our potential for violence. There at the center, but on our behalf, the state is given the legitimate right to possess and use violence, and as such—that is, in being used as justified force—violence often loses its character of savagery and becomes civilized. Thus from beyond or even from inside the boundaries of our community, the warrior savage provides us with the necessary grounding for our moral presence. Indeed, when we can no longer see the specter of war on the horizon or in our midst, when we no longer hear the roar of battle and, instead, stand facing an empty field of silence, we confront more than a mere dark and formless void. The silence and absence of the savage deny our civilizing presence.

The tongue-in-cheek use of the term *savage* by Clastres—when referring to the Amerindian person—places the burden of interpreting on us. At one level we want to understand this savage as the ideal lack or absence in us of barbarism. Savagery and its barbarism are out there, in the forest, hiding behind primordial beliefs. We in fact need them there, on the boundary or limit, as "the visible frontier of our culture" (Clastres 1998:141). They help to bring us into being. One might imagine the alternative, imagine their silence and, of course, to our horror, our own lack of being as presence. At another level we seem to want to understand the savage as existing within the confines of our control, within reservations, ghettos, prisons, and asylums of modernity. Here, given the status of "Ward of the State" or even that of legal citizen, the savage Amerindian has, by occupying the lower ranks, historically helped to shape the form of our social hierarchies. We are already afraid that Amerindians may not be responsible enough to commit to and be loyal to the concept of the nation-state. We have given to them an autonomous subjectivity that should proclaim on its own behalf its identity, its needs, and its representation in the modern world. Yet we remain uncertain. Let us suppose, however, that we were no longer afraid of the silence of the savage. If we were more secure in our knowledge and experience of the world, how would we reconsider their being?

When, in our interpreting, we uncritically attribute to the Other our notions of being as presence, we run the risk of misunderstanding how culture and society perform the work of constructing human subjectivity and how culture and society take on their particular forms in relation to the human subject (Habermas 1987; Rorty 1989). With particular reference to Amerindian sorcery and specifically to Waiwai shamanism, let us begin by trying to place in abeyance our terror of the Other's silence. Let us grant to their society the power to produce and place in prominent positions a wholly radical kind of human subjectivity with positive and legitimate being. Let us also proceed to pose the question as to why in these societies death is invariably murder and, furthermore, murder is always the work of the dark shaman. Can we go so far as to find a place for this killer savage that does not reduce murder to "a moral wickedness" and "the most heinous kind of criminal homicide" (Little, Fowler, and Coulson 1980:1374)? I would argue that it has been this prejudice about such violence — from the knowledge that its source could only be attributed to a universal autonomous subjectivity — that has for so long forced us to ignore the shaman from the dark void and instead place most of our scholarly efforts into analyzing the shaman from the light of life.

- diy to rise of born-again hippies interested in healing
  - ↳ population, life
    - ↳ not interested in role of dark shaman
- ↳ busy trying to protect/defend ourselves against argument of dec

go to shamanism (not shaman)

↳ not tracing in field to individual - everyone has the capacity

to be shamanic

ex: Guayuki: pregnant women = shamanic - walking

around w/ power of spirituality/vitality inside her

Access to shamanic/healing not specific to individuals

(tendency to individualize)

Nobody really wants to play shamanic role but all can

humans made up of vital/spiritual power

The Archer and His Bow

A Purple Passage

We beached on Pebbled Landing. Dark dolerite sentinels loomed on the murky shore. Burrowing beneath frond embankments, fretting fitfully in persuasive soliloquy, the sable river glided gently by. A toucan quizzed from the upper canopy. A legion of beetles, in metallic crescendo, instantly replied. The exhaled breath of a howler monkey, cushioned by the damp morning air, boomed across the leafy landscape. All seemed unrehearsed, yet not a discordant sound could be heard. We had been on the river for ten days. Our task had been to bring back meat for the festival of *kesemanïtopo*. The hunt completed, we were now preparing ourselves for the triumphant entry into the village. A single point bar in the river hid us from those we were about to rejoin.

For me it had been a grueling ten days. This was my very first hunting trip with the Waiwai. I had volunteered to accompany the hunters, not only to observe the occasion of an arranged communal hunt but also to show to the community my willingness to contribute to the collective village effort. [1] I was not, however, prepared for the rigors of the hunt.

We had left the village early in the morning while it was still dark. Two canoes each manned by six hunters. The leader of the party was Ipamar; he had been the first to say "oho" when Shamawa had asked for hunters. He commanded the first canoe, taking the *mapitaw* position in its stern. His brother, Ponu, took up the poturu position at the prow of the same canoe. In the seat behind Ponu sat Amakayan and Itup. Anawach and I sat in the seat in front of Ipamar. In *iyotaw* (between) the front two seats and the back two seats, a platform of cut sticks had been placed inside and across the canoe to carry our baggage and any game caught on the trip. Yawa, who was accompanied by Iwap, Anya-am, Isokikor, Awawatak, and Emtushen, commanded the second canoe. Every man carried a paddle, his weapons, and provisions.

Ipamar led us upriver. For three days we paddled and hunted. The hunter at the poturu kept watch for any signs of game up ahead. If he sighted a tapir crossing the river, we would speed up our paddling and chase it to the shore. The hunters in the leading canoe would then disembark and track it down. If we spotted a troop of spider monkeys feeding on the fruits from trees on the embankment, we would stop under the tree they were feeding from and shoot them down with curare-tipped arrows. In the late afternoon we would stop in a lagoon to fish. After the three days (presumably three days away from the regularly hunted areas around the village), we made base camp.

We hunted continuously, sometimes in shifts and sometimes all together. Two of us always remained at base camp, however, to tend to the meat. We had built two low platforms for smoking the meat we had caught. Under the platforms, made of green timber, we kept the fires burning day and night. Periodically, the meat had to be turned. Already, the platforms creaked under the weight of roasted meat. On the first night of our landing at base camp, Ipamar and Anawach had killed two large caimans. During the night, while fishing and hunting for paca, they also brought down a deer and a curassow. The routine remained harsh throughout the trip. Most days we paddled upriver or downriver, but some days we ventured deep into the forest, climbing up the steep inclines of the valley head to hunt for peccary and howler monkey. We had little sleep (maybe three to four hours between eleven p.m. and three a.m.) and little time even for rest. To me it felt like a ceaseless round of rigorous paddling, chasing, carrying, and cleaning of meat. Each hunter displayed an overall intent and concentrated focus upon catching as much game as possible.

They possessed a discipline in their every action. Although I heard no given command, each hunter moved to perform his every task with precise deliberation and in a well-coordinated sequence. From who would hunt to who would stay in camp, from who would take the prow to who would command the stern of the canoe, from what would be the necessary direction to take in a chase to where to go for the best fishing, the hunters accomplished all with a minimum of words and without a single directive from anyone. In my intended generosity and in the face of their unfettered deliberations, however, I became a self-conscious spectacle of confusion and hindrance. Yet to my abiding gratitude, they patiently tolerated my ineptitudes. I concluded that this was because the knowledge they displayed and the skills they possessed were all turned to the single task of procuring meat and had little room for pointless criticism.

While this simple conclusion seemed apt, it nonetheless kept me searching for the actual source of their organized control. It kept me looking for a base to the seemingly hidden force that directed and guided their every action—a source that at the time, in the midst of the hunt, I could not locate. In the end, however, it became but a matter of resigning myself to the well-tested anthropological mainstay that, regardless of its source, causal force had to rely upon the collective human imagination. Only the human capacity to share ideas and be similarly influenced by those ideas could result in the kind of order I saw manifested about me. Such conceptual power could only be produced by the facility to understand the self within the cultural paradigms shared by others—faithful, taken-for-granted paradigms. Hence I came more to appreciate how the invisible but effective forces directing the knowledge and skills of the hunters resided both among them in the moment of the hunt and in the imagined ritual spaces of the village three days' journey downriver.

Unseen and quiet but made objectified and tangible, strong imagined bonds linked the hunting party to the village. What governed the deliberate focus of the hunters' actions were not just the particular social bonds between them—that is, those helping to organize the tenor of behavior between each of them during the hunt—but rather the greater community bonds between them and the village. Revealingly, these bonds appeared to take their specific cast from the cultural figment of gender. Every time the twang of the bowstring disturbed the serene rhythms of the forest, the hunters confirmed their immediate project as an attachment to the village. With the use of the bow and arrow, the conceptualized and acted force of gender forged the hunters together in what they were doing and whom they were doing it for. Every pull of the bow implicated a pride and an achievement in represented masculinity. Throughout the hunt, the bow and arrow took the dominant role as the instrument of labor and the active symbol of masculine identity. Through the bow and arrow and their effective use, masculinity formed the elements of the ideas for its shared meanings. In the very act of archery, masculinity molded the image of itself. The foundry of the forest provided the working space in which manhood could shape itself as archer. There in the forest, it tracked living flesh and bone to open and to brake. For this work, however, it had to be deliberately sent out of the village; it had to travel away from the village community to kill in order to formulate itself as the bowman of death. Yet this formed meaning could not sustain itself by itself; to confirm manhood with archery and as archer, the hunter had to return to the village. There was no logic to perpetually wandering the forest, hunting and eating among ourselves men to men. Waiwai moral values had provided no conceptual space for the legitimate existence of an autonomous all-male community of hunters. Masculinity forged in the image of the archer could only confirm its meanings and values in its relation to the village. It required the forest to give it shape, but it needed the village to confirm this shape in its image of a lethal killer with a bow. What each returning hunter looked forward to, what each favorably anticipated, had to do with the display—and through the display, the confirmation—of his masculine prowess. The proper place for this performance was in the village and in the archery ritual of *tïwosom*.

On Pebbled Landing we took turns painting each other with black *channa* seeds. We placed on our heads and on our arms the feathers of the birds we had killed. We made bark horns that we would blow on entering the village. On the end of every horn we tied the roasted carcass of a small animal we had killed. We distributed the meat among us, each hunter making a leaf backpack in which to carry the meat. Ipamar made the largest backpack and carried the most meat. I made the smallest and carried the least. When we had completed our preparations, we left the landing. With each stroke of our paddles, we hit the sides of our canoe. We began to whistle, and as we approached the main landing of the village, the people cascaded down to the levee to greet us. We were ready for our entrance. We had returned once again to the *tawake tahr̃unkaši ewto r̃or̃o* (happy open center of the village).

Tïwosom: An Archery Ritual

Society always takes persuasive hold of its individual members, and in return the individual as social person clings to society. On the occasion of tïwosom, a Waiwai archery performance, we can witness this intimate embrace taking place. Applying the distinctive cultural techniques of ritual activity, Waiwai society and the individual use the body of the archer to display and implement their fundamental logic and moral philosophy for both participants and spectators. In the archery ritual, society and culture confirm gender roles and artifacts for the actions of participants. These actions in turn depict and reinforce the strong ideological beliefs that work to shape social relations. For example, in the central presence and use of the bow and arrow in ritual, the exclusive role that Waiwai men play as hunters is set off against and complementary to women's exclusion from hunting. Women do not hunt and do not use the bow. Hunting belongs to the domain of the forest, and archery belongs to the domain of hunting. Both have attained exclusive association with men. The archery performance helps to confirm such knowledge. It does so in small part by possessing the same name as that given to the carved wooden animals used as targets by the archers. More substantially, however, while it may indeed be a general purpose of all competition to decide winners and losers (Bailey 1969; Scarry 1985; Armstrong 1998), in tïwosom participation serves principally to place the hunter as archer at the center of the social gaze. In this ritual position, masculinity not only displays and makes claims about the predatory character of its archery prowess but also reinforces its legitimacy at the center of the social gaze. It is not just a question of how society takes hold of its members or whether it can, in fact, show us it does so through an instance of an archery performance, but rather that it does so in ways that make the exercise of power appear immanently appropriate and seemingly unimpeachable.

Every year around December or January, during the shorter of the two rainy seasons, the village community prepares for the ceremonial festival of kesemanïtopo. The festival always begins with an announcement of its forthcoming proceedings and a formal request from the village leader for *woto-yeposo* (seekers of [raw uncleaned] meat). In the formal request for hunters to go out into the forest to kill animals, the festival, in its commencement, does not differ much from other, more routine community activities.

As I have already mentioned, the daily routine of a Waiwai village often revolves around some form of communal activity. Farming, building canoes, constructing and repairing houses, and a number of other activities keep a village in regular if not constant collective action. To entice and repay the labor for such work, the communal meals of onhari have to be provided. Initiated by the village leader but actually administered by specific *antomañe-komo* (work leaders), collective work and communal meals always begin with leadership's formal request for hunted meat.

It is the karipamšam-komo who usually comprise the greater proportion of hunters in the group, but the porintomo-komo also participate. The village leader's authority to request and contract the activities of these hunters stems overtly and immediately from the persuasive eloquence of his voice—that is, in Waiwai parlance, from his ability to speak publicly without fear, shame, or reluctance. More substantively, but less obviously and immediately, his authority to initiate and direct communal activities derives from the influences

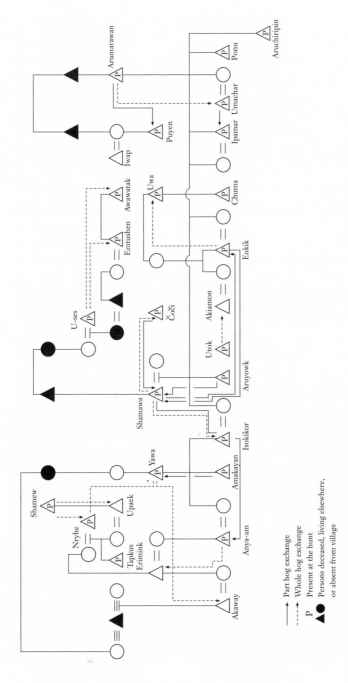

Figure 1. Kinship relations and hog exchanges

of his kinship and marriage relations to village members. Indeed, he is village leader because he can be found at the center of a core group of filial and affinal kinsmen who constitute the interrelated relations of the village. He is in this sense understood to be more prominently associated with the village than any of its other members. The authority of his request for hunters does not, therefore, depend solely upon his public and formal entreaty but rather on the combination of his persuasive voice and his informal influence over immediate kinsmen. Both effects create an obedience that ultimately benefits the village community. The labor of hunters in the provision of meat for village activities and, perhaps more importantly, the village leader's political capacity to govern depend upon the particular stylistic hold Waiwai society has on the compliant bodies of its village members.

The festival of kesemanïtopo probably most cogently departs from ordinary village activities in its sustained sequential efforts at collective enjoyment. On the day they return to the village, the hunters, with great pomp and ceremony, dance around the plaza carrying their packs of freshly killed meat on their backs while whistling and blowing their bark horns. They ceremoniously present their backpacks of meat to the village leader, after which every returning hunter receives a bowl of palm drink from the women of the village. The festivities can now begin in earnest. Each day various games and activities take place, from dancing to the music of the deer-bone flute and tortoise-shell resonator to chasing and pretending to kill different forest creatures whose image and behavior the villagers very convincingly mimic. The festival itself may last from three to five days or as long as the food and drink will last. It often ends simply with the exhausted participants remaining in their hammocks and later returning to the regular routine of daily life. It is within the festivities, after the "seekers-of-meat" have returned from their hunt, that the ritual of tïwosom takes place. The archery ritual is usually held on the day after the hunters have returned.

Before the festival begins and while the seekers-of-meat occupy their days hunting from canoes along the rivers and in the high forests of the mountains, the etïnomshapu-komo—the men who have remained in the village—make the arrows and targets to be used in the ritual. Each *etïnomshapu* fashions the finest arrow he can possibly produce. There is a good deal of friendly rivalry as to who can make the best arrow. These arrows are given to the returning hunters to use in the archery ritual. One man is commissioned to carve from soft wood the life-size figures of the birds yakwe (toucan) and *potwo* (grouse). When completed, these figures are placed as targets around the axle of the central pole up inside the large conical roof of the meetinghouse. If a village does not have such an edifice, a scaffold is specially built for the performance, with the carved birds perched up on its frame. The targets are usually about twenty-three meters from the ground, and the archers shoot upward as they do when in the forest hunting birds and monkeys.

Every male member of the village takes part in the ritual.[2] They all line up one behind the other, with each participant taking a single shot at his target, seeking to lodge his arrow in either one of the carved and painted birds. A fair amount of jovial banter takes place between the participants and the spectators, particularly between the archer taking aim and the female spectators. For example, as he is about to shoot an archer loudly boasts, *"onpoyiero opichi oyasi"* ("this is why my wife took me as her husband"). Everyone smiles, but if he misses, tremendous laughter bursts forth from all those present. The laughter in this context may well be embarrassing for the archer who misses, but it also helps to deflect the greater shame incurred from his inability to hit the target. When all the participants have fired off their arrows, a work leader brings down the birds festooned with arrows. From these arrows only, he chooses the most attractive and presents it to the village leader. The rest he distributes to all the attending archers who have hit their target, but no participant ever receives the arrow he has shot. In this and other aspects, the distribution of arrows copies the sharing of meat by work leaders at communal meals, where careful attention is paid to the custom that no hunter should eat the meat from his own kill.

The best hunters, *woto-waparï-komo* (renowned-killers-of-meat), and/or the best fishermen, *otï-waparï-komo* (renowned-killers-of-

fish), will often take the opportunity during the festival hunt to demonstrate their esteemed talents. The festival is also an occasion when the public secret about what has been the particular contribution to their success as hunters gains its disclosure. *Woto* specifically refers to meat from animals that live generally on land. *Tarĩnim* refers to meat from birds. *Otï* refers to meat from fish or animals that generally live in the river. The best hunters bring back all categories of meat, but they nevertheless acquire a reputation for having a greater familiarity with one of the principal guardian spirits of a domain and, therefore, receive more meat from that spirit's domain. Erimink, for example, had an impressive reputation as a fisherman, oftentimes bringing home large fish and catches of fish when other men brought home nothing at all. I never once saw him point an arrow in the direction of wayawaya, the river otter, or even attempt to chase one (not that the Waiwai ever hunt this animal for its flesh, but they often play at shooting at it from their canoes, and indeed there was a time when Guyana and Brazil had an active market for otter hide). The rumor was that Erimink's achievement as an accomplished fisherman came from his familiar relations with the Great Spirit of the Otter. Many other men also privately engaged assistance from the primary spiritual entities of animals, but their degrees of success varied. Obviously they sought these spiritual engagements or "contracts" in order to improve their efforts at hunting and fishing, but the desire for improvement came directly from social pressure. The high regard given to the more successful hunters derived from the privileged location hunting and fishing had in the regular routine of village life.

The Waiwai can quite correctly be referred to as slash-and-burn agriculturalists, but it is also the case that hunting takes pride of place in their economic and cultural life. Yuca is indeed the staple root crop and the basic source of bread and many beverages, but hunted meat completes the ideal daily meal. It could be argued that tïwosom actually celebrates or, more correctly, dramatizes the contribution hunters and their hunted meat make to collective village life. Perhaps no better illustration of this can be found than in the prominence of the bow and arrow both in the regular round of hunting activities and in the ritual of tïwosom.

Feminine Bow, Masculine Arrow

The *krapa* (long bow) has remained, even after the introduction of shotguns into Waiwai society, the quintessential instrument of labor and the primary symbol of masculine identity. When a man dies, his family normally burns or buries his bow with his body. Every man knows which trees produce the best wood for bows and can, with varying degrees of skill, make his own bow and arrows. As soon as a boy can conceptually grasp the connection between gender and social activity, he can be seen carrying a bow and a couple of blunt-tipped arrows and, at every opportunity, playfully taking aim and shooting at the various domestic targets in and around the village plaza. So deep and strong are the cultural connections between masculinity and the bow that their meanings have become intricately interwoven at many different levels of material and intellectual life.

A Waiwai bow, a simple yet remarkably efficient weapon, consists of a single stave of wood tapered at each end where the *krapa yawyechi* (knotted bowstring) is attached.[3] The cross-section (classified as "elliptical concave high stacked," following Heath and Chiara 1977:167) reveals the *krapa tïmkakim* (back of the bow). The *krapa yawyechi tipurï* (bowstring's terminal knot), a semidetachable loop, goes over the top nock or *krapa ewnarï* (nose of the bow) and sits on the shoulders or more correctly the *krapa itepurï* (head of the bow). The permanent middle knot sits on the bottom nock or *krapa mapirï* (buttocks of the bow). It is only removed when the bowstring breaks and has to be remade. For this purpose, particularly in emergencies, the length of another bowstring continues on from the middle knot and wraps around the lower end of the stave to about halfway up the bow. The Waiwai call the bowstring wrap *krapa katami*. The word *katami*, the same used for referring to the back apron traditionally worn only by adult women, tantalizingly suggests the bow as being in possession of a feminine body.

Indeed, a bow remains "naked" until adorned with the "clothes" of its traditional adornment. In Waiwai ideas (as in many other Amerindian conceptual schemes) an adorned human, animal, or object produces cultural and social meanings that go beyond the mere aesthetic, providing perceptible and, hence, distributive realities to intangible concepts (Seeger 1975; Terence Turner 1980). Significantly, a bow remains bare and in fact unusable until dressed with its bowstring. The krapa katami—that is, the bow's "back apron," marks a gendered functionality. Like the decorative aprons on women's backs, the wrap begins at the *krapa yasitopo* (center of the bow)—the thickest and most powerful section of its stave. This seems to connote the compressing of an energy at the center, emphasized by a two-inch cotton bind interlaced above the bowstring wrap. Here red and yellow breast feathers of the macaw hang in tied tassels. The only other place where decorative feathers can be found is at the terminal knot of a bow's top nock. The feathers seek to enhance the significance of the energy source located at the center and along the back. Their vibrant colors, suggestive of heat and strength, convey and confirm the Waiwai knowledge that such forces possess spiritual as well as material energies.

This, in fact, is why the word particle *yasi* in *krapa [yasi]topo* refers to the center of the bow. To reiterate, *yasi* is the same particle used in the first syllable of *yaskomo*, the Waiwai word for shaman. Corresponding to the way the source of shamanic power finds a temporary shelter at the center of a shaman's body (and indeed the way women's backs gain the strength to carry routinely their heavy backpacks of firewood and yuca tubers), the intrinsic spiritual and material power of the bow can be found in its back and at its center. From inside the shaman's body, the heat and strength of his spiritual energy gives birth to his powerful words, sent like arrows to kill or to heal. Correspondingly, to support her pregnancy a similar vibrant vigor converges in the back and at the center of a woman's body. Indeed, in Waiwai ideas it is the very same spiritual force originating at the center of the universe that permeates and finds a presence in the bodies of the bow, the shaman, and the woman. Feminizing the bow (and arguably even the shaman) amounts to making the claim that the power of the bow derives from spiritual and material qualities beyond its immediate form. Thus the bow's feminine and spiritual features subtly interchange and carry over into each other to provide the bow with its distinctive quality of centralized energy. To make authoritative and competent statements about their manhood, Waiwai men must set themselves in proper relation to their bow, their women, and their shamans. The following representations can hence be found in the archery ritual of tïwosom: the spectacle of each archer taking aim at his target; the overtly stated connections among hunting, meat, and marriage; and the whimsicality of an arrow's flight. It is these same elements that recur in owning a bow, having a wife, and existing on good terms with the certainty of shamanic forces (all highly desirable conditions for Waiwai hunters). And in each, a man must align himself to the emanating forces of the center.

It has long been recognized that for Amerindian societies of lowland South America strong oppositions, particularly between male and female, must first be established and maintained in order to be finally brought together in mutual interdependence (Lévi-Strauss 1972; Stephen Hugh-Jones 1979; Crocker 1985; Christine Hugh-Jones 1988). In such societies it is considered part of the social dynamics of human existence to know and understand the limits of elements believed to be in complementary opposition to each other. It may seem to us like high irony that an artifact used to objectify and bring full meaning to Amerindian masculinity should be given a distinctive feminine feature. In our world, for example, where much of modern sport has been restricted mainly to men, the feminizing of athletic equipment can often be interpreted as a form of endearment or familiarity conducive to making the relation between the athlete and his essential instrument of play more intimate. Such feminizing, it could be argued, betrays a desire to subordinate sporting equipment—that is, to bring the instruments of play under greater control and to bend them to the will of the athlete. For us, suggestively, a telltale correlation apparently exists among politics, work, and play. Yet for Amerindian societies, and certainly in Waiwai

culture, the logic carried over from politics and production to play is not so much that of domination as that of accommodation. To be political and economically productive, oppositional forces must be brought together in mutual cooperation; here it is not a question of defeating the opposition but of bringing opposing differences into effect by coupling them in mutual interaction.

Feminizing the bow in Waiwai culture is not a case of seeking greater intimacy with the bow in order to subordinate its energies to a more efficient masculine will, but rather one of bringing the essential requirement of feminine opposition into action to make masculinity actual and effective. To be a Waiwai man, in other words, means to be a hunter with a bow—that is, to be in proper relation with feminine forces that do not just enhance masculinity but actually bring masculinity into socially productive reality. By considering some of the physical and symbolic features of the bow, its feminizing contribution to masculinity can be best interpreted, in the ritual of tïwosom, as a dominant stylistic hold on the individual bodies of men.

If it can be reasonably determined that the bow contains certain features of femininity, then by the very form of complementary opposition, it can be deduced that the *waywu* (arrow) holds certain aspects of Waiwai masculinity. To do so comprehensively, however, would involve moving through the appropriated symbols of Waiwai manhood to meet once again the metaphor, "men are like birds"—a complicated analogy to interpret, yet it has a place in many different aspects of Waiwai material and intellectual life. From body adornment and house thatching to the defining characteristics of the layered celestial realm, men and birds operate as dynamic tropes. Particularly with arrows and their principal motion of flight, men and birds sustain strong associations. Here the somatic reference allows the wings of birds and the arms of men to combine specifically at the fletching of an arrow. In Waiwai the word *yaporï* means both arm and wing; hence calling the fletching of an arrow *waywu yaporï* (arm/wing of the arrow) assists in carrying all the symbolic load of men and birds to the arrow.

The body or *waywu* (shaft of an arrow) has a *waywu mapirï* (butt end), a *waywu putirï* (head), a *waywu takpo* (foreshaft), and a *waywu ponumchi* (fore end).[4] The butt end usually has about an inch of cotton or fiber binding, which holds in place an inserted, grooved hardwood plug serving as the *waywu mayewnari* (arrow's nock). The binding also has an additional coating of maani (black adhesive latex). Above the fletching, held between the overlapped, spliced ends of the main feathers' quill, are the *waywu mawyuru* (red and yellow tufts of parrot feathers). Some arrow makers add colored tufts of feathers below the main fletching, applying these ornamental feathers so as to distinguish the "dress" of the arrow and, in so doing, to be able to identify the arrow with its maker. For the main functional feathers of the waywu yaporï (fletching), the Waiwai always use the black primary flight feathers of the powïsï (curassow).[5] On and along the fletching bind, some arrow makers paint their special individual designs, once again allowing any arrow to be identified with its particular maker.

Waiwai arrowheads come in many different sizes, shapes, and materials, with the type of head used being primarily dependent upon the kind of animal hunted. The most versatile arrowhead is called *tiyashkem*. It is a long, pointed rod of hardwood with barbs carved either on both sides or on only one side. It has a long tang that is inserted and bound at the fore end of the arrow shaft. So well balanced is this arrow that if an archer misses his target when shooting upward into the treetops, the weighted arrowhead will turn the arrow back down to land near the archer. The Waiwai use tiyashkem principally to shoot large birds. However, because it is the arrow most frequently made and most frequently carried by the hunter, it can be used to shoot small monkeys and at times even larger game such as deer and peccary. The proper arrowhead for big game, however, is *rapu*. Traditionally carved from segments of strong, thick bamboo (although today some can be found made from hammered and sharpened pieces of an old machete), rapu arrows have a broad-bladed lanceolate head, which hunters use at close range on animals such as the tapir, peccary, and capybara. When newly made, both tiyashkem and rapu arrowheads can be seen adorned with white cotton thread and red painted designs. There are many other arrowheads belonging to the arsenal of the hunter, but to mention them all would merely serve to make the technical ingenuity and craftsmanship of Waiwai arrow making that much more obvious. Yet with all this diversity, there remains the noticeable fact that the one type of arrow Waiwai men most identify with happens to be the tiyashkem—the only arrow used in the archery ritual of tïwosom. Tiyashkem, more than any other arrow, is most closely associated with masculinity precisely because it carries death to birds.

Death provides the opportunity for an exchange to occur between

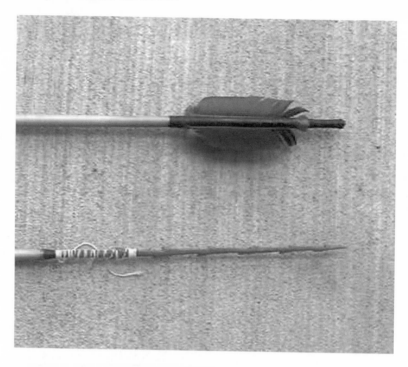

the successful hunter and the spiritual custodian of the deceased animal. Technically speaking, it is the entry of the arrow into the animal's body that dislodges its ekatï and initiates the process of death. Corporeal life actually ceases when the spiritual vitality of the animal can no longer return to the material form of its body. In other words corporeal death occurs when the animal's violently dislodged vitality has returned to its original celestial domain, where the main source of all spiritual vitality resides. In the ritual of tïwosom this process, which normally takes place in the remote forest, is reenacted in the familiar domesticity of the village. The site of the archery performance is a transferred ritual space; nevertheless, it seeks to mimic a domain that goes beyond the forest and the village. The targets of the carved and painted birds, placed in the three-tier canopy of the conical roof, signify not earthly but celestial beings.

Sky or heaven (or more accurately its three-tier realm of kapu) houses the main source of vitality that gives life to all living things. The Waiwai speak of kapu in avian terms. Its lower and first stratum, Maratu-yena (Guan-people), has the characteristics of dull-colored birds that keep mostly to the floor and lower levels of the forest.[6] The middle and second stratum, Kwaro-yena (Macaw-people), possess the characteristics of gregarious and brightly plumed birds who live in the upper reaches of the forest and fly above the forest canopy. The upper and third stratum, Kurum-yena (Vulture-people), possess the characteristics of high soaring carrion and carnivorous birds. The predominant avian attributes of flight, talon, and beak—which converge around ideas about missiles that rip and cut—belong to the cosmic birds of kapu, but they also get transferred to the hunter's principal weapon of death: the arrow. In this case they become the features of the arrow used primarily for killing birds: the tiyashkem.

After tiyashkem has dislodged the spiritual vitality of its victim, the bird's vitality must find its way to kapu and the custodial cosmic energy of Kwarokiyim, the Great Spirit/Father of the Macaw. This can occur successfully only if the hunter has properly killed his prey and correctly distributed its meat—that is, not "tortured" or "sickened" or wastefully left its carcass to rot. To allow a wounded animal to suffer needlessly or to leave its carcass behind after its death is to maroon that animal's spiritual vitality on the earthly stratum, where it not only can do vengeful harm to humans but also avoids being properly received by its spiritual custodian. When the hunter carries out his obligations successfully to the dying bird, the meat of its body becomes a gift in exchange from Kwarokiyim. It is in this sense that the tiyashkem arrow presents an opportunity for an exchange to take place between the hunter and the spiritual custodian of the deceased bird. The ripping and cutting missile of tiyashkem, an instrument of death, becomes masculine because it is made and used by men and in its making and use emulates the single most important force with which men identify: the Great Spirit of the Macaw. With its cosmic avian attributes, the Great Spirit of the Macaw empowers tiyashkem by offering the object of its custody to the hunter, thereby placing the hunter under an obligation to reciprocate. This occurs precisely because the hunter is the immediate beneficiary of the effect of the arrow's flight—that is, the meat of birds. In due course and through the hunter's relations with other village members, the meat changes into the social currency of masculine honor and esteem, which, in Waiwai understanding, has to be reciprocated with subordinate behavior toward the Great Spirit of the Macaw. In part the ritual of tïwosom is exactly this—an objectified, annually repeated statement of subordination to forces beyond Waiwai society.

In its process, however, the ritual plays out an additional and strange appreciation for the hierarchy of relations between the forest and the village. The suggested superiority of the village over the forest may only be offset by the superiority of the celestial spiritual realm of kapu. It is multidimensional in all its parts, but in its motion the world affects a concentric reality. At the margins is the forest. At the center is the village. At the center of the village can be found the entrance to the three-tiered upper world. The pull on the individual bodies of hunters out in the forest back to their village can thus be spoken of as more than just the force of social obligations and moral responsibility; it is, at least in ideological terms, the manifest energy of the spiritual world located at the epicenter. The torque force of its power reels in the wandering hunter. The properly lived social world depends upon spiritual force, the value of which the ritual of tïwosom helps to confirm.

Waiwai society, through the archery ritual of tïwosom, reaffirms its hold upon its individual members. By persuading its archers to take part and requiring them to follow the rules of participation, society demands and receives a reassuring obedience. Tïwosom makes the archer use his bow and arrow in competitive display, publicly testing his skills in archery. This style of retrieving obedience succeeds in projecting to members some of the concepts critical to the opposition and accommodation between men and women. The archer's equipment and actions, for example, assist in rationalizing and legitimizing not only the complementary differences between men and women but also those between husbands and wives and, indirectly, those between hunting and farming. Men's instruments of labor (the bow and arrow) as well as the products of their labor (meat) and, hence, men themselves become celebrated in and privileged by the performance. The repetitive actions of the archers in taking aim and shooting at the target of birds draws attention to the particular predatory relations men have with their prey as hunters. These relations have the capacity not only to provide men with the opportunity to fulfill their obligatory subordination to higher divine authorities; they also substantiate a seemingly inevitable hierarchy between humans and the divine. In the substantiation the ranking between humanity and divinity surreptitiously translates into a ranking between men and women. The overall ideological statement from the ritual archery of tïwosom carries the principal message of a hunting man's reciprocal subordination to the great cosmic spirit of birds. At the same time, however, tïwosom also makes the claim that men are, by their exchanges with the Great Spirit, closer than women to this eminence. The cultural drama of tïwosom fixes and frames the form of bodily obedience into the social substance of Waiwai society, and it does so in a style that allows society to maintain unchallenged the exercise of its power.

Styles of Obedience and Playing the Game
The comprehensive argument should be that when looking at the games of different societies, from centralized states and capitalist economies to acephalous societies and barter economies, however different they are—from the Olympics to kesemanïtopo—the actual elements producing the differences remain, in terms of anthropology, much the same. The argument should be that there exists a relation between the ways in which society takes hold of its individuals and the effect of the social persons it produces and also, provocatively, that even sport, as a dramatic form of emphasizing the body, functions to assist in producing a local style of social personhood. Because the ambience of Western capitalist societies is more familiar to us, it can serve as a comparison here, making a coherent point of departure for a discussion of the Waiwai and their ritual performance of archery.

I have been arguing that society constantly seeks to retrieve through the individual human body the substances for its own existence. There is no society without the individual, yet because the individual needs social roles and moral terrains for its meaningful existence and agency, there is no individual without the potential existence of society. The individual body acquires its agency and moral values by being made into a social person. Using the specific techniques of culture, society takes hold of the body and provides it with the categorical features of personhood. To constitute and perpetuate itself, society forcefully persuades the body to give itself up to the social. It makes sons and daughters, fathers and mothers, clansmen and citizens; it turns girls into wives, boys into husbands, civilians into warriors, athletes into heroes, but, most emphatically, it insures its own existence by securing the individual as social being.

To make the person and to substantiate itself, society continues into the body of the individual. It has first to wait patiently for the individual to arrive and then to extend itself into its somatic form. Long after the mortal body has come and gone, however, society remains in occupation as the social categories influencing other individual bodies. Within a single social biography, it can produce many categories of the person, allowing the individual to switch roles and moral terrains. At one moment a daughter, at the next a wife, and at yet another a mother, the individual can be mutable and capable of being multiple persons. This requires knowledge of the correct parts to play and perception of the moral attributes governing social roles. It also necessitates a certain attributable history to the categories of the person and a regular display of collective values as social power. In these ways both personhood and society can and do objectify themselves in, on, and through the individual.

Objectification allows the categories of personhood and the values of society to be shared and in so doing provides confidence in the kinds of behavior and beliefs expected from others in society. Objectifying, which can be said to become culture, certainly serves both individual and society. In this capacity it helps in organizing the world of the individual, making it possible for the individual to interact with the world in meaningful ways. At the same time it provides the means by which a society can achieve its distinctiveness, thus allowing that society to distinguish itself from others. Because not all societies take hold of their individual members in the same way, not all effects of cultural objectification will be the same. The different styles in which societies appropriate the body of the individual can be said to be the cultural means by which they distinguish themselves one from the other.

Hence the style in which modern capitalist societies seize their individuals—as "natural" autonomous entities ideally possessing "equal" rights with one another—can be identified as the cultural means by which they distinguish themselves as being, for example, politically democratic. In such cases the ideology of democracy tends to turn back upon its formative economic structure to assist it in shaping individuals to be, for example, independent and equal consumers of commodity goods. In these instances individuals receive the legitimacy to desire access not only to political polity but also to economic goods. In taking hold of members in ways that objectify them as autonomous individuals, Western capitalist societies allow their states and markets to engage individuals principally as persons understood to be citizens and consumers respectively. Yet at the level of belief, the cause of the desire for polities and commodities is placed not in political and economic forces but rather in the human individual as the source of self-conscious being. Perhaps because of this location of desire, what modern state societies judge as being most uncertain about their own existence is the depth of commitment of their individual citizens.

Modern state societies build community membership from the body of the individual and assume for each individual the capacity of a motivated conscious self of which they can never be fully certain. They constantly seek reassurances of commitment from their citizens, and to this end the disciplined body of the individual plays its crucial part in helping to deliver its own awareness into the safekeeping of the state. In obediently responding to government and market forces, for example, the disciplined body presents the possibility of corroborating the effect of the state's claim over the individual. In addition the disciplined body can confirm with its docility the individual's sense of meaningful existence in the known value system of the state. Regular obedience to culture makes the world real for the individual. Dramatizing this necessary character of relations between the individual and the state thus becomes a means of satisfying social desires. I would like to argue (as others have done) that in our modern Western world of belief in the autonomous individual and the democratic state, even competitive sports function to present and satisfy certain social desires for the individual and the state (Hargreaves 1986; Bourdieu 1990; Faure 1996) by repeatedly reenacting the dramatic obedience of the athletic body to spectators.

For the obedient bodies of individual citizens living in modern Western states there arguably appears a sense in which, when seeing two teams competing upon the field of play, such concepts as equity and fraternity become objectified and subliminally desirable. Two teams with an equal number of players, two goals or baskets with the same dimensions, matched halves to be defended and attacked, and equivalent time to determine the length of play are all forms of balances that help to convey the perception in competitive sport that a natural equity of sorts exists in the world and that obedient bodies merely mimic this by organizing their playful confrontations in its image. In addition by helping to maintain the rules, safety, and proper "spirit" of competition in the drama of sporting events, referees, linesmen, and officials reiterate the idea that the "brother-hood" of team play is a desirable ideal. Hence equity and fraternity appear to be like the "natural order of things." In fact citizens and states perceive and even find reassuring that winners and losers (in other words, an inevitable hierarchy) essentially come about because of a natural fraternal justice. What tests this perception and brings about the appearance of its certainty is, in fact, the playing of the game.[7]

What has been called the godlike role that athletes perform in the game—by making winning and losing actual—opens up the possibility of perceiving and finally understanding that which is just (Barthes

1981:25). Athletes, as winners and losers, turn the forces of the unpredictable and the asocial into the consistent and the social. In this regard they act like gods seeking to subordinate the forces existing beyond ordinary human will. These forces, like their representatives, behave like natural justice; they determine winners and losers. They are tested and confirmed by the game being played. Playing the game provides the possibility of perceiving and confirming that a natural fraternal justice exists—one to which citizens and states may indeed have access and to which they may be subject but which ultimately exists beyond their immediate and direct control.

With each game played citizens share in moments of collective moral order. In doing so, however, they make available to the state the single most important property for its own legitimacy—that is, the apparent objectified commitment of citizens (or, as some would say, "public consensus").[8] This is because both sport and the state feed into and depend upon the same style of governance and, hence, demand the same rational response from their participants. Obedience to the natural order of things becomes palatable when the responsibilities for obeying reside in the external forces of the inevitable. Obeying the governing authorities of sport or state quite literally translates as obeying nature itself. To use what already appears to be an in-place fact (citizens and states following "natural law") can be construed as highly efficient and rational. Sport has the unobtrusive ability to convey the apparent fact that public commitment and obedience to the state appear in unison with each other as well as with nature. It is therefore hardly surprising that for the modern state, sport has developed into a dominant style of expressing the nation-ness of committed and obedient citizens.

Sport captures and presents the qualities of individuality while at the same time demonstrating how such individuality, when disciplined by rational order, can become aesthetically pleasing and desirable as fraternal communality. Distinctive sports with athletes who attain substantive esteem and renown draw individuals together not just at local levels but also at the level of national consciousness. National sports become the vehicles for collective consciousness because they can appropriate and redistribute the simultaneity of human sentiments (Anderson 1992). Sharable emotions and revealed values objectify individuals as persons who can possess nation-ness.[9] They are fans, yes, but how smoothly such fanaticism turns into national pride and patrimony when "blessed" by the game.[10] I would argue that it is the repetition of playing the game that performs the bulk of this basic socializing work for sports.

With all its qualities of repetitive ritual drama, sport is the fixing and framing of form against the indeterminacies that can work against the possibility of imagining the community (Victor Turner 1988; Anderson 1992). From the repeated appearances of similar sanctioned athletic equipment, the reiterated normative and pragmatic movements of the athlete, and the reenacted procedures of how, when, and where the game should begin, pause, and end, the ritual performance of sports culturally dramatizes a bodily obedience made into the social substance of community. Particularly in its mimicry of obedience, sporting performance determines the capacity of the individual to possess community. In the Western world, for example, to find a modern state without a national sport or a citizen without a nationality would indeed be extremely difficult. Every time the game commences and every time the athlete repeats the disciplined actions that define or give form to the game, shared sentiments and knowledge make the individual perceive social community. To be part of the proceedings, to support one competitor or team rather than another, even to anticipate the actions of the athlete or the sequence of the game can all be turned to the cause of making the individual into a person with community. Such aspects of human behavior seemingly accomplish their socializing work well when they are formed by the repetition of sport's ritual performances. I would like to conclude that, as in the sporting performances of Western societies, they do so in the Waiwai performance of tïwosom just as well.

When the Cicadas First Sing

From the Translucent to the Freestanding

The Waiwai say that when they hear the sound of the *taritari* (cicada), they know that the making of farms and the planting of crops should begin.[1] They profess that after *porin tuna* (the big rains), the heat of the sun warms up the *ŕowa* (earth or soil) and energizes not only the *ŕowačew* (underground or underworld) but also the Taritari-yena (Cicada-people) who live there. Like the principal bird spirits who occupy the upper three strata of the cosmos (giving to the heavens its particular avian character), the Cicada-people pervade and master the insect domain under the earthly realm. The sounds of activity from the Cicada-people indicate that the earth is *očoro* (hot) and ready for cultivation. This regular round of knowledge exchange between the Waiwai and the Cicada-people not only helps seasonally to galvanize the agricultural labor of the village but also, more importantly, helps to maintain the continuous supply of yuca. To satisfy their constant demand for the staple crop, the Waiwai must respond every dry season to the "song" of the Cicada-people.

Waiwai culture provides for an understanding of *roma* (hunger) as the absence of *čure* (yuca bread) and/or *woto* (raw uncleaned meat). To be without one or the other is tolerable adversity; to be without both is starvation. Čure and woto can (in cultural transposition) be considered the staple foods of the Waiwai. Nonetheless, the highest percentage of their consumed foodstuffs comes not from the uncultivated forest but from their *marari* (farms).[2]

The Waiwai plant a variety of *šere* (bitter yuca tuber) as the primary crop. Within a sample area of 2,229 square meters—with the aid of Enkik, his wife, Emekuch, Utok, and his wife, Chmaku—I once recorded thirteen varieties of bitter yuca. Interestingly enough, as they reeled off the names of each to me, they included where and from whom the original cutting was acquired. Some cuttings they had acquired while journeying to strange and distant villages and some from faraway peoples who visited. Some came from the nearby Wapishana. All had stories attached to them—stories that helped to identify and name each kind of yuca plant. These represent a wonderful diversifying of the single most important crop, made intellectually approachable by the biographies of each cutting.

In addition to šere they planted a number of important secondary crops, many of which were root vegetables like šere with edible tubers high in carbohydrates. They had, for example, three varieties of ordinary yam, all classified in terms of their color. They also had a bell yam—a great favorite when roasted or when prepared as a drink. They had sweet potatoes (*Ipomaea batatas*), tania (*Dioscorea sp.*), eddoe (*Colocasis esculenta*), *peča* (unidentified), and *kamarataru* (unidentified). At strategic locations in their farms, they planted certain fruits such as papaya, pineapple, and banana but also certain crops for technical use, such as cotton (for bindings), reeds (for arrow shafts), and sisal grass (for bowstrings and rope). Much later on in my years with them, and particularly after their move from Shepariymo to Akotopono, they began to plant citrus trees among the peppers and beans of their home gardens in the village settlement. Many villagers actually collected new strands of seeds and exchanged them with each other, sowing and nurturing them for transplantation into farms or home gardens. While they enjoyed experimenting in this way with condiments and "exotic" fruits, šere still persisted as the principal crop. As the food plant providing the basic ingredients necessary for subsistence, it remains the main focus of Waiwai agriculture.

Early on in my relations with the Waiwai, while I stumbled through learning how to speak their language, I orchestrated my daily activities to make myself feel more productive as a researcher. This work concerned quite simply the main farmland of the village, located about a quarter of a mile behind the settlement.

A well-worn path snaked its way beside huge buttresses, between ancient palms, and under high, overarching boughs to the farm site. Even at this distance away from the river, the farm plots at the lower end of the site flooded in the rainy season. The heavy rains and rising river never waterlogged the rest of the plots, however, for they were situated on the incline of a hill. Here in this circular space, surrounded by the motionless columns of the forest trees, I began the dubious and yet consoling empirical work of measuring, weighing, and calculating Waiwai agricultural life.

When gauged against my emotional discomfort and initial difficulty with learning to speak Waiwai, these tasks gave me immediate satisfaction and comfort. Routine seemed to keep me sane. The learned bodily rhythms from a self-imposed timetable kept at bay the dementia of my isolation among a people living within a language different from my own. I spent long days at the farm in my first few weeks. When groups of family members came to attend to their plots, I would practice some simple greetings and even repeat those now tired questions about where plots began and ended in the farm site or what kind of crops were planted among the yuca. A good deal of what I initially learned of their language came from those early days on the farm collecting agricultural data. In addition it was from this phase of my experience with the Waiwai that my particular formal training in anthropology opened into its substantive materialist-based explanations.

Such trace to the "real" material conditions of Waiwai existence had a very special place in my relationship with anthropology. Significantly, the path reveals that it was the Waiwai and not Marxist theory that made the reality of the data discursively convincing. Holding up the supposedly freestanding theory of political economy was the Waiwai world of translucent facts. To put it somewhat differently, as I moved through the empirical force of material data to find the spirit of an anthropology only the Waiwai could teach me, I heard the song of the Cicada-people not as melody but as measurement. I had, in this phase and influence, set myself two questions to address: What were the social relations of agricultural production, and what factor(s) determined the distribution of farmland? Rather obviously—but also because of the previous ethnographers' claims about the Waiwai division of labor (Fock 1963; Yde 1965; Dagon 1967; Hills 1968)—I began by focusing on the social processes involved in the physical work of cultivating yuca. My own conclusions about the primary structure of the social relations of agriculture developed from my preliminary observations on the labor process. Two very convincing case studies presented themselves to me, both shedding light on what I considered at the time to be the core relationships governing the structure of work groups. The obvious criteria of subsistence farming (that is, cultivating crops not for wages but for personal consumption) and the use of farmland guided my quantitative analysis of individual household claims to farmland, household size, and cultivated-food requirements. These I analyzed in an attempt to understand how the bounds of farmland distribution were set. Yet behind this style of freestanding inquiry there whispered another series of ideas that addressed the same topic, but from a fundamentally different perspective. These ideas did not come from me or my Marxist theory, but from the translucent evidence of Waiwai myth. Before entering the results of the former, let me first present the latter.

THE MAWARI MYTH: THE ORIGIN OF PLANT FOODS

The brothers Mawari and Washi find themselves to be first eating the tubers of a forest vine.
Their host the Jaguar-people gathered and processed the vine like yuca.

While out collecting the vine
the brothers were approached by a little bird
who introduced them to another forest tuber
the name of which was *pitu* [penis].

At the time, neither of the brothers possessed
any sexual organs and it was not until they had eaten the pïtu
plant, slept, and awoke
that they acquired their abnormally long and large penises.

Accordingly the brothers appeared
to be on their way to becoming proper men
but were not quite yet there.

Consequently Mawari demanded
from his hostess the old Jaguar Woman
better food than the forest yuca they had been eating.

The old Jaguar Woman complied by defecating
the meat content of her meal in a cleared field
from which grew the very first domesticated yuca tuber.

A prototype of the present-day plant,
this variety [being the "heated" product of the belly] was clearly
distasteful and not liked.

The old Jaguar Woman once again returned
to the cleared field, but this time
by allowing herself to be burned to death,
she produced the proper and currently cultivated yuca.

Initiating a Farm Site

The Waiwai cultivate their fields in the vicinity of the main village, but they also cultivate and maintain what I have called "auxiliary river farms" at temporary camps upriver and downriver from the main village. A male head of household will initiate a site for a prospective farm by first surveying for suitable land along the river embankment or very close to the river. The initiator of the field cannot make the mistake of establishing a site that will be difficult to clear of its undergrowth, or may flood in the rainy season, or has poor soil and many rocks. What I did notice (after documenting the location of all the functional farm sites as well as all those no longer in use) was that some locations were much better than others and that these better locations had been purposely reused after lying fallow for many years under secondary forest growth. The Waiwai always located functional auxiliary river farms within one day's paddling from the main village. After the initiator of the farm has surveyed and chosen his site, he will *mararï ninanketu*—that is, mark out the area for clearance. Having done this, he will then formally acquaint the village leader with his plan to clear the area for a field.

Of course during the period of surveying, everyone in the village knows what the initiator has been doing. Purposeful behavior of this kind hardly goes unnoticed in the community. Indeed, it is common practice if not the protocol always to ask someone leaving the village, "*¿Ahna mïče?*" ("Where are you going?"). Even when the person asking the question knows what the answer will be, the inquiry will still be made. It is not prying, nor is it an invasion of what we may call personal privacy. It is Waiwai etiquette—both a kind of formal greeting and a request for voiced confirmation of departure. In this way everyone knows more or less what everyone else is doing when not in the village. Note that the request is not "*¿Ahče poko may?*" ("What are you doing?"), which would be too obvious and inane a question to ask a person walking past. Nor is it "*¿Ahče nhe poke may?*" ("What will you be doing?"), which clearly would make the inquiry more interrogative and less of a salutation in Waiwai terms. In a kind of circumlocution, the request seeks confirmed knowledge of where, and from where the why of where, and thus what the passing person is going to do. Such knowledge does not become formal public property, however, until it is conveyed to the village leader. Something as momentous as the clearing of the forest for the cultivation of crops gains official recognition because, in the overall scheme of agricultural production, it directly implicates the collective village community.

The village leader conveys to the work leaders the information that the initiator of a field has chosen and marked out a site. The work leaders, in turn, inform their fellow villagers. Emerging from this sequence of events will be the recruitment of able-bodied men to clear the site. The clearing of the site, like all formal communal village projects, is punctuated with onhari.

Conducive to the very principles of poyino, which ideally congeal the relations of the ewtoto, the scenes of men carrying portions of cooked meat, yuca bread, and/or drink from their homes to the meetinghouse add poignant credence to the social power of Waiwai exchange. The men's gift of food to each other contracts each of them to the day's work. Because the work implicates the collective community and has been officially sanctioned by the village leadership through the formal process, the food officially becomes a gift not from the individual men, or technically speaking from their individual households, or indeed from the women who prepared the meals, but from the village leader to the attending men. To instill the exchange with this meaning, the men, upon arriving at the meetinghouse for the communal meal, immediately place their contributions of food at the center of the circle. From there the village leader and/or a work leader will then ceremoniously hand each man a piece of meat and a section of yuca bread, after which bowls of drink will be passed around the circle. Being aware (as they should be) of the formalized public knowledge pertaining to the site clearing, each man (as I interpret it) should then offer his labor to the project in counterprestation for eating the food from onhari.

Underbrushing and Tree Felling

There exist two stages to the clearing of a field site: *načpokyatu* or *ačipso* (underbrushing) and *nametu* or *amaša* (tree felling). Clearing usually takes place at the end of the big rainy season (the beginning of August), with the intention of felling the trees in time to allow the hot midsummer sun to dry out the felled trees before burning.

To clear the underbrush, the men form a work line that moves in one direction, chopping and breaking until the designated area has been cleared. It is uncomfortable and irritating work due mainly to the bites and stings received from the multitude of angry insects that are disturbed as the men level the undergrowth of bush and sapling trees. Whenever I joined them in underbrushing, I always recall to myself a sense of what the pragmatic intent might have been for the ant-biting ritual of Waiwai manhood.

The fact that the initiate of the ant-biting ritual had to display the will, strength, and fortitude to overcome one of the single most pervasive irritants of the forest must have been, it seems to me, reassuring to both the initiate and the community dependent upon his triumph. During the sustained attacks from the irritants of bite and sting, both the displayed body in the ritual and the working body in the forest have to express the resilience for which they have been tested.

As in the ritual of the displayed body, so too in the clearing of a field site—the working body complies with the staged rigor of a cultural logic and must succeed within it. Without the triumph of this resilience, the process of clearing a site would neither be as productive nor carry that particular sense of collective village co-operation. Once the underbrush has been leveled and has provided more room for the workers to maneuver, the men then cut down the trees.

Physically demanding, this lumbering among some of the world's largest and hardest trees can also be dangerous. The work has to be well coordinated, with every man knowing what he is doing and how what he is doing will affect those working around him. The men work in groups that do their best to progress together in the same direction. Sometimes two or three of the men work together, chopping at one giant until it falls. The cuts opening up on the trunk usually allow them to predict where the tree will fall. The difficulty, however, lies in knowing when it will fall and how soon one needs to warn those working in the area of its impending plunge. Normally, when the remaining thickness of trunk can no longer hold the weight of the tree, a loud crack will warn the nearby workers. Before cutting down the giant, all the surrounding smaller trees are partially cut into but left standing. As the giant plunges, it falls on and brings down the smaller trees. The concertina effect is unpredictable, and men have been seriously injured while scurrying away as trees fall to the ground one after the other.

The Waiwai have many uses for the few cutting tools they possess, but the principal use of the ax, machete, and file is clearing the forest. Every household seeks to obtain and possess at least one of these tools. Historically it would have been a case of knowing how to make or have access to a stone ax or other cutting implement. The metal ax, machete, and file—manufactured outside Waiwai society—became coveted tools through regional exchange. In the past they were main items for trade between neighboring communities. Used and new, these particular metal tools were carried from the Guiana coast and Brazil through the extensive trading networks of the hinterland (Butt Colson 1973; Todorov 1987; Clendinnen 1989). The trading networks existed long before European contact with the Americas. They later became the means of acquiring valuable European goods without having to travel to the source of manufacture. Bartering for metal tools has acted as a longtime justification for visiting neighboring communities, perhaps second only to the search for spouses. The *yawaka* (ax), *kachipara* (machete), and *kuru-kuru* (file) have today become indispensable instruments of labor in Waiwai agricultural work.

I would like to add that in my estimation the demand for these items comes not only from the social pressure to contribute to the collective in ways that others do, but also from the pressure to contribute with the objects that others do. This stems from the observed Waiwai wish to bring the very best effort to the communal arena of agricultural work, which includes bringing high-status trading items such as metal tools. The willingness to apply these tools to the work effort signals the high priority and social esteem the contributing worker ascribes to the collective effort. The Waiwai believe that the collective effort becomes enhanced by the presence of the metal tool. Thus every household covets them because every household desires to be observed as a contributing member of the community, confidently supporting and strengthening the collective effort with its labor and prestige tools. The individual, independent attempts to acquire such tools through trade additionally confirm this commitment to the collective. Their ultimate success is the result of a vigilant appreciation not necessarily of the externally manufactured metal tool, but of the particular communal means of Waiwai food production.

Kati and the Double Burn

The burning of the dead trees and dried leaves in the clearing takes place during the middle of the dry season (ordinarily in September). The Waiwai call this process *natniyatu* or *athiso*. Burning has to be correctly executed in order to achieve a properly productive field. Many villagers can recall and identify numerous cases when large sections of fields were not planted because of inadequate burning. They can also recall cases when a field had been burned too early (that is, when the leaves and timber were still fresh and green), so that its initiator had few people taking up farm plots there.

It has been claimed by certain Western experts that, apart from being an excellent way of getting rid of the obstruction of fallen trees, the burning process adds desirable nutrients to the chemically and mineralogically poor soils of the region (Dagon 1967; Hills 1968). Given what we can interpret from Waiwai ideas about heat and the body, however, the burning of felled trees and undergrowth may be better understood not as some cultural "limit" to their knowledge of nature nor as a "lack" in the communication of new techniques, crops, and market system (Hills 1968:44), but rather as the result of their own informed theories.[3]

From the Waiwai point of view the application of heat from the sun and from fire transforms the site of the now dead forest plants into a field for cultivated food plants. The applied heat infuses a transformative energy, so that whatever it burns turns into an area of potential fertility. It is as if the very ground heats up to help gestate the planted crops. Starting from the initial condition of that which is burned, it should properly undergo this kind of double burning from the sun and from fire—a double process involving a positive transformation of the nondomesticated and the raw into the domesticated and the cooked. One might note here how, so like the bodies of animals and humans, the "bodies" of trees and undergrowth exact a diligent circumspection from the Waiwai. Moreover, the caution arises for the very reason (and much-celebrated insight) that continuity prevails between human and nonhuman beings, however different (Århem 1996; Bloch 1998; Rival 1998b).

Mortal life requires the substantive heated energy of katï (oil or fat or resin) flowing in the body. Unlike the spiritual vitality of ekatï, which departs from the living body and actually contributes to its death, katï remains as the dying organic substance of corporeality. When burned, the katï of the body will intensify the heat, further infusing the transformative process. In the cleared fields of meat/wood and fat/resin, this double burn has obvious value, reinforced not only by the pragmatic world of subsistence agriculture but also by the Waiwai world of myth acting at a deeper level of consciousness.

In the same way that the old Jaguar Woman enacted the double process of her heated belly and cremated body to produce the final and correct food plant, so too do the felled trees and undergrowth of a cleared field become subject to the double burn of the sun and fire to ensure the proper cultivation of yuca and other food plants.

Marking Up and Distributing Farm Plots

The Waiwai do not clear away any further debris from the field, as very soon after the burning they will begin planting. Before this, however, the field must be divided into farm plots. It is expected— and indeed it is the regular practice—for every initiator of a field to claim a farm plot in the field he initiates. Custom declares that the heads of households who assisted the initiator in the underbrushing and/or tree felling may also receive farm plots in the same field. No household ever has more than one plot in any single field. The initiator agrees to claims for plots depending on the availability of space and the number of requests. Only those who have made a request will be assigned plots. The initiator apportions strips of land by marking out traverse parallel boundary lines along the length of the field. The area between the lines will contain the amount of land allocated to each recipient household. The field will not, however, be divided to accommodate every legitimate request if these exceed reasonable availability. To divide the field in such a fashion as to reduce the reasonable size of plots would be to reduce the potential individual yield of each plot. Depending on the size of the field, there seems to be a standard area requirement for each farm plot that is not determined by any precise form of measurement but nonetheless fits acceptable social criteria. Some small fields have an area that will allow for only two plots. The more familiar regular-size field averages six to eight plots.[4] Of course if as few as two households request plots in a field capable of further division, farm plots can be larger.

After the marking up and distributing by the initiator, the new occupants put down their own boundary markers, called *wokpo*. This merely consists of picking up lengths of burned timber and laying them down along the assigned lines already demarcated by the initiator. Once in place, the wokpo become the formal boundaries between farm plots and establish the occupancy of the plot with the occupant's household. Later, during primary-phase planting, the occupying householders will make a point of planting noticeable high-growing crops such as sugarcane and bananas at strategic points along the wokpo. Long after the growth of crops has obscured the placement of the wokpo, the boundary lines will still remain distinguishable.

The custom of land occupancy establishes that while the household occupants of a farm plot continue to be resident members of the village, no one outside their household can harvest from their plot. There is but one exception to this, applying to travelers from other villages who, on their journey, sojourn temporarily at an auxiliary river farm. From these farms the travelers may take, with discretion, whatever foodstuffs they require. If, however, an occupant of a farm plot happens to be present on the site, the travelers will not take from any of the plots. On the contrary it is courteous for an attending farm-plot occupant to offer provisions to the travelers before the latter have recourse to asking or taking. This custom of travelers'

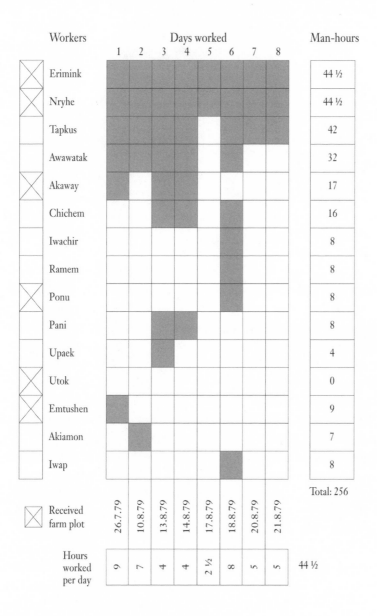

Figure 2. Result of study on work for field 9

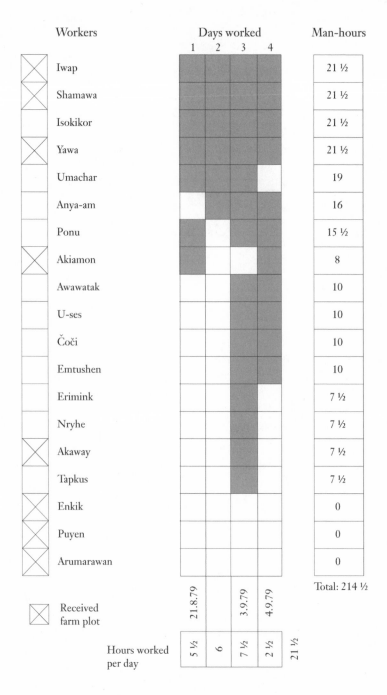

Figure 3. Result of study on work for field 4

use applies only to auxiliary river farms and not to the main village farms, where, by implication, hospitality should always be present.

Planting Phases

Planting begins in earnest during October, November, and December, the period after the dry season, and—if for some reason a field has been cut late—sometimes even in January, after the short rainy season. The Waiwai system of intercropping entails a sowing sequence that consigns yuca to the last phase of planting. In the first phase, *yamso*, they plant the secondary (nonstaple) crops. In the second phase, *umonoso* or *nïmarïčetu*, they plant the primary (staple) crop, yuca.

They first plant the banana suckers and sugarcane cuttings, then the yams, sweet potatoes, tania, eddoes, corn, and pineapples. They keep the pineapples, sisal grass (*Bromelia* sp.), and even sugarcane in regular groups and never plant them individually between the yuca, saying that the pineapple and sisal grass in particular choke the yuca, while the pointed and serrated leaves of these plants scratch the legs of the women when they come to reap. They allow only the sweet potatoes, tania, eddoes, peča, and kamarataru to grow in between the yuca. Although dictated by the privileging of yuca, yamso does not negatively affect the secondary crops. During yamso good farmers will effectively arrange their plots in such a manner as to gain the most benefit from all their crops, both primary and secondary. For instance the plant suckers of sugarcane and bananas will not be unduly harmed if they are located in waterlogged ground, while yuca tubers, if placed in such terrain, would certainly perish. The household members of a farm plot actually control this procedure during yamso by planting the secondary plants in strategic positions in and around their plot. Through this procedure only the remaining ground within their plot will be allowed to accommodate the subsequently planted yuca stems. They reserve the largest portion of the land for the primary crop of yuca.

The remarkably simple process of secondary-phase planting belies the fundamental significance of yuca in Waiwai agrarian life.

Umonoso is invariably a collective village activity performed primarily by the men, although women can and do take part. First they collect the yuca cuttings from the old farms, fellow villagers collecting the cuttings from their own farms and donating them to the household occupants of the new farm plot. Once they have collected and assembled the cut bundles of yuca stems at the site of the new farm, the work leader will then distribute them among the gathered workers. Each worker proceeds to insert two or three stems of yuca (about 0.3 meters long), by half their length and bud upward, into the already prepared mounds. About the size of a football, the mounds are set about 1.2 to 1.5 meters apart from each other. Nothing else is required. When the space remaining after the primary-phase planting has been filled with the yuca cuttings of the secondary-phase planting, the major work on farms has been completed.

Harvesting Cycles

The approximate growing period of nine moons for yuca tubers requires that crops planted during or by the end of the dry season will be mature by the following big rains. All *amokaši* (harvesting) has, therefore, to take place from fields planted in the previous dry season.

Harvesting from a new farm will occur when the crop has ripened and, if replanting takes place on the same farm, it will continue for three or four dry seasons. Weeding and general maintenance of a field, called *aywaši*, takes place whenever household members harvest from their farm plot. Every season the farm sustains a reduced rate of crop yield; therefore, whenever they reap, farmers replant in the same mounds from which they take their tubers. This kind of intermittent planting, concomitant with the regular clearing and planting of new fields, offsets the gradual loss of a field's productivity.

The season after the first field has been planted—that is, at the time of its first fruiting, a second site will be cleared, burned, and planted on. By the third dry season the crop yield from the first field will be markedly reduced and reaping will be more concentrated on the second field, which has begun its output. In the fourth season the yield from the first field drops off drastically, and it is soon left to fallow. The yield from the second field has likewise been reduced, and major demands now become placed upon the third field. This cyclical process is perennial to the Waiwai agricultural system. The seasonal planting cycle, in coordination with the four-season production capability of a field, offers a constant supply of food plants.

Communal Work Groups
Two types of communal groups can actually be identified as operating the agricultural work and the processing of plant foods—a large and a small communal work group. What I have called "an interhousehold work force" gives form to both types of communal work groups. The large communal work group principally performs the tasks of underbrushing, tree felling, and yuca planting but on irregular occasions may be seen weeding and harvesting yuca. The small communal work group, in its turn, principally performs the tasks of yuca peeling and grating but may also occasionally be found surveying and marking up as well as underbrushing and tree felling. The communal groups for underbrushing and tree felling are exclusively composed of men, while the communal group for yuca planting is predominantly composed of men but not exclusively so—for on occasion women may be found helping with yuca planting. Very infrequently men may be found assisting women's small communal groups with the peeling of yuca but never in a group grating yuca, which would exclusively comprise women.

An intrahousehold work group also provides the social labor for agriculture and plant-food processing. In other words it is the specific personnel inside of a single household who give form to the intrahousehold work group. Defined and determined by marriage and the individual family, a household can—at its most comprehensive—be comprised of a husband and wife, their non-married children, the wife's nonmarried siblings, and any unmarried parents of the spouse. The intrahousehold work group principally performs the tasks of primary-phase planting, weeding, harvesting, peeling, grating, squeezing, sifting, and baking. On an irregular basis it may be seen surveying and marking up or even planting yuca. Both men and women of the same household do the primary-phase planting, and occasionally a single household (usually that of resident Wapishana) may be seen planting its own yuca without help from others. The intrahousehold work group also shares equally with the small communal work group the tasks of peeling and grating—that is, one may just as likely see a group of women from joint households peeling and grating together as one would see women from the same household doing the same thing. Only women of the intrahousehold group squeeze, sift, and bake yuca. Very irregularly one may see a woman grating, squeezing, sifting, or baking yuca by herself. It is, however, the standard practice for a man to survey and mark up or burn a field on his own.

All the preliminary stages in transforming the forest into a field—that is, surveying and marking up, underbrushing, tree feeling, and burning—are exclusively the work of men. The planting of yuca can also be considered predominately the work of men. This is not to say that the observed labor of women does not contribute to these stages of "men's" work; the Waiwai reference here is specifically to the principal task at hand, which in their paradigm does not include, for example, the work of women in preparing and cooking food for onhari and the midday meals, which the women oftentimes even carry to the location of men's work in the forest. They classify weeding, harvesting, and peeling as predominately women's work, but from time to time men can be seen helping the women of their households in these tasks. Grating, squeezing, sifting, and baking are exclusively the work of women. Again, I should mention that even in these "women-exclusive" tasks, the labor of men could well be acknowledged in the Waiwai paradigm, but it does not hold an overall prevailing presence in representing the task at hand. I am speaking here especially about the various indispensable baskets used by women during the conversion of yuca into bread. In every single case the making of these baskets is the exclusive craft of men.[5] In keeping with the Waiwai paradigm, therefore, only with yuca (the primary crop) and in the process of umonoso (the secondary-phase planting) does their formal classifying acknowledge the equal labor of men and women.

The agricultural paradigm denies the presence of the labor of women during the transformation of the forest into field. In its turn the culinary paradigm denies the presence of men's labor during the transformation of yuca into food. In other words the "killing" of the bodies of trees is the work of men, while the "killing" of the bodies of yuca is the work of women. The classifying organizes relations between humans and plants principally in terms of gender. It also appears to give priority to the labor of men. Cultivated foods cannot be processed without the conversion of forest into field and of forest plants into fibers (for the making of baskets by men). In this sense the classifying gives preeminence to masculine labor. This privileging of the interface between the forest and human masculinity extends from the sector of hunting to that of agriculture. The legitimacy for the privileging stems from the logic of relations drawn between the bodies of men and the dangers of the forest. Human susceptibility to the dangers of transcendent ekatï is at its very highest during the killing of living beings. The forest is filled with living beings that humans kill. Their transcendent vitalities place the human killer in mortal danger. As I have suggested earlier, Waiwai collective ideas about humans consider the individual bodies of men to be more closed than those of women, and body adornment has the function of further containing men's bodies to make them less prone to any loss of spiritual vitality. Women's bodies, on the other hand, being more open—indeed, more vulnerable—to the loss of bodily substances, can only be protected from the possibility of vitality loss by reducing their contact with the forest and the acts of killing in the forest. Only when converted into the circular realm of a village settlement can the forest become the benign site in which women regularly dwell. Within the safe confines of the household group and the village community, women accomplish their task of converting farm products into edible foods. Men make the dangers of the forest safe with their bodies, while, with their bodily efforts, women do the same to the elements that have been brought into the domestic setting.

It can be reasonably argued that Waiwai ideas do convincingly constitute and associate the social categories of gender with particular authoritative knowledge about land and labor. It can even be concluded from this that their social relations of agricultural production begin specifically within gender categories and direct factors determining both the distribution of farmland and the consumption of cultivated products. It should come as no surprise, therefore, that the principal social domains charged with the production of food and the sustenance of the body can be construed to be the gendered spaces of the domestic household and the collective village community. Yet what relations offer the Waiwai paradigm its means to represent gender with household and communal groupings?

Labor and the Cultivation of Fields

Land clearing and field preparation for Shepariymo in 1979 continued as usual even though at the time many able-bodied men were absent from the village. In my records for July 26, 1979, Erimink, the initiator of field 9, arranged for underbrushing on the field he had surveyed. The men who attended the session on that day worked for nine hours. Working a total of forty-four and a half hours, it finally took the men eight days to clear field 9. A varying number of men and boys attended the work sessions on each day (see fig. 2). When the land was cleared, only five of the eleven men who contributed their labor received farm plots within the field. Erimink and Nryhe attended every day of work and contributed the same amount of labor time as each other. In terms of household contribution, however, Nryhe's household provided more labor time than Erimink's household—that is, if the working hours of both Nryhe and (his visiting relative) Tapkus are added together as a single contribution representative of their household effort in communal work, they would total eighty-six and a half hours, while Erimink and his son Pani together total only fifty-two and a half man-hours. Both households received farm plots, but the combined working effort of

Awawatak and his three sons, Chichem, Iwachir, and Ramem, who totaled sixty-four man-hours between them, had no reward of land. This was in marked contrast to Utok, who received land but did not attend any work session. In the short term (and in my recorded calculations on the amount of work time put in and the direct concrete gains received), there seemed to be little if any correlation between labor and land. The manifest advantages of attracting men who have able-bodied household dependents to communal work sessions would seem, however, to be obvious.

On August 21, 1979, Iwap, the initiator of field 4, began proceedings for underbrushing and tree felling. I recorded both underbrushing and tree felling to have been accomplished in twenty-one and a half hours (see fig. 3). Field 4 was larger than field 9, but it nevertheless took almost half the time to clear. One explanation for this has to do with the greater number of workers attending daily sessions for field 4 than for field 9. During the four days of work Iwap attracted sixteen men, who all but cleared the entire area on day three. This can be compared with the eight days it took to clear field 9, two of which took place when Erimink, Nryhe, and Tapkus were the only ones working and another when Erimink and Nryhe were the only workers at the site.

Eight men received farm plots in field 4. Three recipients of farm plots were absent from the village during the period of work on the field and hence did not contribute to any of the sessions. Eleven men worked and did not receive farm plots in the field. I recorded that some of them (such as Isokikor, Umachar, Anya-am, and Ponu) had high man-hour figures. In this case as well, the results of distribution do not offer a commensurate balance between labor and land. There were no instances of intrahousehold members taking part in work sessions for field 4. Even if we included the workers of field 9, the major form of contributed labor for both fields would still come from the interhousehold relations between men.

With the working group of field 9, the predominant linking relationships came from those of wife's father / daughter's husband, wife's brother / sister's husband (see fig. 4). These were between

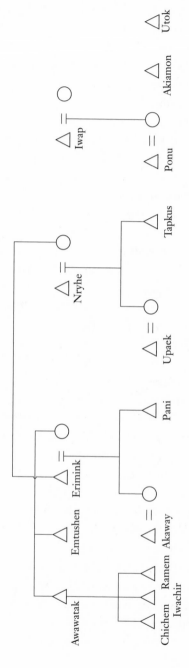

Figure 4. Kinship relations between men working on field 9

Erimink and Awawatak = wb/zh; Erimink and Emtushen = wb/zh; Erimink and Akaway = dh/wf; Erimink and Nryhe = zh/wb; Iwap and Ponu = dh/wf; Upaek and Tapkus = wb/zh; Akaway and Pani = wb/zh. This excludes the (affinal and) potential in-law relationship between mother's brother and sister's son, which existed between Awawatak and Pani, Emtushen and Pani, and Erimink and Tapkus. There was also the affinal tie between Erimink and Awawatak's sons expressed by a wbs/fzh relationship. Of the ten represented household groups, Erimink's formed the axis to a linked cluster of six. The interhousehold kinship tie brought together the groups of Emtushen, Awawatak, Akaway, and Nryhe and, through Nryhe, Upaek. Iwap and Ponu formed a separate cluster bound to each other by the dh/wf tie. Akiamon and Utok exchanged fictive sibling ties. The only other relationship linking household groups was the full sibling tie between Awawatak and Emtushen. Thus, with the exception of Iwap, Akiamon, Ponu, and Utok, all interhousehold ties between Erimink and the men who attended work on his field were in-law defined.

Among the working group of field 4 the ties of relations were numerous and more complex (see fig. 5). There were seventeen household groups represented, forming nine separate clusters, each one structured by a wf/dh and/or wb/zh relationship. Categorically, the dominant binding tie was the in-law relationship: Shamawa and Isokikor = dh/wf; Shamawa and Enkik = dh/wf; Shamawa and Umachar = wb/zh (Umachar and Shamawa's wife, Awam, called each other brother and sister—Umachar's father was once married to Shamawa's wife's mother); Enkik and Akiamon = zh/wb; Isokikor and Anya-am = zh/wb; Anya-am and Yawa = wf/dh; Umachar and Arumarawan = wf/dh; Ponu and Umachar = zh/wb; Iwap and Ponu = dh/wf; Ponu and Puyen = wb/zh; Puyen and Akaway = W (classificatory) B / (classificatory) zh; U-ses and Puyen = wb/zh; Iwap and U-ses = wdh/wmh; Erimink and Akaway = dh/wf; Nryhe and Erimink = wb/zh; Erimink and Emtushen = wb/zh; Erimink and Awawatak = wb/zh; Arumarawan and Yawa =zs/mb. All other ties that existed outside the household and linked household to house-

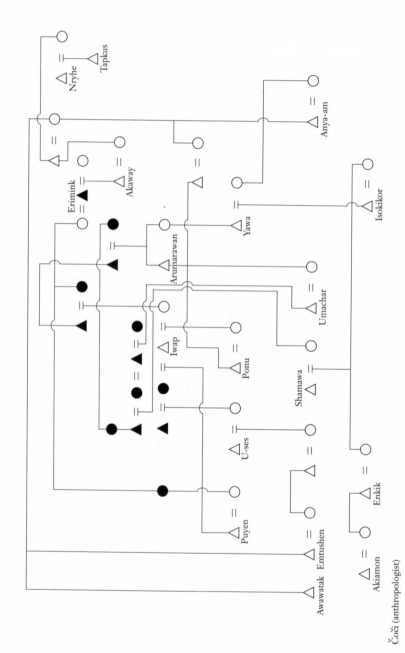

Figure 5. Kinship relations between men working on field 4

hold through men were: Arumarawan and Ponu = F/S; Yawa and Isokikor = F/S; Erimink and Anya-am = WS/MH (F/S); Iwap and Puyen = F/S; Awawatak and Emtushen = B/B.

Marriage forges formal alliances between affines. These alliances tend, particularly for men, to be consolidated in the coresidency custom of uxorilocality, where the social commitment between in-laws expresses itself through such activities as assistance in yuca production. Assisting each other in the pursuit of quelling the provocative forest partially fulfills the moral duty implicit in the in-law relation. Hosting or attending work sessions for an in-law satisfies a good deal of the expectations from the relationship, regardless of any material remuneration. The immaterial but calculated deposit (that is, the moral worth thought to be placed in the work sessions) could be interpreted as a kind of social investment. Configured in terms of what I would call affinity, the investment does not necessarily amount to any immediate rewards to the individual investor, but rather to further assistance promised in the long term to the community as a whole. The amount of calculated investments gets "banked" in the collective community as the expected reserve from the affinal relation.

In temporal and quantitative terms this is not a case of an accumulated time or an ever-increasing amount, but of repetition and supplement. As I understand it from Waiwai ideas about the character of the wošin and its contrast to the epeka (when making community into poyino), in sequence, the special in-law feature of social distance comes after the regular relation of epeka. As it does so—that is, as it follows epeka, it becomes an addition that supplies the collective community with a significant reserve for social life. Unlike the repetition of itself or the repetition of epeka, the wošin relation supplements a village community built upon epeka relations. There could be no poyino without it. In communal masculine work sessions (such as underbrushing and tree feeling), affinity acts in supplement and, in so doing, permits the ideal of community bounds to consolidate its fulfillment in filiation. In this way marriage and the in-law relation guarantee a cycle of intimate gender relations not only among humans but also between humans and the social world of plants.

The social distance ascribed to affinity allows the in-law relationship to be the correct representative means for providing gender with its basic work groups in agriculture and cookery. In the Waiwai paradigm the ascribed social distance in affinity serves to facilitate the human curtailment of the provocational harm from the forest. Within agriculture and cookery, the acts of human violence against plants seem to be more appropriately dealt with through the formal space of relations between in-laws. One could argue in Waiwai terms that a greater dispersal of the wrongdoing involved in killing occurs when in-laws share in the wrong or ugliness. The logic of the retribution from the family of the deceased stipulates that vengeance will target the spiritual vitality of the killer. Sharing the wrongdoing of the killing with relatives connected by the distance of affinity protects all concerned, because the avenger has too wide a social chasm to traverse in order to exact vengeance. Even the act of violence against plants seems to be facilitated by the affinal relations maintained between humans and plants. In general the predatory act itself acquires its most justified means through the formal distance ascribed to affinity. I would like to reiterate, however, that in the conclusiveness of the ideal, the very act of assistance from the affine takes its reference from and behaves very much like the desired altruism of poyino—the ultimate attainment of the collective village community. In other words the actual gender relations of household and communal work groups active in agriculture and cookery, while providing the groups with their affinal means of representation, nevertheless permit affinity to copy the expected moral outcome of filiation. It seems that in order to make the dangerous intercourse between humans and the forest safe, gender encourages affinity to disguise itself with the mimicked attributes of filialness. The tactic of mimicry works by diverting the spiritual retribution of plants away from the original altruism of filialness and redirecting it toward its copy. There the retribution will inevitably be lost and made harmless, unable to contact and hurt not only the original but also the affinal mimic itself. It is as if—were filiation openly used to accomplish the task of dealing with plants—the wrongdoing and vengeance from the killing would run too easily through its relations and destroy them. Thus, between men who work together, between women who work together, and between men and women who work together in managing the forest, gender and affinity instigate an apotropaic means of dealing with the will of plants.

Waiwai labor organizes itself to transform the forest into cultivated fields in order for humans to eat the body of plants on a regular basis. The way of determining access to such fields and the safe consumption of plants begins with membership in an individual household of the village. The household can only come into being as a result of marriage. When a man and a woman form the social space of marriage and develop it into a parental space with a child, society allows them direct access to their own farms. The body of plants becomes available to them from the circular site of the yuca village. Yet only through communal village labor—that is, through interhousehold groups, will the individual household attain the yuca body as a meal. The forest has first to be approached by the collective. In Waiwai ideas the massive, vibrant force of the forest is far too powerful for a single individual to deal with safely. Its vulnerability—indeed, one of the attributes allowing it to be successfully managed by humans—is its divisibility: one collective against another collective, both capable of being divided and made manageable for safe distribution. In the case of the forest collective, its divisibility into cultivated fields and farm plots provides for the human claims and allocations. In the case of the human collective, Waiwai society determines that it is the individual household that acquires priority over the divisible product of the forest. One of the early questions I posed in my quantitative analysis of agriculture was why this should be so.

Household's Priority and Forest's Divisibility

In November 1979 Shepariymo had twenty-two fields in various stages of productivity, with the oldest and the lowest producers dat-

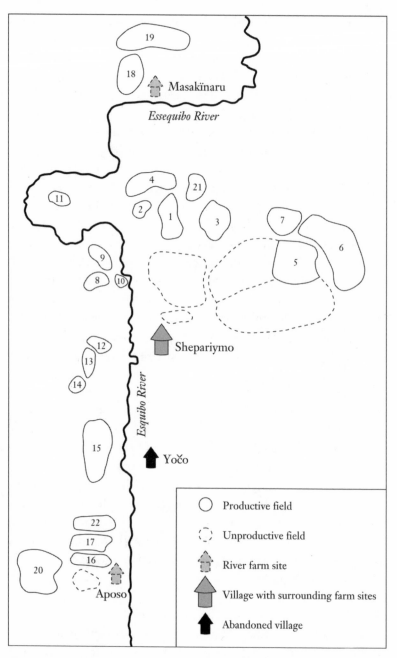

Map 2. Map of Fields

ing from 1975. Six fields were at river locations: two at Masakïnaru and four at Aposo (see map 2). I found sixteen fields in the vicinity of Shepariymo. I calculated that from a total of twenty-two fields there were 101 household farms for an overall population of 139 people, divided into twenty-seven individual household groups. Fields number 4, 9, 10, 11, 12, and 22 (see fig. 6) were the most recent; they were planted in November 1979 and were not yet productive. The fields of 1978 were number 6, 8, 14, 17, 19, and 21. These had their first harvest in mid-1979, thus their yield was very high. So, too, were those of the 1977 fields, number 6, 8, 14, 17, 19, and 21. The fields with the lowest yields, number 2, 13, 20, 5, and 15, were planted in 1976 and 1975. It should be remembered that in any given year fields with the highest productivity are always those of the two preceding consecutive years. In 1979 the fields with the highest productive rates were those from 1978 and 1977, which were in their first and second crop phase respectively. The 1976 and 1975 fields were in their third and fourth year of low and sporadic yields.

Of the 101 recorded farms, 58 were measured, with the names of individual household owners and the history of productivity documented. There were no data for fields 20 and 22. It was known, however, that both fields 20 and 22 were located at Aposo and were initiated (number 20 in 1976 and number 22 in 1979) by U-ses, the head of household R (see table 1 for household census data). There were no measurements for fields 4, 5, 9, 10, 11, 12, 13, 15, and 16, but distribution of household farms in these fields had been documented.

When a newly wedded couple forms an independent household, it is mutually understood that until their first child has been secured in the world after its first twelve moons, they should harvest their crops from the wife's father's farms. This is why there were no farms recorded for households E and F. Similarly, there were no farms recorded for household Y, for in the year of its first child and the clearing of its first field in 1978, its members decided to go on an extended visit to Surinam. The field they cleared (22) had been given over to the wife's father, U-ses.

There is an exception to the custom that only married couples

Number	Name	Sex	Approximate age	Household relations	House
1	Nryhe	M	35–45	Husband	A
2	Wsae	F	35–45	Wife	
3	Iceaw	F	3	Daughter	
4	Anathi	F	2	Daughter	
5	Ethapr	F	15	Daughter	
6	Tapkus	M	18	Brother's Son	
7	Arthtmern	M	11	Son	
8	Erimink	M	35–45	Husband	B
9	Chiwosom	F	35–45	Wife	
10	Pani	M	15	Son	
11	Araip	M	3	Son	
12	Ene-euk	M	11	Son	
13	Inaernest	F	13	Daughter	
14	Inatmert	F	8	Daughter	
15	Chipowi	M	11	Wife's Son	
16	I-ioay	M	4	Wife's Son	
17	Ichamap	M	2	Wife's Son	
18	Puyen	M	25–35	Husband	C
19	Itokmir	F	25–35	Wife	
20	Yawa	M	25–35	Husband	D
21	Utumat	F	35–40	Wife	
22	Amakayan	M	17	Son	
23	Rem-me	M	11	Son	
24	Eya-ays	M	14	Son	
25	Akais	M	Under 5	Son	
26	Sai	M	Under 5	Son	
27	Ayras	M	Under 5	Son	
28	Emiy	F	1	Daughter	
29	Chape	F	60–70	Mother	d
30	Anya-am	M	20	Husband	E
31	Ihar	F	17	Wife	
32	Muno	M	1	Son	
33	Isokikor	M	19	Husband	F
34	Ika0aror	F	16	Wife	
35	Ohnch	M	1	Son	
36	Anawach	M	21	Husband	G
37	Netcha	F	21	Wife	
38	Ominai	F	2	Wife's Daughter	
39	Ponu	M	23	Husband	H
40	Hyawa	F	20	Wife	
41	Wsae	F	2	Wife's Daughter	
42	Ayamatat	M	1	Son	

Number	Name	Sex	Approximate age	Household relations	House
43	Iwap	M	45–55	Husband	I
44	Amishamish	F	35–45	Wife	
45	Akaway	M	20	Husband	J
46	Nisu	F	19	Wife	
47	Riakwo	F	1	Daugher	
48	Arumaw	F	50–60	Mother	
49	Shawu	F	50–60	Father's Wife	
50	Chichem	M	22	Husband	K
51	Atmik	F	21	Wife	
52	Ipamar	M	25–35	Husband	L
53	Iknukim	F	25-35	Wife	
54	Rona	M	8	Son	
55	Unitak	F	1	Daughter	
56	Upaek	M	18	Husband	M
57	T-tawore	F	17	Wife	
58	Utech	M	1	Son	
59	Retawp	M	35–45	Husband	N
60	Ketmar	F	35–45	Wife	
61	T-tecowe	F	16	Daughter	
62	Ithoaw	M	Under 5	Son	
63	Tonchrysos	M	12	Son	
64	Riaaweshanth	F	Under 5	Daughter	
65	Sypat	F	8	Daughter	
66	Yar	F	2	Duaghter	
67	Shamawa	M	35-45	Husband	O
68	Awam	F	35–45	Wife	
69	Aruyowk	M	18	Son	
70	Eriwoch	F	22	Daughter	
71	Eus	F	5	Daughter's Daughter	
72	Arym	F	12	Dughter	
73	Ncifran	F	5	Daughter	
74	Shoa	M	10	Son	
75	Sorewea	M	14	Son	
76	Enkik	M	25–35	Husband	P
77	Emekuch	F	25–35	Wife	
78	Inat	M	Under 5	Son	
79	Rayi	M	Under 4	Son	
80	Uewmas	M	1	Son	
81	Emtushen	M	20–25	Husband	Q
82	Apimach	F	20–25	Wife	
83	Rance	M	Under 5	Son	

Number	Name	Sex	Approximate age	Household relations	House
84	U-ses	M	45–55	Husband	R
85	Etap	F	35–55	Wife	
86	Chichem	M	18	Son	
87	Iwopar	M	11	Son	
88	Wra-a	F	15	Daughter	
89	Owimar	F	9	Duaghter	
90	Ochimorok	F	5	Daughter	
91	Awawatak	M	25–35	Husband	S
92	Anawochek	F	25–30	Wife	
93	Smaro	F	Under 5	Son	
94	Aswa	M	Under 3	Son	
95	Iwachir	M	12	Son	
96	Chichem	M	11	Son	
97	Ramem	M	7	Son	
98	Apakan	F	50–60	Wife's Mother	t
99	Akiamon	M	35–45	Husband	T
100	Akuchiruw	F	35–40	Wife	
101	Uchimauk	F	1	Daughter	
102		M	Under 3	Son	
103	Ukupanasur	F	13	Daughter	
104	Iwatarie	F	5	Daughter	
105	Shamew	M	45-55	Husband	U
106	Aruim	F	35–45	Wife	
107	Ramem	M	11	Son	
108	Sayama	M	4	Son	
109	Utok	M	25–35	Husband	V
110	Chmaku	F	35–45	Wife	
111	Aynat	F	8	Daughter	
112	Ierthan	M	Under 5	Son	
113	Staneta	M	Under 2	Son	
114	Arumarawan	M	45–55	Husband	W
115	Yenayaw	F	35–45	Wife	
116	Aruchiripin	M	23–25	Son	
117	Ska-a	M	4	Son	
118	Eyapen-n	F	15	Daughter	
119	Akasar	F	13	Daughter	
120	Umachar	M	35–45	Husband	X
121	Akuis	F	20	Wife	
122	Orus	F	2	Daughter	
123	Uraet	F	1	Daughter	

Number	Name	Sex	Approximate age	Household relations	House
124	Akow	M	25–35	Husband	Y
125	Apuw	F	25–35	Wife	
126	Ionk	M	1	Son	
127	Aywek	M	25–35	Husband	Z
128	Awa-ach	F	25–35	Wife	
129	Ysae	M	8	Son	
130		M	2–6	Daughter	
131	Itup	M	15	Husband	Az
132	Iam-mir	F	17	Wife	
133	Uwa	M	45–55	Husband	Bz
134	Akach	F	35–45	Wife	
135	Iyakar	F	1	Daughter	
136	Riama	M	3	Son	
137	Chuma	M	10	Son	
138	Erik	M	7	Son	
139	Owipat	F	17	Daughter	
140	Čoči	M		Visitor	Cz

can be identified with farm plots. For example, when a married man dies, his eldest son takes over the principal masculine identification with the farmland. He has to be unmarried and living in the household of his deceased father. When he marries, however, the land remains with the deceased father's household—that is, with his mother and her remaining dependents. If his mother remarries, masculine identification with the land passes on to her new husband. Throughout this scenario, the land continues to be identified with the household of the mother and her young dependants. This was the situation for households B and E. After succeeding to the head of his dead father's household, Anya-am subsequently married and formed his own household group (E). When he did so, he forfeited his identification with the land he held as trustee from his father for dependence upon his wife's father's farms. His widowed mother remarried into household B, carrying the use of her ex-husband's land with her. Thus household B acquired not only a wife but also her three dependent children and her household land.

Given these qualifications, it can be seen that all households in

Shepariymo, barring those mentioned above, had access to farm plots for their own subsistence requirements. The actual size of fields varied from 0.6 (21) to 4.8 (6) hectares. The number of farms in a field did not exceed ten. The farm size with the highest frequency (that of seventeen) fell within the class interval 0.2 and 0.3 hectare. There was a cluster of 48 farms within the 0.1 and 0.5 hectare-range, which constituted 82.8 percent of the total number of cultivated farm plots measured.

Households Y, E, F, H. and S were excluded from the survey comparing the size of household with the total size of farmland identified with each household. Households Y, E, and F were all newly formed and dependent, without direct access to cultivated land. Household H did have access to two farm plots in 1979, but previous to this it was dependent on wife's father's farms. Household S was not a full village member, although it did have access to one plot in field 15, which it had previously acquired as a member of the now abandoned Yočo village. From the twenty-two households compared, three were composed of a minimum of two occupants. All three were exceptions to the norm. For example, Itup and Iammir, the young couple of household AZ, instead of being dependent upon the wife's father, Erimink (B), was in no position to support additional members at the time. The two other households were composed of Puyen and Itokmir (C) and Iwap and Utumat (I), two couples who were many seasons into their marriages but had no dependents living with them. The rest of the household groups varied in number from three to as many as ten to a household.

Even with the exceptions of households P and B, a pattern of correlations can be shown to persist between size of farm and size of household. Those exceptional households with a minimum of two occupants and direct access to farmland had the smallest total farm area of between 0.20 and 0.80 hectares. The households with the maximum of ten occupants (barring B) had the largest total farm area of between 1.60 and 1.90 hectares. In other words as the numbers in a household increased, so too did the total area of its farmlands. The relation between size of household and size of farm was quantitatively verified.

I had thought at the time that by measuring the subsistence requirements of the household, I could further corroborate the correlation between household size and farm size. To this end I used figures from the Medical Research Council (UK) as my source for comparative analysis. The council had presented their estimates for daily energy needs in terms of age, gender, and physical activity (Nuffield Biology 1966:61). Their standard figure was 5,000 kilocalories, which they estimated to be the daily energy consumption for men nineteen years of age and over, performing extremely heavy work. I converted this figure into a single unit (or 100 percent). I then estimated all other calorie findings to this unit figure. I represented the daily requirement for each household (determined by each member's age, gender, and physical activity) by its maximum calorie unit figure. That is, each individual's highest unit figure, tallied with that of his or her fellow household members, constituted what I awkwardly called a "Household's Estimated Maximum Daily Calorie Requirement"—HEMDCR. When, for example, I established that household X had a total calorie standard figure of between 5,700 minimum and 10,500 maximum, I transposed this into the unit figures of between 1.15 minimum and 2.1 maximum. In other words household X—composed of a man and his wife both over the age of nineteen with two children ages one and two—would have a HEMDCR of 2.1. When I applied this scale, I corrected for age, gender, and work performed, which I could not do from simply counting heads.

The results of comparing HEMDCR with size of farm area supported the distribution pattern of that between size of household and size of farm. The frequency composition was very similar, revealing that when the level of HEMDCR rises, so too does the size of farm area. The HEMDCR and farm-area figures offered very different clusters and frequencies. The HEMDCR figures had a short range of 1.00 to 5.40. The largest cluster occurred within 1.00 to 3.00

Head of household	Household reference	Number in household	Fields									
			1	2	3	4	5	6	7	8	9	10
Nryhe	A	7	0.23517					0.4047		0.40825	■■	
Erimink	B	10								0.35136	■■	
Puyen	C	2	0.22855		0.175896	■■						
Yawa	D	10	0.23517		0.21435	■■	■■	0.5908				
Anya-am	E	3										
Isokikor	F	3										
Anawach	G	3		0.7935044								
Ponu	H	4									■■	■■
Iwap	I	2	0.409227		0.2349887	■■						
Akaway	J	4	0.2823623		0.224254	■■	■■			0.6794	■■	
Chichem	K	3										
Ipamar	L	4	0.44980									
Upaek	M	3	0.3769									
Retawp	N	8		0.7843				0.16722				
Shamawa	O	9			0.06390	■■		0.6652	0.2861			
Enkik	P	5				■■		1.0145	0.2898			
Emtushen	Q	3	0.31622								■■	
U-ses	R	7							0.2979			
Awawatak	S	7										
Akiamon	T	9				■■		0.45709	0.3158			
Shamew	U	4					■■	0.3902	0.1374			
Utok	V	5						0.1412			■■	
Arumarawan	W	6			0.154108	■■		0.7655	0.1783			
Umachar	X	4	0.28236									
Akow	Y	3										
Aywek	Z	5							0.4106			
Itup	AZ	2										
Uwa	BZ	7						0.2378				

Figure 6. Fields and farm plot size, plus distribution by household

| | | | | | Fields | | | | | | | Total Household farm-plan hectares |
11	12	13	14	15	16	17	18	19	20	21	22	
■■												1.04812
		■■		■■								0.351367
				■■						0.1073487		0.5117947
	■■	■■				0.4197523	0.2300331			0.134244		
	■■		0.2765044	■■								1.0700088
								0.114029				0.7582447
		■■										1.1860168
	■■		0.5592825									1.0090825
■■												0.3769
				■■								0.95152
	■■	■■				0.3659617	0.1835617			0.0855653		1.6502887
				■■				0.4458924				1.7501924
					■■							0.31622
					■■	0.406159						0.704059
				■■								
		■■				0.2425803	0.3530079	0.2432774				1.6117556
	■■											0.5276
								0.1284932				0.2696932
		■■								0.22852		1.326428
	■■	■■	0.3650323									0.6473923
					■■	0.333199						0.743799
			0.1912295									0.1912295
		■■						0.4937579				0.7315579

and the highest frequency rate appeared in the 2.20 to 2.60 range. Farm-area figures were spread out along a low horizon of 0.10 to 1.80 hectares. The largest cluster and the highest frequency were between 0.50 and 0.80 hectares. The correlation appears after comparing each variable. Only household Q had a HEMDCR equally proportional to its farm-area figure (see fig. 6). There were only three examples—households B, R, and V—in which farm-area figures fell below HEMDCR figures. All other households had farm-area figures proportionally larger than their HEMDCR. If households S, H, Y, E, and F had been reintroduced, it could have been calculated that 18.5 percent of households had no recorded farm measurements (note that 14.8 percent are dependent in-laws without land); 3.7 percent had a HEMDCR equal to farm area; 11.1 percent had a HEMDCR in excess of farm area; and 66.7 percent had a HEMDCR below farm-area figures. The two most conspicuous households, B and P, fall at the extreme opposite ends of the comparative scale. Household B's farm area was eighty-one times smaller than its HEMDCR. All the other households fell within a block cluster of twenty times greater farm area than HEMDCR.

The culminating point seems to be one not unusual for findings in small subsistence economies reliant upon agriculture. Where the vicissitudes of climate, pests, and soil deterioration combine to effect crop failure, farmers implement various protective techniques. To produce more than is required seems an obvious step towards covering the possibility of crop loss. In the Waiwai case up to 66.7 percent of households did this in varying degrees. It would not be too contentious to assume, however, that they produced proportionally more than their subsistence requirements in order to compensate for those households whose land holdings did not meet their known needs. Indeed the disparity between households that overproduced could be interpreted in this way. The individual overproduction absorbed back into the system by those who underproduce could suggest an economy expressive of "production for use." Households do balance their subsistence level, and very few if any of their farm products enter into the flow of trade. The exchange of agricultural goods remains institutionally restricted to what we would call the non-commercial sectors. Such goods are distributed and redistributed through the regular occurrence of social intercourse. At this stage they have become part of the very medium of social existence and even express an important aspect of community membership. And yet if they were all taken from the logic of Waiwai relationships, these findings would return us not to the theme of the economic or the political but rather to that of the body.

The Volition of the Cicada-people

It may seem odd to us or may just be taken for granted that the term *staple diet* means having to produce and to eat the same kind of food day in and day out. The idea of an apparent lack of choice and an absence of variety in the foods produced and eaten has deep objectionable significance for us in modern Western societies. In no more meaningful place than in our meals do we take seriously the adage that "variety is the spice of life." At least in the idea if not in the actuality of diversity, our daily meals seem to provide us with a sense of subjective as well as gastronomic fulfillment. Today the not-so-hidden relations between the global food supply, its retailers, trade organizations, and government agencies help to promote the ideological "truths" for eating more in variety, content, and quality (Nestle 2001:3). This often takes on the political rhetoric of individual "liberty," it being a matter not just of greater expressive choice in the food one eats but also of "increasing one's freedom of choice" (Mintz 1986:203). Furthermore, the so-called "insoluble shortage" of time experienced in modern society encourages this "condensing" of eating pleasure. "Consuming different things . . . simultaneously" suffices to codify consumption as a thing unto itself; a thing that can demand "maximum enjoyment in minimum time" and even a "higher frequency of occasions for consumption" (Mintz 1986:202). In the subtle obliqueness of ideological processes, the ideas about the circumstances leading to consuming in such a heightened fashion often obscure the fact that "food has a constant tendency to transform itself into situation" (Barthes 1975 [1961]:58).

The situated food sign of simultaneous consumption emphasizes a heightened way of life seemingly bereft of starvation and structurally opposed to poverty. We often forget that the discriminatory political structures (indicative of such an "evolved" sign) distribute and differentiate wealth against poverty from within their own criteria of meaning. For example, lack of possessions (purchasable with money) becomes a primary mark of poverty.[6] Here the food sign situates poverty and hunger not as the structural "relation between people . . . a social status . . . the invention of civilization" (Sahlins 1974:37) but rather as a lack of goods, subjective choices, and, of course, proper deployment of means and ends. Suffice it to say, however, that in Waiwai society, the daily repetition of the same foods does not in any way transform itself into a situation of poverty and certainly not into any kind of hunger.

This is not merely because Waiwai economy does not readily support a monopolizing food industry where the consumers of mass-produced foods do not control or even have to cook the food they eat. Nor is it merely that they do not live within a temporal world dictated by the tyranny of the clock. Rather, I would argue, their notions of the self and the body cannot accommodate, within their traditional social and cultural forms, the tendencies of an individual autonomy susceptible to the disciplinary techniques of a rigid centralized power (Foucault 1979; Deleuze and Guattari 1987; Gil 1998). Waiwai ideas about subjectivity do not privilege the self to the degree where, for example, selfhood demands fulfilled presence in heightened diverse consumption and, in the process, acquiescence to economic and political institutions that actively cater to such presence. In their understanding, meat and yuca complete the need for food. If eating did elevate their experience of self, it would do so presumably with these primary foods, which they do control and cook within the intimate confines of the village community. Lack of these foods does mean hunger and a weakness of the body. Men on long journeys, for example, complain bitterly if their rations of yuca bread run out, insisting (even when they have other purchased alternatives such as rice and wheat flour available) that the energy they need to paddle the canoe cannot be replenished with any other kind of foods. They certainly do look forward with joyful anticipation to the annual festivities, when a larger variety of different meats, yuca bread, and drinks are prepared and consumed. They also relish the seasonal change in their diet, when the forest blooms with the seeds, flowers, and fruit that attract and feed the fish and game they eat. Yet in all of this, the self never seeks the liberty of choice; it does not demand the fulfillment of an experience of freedom through choice or in the individual consumption of plenty. If the force of a restriction or a denial can be attributed to hunger in Waiwai cultural understandings, it would not be a force applied to the self but rather to the body. In this regard the principal social domains charged with the production of foods for the sustenance of the body are situated in the domestic household and the collective village community.

In general, for a subsistence economy like that of the Waiwai, the food products of agricultural work tend to be the main material rewards of human labor. Not necessarily a celebrated return emphasized by formally situated moments such as those of daily meals or ritual festivals but a return nonetheless; one identified in relation to the producer and situated as the outcome of an agrarian effort. Here, in its productive agrarian activities, the operating force of the body is usually categorized as work. Not all subsistence economies, however, display the objectification of labor superordinately reckoned in terms of its calculable returns. Unlike the sometime obsessive concern for greater efficiency and for modern rational relations between consumer and commodity in Western economies, subsistence economies vary in their systemic aspirations for labor. Contrary to the view that this is because their "means of production . . . are simple and accessible" and thus "cannot be used as a means for controlling the producers" (Meillassoux 1980:136), the contrast may have something to do with the different structural configurations of the material base and the contents of ideology, both levels of which can engage each other to articulate the different economic conditions (Hindess and Hirst 1979).[7] In the Waiwai case the *yetapičke* (work) for the social product of *esereme* (a meal) could be said to involve not only the particular structural relations between labor and land, but also the particular Waiwai understanding about what labor and land constitute and how they come together to be the means for making the food eaten at meals.

Waiwai agrarian knowledge considers the land and its plants as living entities filled with moral as well as subsistence value. The very fact of the systemic human processes involved in the clearing of forest, the planting of fields, and the harvesting of crops informs the farmer about the character and capability of land and plants. The repetitive intimacy between human, land, and plant, in addition to the fixity of the sequence of their engagement, make the systemic processes not just a way of life but also a way of being. Not surprisingly, therefore, the people's diligent attention to the bodies of plants responds to the heating of the earth and the seasonal song of the cicadas as phenomenal experiences.

Traditional Waiwai culture does not possess any other knowledge about producing large amounts of subsistence food plants—at least not one that could be considered historically and culturally Waiwai. The theoretical paradigms and procedures for engaging the land and its crops have no marked alternative form. The Waiwai may imagine what it would be like not to cut down the trees and simply to plant their crops under the forest canopy or even out in the small savannas found spotted here and there in the forest. They may imagine not waiting for the song of the cicadas in order to begin planting or even not burning the falling trees and undergrowth before planting. Such imaginings would, however, be counterintuitive to the established beliefs and ways of farming, for they would not be the product of a knowledge tried and tested by previous successful engagements. As it is, their knowledge of land and plants has a distinct place and presence of authority, extending beyond mere human attainment and possessing a weight and a force seemingly all its own.

The orthodoxy of the sequencing in the cultivation of yuca appears to be consistent. It stipulates a regularity of the process so unchallenged that the regularity itself seems to come of its own accord from the land and the crops. In a setting of such knowledge and experience, land and crops can even be said to dictate to their human producers what they should produce and how they should produce it. In other words, from this perspective land and plants manifest an avowed intentionality—a criterion of being that, from a Waiwai point of view, can be noted as a valid attribute of life. The volition of the Cicada-people to sing and, by the singing, to inform the Waiwai about the procreative heat of the land indicates a willing collective interaction and a communicative corporate relation between social beings. Even the generative growth of plants can be interpreted as the self-evident intent of the plants themselves. Thus does the effect of such intent upon humans amount to a compliant response—that is, to a specific action from humans to the distinct bodies and will of the plants. In verifying the living, active identity of land and plants—by complying with a regular round of agricultural activities—humans also confirm their degree of communality with plants. Communality in return insists on moral worth and the subsequent need for properly engaged social relations with plants. The consequent fact that cultivated plants become the object of human consumption therefore takes on almost the same level of meaningful concern as does the human consumption of animals.

Negotiated Subjectivities
Although it categorically includes the eating of meat, the Waiwai meal semantically privileges šere. As the word *e/sere/me* suggests, the intellectual focus of meals is upon yuca. It is as if the cultural appropriation of the idea of meals places the yuca tuber at the very center of a persistent contemplation of what humans eat for food. It is not čure—that is, yuca bread itself—but the transformable body of the tuber plant, with its deadly prussic acid, that becomes the focus of a culinary contemplation. Hence, in addition to the transformation of the forest into cultivated land for yuca, the technically elaborate process of transforming tubers into edible bread also becomes the linguistic and cultural target of meals. In the Waiwai paradigm these categories of activity are interlinked and indeed thought of as joint processes. In the literature (Yde 1965; Stephen Hugh-Jones 1979;

Christine Hugh-Jones 1988; Balée 1994) and in Waiwai society, the later stages of the process to transform tubers into bread, while not more important, nevertheless appear the more familiar.

For the Waiwai the production of yuca cannot be complete until they convert tubers into their basic consumable form of baked bread. The technique among Shepariymo housewives varies little from that of other documented users. As soon as they uproot and carry home the tubers in their basket backpacks, *šereñipiketa* (peeling) and *šereñikna* (grating) begin. The women usually schedule these activities for the morning. Peeling and grating can be long and tedious jobs, but by midday most women have their pulp ready for the *kwašï* (woven basket squeezer). They place the pulp into the kwašï and squeeze out the prussic acid by tightening the cylindrical basket and allowing the liquid to run through the woven material into a container. This stage of the process they call *šerenamoso*. The dried flour, now shaped in compact tubes, can at this point be heated a little and preserved for future baking. In the next stage they crumble, grind, and sift the flour. A flat woven basket with slightly raised edges, called a *manari*, is used to separate the *kwašarï* (fine grains) from the *aparicho* (coarser grains). They feed the aparicho to their dogs and use the kwašarï to make bread. They *čïrenayna* (bake) by pouring the flour onto a large heated *eripo* (griddle). This, when assisted by the small amount of acid still remaining in the flour, binds the flour, which then turns into bread. The entire process, from šereñipiketa to čïrenayna, involves the maker in a good deal of creative work, often unavoidably submerged in the details of precision and repetition.

Like the primary work of men in converting the forest into farms, the creativity, precision, and repetition seem instilled by a firm belief in the collective will of yuca. The Waiwai agree upon the belief and state quite categorically that the evidence for the volition of yuca exists in the fact that it can kill. Like animal and human predators, yuca can, if not properly treated, kill its consumer. Hence the interlinked processes of cultivating and detoxifying the tuber can be interpreted as the sum of practical knowledge and action for safe and proper relations with yuca. Indeed, like the known affinal relations between humans, the cultivating and detoxifying relations between farmers and yuca have to be established in order to avoid the dangers of the potentially lethal Other. The basis for the ideal state of familiarity achieved between farmer and yuca takes its paradigmatic reference from the developed relations of marriage. It assimilates the attributes of the initially strange relations of newly married couples, which progressively change into the more familiar relations between spouses well established by their subsequent parenthood. The Waiwai avoid the lethal potential of yuca when they properly transform the body of the tuber into safe and edible food through the systemic processes of agriculture and cookery. From their point of view, by being both a major source of potential food and violence, yuca provokes the specific kinds of processes used in agriculture and cookery. In other words its character forcefully influences humans—with their recognizable appetites and vulnerabilities—to help organize and control the cultivating and detoxifying of its body.

Yuca lives in a "village" of cultivated plants. It lives within the cleared circle of the field. Sometimes, when it has been eaten out and can no longer reproduce from within the same field, its plant village becomes the actual site of human occupation. This was the case with Sheparyimo, which first came about at a field site initiated by Shamawa. Humans often build their houses where cultivated plants once lived. They clear the forest initially for cultivated plants and subsequently for themselves. It is no accident, therefore, that the circular shape of the agricultural landscape repeats itself over and over again. The social identity of plants influences this aesthetic. Setting into motion the positive change toward the domesticated and the cooked, the double burn from sun and fire do not infiltrate the surrounding standing trees; the living trees provide the protective circular form for the site. The fallen bodies within the cleared circle, however, contribute their heated substances to the growth of the cultivated plants. They had been literally attacked by an army of men, chopping, hacking, and cutting at their limbs. Their only means of resistance had been to retaliate with their own army of biting and stinging insects and sometimes, in their final death fall, by crushing some of the enemy. The victorious army of men divides up the site as it would the body of hunted game. The men then repopulate the site first with their own plant kinsmen and then, sometimes, with themselves. Their yuca affines in particular gain privileged status, occupying most of the site and dictating the length of plant occupancy. Almost every day the women come to the yuca village, uproot the mature bodies, and carry them off to their own homes. There in the house of humans, the women prepare and cook the yuca body for food.

The continuity of ekatï, of spiritual vitality, flows not just inside all living beings but also between all living beings. To harm other living beings is tantamount to harming oneself. A principal object in transforming some living beings into edible things is to make sure that the shared ekatï, expelled from the victim at death, does not depart with some elements of one's own spiritual vitality. When women take home the reaped crop of yuca to detoxify and bake, one main concern of their culinary paradigm is (as in the case of burning the fields) to eradicate the danger from tubers, which can extract human spirituality permanently out of the body. The long and elaborate process of peeling, grating, squeezing, sifting, and baking yuca makes the tuber safe for eating by removing as much of its ekatï as possible. The visible viscous substance—that is, the katï of the plant (its evident material carrier of spiritual vitality)—must be separated from its corpus, its hard original body. The technique for removing works by systematically breaking down the corpus of the tuber into fine grains where no dangerous vitality can amass and be strong enough to influence a human spiritual entity. When, over the heat of fire, the grains of flour coagulate as a flat, round wafer of bread, yuca has finally lost its subjectivity and becomes the situated object for a meal.

Bodies can be eaten, but if known to be the constituted corpus of subjective beings, they must be reconstituted into nondangerous substances before humans can consume them. When thought of in this way, the consumable body takes on the character of the quintessential plant food—yuca—and becomes a meal, or the object of eating. As I mentioned earlier, in the Waiwai culinary paradigm even the cooked bodies of animals reconstitute into the consumable quality of vegetable food. It is the heat of cooking that finally turns meat into a plantlike food. As the message of myth suggests, the deep association among death, eating, and women places an articulated emphasis on meat and plants. To the extent that the body of woman can in myth be both feline and plant, this would seem to address, in Waiwai ideas, the known predatory potential of yuca. From the perspective of a manifestly masculine ideology, the predicament of the relations between women and food needs to be resolved. The approach taken settles upon the technique of reconstituting the threat. In other words rather than having nothing to do with women or yuca, the paradigm makes women and yuca the initial project of men but then makes the final conversion of the threat the particular object of women's concern and work. One main message of the origin myth of plant foods addresses the topic of having to identify, by trial and error, the correct plant for human consumption. Another main message deals with the proper preparation of the plant for human consumption, which, in the myth, is also achieved through trial and error. As the heated product of the earth, yuca transforms into a giant penis and cannot be safely used for sexual intercourse. As the heated product of a woman's stomach, yuca transforms into excrement and again cannot be safely used. However, as the heated product of the cremated woman's self-immolated body, yuca finally becomes the situated food of meals. Like the heated body of an erotic marriageable lover and like the cooked meat of tasty game, yuca can at last be safely enjoyed after it has been prepared and cooked by woman.

To reconstitute the outside dangers of the forest, the consuming human bodies that subject themselves to the risk of such threats must bring into effect the cultural forces at their disposal. The successful operatives in this project happen to be the forms and sequences active as the systemic processes of agriculture and cookery. From the view of an agreed upon, formalized anthropology, it can be said that gender, household, and the village community function as the principal social operators for these processes. The bodies of humans live in the circular space of the village community and within the safe confines of the household. The bodies of cultivated plants, particularly yuca, live in the circular space of the field and within the protected confines of the farm plot. Access to each other can only be achieved, in the first instance, through the collective community and, in the second instance, from within the formal segments of the collective community—that is, from within the individual household for humans and from within the farm plot for yuca. In the Waiwai paradigm the size of households and the size of farm plots achieve their commensurability because of the bodily demands to stave off hunger and because of the affects to satisfy this demand by the act of killing. The assistance from other humans—the men and women with whom an individual lives—not only brings about the particular forms of groupings that serve to achieve these ends but also directly protects the individual from the dangers incurred from the killing. The result of the commensurability between household size and farm-plot size can be said to derive from such beliefs and actions. In Waiwai terms household subsistence requirements cannot be intellectually divorced from the dangerous agency of plants and from the specific role the household relations serve in protecting the consumer from cultivated plants. Indeed, it is precisely because the human household already has assigned the work of the most shared vitality between individuals to its form and domain that it acquires its prior claim to the divisible product of the forest.

The Waiwai say that the *taponukew* (lightness) the body feels when it is hungry is due to the fact that its normal *awsina* (heaviness) has not been attained by the consumption of yuca bread and cooked meat. The foods of the body have been detained in some other place and consequently cannot make the body heavy again. The lightness itself they attribute to the departure of particles of spiritual vitality from the body. Close to but not quite in the same category as feeling *karipera* (sick), the bodily lightness of hunger amounts to a depleted vitality of being. Some inevitable loss of the spiritual vitality of the body has to be assumed to take place because of the body actually having to live in the world and share vitality with other beings. Indeed, to be a social being and share the same space with other individuals must result in some degree of spiritual loss that the eating of proper food aims to abate. The subtle and perhaps sublime project of life thus appears to be the sustaining of contact with those who share vitality with you. Of course the other side to this project would be to reduce contact with all those who do not have sustained relations with you. The argument I am assuming the Waiwai paradigm makes is that the household—the place where the most intimate and sustained contact between humans takes place—derives its prior access to food because it has the strongest defense against the depletion of bodily vitality. In the intimacy of the household, the body can expect to be weighed down by the responsibilities of kinship and marriage, for it is in the household that bodily sustenance can be most effectively replenished by the filial and affinal relations expressed by the meal. When the Cicada-people first begin to sing and tell about the oncoming dry season, the Waiwai prepare, by attiring their bodies with the social adornments of kinship and marital relationships, for the cultivation of new fields and a fresh round of assault upon the forest. The shared subjectivities among humans and between humans and plants have once again to be diplomatically negotiated.

The Plaited Design of Human Life

Contrasts in the Pleasures of Space

Waiwai cultural aesthetics emphasize balance and harmony in regard to the pleasures of residential space. A proper complement to life itself has to be produced. A necessary human sense of confidence about the forest and the village must be attained and factualness about the position of humans within the world achieved. To accomplish all this the cultural aesthetic of Waiwai life creatively opens by contrasting and opposing the qualities of spatial content. The distinct features of the trees of the forest and the waters of the river as well as the animals, plants, and insects living outside the village settlement contribute to the understanding of space. It is with such an understanding that these features elicit a certain kind of confidence from humans about lived spaces.

Established as the effects of spatial knowledge contributed to this end, the settlement itself develops features that possess an aspect of bodily encompassment. Protective and predictable, in the world and of the world, the settlement serves as the place of the body surrounded—a fact that is made. This derived knowledge about its encompassing powers informs and sets its equilibrium. The self-orientating body learns its temporal rhythms from knowing and experiencing this encircled space. In the Waiwai pedagogy of the aesthetic, the balance and harmony of the eternal circle teaches the pleasures of containment.

At the point where the practice of being contained finally marks the body with its distinctive comportment and sense of self, the practice takes over from the teaching. Perhaps more accurately, they become one. The doing teaches and the teaching informs for further action. Particularly in its architectural features—that is, in the made design of its circular representation, the lived space of the settlement aids in the bodily process of understanding encompassment and containment as safe and assuring pleasures.

What, if anything, do we who live in the so-called modern world lose when—as in the case where we no longer cook our own food—we no longer build our own houses? We rent. We lease. We buy. We move into new or ancient homes. We may design the house in which we live. We may even have our names permanently associated with the design and edifice of the house. Most of us, however, will hardly have lifted a finger in the actual construction of the place where we sleep, eat, love, cry, and establish lifelong memories. By our own individual contribution to building the house in which we live, what, if anything, could we keep and come to know about the personal experience of being in the world? Some of the lessons we could learn from the Waiwai suggest that we may be missing a considerable amount.[1]

Watching and helping the Waiwai build their circular house once forced me to pay attention to details such as the materials used, the kinds of labor involved, the distinct parts of the edifice constructed, and particularly the ways in which the parts related to each other in position, shape, terminology, and meaning. Yet it also occurred to me at the time that in my own recording, the very "magic" of an emotion, possibly attained only through the act of making, hardly ever received a mention. Later on I took note of the incidental fact that even in the historical records about those monumental ceremonial edifices of the ancient Americas, little if any credit went to the individual or even to the collective social experience of physically building the sites.[2]

The records showed little if any pleasures gained by the people from handling or thinking about the handling of materials for building. They offered very few examples of the delights in having the skills and/or being associated with the skills of construction. They often suggested that little satisfaction could be found in demonstrating the knowledge it took to make the forms for human space. And they invariably reduced the explanation for the appearance of the obviously human-made forms to the imposition of elites who, in many cases, did not actually participate in constructing the edificial forms themselves. Our records so frequently ignore the input of the individual builder and the very experience of creative human production. Surely this cannot all be explained by the prevalence of our modern stigma against the masses and manual labor or our partiality for a certain kind of reasoning and the "men of ideas."

Admittedly, the persistent modern desire for more individualism often appears more convincing when set against the great horror of anonymity and invisibility attributed to living among the masses. One cannot help but notice, however, how the modern desire and its horror of obscurity hides an even greater fear that an alternative liberty may be obtained by the individual in the very indistinguishableness of living among the masses. From the consequences of schizophrenia (where the "illness" allows the "insane" to live among us but without us in their own invented world) to the moral illegalities of ethnic groups (where their "crimes" often derive from different forms of honor and justice), the view of the individual, particularly for the modern state, cannot be obscured. A strict bureaucratic order operates to keep the individual visible, quickly attainable, and obedient. The logic of linked hierarchical offices based on the precedence of impersonal rank has helped this agenda in the modern construction of space and time. The boundaries between the urban and the rural, the finitude placed on time, paved roads, electricity, inside plumbing, and bills all seem to work through the logic of monitoring the individual. The fear that a whole new logic may be obtainable and not shared so as to privilege the state seems to be prevalent. One must always be vigilant. Such an alternative logic must never become possible; it must always be made to appear outside the bounds of possibility. Keeping it at bay by keeping it outside what is discussed or even thought about has been a successful tactic. Hence most of our historic heroes and their heroic attributes tend to accommodate and represent the prevalence of a conservative individualism. The feelings of the masses must be denigrated or lost in a faceless history, for it may be possible that they secretly pose a threat to the modern rational order of things. The "magic" of the masses, the inspiration of the rabble, can only lead to madness and chaos. The triumph of our more modern, efficient order and of all those privileged by it lies in maintaining a being that can be individualized by an empirical presence, an individualism that cannot be achieved without thoughts about the horrors of obscurity—of a silence.

The Caution of the Sonorous Ideal

One of the earliest accounts we have about the houses lived in by the people who today call themselves the Waiwai mentions the *tamnoñim* or *maporku* (circular- or conical-shaped domestic dwelling).

> After an uninterrupted march of 5 miles they arrived at the provision fields of the Maopityan [Mawayena] settlement, which consisted of two large bee-hive houses: on the tops of these there rose a second smaller bee-hive roof from which hung several flat pieces of wood shaped into all kinds of figures that were swayed backwards and forwards by the wind. (Richard Schomburgk 1922 [1848]:377)

The account also claims that "the larger of the houses" had "a height of 100 feet, and a diameter of 86" (Richard Schomburgk 1922 [1848]:377). Years later, this time in a report on the Waiwai themselves, another account states:

> The large communal house was 66 feet in diameter, a perfect cone, 60 feet high to the apex. The centre pole continued 35 feet above the house and was topped with a Brazil nut. Two feet

above the top of the house a canopy 5 feet in diameter, attached
to the pole, covered the smoke hole in the roof. (Farabee 1967
[1924]:164)

The Waiwai call all houses *miïmo*. They use different terms for the
different forms and functions of houses: from the tamnoñim to the
tiïči (rectangular-shaped domestic dwelling), *yawarimta* (rectangular-shaped workhouse), and *umana* (circular-shaped workhouse).
Today they build their houses much smaller, but whenever they use
their most favored design, the conical shape and the canopy over
the roof's central vent remain the distinct and consistent features of
their domestic dwellings. It has been remarked upon that "conically
roofed houses with vertical wall are quite common in northern
South America, but almost absent in the area south of the Amazon" (Yde 1965:156). In addition, at least among the Waiwai and
their neighbors, the "singular feature of these houses, not reported
from elsewhere, is a conical canopy erected over the opening" (Yde
1965:155). When we consider that the Waiwai word /miïmo/ has its
root in the noun *mina* (their term for the dallibanna leaves used in
the construction of the roof) and that the word /tamnoñim/ actually
means "circle" or "in the round," it should come as no surprise to
find that the most noticeable architectural feature of a house pertains
to its roof. In many respects the roof is the house, and the effect
of its thatched completeness goes a long way in contributing to the
Waiwai understanding of the ewto as one of the most important
cultural statements about their humanity. The roof is a fundamental symbol whose form and features address issues of relevance to
society. Therefore, as in other aspects of Waiwai life, one cannot
ignore how the implementation of collective social labor brings the
house into existence.

House construction depends primarily upon the collective labor
of men. One explanation for the exclusive identification of men with
this task can be found in the Waiwai claim that the forest provides
the materials for house building. In their ideas the forest registers
as the realm with which men associate the most, and with this asso-

ciation they gain knowledge of the things in and of the forest. This knowledge legitimizes the access men have to the materials found in the forest and at the same time delegitimizes such access to women. What men know of the forest, what turns into the internalized wisdom of their being, becomes substantiated in the objectified world as the practical outcome of their gendered bodies. In being useful to society, in having an imperative place of value constructed for it, men's knowledge of the forest enables their gendered labor to take up occupancy in the essential space of an applied social service. As the consequence of the labor of men—that is, as the product of men's bodies, human shelter manifests itself as the knowledge of men. In this way, being dependent upon men's knowledge and men's bodies, the constructing of human shelter convincingly appears under the auspices of men.

The labor of men clearly invests the house with recognizable social value. Nevertheless, because house construction also involves an ongoing cycle of ceremonial exchanges expressed in terms of the ritual meals prepared by women, the house cannot be built without women. As with all other scheduled work sessions involving collective labor, the ritual meals of onhari have to come into affect. Hence even for house building, the women prepare the food in their individual households and present it for communal consumption at the village leader's house or at the meetinghouse. If the place of work happens to be near the village, the women will carry and serve the food to the men at their work site. More often, however, the men partake of the communal meals in the village before and after each work session.

During the preliminary stages of house construction, the forest becomes the workplace. From it the men procure all the materials required for house building: the latching vine, the rafter poles, the purlin beams, and the hardwood house poles. Working in small groups, they cut down and drag the lumber back to the cleared ground of the village. There they erect the posts, secure the rafters, and tie down the purlins. Later, at their own convenience but before the time fixed for the *turu katopa* (plaiting of the roof), each man will go deep into the forest to collect the mïna leaves. The large "vagina-shaped" dallibanna grows in huge groves low on the forest floor. As his contribution to the building of the roof, every man must return to the village with at least one backpack of leaves. It takes many trips and many backpacks of mïna to make a traditional tamnoñim.

The informal event for the plaiting of the roof is a convivial and relaxed affair.[3] Throughout the entire process casual talk, jokes, teasing, and soft laughter can be heard coming from the undulating voices of the men. It is possibly the one occasion when men as a collective group sustain a long stretch of time together in the open space of the settlement. In the normal cadence of daily life, men usually spend most of their time in small family groups out on the river, in the forest, or around their houses in the village. The responsibilities of the household mostly keep them to the smaller groupings of the family or, as in the case of the young unmarried men, it is the companionship of their age-grade mates that has them roaming together in small gangs. Even after a long day working with a collective group on a major communal task, the men can be seen carrying out their various domestic duties with close male kinsmen and/or their wives. In fact one understood and well-kept custom of all communal work is for work sessions to be concluded by the late afternoon at the latest—that is, with enough daylight time for individual chores to be carried out. When they are together in a collective group, particularly in the relaxed atmosphere of the village, the men commune with each other in ways that allow the day to pass in pleasurable circumstances. No raised voices. No anger. No singing. Just quiet talk and noncompetitive work. No need to objectify work as an obstacle, as an imposition, as an enemy to be defeated. The joy of being together, of unison, is not to compete and to overcome but to balance the divided containment of each other as a sweet concordance. The sonorous ideal seeks to avoid any remainder—that is, any individual from the inside left outside after the subtraction of work. Handling the elements of the forest always requires such caution.

On the appointed day of plaiting, the men carry their backpacks of leaves nearer to the framework of the house to be built. They also drag their collected strips of *maripa* (kokerite palm), *kupa* (socratea palm), and thick turu bark to the same location. Each man sits himself down comfortably on his low carved stool or on an old chunk of wood and, with his materials around him, prepares to make as many *pačanay* (tiles) as his leaves will provide.

The process begins with the folding of the leaves. Every man divides the leaves from his backpack into two piles; the leaves from one pile are kept flat and open, and the leaves from the other pile are used for the folding. Each leaf to be folded is bent along its middle rib, starting at its heel and up to about two inches from its top, where a dexterous fingernail cuts across the interfacing sides, leaving the remaining upper portion in its original open position. Two folded leaves, one on top the other, are then placed on two unfolded leaves. All four leaves have their stems trimmed to equal lengths. On the ground in front of each man plaiting, two already prepared palm-wood strips lie parallel to each other at about an inch and a half apart. The man plaiting takes the stems of the four leaves and pushes them under the top strip of the maripa and over the bottom strip of the kupa palm wood. He then bends the stems back behind both strips and, with a length of thin inner bark from the turu, ties them to the top strip. Another set of four leaves is placed next to the first and secured in a similar fashion, but this time they and all subsequent sets of stems placed along the two strips of palm wood are held in position by the bark skin wrapped around the top strip and behind each set of stems. The upper right side of every top two folded leaves is placed over the left side of every following set of leaves. Each completed tile measures about thirteen feet in length. The final result is a very waterproof tile looking every bit like the wing of a giant bird.

All the individual tiles of leaves—the fabricated "wings of birds"—have to be tied to the rafters. The tying requires teamwork. The men form themselves into groups consisting of two or four workers. While one or two men from each group climb onto the frame of the house, those on the ground pass the tiles up to be tied down.

(I should say that at this stage of construction, because all the poles used for the framing have been stripped of their bark, the fresh white wood makes the house frame look like the bleached bones of a huge animal.) As the men on the roof put the tiles in place and secure them—progressively covering the lower section of the house—they recede further away from those passing the tiles up to them. When they can no longer reach each other, the ground team uses poles with forked ends to hoist the tiles up. After all the pačanay have been positioned and tied down in this way, the men complete the roof by laying the long leaves of the *kumyarï* palm vertically around the top section of the roof.

This design feature of the low, horizontally laid mïna leaves and the high, vertically laid kumyarï leaves has been noted and compared (Yde 1965:156) to a similar roofing design cited for the Yekuana people in Venezuela (Koch-Grünberg 1916–28:323). It is an intriguing comparison, for it has recently been claimed that "the Waiwai . . . remain one of the most closely related groups, linguistically and culturally, to the Yekuana" (Guss 1990:236). Indeed, the Yekuana and the Waiwai emphasis on roofs as well as their nomenclature for house parts do seem remarkably similar. I would like to argue, however, that maybe the similarities appear less because of the design features of the house or even the Cariban ethnicity of both peoples than because of a shared cultural logic on the theme of the body. It could even be further argued that a more widespread lowland Amerindian engagement with the copresent thoughts about house and body already transpires (Reichel-Dolmatoff 1971:232; Butt Colson and de Armellada 1983:1232; Christine Hugh-Jones 1988:218). It seems that whenever Amerindian cultures of this region present ideas about the house, they invariably do so within the paradigmatic idiom of the body. In the Waiwai case, as I will explain below, the bodily reference occurs all over the thatched design of the roof.

Reducing the Strangeness of Difference
When concepts and beliefs come into the world and become what we can call the empirical cultural products of the mind, they do

not necessarily do so because they manifest a less "real" or a less "true" reality of the mind. It is not because concepts and beliefs can be considered unseen, inaudible, or intangible, and hence somehow unperceived, that they need to become part of the cultural world. The public and social revelations of concepts and beliefs do not result as a necessary by-product of being unperceived. Certainly, for anthropology, concepts and beliefs occur as the substance of a cultural world because in such a domain they give life to the embodied human experience. Indeed, "the cultural world . . . is [where] our existence finds its sustenance" (Merleau-Ponty 1992:24), and human perception—with its ability to perceive significance—seemingly relies upon cultural symbols that "elicit emotion and express and mobilize desire" (Terence Turner 1974:54). Culture certainly mediates between the body and the world, yet it is also the signifying realm in which embodied thoughts and experiences live. This is not to reduce thought and experience to a crass materialism but, instead, to understand the possibilities of human existence to be limited by nothing other than its own thick cultural universe.[4] Far from being an illusion requiring substantiation from, for example, a more "real" and "natural" world, culture enables the world to be brought into being. Thus do the Waiwai house and body carry and exchange between them not the concepts and beliefs of a counterfeit reality but those of a very substantive life.

The paradigmatic transference of ideas about and from the body to the house provides an immensely powerful means not only of producing a difference of otherness, but also of knowing and experiencing that difference with a certain degree of intimacy. The extension of the primary intimacy between the self and the body into the cultural world permits the individual to transfer aspects of subjectivity. Presented as the objectified entities of culture, these aspects of the self can be said to serve as exchange items between the self and the Other. In this way individual conscious or subconscious thought and experience about the solitude of the self may be relieved in the reciprocal relations of an exchange. It could be further claimed that by seeking to repeat or mimic the familiarity between the self and the body, this kind of sanctuary by culture in society achieves a secondary intimacy between the individual and society. It is the attainable means of reducing the strangeness of difference. The individual in society can now anticipate the world with a confidence that takes its lead from the relations between the self and the body. Anticipated and, of course, recognizable, the coded world guides human action. In the specificity of house building, the intimacies between the body and society carry the very recognizable code for Waiwai gendered behavior.

Woven Thoughts and Gendered Bodies

The learned dexterity of the fingers that gather and plait the leaves and the stored agency of house-building skills all become fundamentally associated with the experience, knowledge, and bodies of men. The subjectivities of masculine bodies anticipate, recognize, and participate in the coded regime of their transcendent selves. At the same time, however, legitimizing access to the knowledge of house building as well as the actual ability to build houses has to include the willingness of femininity to forego any of its own incipient claims to such knowledge and practice.

House building becomes the work domain of men as much because men claim access to it as because women deny themselves such claims. Part of the personal understanding about being gendered woman or man incorporates comprehending and, of course, acting upon the comprehending that house building either includes or excludes the masculine or feminine body in particular aspects of its process. Such understandings appear not only from the customs of making the house but also from the actual form the house takes. At least within the traditional realm of Waiwai thought and behavior, the extent of cultural power remains logically consistent with its effects.

The guided actions, beliefs, and feelings associated with house building tend to determine the objects transformed into the material manifestation of architectural knowledge. In this way the forest leaves that become the roof help to proclaim the validity of gender and the knowledge attached to different genders. It is from such a perspective that we can speak anthropologically about the roof's taking shape as the woven thoughts of gendered individuals and as the objectified representation of collective ideas about masculinity and femininity. Objectified in the roof, these thoughts and this representation affect both men and women.

Leaf, Feather, and Hair: The Embodied Roof

All Waiwai incorporate an understanding of the clear differences between leaves, feathers, and hair, yet by the use of the same word /*yepoči*/ to refer to leaf, feather, and hair, an overriding of the differences for a cultural emphasis upon the similarities exists. They speak of leaves as the "covering" of trees, feathers as the "covering" of birds, and hair as the "covering" of humans. This covering represents a kind of *hanorronome* (proper completion) of objectified being that is *kirewani* (good). In its adornment state, the covering that yepoči produces not only suggests a moral completeness of being but also a *yenpori* (beauty). It is this moral completeness of beauty that yepoči carries over to the roof of the house. Hairlike and featherlike, the leaf tiles of the thatched roof cover in an adorned fashion the naked "bones" of the embodied house. The covering instills a beauty to the structure—a moral splendidness experienced by appreciating the fact that the covering has achieved its proper end. Part of the achieved aims of this beauty includes the form the covering adornment takes. In the circular, corrugated regularity of the roof, as in the well-groomed coiffure of the Waiwai head and in the careful plumage of birds, beauty attains its desired forms of harmony and balance.

In Waiwai ideas leaf, hair, and feather constrain as well as cover the body. Leaf, hair, and feather are, by the observable fact of their generative and regenerative properties, living substances. They grow from the "skin"; they protrude through tiny orifices to cover the body. With the force of their obvious energy, brought into effect by design, they cover and "constrain" the inner capacities of the body. (My use of this word is clarified below.) They can hold together the *tikotonoyime*—that is, the various volatile "parts" of the body. In the particular case of leaves, when they no longer cover the body of a tree, they expose the death of the tree. As they lie on the forest floor or become the tile of a seasoned roof, the leaves display an aging. Like hair and feathers, they last beyond the life of the body from which they are plucked. The life they possess beyond the body can, therefore, be further used to cover the bodies of others. As the artifice of serviceable and creative expression and through coherent reference to hair and feathers, the leaves of a roof can be understood as the proper covering and containment of human life.

With the high and vertical position of the long, narrow kumyarï leaves plus the low, horizontal thatch of the vagina-shaped mïna leaves, the design of the roof sends more than just the obvious message that the house is an ewto, a "place-where-people-live." It also conjures up a whole host of ideas about the people the house contains and the kinds of ideological principles governing their residence. It prominently stimulates the fundamental social axiom, for example, that for people to live together correctly, they should possess certain self-evident qualities that cast them in complementary opposition to each other. Caught and conveyed in the design, without any need to demonstrate its veracity, is the cultural view that the successful bringing together of oppositional features has been achieved by the influence of circular containment. Contained within the same space and time, the particular manifest oppositional qualities of human gender have been subjected to the cultural covering of the house. The retained oppositional qualities of masculinity and femininity—interpreted as such by the design features of the roof—find their differences complementing each other as the very beauty of residential containment. Thus the detailed differentiation between the leaves of the roof can be said to express the fundamental internal opposition between the masculine and the feminine, while the thatched completeness of the roof represents the balanced wholeness of the village community.

The designated masculinity of the kumyarï leaf begins in the forest, where it can be found in tree crowns and as the pinnate fronds dangling from stiff and upright stems. There can be no mistaking the sign of the trees; their compound leaves look everything like the large feathered plumes with which men adorn themselves. Meanwhile, the designated femininity of the mïna leaf also commences in the forest, but low down on the ground, where its single splay leaf looks every bit—as the Waiwaï often imply—like a displaced ambulatory vagina. When taken from the forest to be transformed into the roof of the house, both kinds of leaves carry their gender properties with them as the conceptual ideas of their gatherers. When brought together as the roof, through the knowledge and labor of men, the leaves assist the human imagination in transporting their shapes and spatial positioning to the cultural reinforcement of gender differences. The veracity of the one supports the other. While separated in the forest, the leaves provide no productivity for humans. When unified in the village as the roof, they become useful to human need. In becoming thus useful the leaves give recognition, validity, and veracity to the knowledge and labor of men. And yet this alliance between leaves and men, in materializing the knowledge and labor of men, acknowledges, incorporates, and makes perceivable the elements of femininity as well as the relations between the feminine and the masculine. The plaited design of human life (as the bringing together of the long, narrow, high, and vertical kumyarï with the short, round, low, and horizontal mïna) results from an insistence on including the feminine. In other words men have to admit the elements of womanhood into all renditions of proper human existence. The long and short, the narrow and round, the high and low, the vertical and horizontal, they all complement each other in their opposition, just as men and women's masculine and feminine elements complement each other as the harmonious fusion of society.

The Mewrï of the Roof

One of the consequences of Waiwai belief about social being is that, like the body and many objects of human manufacture, the place-where-people-live must be given an outer design; it must receive mewrï. Like our own Western tradition—with the "paradoxical double skin" (Gell 1996:38) in tattooing, or the "shaved, tanned, and oiled skin" (Dutton 1995:301–17) in body-building, or the "eminently osmotic shell" (Cavallaro and Warwick 1998:116) that absorbs clothes as flesh—the Waiwai custom of mewrï communicates about meditative and protective surfaces. The house receives its roof filled with the potency of human rendering about the protective outer design of its inner contents. The individual bodies of its inhabitants have their gender differences depicted by the leaves in the roof as a reconciled, complementarily opposed aesthetic. The mewrï, or depiction, in and of itself encompasses and produces the desired ideal of a protective social harmony. In kinship terms this is always the societal ideal of a compassionate uterine harmony—that is, the epeka. In depicting this social harmony, the mewrï of the house quite correctly retains the tension of opposition between genders. To produce its ideal of proper harmony, society has to operate with the elements of gender and gender differences, yet at the same time it is these very same elements that constitute the source of potential discordance. Without the opposition there would be no need for the mediating encompassment: without the act of encompassment, the oppositions could not be protectively contained. In the Waiwai paradigm, because gender differences carry the elements of their passionate opposition into the active relationships of kinship and marriage, they can only be resolved or contained through the ideal of epeka and by the principle of poyino encompassment.

Poyino encompassment should, for example, be able to restrain incest as well as (perhaps rather ironically) convert the passionate affine into the compassionate uterine. Indeed, the very act of encompassment that the mewrï depicts with the leaves of the roof is one of poyino harmony built upon gender opposition. The act of giving its particular design of the roof to the house, by actually putting the ever-present and ever-emergent differences between masculinity and femininity together in the useful productivity of the roof, restrains and converts. As I mentioned earlier, the internal elements of difference do not disappear; they merely become safely contained in the restraining and the converting. As with the contained internal elements of gender differences, the sustained outer covering, which the different leaves of the roof achieve by being made to complement each other productively, results in the very idiom of an encompassment. It does so not merely to render objective a particular spatial or temporal reality to the settlement, nor even to substantiate a prodigious abstract reality to social being, but rather as the very placelessness and timelessness of a divine eternity.

This placelessness and timelessness are not necessarily assembled —unlike our own modern examples—upon a dominant sense of "sameness" (Bale 1994) or "simultaneity" (Anderson 1992), which would, I think, depend empathetically upon working with a paradigm belief of "being as presence" (Heidegger 1972). The sameness in the placelessness of our own built landscapes seeks to produce rational, democratic spaces eked out from what we understand to be the unruly and despotic encroachment of nature. It repeats itself over and over again in our shopping malls, sport stadiums, and modern cities. The simultaneity in the timelessness of our deeply felt nation-ness allows us to join our autonomous individualities to each other in imagining the national community. In either case a purposeful reckoning occurs inside space and time that gives to the being of placelessness and timelessness a nonetheless spatial and temporal presence; even with the so-called erasure of difference and discordance, their respective sameness and simultaneity provide a measurable presence in space and time. In the Waiwai case, however, it could be argued that the placelessness and timelessness of their divine eternity exist outside space and time and, hence, can have no measurable being as presence.

Divine eternity cannot be repeated nor even be given a language of unison; in the Waiwai paradigm it just continues. It is already the inevitability of the house. It is the imminent roof. It is the impeding tile of leaves. It is placeless and timeless because it has no place to be or not to be and no time with which to begin or end. When objectifying and giving presence—as in the example of the mewrï of the roof—it remains an uninterrupted being, placeless and timeless, merely circuiting through the particularities of site and moment. When it is perceived, for example, as *kamo*, the sun, or *nuni*, the moon, it can live to offer calculability to space and time, but calculable space and time cannot be given to it. Divine eternity cannot be contained; it does the containing. It cannot be encompassed; it does the encompassing. Thus it can indeed have a verifiable existence, but this cannot be irreducible to a spatial or temporal presence. In coming to know and experience the existence of divine eternity as outside of place and time, the Waiwai fulfill their cultural demand for avoiding or reducing the inevitable dangers of social life.

While the results of all placelessness and timelessness can and do arguably produce a similar safe familiarity (perhaps for all societies), they do not all do so from the same cultural premise. Any achieved secure familiarness in our modern spaces and time tends to be driven by ideological concerns for efficiency, growth, progress, and "community conceived as a deep horizontal comradeship" (Anderson 1992:7). The safe familiarity of Waiwai placelessness and timelessness has concern for the balancing and harmonizing of the complementary oppositions in human existence. The mediating and protective powers of mewri do not work (as, for example, in the case of the service from our own modern state) against any hidden failings from its own abusive force, but rather against those from human agency. The divine eternal elements of mewri (of which humans take full advantage) may lose their proper influence upon society, but not because of any weakness or failing on their part—rather, because of human intent. The dangers to human society, which the circular encompassment of mewri serves to mediate between and to protect against, stem from the dark shamanic intent of human ill will. The deadly partnership between divine forces and the dark shaman can be avoided, or at least be reduced to an innocuous relationship, by the attained safe familiarity of mewri. Always imminent, always now, always receding, the balance and harmony pertaining to divine eternity as the placelessness and timelessness existing outside of space and time cannot be influenced, but the particularities of individual body and community that they pass through in order to give them life certainly can be put under threat. For the harmonious fusion of society to attain its safe familiarity and counterfeit beauty from divine eternity, human intent and agency have to negotiate the balance to the complementarily opposed tendencies inside space and time. It is here that the ideological privileging of negotiators takes its effect.

In bringing the kumyarï and mïna leaves together as the completeness of the roof, masculinity identifies itself by means of one of the primary processes signaling the unification and hence the continuance of society. In doing so it is able to articulate its political claims to being principal participant in the creative reproduction of organized society. The cultural meanings established in the leaves and other materials of house construction, as well as the ordered procedures given to the building of the house, all help to validate such claims. Yet it is fundamentally in its rights to the uncontested evidence of men's bodies that masculinity most ostentatiously articulates its access to the crùcial elements of the reproductive social process. Within the cultural space and time of individual mortality, masculinity privileges the bodies of men not just with their distinct gender difference but also with the specific agency to negotiate the formal representation of the feminine.[5] The somatic fact of masculinity acquires the privileged intentionality and agency to produce the safe haven of society not only for men but also for women. It is ideologically the formal political work of men to bring together the opposed gender differences as the reconciled placelessness and timelessness of the familiar house. The supposedly better-wrapped and encased bodies of men have the better qualities of management ascribed to them. Nonetheless, apart from the imperative role of making evident the bodies of women, it is femininity that provides men with the objective elements of difference necessary for expressing their managerial skills. Without the difference of muliebrity there would be no privileged space of manhood, no asymmetrical opposition to be reconciled, and no society to be continued.

This bringing together of the opposed elements of gender differences may not necessarily be a case of men's appropriating the at-

tributes of womanhood. Men do, after all, have to contribute their
own productive masculinity to the combined effect of the whole.
They have to come to know and experience their own masculinity
and, in doing so, come to know and experience both an incompleteness of being and the full force of a social requirement to complete themselves with the complementarily opposed otherness of
the feminine. By what can be interpreted from the accumulated
Waiwai ideas and actions on the topic, the aesthetic of mewri ca-
pably protects this vulnerable gender difference of the individual.
Men's actions with the aesthetics of mewri carefully perform this
apotropaic work by coupling the gendered body of the individual
with its complementarily opposed other and encompassing them
both as the contained elements of moral society. Even so, in the very
act of protective coupling and encompassing, the plaited beauty in
mewri attributes a formal privileging to Waiwai manhood.

Many of the cultural proclamations of Waiwai manhood invariably carry with them an announcement about the asymmetrical relations between the social categories of masculinity and femininity.
When these claims are made and when they specifically refer to
masculinity or femininity standing on its own (that is, like individual
leaves apart from any cluster, or leaves not yet plaited), they can be
interpreted as statements about the ugliness and immoral worth of
asymmetrical gender relations. This particular kind of asymmetry,
the kind that keeps genders separated while at the same time ranking
them, has to be ideologically proclaimed (that is, has to be in the
conscious public domain). This asymmetry has to be so proclaimed
because the very purpose of social life—the actual project of living
in the human world—is to eradicate such ugliness and replace it
with the beauty of mewri. In this regard merely being a man or a
woman without achieving the proper plaited reconciliation (or "accommodation") between the different genders keeps the individual
vulnerable to the dangers of the world. It could be argued (from our
point of view) that just retaining the differences between genders
makes conspicuous the category domain of one or the other gender
and hence the asymmetry between the two. But this could only be

so within a cultural context of dominance such as our own, where the very idiom of proclaimed differences already privileges one over the other as an expression of dominance. In such a context not even the desire to reconcile the opposition between the differences can be made without this privileging of asymmetry as dominance. In the particular Waiwai example, however, one of the functional requirements of the momentary privileging of an asymmetry, even in the attainment of beauty, is to sustain the asymmetry just long enough to manage the achievement of beauty. In Waiwai ideology the achievement of beauty does not necessarily remove gender hierarchy; the plaited beauty of gender relations simply eradicates the ugly spaces between masculinity and femininity, allowing them to embrace as human pleasure and as the beauty of rank without domination. This is particularly the case with the pleasurable sentiment of *wayamnu*.

In no more emotionally felt experience than the wayamnu sentiment of erotic love does the embrace of gender difference relieve the ugliness of dominance and achieve the plaited beauty of fulfilled desire. The "otherness" or "strangeness" of the opposed gender in the category of wayamnu seems in and of itself to stimulate romantic passion. It could even be argued that it is actually in the erotics of a legitimately placed sexual other that the conviviality necessary for society to continue begins. Growing into the proper moral knowledge supportive of the actions and rules recognizable for living harmoniously together as a people, sexual passion flowers into convivial compassion (Santos-Granero 1991; Overing 1996, 2000; Kidd 2000). In the Waiwai case the knowledge of compassionate love stems from the erotics of passionate love. The plaited beauty of entwined bodies relieves any suffering from the loneliness felt by the engorged rush of sexual desire. In eradicating the ugly spaces between their gendered bodies, lovers achieve the "virtue-centred morality" (Overing and Alan 2000:5) upon which the beauty of collective conviviality is formed.[6] The very energy of masculinity passes into femininity to become properly housed in its complementary position and role as the object of a feminine embrace. Only in such reconciliation can the beauty of convivial community be lived.

One should take note, however, that even while in the process of removing ugliness with love, the Waiwai ideology on emotion and thought never displays any veiled attempts or hidden anxieties to alter the particular asymmetrical character of gender relations.

No term for or understanding of "guilt"—as in the sense of a transgressive soul or failed subjectivity—can be found in traditional Waiwai concepts. Certainly no idea of a "sin" against divine law or divine beings can be discovered investing itself in feelings of emotional anxieties pertaining to an autonomous selfhood. No notion of going against the grace of divinity by seeking to alter the "nature" of gender difference is placed between subjectivity and the actions to transform the ugly into the beautiful. If an idea exists about remorse—contained in the feelings of tenderness or compassion—then it is one aroused principally because of thoughts about the suffering of the lonely other. The need to relieve the pain of a conscious realization of loneliness in the other gender creates the compassion that stimulates solidarity. The collective solidarity of the village begins with erotic passion—that is, with sexual longing for the other gender, which then becomes reconciled for the lonely sufferers by a kind of sympathy for each other. What is transformed with love is not asymmetry, but rather the ugly suffering of unsatisfied emotional desire.

Unlike our own Western tradition of seeking and establishing equality in the face of supposedly inherent inequalities (often understood to be in and of nature), Waiwai notions of moral beauty and justice do not demand parity in a brazen compensatory manner. Their notions of moral beauty and justice would not, for example, be immediately instigated as new rules in order to counterbalance recently discovered or slowly developing deficiencies. Such notions would certainly expect an equity, however—that is, a fairness understood not in terms of an equal distribution of moral worth between asymmetrically ranked persons, but rather in terms of a balance between persons and the recognized moral worth due to their social roles. For example, the different categories of womanhood must expect and receive various forms of respect and esteem that match, in moral worth, the different social roles played by women. The same applies to manhood. This is not merely a question of different kinds and qualities of social worth, but one of actually having to match the proper amount of social worth due to differently ranked persons. Village leadership expects to receive and is duly given more respect than ordinary personhood, because the role of the leader has more responsibility in its performance of community duties and even a greater vulnerability to the dangers of the outside. An older married woman with children expects and is given more esteem than an unmarried young woman, because her category of social person-hood has greater varied responsibilities and duties to household and community. The number and diversity of her social obligations do indeed put her in positions of greater vulnerability than her younger unmarried counterpart. Balancing the social worth recognizably due to a legitimate social person is the attainment of an equity. Waiwai notions of moral beauty and justice demand equity between per-sonhood and its established social worth, and yet equality or parity between legitimately different and opposing ranks is not sought. To make the latter work without the imprint of harsh domination, the cultural weight and emphasis of moral notions bear upon the noncontested features of gender asymmetry; hence, the ideological privileging of the roles of men will always be accompanied by their incontestableness. In the particular example of the architectural an-nouncement of the beauty of ranked difference, gender asymme-try and its incontestable features appear conjoined. The syndicated bound between privilege and any lack of challenge to privilege helps to make the general acceptance of ranked difference aesthetically pleasing.

Meanwhile, the completeness of the roof assists in confirming asymmetry as placeless, as timeless, and as the beautiful, safe famil-iarity of gendered life. It is like the proper completeness of being. It is gender asymmetry justified and, as such, predicates itself as ideologically incontestable. Hence, in the practical orchestration of everyday life, asymmetrical balance has itself favorably positioned before any maneuvering can take place. As its paradigm implies, without the superordinate position given to men by the structural accommodation of womanhood, masculinity would find it difficult if not impossible to attain and operate its privileges. Within the political field, for instance, the maneuvering of men among themselves can only become tenable in their particular Waiwai manifestations when the gender asymmetry between men and women supersedes the asymmetry between men. Cultural proclamations announce that without asymmetrical balance, the question of political obedience would have to be negotiated at almost every frontier of difference and not just at those legitimately prescribed to the authority of men. At every other frontier there is no questioning, no negotiating, simply compliance to an overall moral imperative of being. With proper fit, proper equilibrium, proper balancing of the complementarily opposed parts, no remainder can exist. The dangers of any subtraction can be avoided. The single most significant message from the multirepresented statements of the house is that of reconciled difference.

Passionate Human Sexuality and Mewrï

From an anthropological point of view, the house apparently renders such themes as settlement endogamy, gender hierarchy, thatched completeness, balanced wholeness, and forged unification as if they were the reconciled adornment of society. In the material manifestation of the visually overwhelming roof, the house offers the representation of a pleasing community. From a Waiwai point of view it takes all the vibrant contradictions and encircles them, thereby transforming the *kičičime* (badness, danger, and ugliness) of society into the kirewani (goodness, safety, and beauty) of encirclement. The perpetuity of society and the elements of its possible discontinuity coexist in the aesthetics of encompassment. When encompassing and containing, the circular house specifically targets and seeks to reconcile the perceived generated contradictions of human energy. Bodily adornment already encompasses the flow of vibrant energies emanating from each individual, but it is the house and its design that place the combined energies of the collective bodies—as community—under the constraint of circular reconciliation. The ideological argument makes the claim that without this encompassment and containment by the design of the roof, the full combined force of opposing human energies would entwine and pass through each other with such force that they would destroy themselves. Of particular concern in this regard—and indeed what the Waiwai keep returning to as a form of explanation—are the sexual energies of gender differences.

They say that the sexual energies of men and women are most active and felt most intensely by those in the wayamnu (potential spouse / tortoise) category. In the cultural statements of a manifestly masculine ideology, it is invariably the particular excessive flow of women's erotic energies that most threatens and, hence, requires the most vigilance. In Waiwai logic any overflow of women's sexual feelings threatens the collective totality of community. The interesting sequence of ideas that leads toward this conclusion moves through the thought that by arousing masculine sexuality, the excess flow of women's eroticism can raise the temperature of male passion to such heights that the latter will eventually break out from its encompassed confinement within masculine bodies. This train of thought begins with the idea that because women's bodies are more open, their *ñenkariwa* (female sexual feelings) are more susceptible to passionate overflow. Here the cultural techniques of confinement seem more prone to defeat when confronted by the bodily energies of women—except, of course, when these become the very means of confinement. Whenever the sexual feelings of women overcome their confinement and overflow, the thought is that they work directly upon men's *nankariwa* (male sexual feelings), deliberately seeking them out for feminine satisfaction. Thus do the bodies of men become dangerously reduced by the outbreak of their own erotic passions. Both kinds of gender arousal cause the body to heat up and writhe with excitement. Hence it is perceived that without the asymmetrical balance of mewrï—which successfully combines, then further confines the different sexual energies within manageable degrees—the erotic energies of men and women would boil and convulse into dangerous supplementary passions. The threat to the community stems from mewrï being unable to confine such excess by its technical means of plaiting the differences together.[7]

As I have mentioned, perhaps of all the constraining adornments of the individual body, it is the designed mïiso, the man's decorated hair tube, that most obviously analogizes the thatched roof. So similar in name to the house (mïi[m]o / mïi[s]o), the hair tube traditionally encompasses and contains the exuberant energies of men's long hair. Relying on the shared analogies of form and function, both circular artifacts proclaim their constraint over the sensuous human body. They provide an acceptable beauty to the management of the procreative flow of sexual fluids, of the fecundated flow of growing hair, and of the passionate flow of the wayamnu sentiment. The head hair of a young girl who menstruates for the first time has to be ritually shaved off and (in her confinement hut) be allowed to grow again, with all its fresh new eroticism guided by the cultural constraints of society. Like the procreative vitality of her sexual fluids, her coiled hair must display the body's willingness to submit to society and be representative of its beauty. The same applies to the procreative and erotic vitalities of men. With the circular reconciling of men's bodies by domicile and hair tube, masculine vitalities assist in the adorning of the status of marriage; they beautify the conjugal union not simply as the completeness of adult status (Rivière 1969b:155; Stephen Hugh-Jones 1979:205), but more fully as the physical being of impeding parenthood. For masculinity the achievement of manhood does not merely come about with marriage and its legitimacies of sexual intercourse in marriage, but with the success of being both husband and father in entwined embrace with wife and child. In this way successful manhood accomplishes an arrival.

The point that vulnerable masculinity succeeds in reaching may not (at least for the Waiwai) be "the most humble and painful truths" (Clastres 1998:50) about its mortality. In Waiwai concepts and beliefs, there is nothing "inevitable and cruel" (Clastres 1998:51) about the death of the body, only the clear certainty of the ill will and dark, shamanic words of humanity. By using mewrï to protect against such dangers with passionate and compassionate love, the individual and the community can arrive at the experience of balancing the complementarily opposed parts of existence. If in Waiwai culture death is to be understood as a kind of subtraction to be avoided, this is not because of its inevitability and cruelty (to body or to emotions), but rather because of the ugly imbalances and unreconciled differences it brings about. The issue, it seems, does not concern an absence, a void, or a silence (which supposedly cannot express a being), but the creative management of a life of love.

The Waiwai do not sit around waiting for death, nor do they live in constant fear of their own mortality. They do not have what to us would be the familiar institutional sites or formally prescribed social spaces for intellectual debates about the meaning of life. A confidence and certainty about existence already occupies a secure position, one that does not require a culture of interrogation. Indeed much of what goes on in the daily lives of villagers takes place without any need for questions. The creative process of a human life of love is about seeking to maintain the proper balance and harmony between manifest differences. Knowing the prescribed route toward complete being and understanding mewrï to be the preparatory means for all contingencies provide a confidence for living. A part of this contingent confidence also comes from the Waiwai appreciation of the full effects that spiritual vitality has upon the material world.

It would not be an interpretation exclusive to psychology and anthropology to corroborate, for example, that hair can symbolize "genital displacement" (Berg 1951; Leach 1958; Rivière 1969b; Seeger 1975; Terence Turner 1980) and that the Waiwai hair tube can represent the containment of men's "libidinous energy" (Rivière 1969b:156). In Waiwai ideas the relation between hair and genitalia produces and sustains the meaning of sexual potency precisely because of the understood attributes of spiritual vitality that run through it. Thus when the generative force of spirit "associated with sexual incontinence and the lower cosmic levels" (Rivière

1969b:161) accommodates the hair tube with its constraint, it is because the circular harnessing by mewrï works indirectly through the impassioned body to balance itself with divinity.

As in its architectural encasement by the conical roof, in its sartorial encasement by the bamboo tube, and in its institutional encasement by marriage, passionate human sexuality finds safe expression in the familiarity of mewrï. The spiritual entities in human sexuality and mewrï converge, as it were, to become material manifestations of divine spirit. To be asymmetrically balanced and harmonious as the convivial goodness and beauty of the compassionate body, divine spirit accommodates its own transcendent potency in human sexuality, hair, leaves, and mewrï. Without the effect of this accommodation, the generative force of divine spirit would be too excessive and, instead of being creative, would be destructive for humankind. The evoked fractional, interactive, and dependent human ekatï would refract, diffuse, and return to pure spirit. In the Waiwai paradigm of human existence, people who live together have to seek each other out for assistance in order to achieve the safety, goodness, and beauty of spiritual vitalities. The circuit of divinity, in giving proper life to humanity, must flow through a community of complementarily opposed individuals in passionate and compassionate love.

It is difficult to conclude this discussion without a reminder. For the Waiwai it is obvious. For me, however, it has been difficult to sustain the point within the linearity of the argument. The reminder is that even though, by the tubular constraint of male hair and sexuality, mewrï confines the excess of its own spiritual vitality, it must not be forgotten that as part of a feminine moral aesthetic, it is the mewrï of womanhood that takes on the responsibility of assisting masculinity in its adorned encompassment.

The hair tube of men, in its more dramatic ceremonial beaded form, is the product of a woman's bodily energy. In the division of labor between men and women over the production of ceremonial costumes, it is women who string and twine the beads around the mïiso worn by men. In other words it can be said that not only is femininity capable of enticing masculinity to dangerous excesses, it also has the more social and moral responsibilities of directly contributing to the attainment of manhood and to the manufacture of masculine beauty. This service of femininity can, from an anthropological view, be considered an appropriation of the formulated individual awareness about being woman—an awareness that society uses (at the level of collective consciousness) to verify its own existence.[8] Womanhood and society exist transcendent of the individual—beyond the body of woman. What femininity provides becomes a service on behalf of society. No longer just a custom, the making of mïiso appears like a duty. It could be argued that it is in this respect similar to the plaiting of the roof by men. The duty of masculinity here provides the services of its bodily energies as if they were representative of society. There does not appear to be any sense of alienation on the part of the individual about such a contribution.

In Waiwai society the politics of identity does not operate as if a great chasm exists between individual desire and the fulfillment of beauty and goodness. With particular reference to the feminine designer of mïiso and her masculine client, the social determinant provides them with the inalienable intimacy of the wayamnu sentiment and the epeka relation. Invariably, the relationship between the designer and her client is defined in the terms of passion or compassion. Between a woman and a man involved in the making and wearing of the hair tube, their relationship carries the simple message that it assists them in keeping their sexual energies under constraint and, in so doing, aids them in the achievement of their gendered beauty.

The Wayamnu Sentiment

The look in their eyes spoke tenderly of romance. Its voiceless words we could hear from our involuntary oblivion. Lost from the concentrated gaze of desire, we basked in the lyrical rendering of their deep affection. The gendered beauty of their entwined bodies achieved a passionate poetry. Its plaited aesthetic was erotic. It stimulated the blood. It kept the body hot. It forced attentiveness upon the object of desire. It served to contain and encompass a mutual devotion, made time irrelevant, and turned space in upon itself. The two lovers felt the counterpoised emotions of their gendered passion. Only the design of their sexual bodies could reconcile the differential heat. In their emotional spirit and in the limit of their cultural understanding, Eup and Uracharak lived in the full flush of the wayamnu sentiment.[1]

One has only to mention the word *wayamnu* in Waiwai public life to receive a cascade of giggles and beams of knowledgeable smiles. People understand the personal nuances of the sentiment and the effect of its eroticism upon individuals. Their shared understandings about the thrill in meeting, containing, and quelling the dangers of aroused sexual passion produce the somewhat embarrassed reactions when the word *wayamnu* is mentioned. The wayamnu sentiment belongs to the domain of the personal, the private, the intimacy of a coupling. When it meets the objectified public world in the voiced word, it sends ripples of involuntary joy among its listeners. Using the word in reference to the romance between Eup and Uracharak brought joy to the village.

This was not simply the selfish euphoria of a community knowing well that the romance of the young couple held the prospect of marriage, parenthood, children, and, therefore, the further prosperity of the village. Rather it was the immediate, heady stuff of appreciating beauty—of seeing the all-consuming happiness of the young couple fill the entire public space of the village. It was intoxicating. Everyone knew about the romance, and everyone appeared drunk on the knowledge. It was all we could talk about. On the river, in the farms, lying in our hammocks, our complete attention rested upon the two lovers, while all else wobbled by unheeded. The exemplified beauty of their wayamnu sentiment had become a palpable thing. It had even been spoken of in terms of that infamous Wapishana concept of *bina*—magical spell. The "magic" of love had affected us all, but its concentrated force had its greatest pull upon the lovers, drawing them together and encompassing them with the design of pleasure.

Uracharak had, since his recent arrival from Brazil, purposely and single-mindedly courted the ebullient Eup. As a visitor and a guest in the village, he had few if any formal chores to carry out. He had arrived with his father and a few other men on the annual, short rainy-season visit. Now that the small villages of the past have agglomerated into large, widely dispersed settlements, visits by wayamnu from other settlements have had to be well thought out, intense, and emphatic. In this way the act of courting itself, and not the arranged visit, becomes spontaneous, creative, and full of strong sentiment. Before arriving in the village, each suitor already knows the names of the women available to him as wayamnu. With all other preliminaries taken care of, suitors can devote their entire attention to the weave of romance. While in the village, the suitor will settle upon a particular wayamnu. His intent will be to stimulate an interest in her for him—an interest so intense that the result has to be the plait of love and its encompassed design for marriage. Paying absolute attention to the loved one—by being close to her, touching

[handwritten: trying to create communal living through courting]

[handwritten in right margin: theme]

[handwritten in right margin: same ideas about love]

her, talking to her, in fact closing out all of her daily activities so that her only thought remains that of her suitor—gives the impression of a chase. It is the kind of chase whereby the object being pursued becomes trapped through the constraint of its actions. The suitor in effect mesmerizes the loved one. If all goes well in the suit, no harm results from the chase and the entrapment. Both parties appear to gain the gift of each other's love and pass into each other to become the perfect complement of one another. The longing, the desire, subsides into the institution of marriage and the perpetuation of the village community.

At every opportunity that they could muster, Eup and Uracharak found themselves together. Who was entrapping whom, however, seemed to be highly debatable. After all it had been Uracharak who had traveled all the way from Brazil to court Eup. It was Uracharak who had to untie, with fretful anticipation, each knot in the long string marking the days between him and his arrival at his beloved's village. It was Uracharak who wandered around the settlement without anything to do but be enchanted by Eup. Both lovers shared in the embarrassment of their bodies. Both displayed the telltale signs of their desire. The shy smiles, the awkward laughter, the clumsy fumbling with words, all betrayed the knowledge of their longing. They wanted to be together. They seemed right for each other. Eup, the daughter of the village leader, had attracted a young man well known for his skills as a hunter. The match had no dissenters; no one, not even Shamawa, her father, interfered in their courtship. The logic of their bonding—the reconciled differences of their genders—made perfect sense to everyone. The problem for the village community was how to keep the couple resident in Shepariymo. After setting the passions of love into motion, where were the lovers going to resolve their desires?

The day had come for the party from Brazil to return. We had all been feeling the emotional pull of the moment. No one had offered an interpretation of what to expect, so an empty point existed toward which we were all headed. Not knowing what to expect had made us tense and restless; no one could settle down to a single task. During the morning, as the visitors prepared their canoe, loaded their backpacks, and untied their hammocks, we all moved hesitantly, hoping for the best but expecting the worst. By midmorning it became clear that the worst was on its way. An outburst of wailing so sudden, so pitiful, tore its way from the house of Shamawa. Someone had told Eup that Uracharak was packing and preparing to return with the visitors.

This was no ordinary crying. This tearful expression of sorrow was not the sound of a fleeting agony. Everyone knew this and everyone became instantly troubled. It was not that Eup cried. Everyone had anticipated that she would have been saddened by the departure of the visitors, even if she had been going with them, leaving her own family and friends behind. It was not even that she cried at the news of Uracharak's intent to depart without her. No, her crying became perturbing because, once she had started doing so, Eup would not stop. Her crying was incessant. It went on and on without pause. She cried throughout the morning, the midday, and into the afternoon. And she cried alone. The sound was eerie. It cut through the air like an ancient wind. It blew over the river, into the forest, and toward the distant mountains—a plaintive sound of distress to which any predator would be attracted. It brought a horror down upon the community, and we all cast around for an explanation of this unusual event.

The affairs of the heart always produce reams of ideas about the human passion for love. The wayamnu sentiment certainly had volumes to contribute on the topic. For the Waiwai the effect of its beauty, the deep feeling of joy it brings about, exemplifies the pleasurable plaited design of life itself. In all regards the wayamnu sentiment begins with the body. Gendered bodies entwine in complementariness. Oppositional sexes pass into each other, not to eliminate each other but—like the leaves of the roof—in order to make a single entity with their differences. The impact upon the senses by the wayamnu sentiment does nothing more thoroughly than to inform human consciousness of the very vibrancy of the body. In my understanding from the Waiwai on the topic, the ecstasy of life

BODY → love

has its most rewarding existence in the sentiment of love. They say, for example, that the wayamnu sentiment makes all those under its influence more generous. Giving becomes an enjoyable act. So complete do lovers become in their sense of what they are while in the comfort of their beloved, they happily fulfill the want in others without a sense of lack on their own part. But perhaps more thrilling than the joy of such altruism is the way in which love makes the notions of time and space integral themes of its character, for to be in love is to bring to the foreground the finite modes of a human mortality that shamelessly confronts death and denies it the one and only means of existing—the body. What the sentient body permits while in love is the temporal and spatial experiences for feeling the living tissue of romantic life. The capillaries of experience send the sentiment of love back and forth within the body. The passion felt at the sight of a beloved, or even the pain inflicted by the absence of a lover, conveys an awareness that tells the body it is fully alive. Death has no quarter while love can be felt. What we had figured out as a community about the strange malady of Eup's crying was that death appeared to be taking steps to challenge love and to claim the body of a wayamnu.

The incessant, lonely crying of Eup was harrowing for the community because it clearly signaled to them the presence of sorcery. On the breath of a dark shamanic influence, mystical words had taken an inadvertent effect. The general opinion had been that in his courtship Uracharak had used the powerful love magic of the *torowo* (small songbird) erem (silent predatory words) in order to gain the affections of Eup. In the same way a hunter would employ the assistance of various forms of hunting potions to assist him in capturing game, so too can a lover engage the persuasive forces of the relationship between the shaman and the spiritual world to constrain the actions of a beloved and stimulate a desirable interest in her for him. As in any human entanglement with spiritual powers, however, no one can actually predict the outcome of engaged spirituality. In the case of Uracharak and Eup, the mesmeric influence upon the latter by the spiritual vitality of the songbird magic worked with such thorough effect that it took on an intent and intensity of its own, beyond the demands of Uracharak himself. At least in the mechanics of its actions, the incessant, lonely crying of Eup mimicked the plaintive, repetitive song of the bird so accurately that it took on the danger of disappearing into itself. The horror of Eup's predicament was that her now unfulfilled desire for Uracharak had taken on a sentiment so strong it could easily turn into one that could destroy her—she had to be "plaited" to Uracharak; she could not now be left on her own as a woman in love. The empty space between the two lovers had become an abyss into which the incessant, lonely crying of Eup could travel and never return. The objectified continuous and repetitive crying—manifested as her spiritual vitality—would find, in the space between, merely itself and not her body in which to return. It would, like any dislodged and/or wandering spiritual entity, find only the original and welcoming pure spirit of divinity. What we all found worrying was how many of us—that is, how much of our own collective spirituality—would Eup's transcendent self carry with it in its plaintive agony. The presence of sorcery indicated an attack not just on Uep but also on the whole community. It had targeted the separation between the lovers and had in that motion attacked the plaited design of village life. In other words it would not allow the gendered leaves of the roof to become a balanced beauty of harmony.

To remove this ugliness and deflect the threat of death, we all had to take quick and deliberate action. Uracharak and his party had already loaded their canoe and were preparing to depart. For some odd reason (only made clear much later on) the visitors had chosen to leave while Shamawa was not in the village. It may have been a ploy by Uracharak to have eloped with Eup, or at least to take away from her family the option of a refusal to take her with him. Only Shamawa, as father, as village leader, as exemplary human representative of house and community, could actually approve the move by Eup to go and live in another village as a wife. He was not available for this approval. Uracharak was on his way, and Eup could not leave with him. For Shamawa not to have been on the scene when the visitors were departing seemed staged to me. I even thought that it might have been his way of testing his daughter or the very love she and Uracharak felt for each other. After all, daughters are supposed to stay in the village of the parents; they are supposed to attract husbands who will remain and add to the life and prosperity of the community. It would not have been the proper duty of leadership nor even in the best interests of the community for Shamawa not to be seen influencing the couple to remain and live in the village. We understood his absence as a political strategy in forcing Uracharak to remain and become a husband and member of the village. As it turned out, the strategy was not working. We had to send for Shamawa.

He had been fishing downriver. Uracharak and his party had left upriver for the Brazilian border. By the time Shamawa had arrived, the visitors were half a day and many bends of the river on their way home. After he had been informed of what had transpired and with Eup still crying dangerously, Shamawa and four of the strongest rowers in the village manned our fastest canoe. In the canoe, as its principal passenger, sat Eup with her hurriedly tied-up bag of belongings. As we heard the rhythmic thud of paddles upon the hull echoing hollowly across the water, as we watched from the embankment the powerful shoulders of the rowers rapidly pulling the canoe across the river, a familiar tranquility returned to the village. Eup had stopped crying.

We were told, when Shamawa returned, that they had caught up with the heavy, slow-moving canoe of the visitors, whereupon they had transferred Eup to the visitor's canoe and to the arms of her lover. Shamawa blessed their union and said good-bye to his daughter. What he had failed politically to achieve for his community he had succeeded morally to achieve for the wayamnu sentiment of his daughter. The love between Uracharak and Eup would now go toward the beauty and balance of another village community. Their gendered complementary opposition would now contribute to the plaited design of mortal life in another covered and encompassed place-where-people-live.

significance (?)

Notes

Prologue

1. If the logic of text does indeed obtain and offer meaning by enforcing coherence in its inscribed representations, it must do so, it seems to me, through simulating the exile of certain procedural patterns. In the same way that writing apparently "murders" or supposes the "death" of its own author in order to be communicative (Derrida 1991:87–88; Foucault 1993:117), textual logic has to exile specific aspects of itself in order to produce meaning. Each seeks an absence on behalf of coherence. To understand and to be understood, particularly in our literate world, requires an enforced coherence, a closure that limits, a shutdown that, when opened or even in the opening, closes again in mimicry of death, absence, or exile.

   I am here, of course, making inference to Michel Foucault's view of writing as a "voluntary obliteration of the self," where the author's work has "the right to kill" (1993:117). The author serves as victim, a sacrificial victim of a writing that cuts itself off from and continues beyond the life of its absent producer. It is this absence, in Jacques Derrida's terms, that "belongs to the structure of all writing" (1991:88).

2. I am using the term *author* in the same limited sense as Foucault, who concentrates on "the singular relationship that holds between an author and a text, the manner in which a text apparently points to this figure who is outside and precedes it" (1993:115), and on the "author-function" that "characterize[s] the existence, circulation, and operation of certain discourses within a society" (1993:124). What interests me

most about the use of this term is the double way in which it turns upon the ethics of writing, or what Roland Barthes has called "the morality of form" (1988:15). Here the anthropologist as author not only obligatorily reproduces and sustains the anthropological discourse but, in doing so, also casts the textually objectified Other in the morally acceptable role of subsidiary—one subordinate to the relation between author and text.

3. I am working here with the view that we come to know the past through formulated notions of time. For us brought up in the Western tradition, it is our formulated ideas of time as systemic interdependent elements that serve to introduce us to the past. It seems we cannot know the past without knowing it in relation to the present and the future. Yet when we think of temporality, we tend to do so in terms of a series of perishable, constantly changing points of now. Hence our theory of time only offers us the past and the future from the view of the present. The past seems always to be understood first and foremost as an elapsed period; constituted as a completion of preceding moments or as a duration before the present, it implies a notion of time meticulously measured and divided into a series of "nows." It is this calculable character of time that we use as an aid in our interpretation of living in the world. It is this notion of time serially construed that gives substance to our understanding of the past.

4. We can see, specifically with ethnographies, how the significance of the author's role makes itself intensely felt by anthropologists. I particularly have in mind the contrasting objectives and text of Jean-Paul Dumont's *The Headman and I* and Jacques Lizot's *Tales of the Yanomami*. In each case the distinct cast of the author's relation to his text provides a different rendition of the anthropological Other. I am certainly convinced by Dumont's concern for the "distancing effect" (1978:47) of temporal and spatial delay, for it allowed him to locate himself and the Panare in a sensitive retrospection, one in which we constantly see him negotiating the logic of their statements. I am equally convinced, however, by Lizot's attempt to reduce the distance of time and space between his field experience and "the book," for it clearly affected his desire "to recede into the background as completely as possible" (1985:xiv). His

"book was written in the field" and sought "to describe . . . Amerindian society . . . while reducing sociological interpretation to a minimum by suggesting rather than stating it" (1985:xiii).

5. This brings to mind what Michael Taussig has called the "mimetic faculty," where "granting the copy the character and power of the original [allows], the representation the power of the represented" (1993:xviii). We could, with some historical irony, view anthropological literacy not so much as a case of mistaking copy for original but as a distinct example of sympathetic magic.

6. British Guiana changed its name to Guyana in 1966 when it gained independence from Britain.

7. Anthropology can openly declare its guilt (even if it is merely to avoid being accused of hypocrisy); it can plead guilty to the charge of exiling knowledge about the ways in which its own constructiveness influences the articulation of otherness. By succumbing to the silence of innocence, anthropology surely displays an unwarranted insecurity. Because an official announcement of guilt might deny belief in its textual facility to reflect the world and, consequently, might undermine its authority over the objectified Other, its silence serves to represent a vulnerability. Yet drawing attention away from this vulnerability does not necessarily function as justified practice for protecting the discipline. If one extends the discipline's own rationale, one finds that it has no actual autonomy to protect; it is as dependent upon culture and society as any other manifestation of human endeavor. In fact because it is subject to the same determinants of intelligibility, when it articulates about the Other it articulates about its self. This should always be affirmed. With such an affirmation, the potency of otherness can indeed be expressed in text. With guilt affirmed anthropological literacy can surely articulate the Other's full potential for constructing the world in ways so different they openly challenge our own and actually make us question our own firmly held veracities. I believe this kind of articulating in anthropology could be so adept that it could cogently represent the challenge to itself; it could indeed be the impressive result of an experience with otherness and still be recognizably anthropological.

8. As anthropology continues to be expressive as an innate feature (rather

than as an acquired product of culture and society), it induces us to honor the discipline with its exclusive authority to articulate a coherence about the anthropological Other. I, for one, openly admit to a confidence in its mimetic artifice of closure. I am confident that through this means it seeks to contrive meaning around forms of being and knowing that seem far too threatening for the literacy of other academic disciplines. Yet I remain sensitive to the possibility that such immunity has systematically worked against some of the most yearned-for goals of the discipline. Suitable and legitimate in articulating the Other's constructiveness, yes, but anthropology's own exiled constructiveness never appears to benefit overtly from the craft. I want to think that introducing its constructiveness to scrutiny could help to animadvert a kinder disposition. An introduction of such a disposition should, for example, help to greet more graciously such outrageous claims as "my reconstructions hardly differed from reality" (Malinowski 1984 [1922]:376). Claims like these can be more courteously understood not as products of false reasoning or even as "obsessional empiricism" (Leach 1970:120) but rather as the overall effect of an anthropological coherence. Exiling the prospect of text's inability to mirror the world and exiling any conscious part one plays in creating the effect of mirroring succeed as very skillful expedients of an anthropological literacy. To close around the being and the knowing of the Other in this way allows anthropology both to shield itself against the problematic(s) of its own devices and to make innocuous any harmful results that may emanate from otherness. Through the expedience of an anthropological literacy and as part of its own hard-won legitimacy, the discipline possesses and uses techniques to reduce attacks against itself from the Other's potent ways of being and knowing, but in doing so, it also limits itself.

Shepariymo

1. I will be referring throughout to the plant *Manihot utilissima* not by its older name of "cassava" (originally from the Antillean Arawakan word *casavi* and since 1555 altered to its present form [Little, Fowler, and Coulson 1980:291]), or by its mainland Tupi-influenced *mandioca* and

Guarani-influenced *mandio* (Little, Fowler, and Coulson 1980:1272) name of "manioc," but by its common Carib name of "yuca."

2. In our racial terms *panakuri* can be interpreted as "white people." In Waiwai terms the similarity between the protruding proboscis of the sunfish and the nose on a "white" person's face has allowed them to carry the name of the fish into the linguistic marking of the human.

3. While it would indeed be difficult to argue that among the Waiwai an overall strategy of illegalities containing legal punishment exists or that a mediation of penalty forms part of their mechanisms of domination, it could nonetheless be reasonably maintained that for their society "penalty does not simply 'check' illegalities; it 'differentiates' them, it provides them with a general 'economy'" (Foucault 1979:272). Here the subjugation of the individual to society proclaims punishment to be working upon distinguishing the offences that society can use to justify further the particular configuration of its own existence and not upon eliminating individual offenses that would lead to a "purer," more "moral" individual or society. The crux of the issue has to do with maintaining the pliable movement of power between the body and its social context.

4. In Waiwai a series of meaningful links are drawn between and marked by the words *manmo [man][mo]* and *nasiya [na][si][ya]* (to capture or be captured by aquatic or terrestrial animals) and *yasi [ya][si]* (to capture or be captured by spiritual vitalities). The word for marriage is *man-siya [man][si][ya]*, which appears to carry with it some of the meanings derived from hunting.

5. Anthropology often begins to make sense of human social organization by noting which different kinship relations are "classified" by the same term (Morgan 1870; Royal Anthropological Institute 1951 [1874]; Fox 1967; Radcliffe-Brown and Forde 1975 [1950]). Much of lowland South American anthropology considers the societies of this region to be "characterized by the kind of kin classificatory system commonly referred to as 'Dravidian': the universe of kinsmen is bifurcated along the lines of a cross/parallel distinction and terms for cross relatives are the same as terms for affines" (Kensinger 1984:2).

6. Here I am referring specifically to the brothers Neill and Robert

Hawkins and their family from Dallas, Texas, who came to the Essequibo under the auspices of the Unevangelized Fields Mission—a Pennsylvania Protestant missionary sect intent upon Waiwai Christian conversion (Dowdy 1964). Their mission of conversion hinged crucially upon being able to live among the Waiwai-speaking community, because only through this pedagogical strategy (inaugurated by William Cameron Townsend in 1919 and possibly taught to the brothers through the Summer Institution of Linguistics) could they hope to translate the English version of the New Testament into Waiwai. Thus we have the statement that "field work was done in periods of three, four, and seven months respectively in 1949, 1950, and 1951" (W. Neill Hawkins and Robert E. Hawkins 1953:201).

7. The Unevangelized Fields Mission maintained their presence among the Waiwai of the upper Essequibo River for about twenty-four years (from 1949 to sometime between 1971 and 1973). They currently live and continue their work, reconstituted as MEVA (Missão Evangélica da Amazônia), with the southern Waiwai on the Mapuera River in Brazil (Ricardo 1983:234; Caixeta de Queiroz 1996; Ramos 1998:30). Though their Christian morality and its early influence upon residential space came face to face with contrasting Waiwai customs, the record shows no radical changes to Waiwai architecture and living space in 1958 (Yde 1965). Even by 1966, at the height of missionary activity on the Essequibo, good documentary evidence reports only two Waiwai houses shaped and built like missionary homes.

8. The rather old-fashioned word *filial* has been used here and throughout the book as the best of two poor choices in translation from the Waiwai. I toyed with using *consanguineous* but decided against it because of its unavoidable association (for us) with ties defined in terms of blood.

9. One might consider that in 1934 it was said that "I should have very grave doubts as to the future existence of the tribe, but for the fact that a male Wapishana has settled among them and that now the Commission has opened lines of communication with the Rupununi Savannah, others may do so and so preserve the community, though not retaining the pure strain of the Wai-Wai" (DeFreitas 1993:121). Later, in 1952, it was claimed that "Protestant missionaries, as well as the effects of Euro-

pean diseases and other disrupting influences, made it evident that Wai Wai culture would not survive many more years" (Evans and Meggers 1964:199).

10. This Akaway is not the same individual mentioned above as Atmik's brother, but one might note the use of the same name from a deceased mother's brother by a sister's son.

11. Here I follow the assumption that "the rectangular houses attributed to European influence are the gabled ones, whereas the other rectangular type, with rounded ends and the roof sloping all the way round, is an autochthonous one, originated in South America" (Yde 1965:157).

12. From Evans and Meggers 1964:201 (fig. 2), the reasonably accurate and certainly very useful genealogical chart showing the residents of Weelya (Weeřia-turï [Laba or Paca-village]) in 1952 documents Erimink's genitor to be "Marunao" and his genitrix to be unnamed but married to "Waiwai" Weychar. While Erimink may well have called "Marunao" father because "Marunao" had been married to his mother, my own records have Erimink considering Weychar as his father and Ika-ar as his mother.

13. A written record of this notorious episode exists in which the author renames Erimink "Rikaru" and gives the cause of the murders as a quarrel "with a woman over a string of beads" (Dowdy 1964:109). But the Waiwai frequently recite the events of that fateful night when Arukaram, Erimink's stepmother, refused Erimink's sexual advances only to become, with her companions, the victim of his violent rage.

14. Even despite the obvious but subliminal attempts by the Guyanese and Brazilian states as well as the North American missionary sect to instill the virtues of a modern Christian ethic built upon a responsible autonomous selfhood, the (to us familiar) cultural products of such crusading were not evident in Waiwai society. The pertinent absence of any physical structures or sites for the incarceration of the "criminal" and the absence of any moral attempt to reform the "delinquent" draws our attention to the similar absence of any collective notion about a naturally unique autonomous subjectivity. No Waiwai history of legislation or penal procedures can convincingly be said to exist.

This is not because Waiwai society has no history, no law, or no functioning ideology of punishment. It is rather because Waiwai social knowledge and power influence the cultural processes of individualization in the direction of balancing the complementary entities constituting a presence evocative of a fractionalized, interactive, and more dependent human subjectivity.

15. This reputation has perhaps been carried over from the Taruma, who, it is claimed, "disappeared" as a people during the 1920s and whose region the Waiwai now occupy (Guppy 1963; Butt Colson and Morton 1982).

16. Such analogy may not be as farfetched as it appears. One might consider the comment:

> Perhaps even more surprisingly, although we tend to think of people as mobile and houses as stationary, we are confronted here with cases in which houses actually move. At its simplest this is a matter of people rebuilding their house anew; for swidden cultivators, periodic relocation and rebuilding is a feature of life that militates against the development of truly permanent prestige architecture. More radically, in parts of Southeast Asia such as Langkawi, the house itself may be lifted up by a group of men so that it seems actually to acquire legs and walk or run to a new site. This image of a walking house emphatically demonstrates its animate qualities. (Carsten and Hugh-Jones 1995:40)

17. One might note that "perhaps as early as 1954 the Barokoto [Parukoto] had completely identified themselves with the Wai-Wai, and no longer recognized their old name" (Rivière 1963:143). In addition "the language of the true Wai Wai people was very close to that of the Parkwoto [Parukoto] people. The language of these two groups combined to become the lingua franca of all these remnant groups, and nearly all who live among the Wai Wai speak the Wai Wai language fluently" (Robert Hawkins 1998:25). One should consider, however, that it has also been suggested that within the Carib language group to which the Waiwai and Parukoto belong, some sources have the Waiwai in an "East-West Guiana Carib" group and the Parukoto in a "Southern Guiana Carib

group" (Durbin 1977:35), while others have them both in the latter
group (Migliazza 1980).

18. Presented to the government of Guyana in August 1969, a "Report by
the Amerindian Lands Commission" recommended new laws of tenure
for Amerindians occupying lands within the official boundaries of the
state. In their consideration of such titles of land for the Waiwai, the
commission deliberated that:

> Owing to the very low degree of sophistication and the need to
> set aside lands for their use, the commission recommends the
> creation of a district to enclose all known scattered Amerindian
> populations within this area with the following boundaries: The
> area commencing at the mouth of the Kassikaityu river, left bank
> Essequibo river, thence up the Kassikaityu river to its source at
> the Guyana-Brazil border, thence south-east along the Guyana-
> Brazil border to the watershed of the Essequibo and New rivers,
> thence north along the said watershed to the source of the Amuku
> river to its mouth, thence down the Essequibo river to the point
> of commencement.
> The commission also recommends that residents have the bene-
> ficial occupation of lands between the Kassikaityu and Kuyuwini
> rivers, left bank Essequibo river. (Report by the Amerindian Lands
> Commission 1969:208, n.14)

From the Sutured Wound of Being

1. Perhaps the most strident and persistent voice on this theme in our
intellectual tradition has been that "it is not the consciousness of men
that determines their being, but on the contrary it is their social being
that determines their consciousness" (Marx 1976b [1859]:3).

2. For an overview of "tribes" in this region see Evans and Meggers 1960;
Fock 1963:5–9; Rivière 1963.

3. So dramatic were the cultural propensities of the Amerindian that their
effect of stimulating the notion—at least in the nineteenth-century
European—of beastly otherness produced some rather curious and even
humorous literature. My own personal favorite comes from that "piece

of genial eccentricity" (Aldington 1949:128), *Wanderings in South America* by Charles Waterton. Possibly as a grand spoof (at the expense of a hated Parliamentarian), the naturalist and pioneering taxidermist Charles Waterton claimed to have found a new species of animal in the forests of Guiana. Illustrated in the frontispiece of his book and titled "A Nondescript," the creature is portrayed with features of a "Grecian cast" (Waterton 1906 [1825]:218). The fact that the man-monkey bore an uncanny resemblance to Waterton's sworn enemy (Secretary to the Treasury J. R. Lushington) says a good deal about the bizarre humor of the Walton Hall squire. He was also accused, however, of slaying and stuffing "some 'native Indian' in order to make an arrogant display of his 'stuffing powers'" (Aldington 1949:126), which says volumes about the realms of possibilities open to the European mind regarding the character of Amerindian otherness. The illustration—of what was in fact the decapitated head of a Red Howler monkey remodeled for the deception—seemed to play cleverly with European assumptions about human alterity.

4. In this sense of a structural otherness, I share much in common with the view that "forests mark the provincial edge of Western civilization, in the literal as well as imaginative domains" (Harrison 1992:247).

5. Like other museums of its time, the Pennsylvania Museum was a centralized house of knowledge whose objects on display bore witness to the accumulated riches the state owned on behalf of its citizens. Museums tended to function as guardians of "native" traditions and, in so doing, expressed the style of civilization the nation-state imagined it possessed. Depicting an imperial, pedagogical, and modern style of culturalness, museums—along with the census and the map—"profoundly shaped the way in which the colonial state imagined its dominion" (Anderson 1992:164).

6. I hope the irony makes itself obvious. Certainly it appears lost on Walter Roth, who never appears to grasp the inner logic of a capitalist market system determining the extraction of latex from the forests of Guiana and converting such material into the commodity of rubber-soled shoes. He openly condemns the very labor used to extract the raw material providing for his comfort. What remains far more significant for me,

however, is the way judgments of this kind hypocritically deny an inner logic to other people's actions.

7. "What is worse, considering their position in life, everyone wears clothes; even the toddling infant has to be covered. And yet clothes are not worn for decency's sake, but for something akin to mimicry and swank, because underneath their European habiliments, the sexes sport the red-cloth lap and beaded apron, respectively. Talismans and charms continue to be employed and the filing of incisor teeth is still in vogue" (Roth 1929:vii).

   In other words—Roth suggests—not having the modern logical reasoning to make proper judgments about their appearance, the Wapishana mindlessly copied their betters at the grotesque expense of their own cultural values.

8. The visitor experiences a curious mixture of "being there" with the native and a distancing from them based upon conceptions of difference. One might note that "it sometimes seemed quite uncanny to hear my own voice, which for what reason I know not, I was almost afraid to use. I was absolutely and indeed alone with these people, but as usual quite content and happy" (Roth 1929:x). This feeling of loneliness by the ethnographer among the natives is not unfamiliar; we become aware of it, for example, in perhaps the first, most notable ethnography, *Argonauts of the Western Pacific*: "Imagine yourself suddenly set down surrounded by all your gear alone on a tropical beach close to a native village, while the launch or dinghy which has brought you sails away out of sight" (Malinowski 1984 [1922]:4). In many ways this imagining of loneliness functioned as an indispensable technique of ethnography and a conformation of native otherness.

To the Mutability of Embodiment

1. Pierre Maranda writes about this similar idea in different terms, arguing that "myths are stylistically definable discourses that express the strong components of semantic systems" (1972:13).

2. Consider Waud Kracke's (1992) wonderfully orchestrated attack on the Freudian position about the "primitive" mind. He shows, for example, how Freud's assumptions—about the dominant ordering displayed by

the rich metaphoric forms of thinking in myths and dreams and their division into "primary" and "secondary" process thinking—merely end up supporting the classical analysts' evolutionary views of a different and inferior "primitive" psyche.

3. This, I assume, is what Lévi-Strauss meant by saying the "pre-constrained" and "constitutive units of myth" are like the "elements which the 'bricoleur' collects and uses" (1974:19). They have a limited maneuverability in language that restricts their recognizable meanings.

4. Without wanting to get too embroiled in the myth/history debate, I nevertheless cannot help but mention how Foucault, in discussing the problem of questioning the *document*, talks about history as *memory*, as the archaeology or tracing of silent monuments transformed into documents (Foucault 1972:6–7).

5. Waiwai social organization, like those recorded from other Amerindian societies of the Guianas, can be presented in the theoretical concept of the "house" or "village," where the notion of community becomes meaningful within the residential category of "settlement" (Rivière 1995:190). Such a residential expression of distinctive social structuring may well be—in addition to the cosmological—the very means for identifying the shared social philosophies of all lowland South American societies. Yet one should keep in mind that for the explanation of human existence "as the proper contact and mixing of differences," the suggested pan-lowland philosophy has a distinctly different twist in the Guianas. One might note that "the dissimilarity is that the Guianese Amerindians in general do their best in social life to suppress such differences, while the Ge, the Bororo, and the Indians of the North West Amazon stress them" (Overing 1981:161).

6. Lévi-Strauss has developed (particularly in *The Jealous Potter* 1988) a similar theme based on what he calls a "psycho-organic code." From a particular series or "family of myths," he reveals this "sexual code" in various metaphors of the female body, interpreting them as representative of Amerindian philosophical and moral values. But see also Alan Dundes's (1962) discussion of earth-diver creation myths, where he talks about the origins of myth in dreams, the psychological concept

of womb envy in men, and the prevalence of the theme of anal birth in such myths.

7. In other words, in more anthropological terms, the Waiwai experiences of becoming and being pater and mater seem far more meaningful to them than their knowledge of becoming and being genitor and genetrix, and these experiences, while being put into action by the conception, gestation, birth, and postparturition of the child, nevertheless stem from marriage.

One should note also that if the Waiwai natal custom of the "couvade" is indeed "motivated by the great child mortality" (Fock 1963:149) and seeks merely the instrumental purpose of protecting the child, then it seems to me that it should be a protecting of the child that also implicates the structural protection of the parents. Perhaps it cannot be applied to the Waiwai in the same way it has been, for example, to the Bororo, where the diet of the parents is the influencing process for the protection of the child, while the conduct of the parents is the influencing process for the protection of the mother and father (Crocker 1985:56), but this kind of concern for the child *and* the parents appears to be of crucial significance for an understanding of the ideas and behavior associated with procreation.

8. Here the "flow of an analogical relatedness" seeks first, as Roy Wagner (1977) has suggested, to create a difference from a similitude and then a subsequent return to that similitude. In their shared bonds of perceived essential humanness, men and women are alike. Yet with difference compelled, in order to initiate the flow of certain kinds of recognition and reciprocity, same-sex relations can become like cross-sex relations. Same-sex siblings can become like cross-sex siblings, for example, with sequential birth, where the first child, a female, can be like a brother to a younger female child, the difference in birth sequence serving to inscribe itself upon the similitude of their gender. Likewise, husbands and wives, at least in the later stages of marriage, mirror the relations of cross-sex siblings; a calm familiarity flows between the couple, their having occupied the same marital space and shared the same parental responsibilities and relations to the same child or children.

9. In the Mawari myth structural transformation has the creation heroes

being born from the cosmological egg of a tortoise and not the egg of a bird. This is, however, the correct contrast to make in the problematization and contemplation of Waiwai ideas on masculine creativity. The transformation and contrast situate the concept of cloacal birth out into the world in the image of the egg. At the same time, through the species of tortoise and bird, they attribute to cloacal birth the divine mutability of the oppositional yet complementary spaces of low and high, earth and sky. The cosmic egg of the ancestral tortoise is here the transformed masculine womb of the avian and divine universe.

10. It has been remarked upon many times that the kinship terminology systems of lowland South American societies seek to separate and even oppose relatives in categories that determine their connubial and nonconnubial accessibility (Rivière 1977; Schwerin 1983–84; Shapiro 1984). In the Waiwai case and from an anthropological point of view, terminologically separating the world of relatives into epeka and wošin does have the effect of obliquely focusing attention on the category of wayamnu (potential spouse). (An admittedly evasive gaze that nonetheless reaffirms the suggestion about capturing the highly charged tension existing between relatives imbued with contrasting moral worth.) It cannot be ignored, therefore, that while such procedures lock principally upon connubiality, they nonetheless begin with the premise of discriminating between categories of close relatives. The critical issue for the system is to allow for the separation of affines from within the pool of close relatives so as to confirm their status as potential in-laws. From this point of view the form of connubial concern—that is, the cultural tension over the kind and proximity of relative one can marry—appears as an epiphenomenon of having to know to whom one is related and how one is related to that person.

11. The ideal of the model is to marry from within the pool of known relatives, but the fact that genealogically unrelated people are also considered potential spouses suggests that the ideal has its pragmatic side. In the practical world not everyone will have an available potential spouse occupying a position in the pool of relatives that is equal or equivalent to MBD / FZS, FZD / MBS, or ZD / MB. The ingenuity of the system is that it allows ego always to claim that his or her spouse came

from the wayamnu category—familiar relative or stranger made into familiar relative by marriage. The marriage itself makes the stranger into the kind of kindred who occupies the position of possible spouse. No contradiction appears.

12. I am very convinced by Pierre Clastres's 1997 interpretations in which he makes the same argument for Atchei homosexuality as I do for Wai-wai incest, whereby homosexuality in Amerindian societies can only be incestuous because, like all incest in such societies, it amounts to the destruction of social bonds through the negation of proper exchange.

13. So tenacious has been the hold of traditional ideas about the beaded apron that even those women strongly influenced by current Western forms of attire still wear aprons under their modern cotton dresses. In such instances the known presence of the apron can be detected by the sound rather than the sight of clashing beads, bells, and/or coins customarily attached to the apron.

And Toward the Body Encompassed

1. I am taking my lead here from the view that "we must cease once and for all to describe the effects of power in negative terms: it 'excludes', it 'represses', it 'censors', it 'abstracts', it 'masks', it 'conceals'. In fact, power produces; it produces reality; it produces domains of objects and rituals of truth" (Foucault 1979:194).

2. Another way of putting this is to say that "truth cannot be out there—cannot exist independently of the human mind—because sentences cannot so exist, or be out there. The world is out there, but descriptions of the world are not. Only descriptions of the world can be true or false" (Rorty 1989:5).

The Hidden Hazard of Generosity

1. We have classified the white-lipped peccary (poniko) as *Tayassu pecari* or *Tayassu albirostris*. We classify the collared peccary (*pakre*) as *Tayassu tajacu*. *The Shorter Oxford English Dictionary* (Little, Fowler, and Coulson 1980:2250) claims to have the precise date of 1698 for the earliest appearance of the word *Tayassu*. It also records the etymology of *Tayassu* to be Tupi—that is, deriving from the Tupi word *tayaçu*, mean-

ing "tania-eater." One should note, incidentally, how the word *peccary* itself originates from the Carib word *pakira* (Little, Fowler, and Coulson 1980:1536) and, indeed, how close this is to the Waiwai word *pakre*. A piglike mammal, the omnivorous Tayassuidae can be found free ranging from Texas to Patagonia. The larger and darker colored "white-lipped" species live in herds of up to three hundred individuals and keep mostly to their primary habitat of scrubland and forest. The "collared" species weigh eighteen to thirty kilograms (forty to sixty-six pounds), grow to three feet in length, and can be found roving in small herds or on their own.

2. There is every reason to believe that household H did not receive meat from any other, because at the time its representative male head, Ponu, was in the process of being ostracized from community life as punishment for adultery with his brother's wife. Ponu did attend the hunt but was unsuccessful. His father-in-law, Iwap, head of household I, was not present at the hunt. It is rather surprising, however, that as an old man without household dependents he was unable to receive meat either from his immediate neighbors or from his son Puyen. In a village already based on close personal relationships, the households of Ponu and Iwap were renowned for their very close exchange of ties. It is highly probable that the punishment of ostracism meted out to household H in this instance extended by association to include household I.

3. After undergoing various adjustments from grandfather to brother, my somewhat anomalous relationship with Shamawa was ultimately expressed in terms of affinity. As a male visitor without an accompanying wife or a local farm, I came under the supervision and guardianship of Shamawa as village leader. This relationship was loosely formalized by the kinship terms of address exchanged among the village leader's wife, Awam, and myself. Presumably to avoid any possibility of a sexually defined tie between the two of us, Awam called me ñoño (brother) and I reciprocated by calling her achi (sister). This meant that Shamawa and I exchanged the poimo (brother-in-law) term of address and consequently played out our relationship essentially as affines.

4. Here my understanding of the Waiwai ideas on "political leadership" concurs with what many other scholars of lowland South American

societies have already revealed about this thorny topic (Kracke 1978; Thomas 1982; Clastres 1989).

5. If one understands power primarily as a kind of material object, a sort of substantive thing in the world capable of being possessed and owned, then it seems highly likely that one would concentrate on how access to such power would be acquired (Marx 1976a). If, on the other hand, one seeks to understand power principally in its exercise rather than in its effects (particularly its negative effects), then questions as to why and how its particular representations become important enough to be targeted as desirable should gain the fundamental emphasis (Foucault 1979:26–27). Concentrating on access to power must of course remain crucial in any rendition of the political, but not at the expense, it seems to me, of showing how power works. In its exclusivity the former approach tends to avoid the crucial participatory role of all those subject to the effects of power (Foucault 1979:194).

6. Quite recently there has been introduced the new term and additional category of "perspectivism," where "if animism affirms a subjective and social continuity between humans and animals, its somatic complement, perspectivism, establishes an objective discontinuity, equally social, between live humans and dead humans" (Viveiros de Castro 1998: 482–83).

7. Given such significant facts, for the Waiwai, about the omnivorous diet of the white-lipped peccary and the considerable amount of meat that not just a single peccary but a whole herd can present for human consumption, it is perhaps not surprising that this animal has high gastronomic status for them. In their ideas it is the eating habits of the peccary that makes its flesh taste so delicious. Indeed, its roaming around the forest in search of the finest palm fruits and some small animals to eat puts it on a par with other wandering, tasty creatures such as the tapir, spider monkey, and great curassow. The Waiwai often give this wandering criterion as the straightforward explanation for why they prefer to eat the flesh of forest animals and not that of domesticated animals. In their opinion domesticated animals "eat the filth" of village detritus. At this level of explanation, they prefer the meat of nondomesticated

game because the animal eaten eats, like they do, the tasty foods of the forest.

8. In anthropological theory and (somewhat revealingly) in Christian theology, to understand the analytical significance of sacrifice usually requires attributing structural priority to the relation between human selfhood and divine otherness, a relation formed by a difference often discussed in terms of imperfect pollution and perfect purity, respectively. Such an understanding attributes the difference to be that of estrangement—that is, of being alienated from the perfect purity of Oneness in God. In Christianity the "One Sacrifice" of Christ's body seeks to reconcile the difference and to redeem the lost purity of sinful humankind, for only the divine remedy of God's grace, in the sacrificial gift of his Son, can achieve this end. The atonement materializes as a covenant—that is, as "an eating together"—of God and humankind at a sacred meal of ritual sacrifice. To arrive, however, at the point in anthropology where the analysis can conclude that "the object sacrificed is almost universally domesticated," suggesting "that it is a metonymic extension of the self" (Crocker 1985:151), requires considering the reconciled difference between the "Son of Man" and "God the Father" as stemming from a Western tradition, where patri-filial kinship begins as familial domesticity.

9. Of course this conscious transformation of the gift in receiving also exists on the other side, where in the giving of the gift—particularly in sacrifice—*intent* is "the only thing of consequence" (Lévi-Strauss 1974:224). In fact intentionality not only permits sacrifice to belong "to the realms of continuity" but also makes it possible for its "fundamental principle [of] substitution" (Lévi-Strauss 1974:224) to operate. The intent to give (perhaps the supplement of self) makes any sacrificial gift appropriate.

10. While this conclusion has been around for some time now in the literature on other lowland South America societies (certainly since Lévi-Strauss 1969 [1949]), principally as the result of the anthropological theories about alliance and filiation, I personally consider Viveiros de Castro's rendition of it for the Tupi-Guarani Araweté as the most rel-

evant for the Waiwai. The convincing example, for me, comes from perhaps his key comment that "the enemy was the center of the society" (Viveiros de Castro 1992:301).

11. I interpret this Waiwai understanding to be similar in kind to those that have yielded the anthropological view that metaphysical continuity and physical discontinuity between beings produce animism in the former and "perspectivism" in the latter (Viveiros de Castro 1998:479).

Grief and Shamanic Breath

1. At least in its celebrated Amazonian form as a "welcome of tears," ritual wailing, it has been said, "marks a return after a prolonged absence" (Urban 1996:153). In this sense we may want to interpret the wailing of the Waiwai mourners here as a desire to reverse the effect of death. For if, as it has been suggested, "the cycles of communal attachment . . . obey a distinctive rhythm"—that is, a variable phenomenal and noumenal periodicity of coming and going—and "perceptual contact triggers the lament" (Urban 1996:153), then the wailing of the mourners may be more than a "mark" of return and a "trigger" of sorrow. In contact with the dead and in vocal expression of the sorrow, wailing may be a willful instrument of the desire to revoke death—to send it back from whence it came and thus to welcome the living once again.

2. Much of the discussion had been carried out, I think, for my benefit— that is, for me to have a favorable opinion of the Waiwai in this most powerful statement about the kind of people they were. I detected a sentiment on Anawach's part to appear "modern" in my eyes with re- gard to the disposal of his father's body. When Aruchiripin had died in one final and fatal bout of grand mal, they had buried him behind the village in what was to be a future cemetery. This idea had come from the Wapishana, who had thought this would be the more "civilized" thing to do. Indeed, they thought it was the kind of thing the more modern Guyanese Coastlanders did in the capital city of Georgetown. Unfortunately, Aruchiripin's grave had been disturbed and some of the bones stolen. Anawach did not want a repeat of this and sought my advice on what to do with his father's body. He wanted to cremate the

body in the traditional way. I encouraged this with the information that even the Hindu-inclined Coastlanders cremated their dead. Yet he was pressured to bury the body. This I also encouraged, with the additional information that some Christian-inclined Coastlanders buried their dead under the house in which they lived.

3. Here is perhaps where the debate between religion and rationality could begin—that is, at the point of intersection between human reason and the mystical. In this regard I admit it becomes somewhat problematic for me to continue using the term "mystical," particularly where the context could infer a meaning of "divine mystery." In the Waiwai case, however, I am so far in agreement with the view that "in an inquiry into witchcraft as a principle of causation, no mysterious spiritual beings are postulated, only the mysterious powers of humans" (Douglas 1970:xvi).

4. I find it absolutely fascinating that given what I understand about the greater relevance the Waiwai place upon spiritual being, the marking that "ritualized lamentation" reveals can just as meaningfully be said to mark "a return after a prolonged absence" (Urban 1996:153) not to the living but to the eternal community of spirits. Indeed it makes just as much sense to say in the case of the Waiwai that "a person who has been, for some time, only" phenomenally accessible "is made once again" (Urban 1996:153) noumenally real—through death.

5. While not having occasion to see oho in its traditional and more structured form, I have many times witnessed aspects of its formal features in different ritual contexts. In its core character and aims, oho remains very much an element of Waiwai social life today.

6. Iwap, an old Waiwai when I knew him, once simulated a traditional oho for me, playing both the parts of lead speaker and of respondent. I have to say that the two most noticeable features of his reenactment were the ways in which the oho captured the musical aesthetics of Waiwai flute playing and seemingly mimicked the dawn chorus of a flock of *karapa* (Horned Screamer [*Anhima Cornuta*]).

7. I would here like to draw attention to the interesting comparison between a Waiwai household cluster (also called "neighborhood" [Howard 1991:53]) and a Trio village (Rivière 1970). The Trio are the Waiwai's eastern neighbors in Surinam. I would argue that outside of the

natal household and in terms of the social relations entrusted to bear the most weight for coresident trust and harmony, it is today's Waiwai household cluster that resembles a traditional Trio village. Marriage brings new households into social existence. The Waiwai prefer and practice uxorilocality. The ideal and usual residential cluster in a Waiwai village would therefore be a core household comprising one married couple with their unmarried children (and perhaps even a widowed parent) and, in close proximity, other conjugal households headed by men related to the core household as son-in-law and/or brother-in-law. A Waiwai village can be viewed as consisting of clusters of conjugal households bound to one another by relationships of extended kinship and affinity. In other words what has been called an "agglomeration" for the Trio (Rivière 1970:246, 1971:294) of three to five autonomous villages would be the rough equivalent of a Waiwai village today. I would even go so far as to suggest that this was the case even when Niels Fock first visited the Waiwai at the time when missionary activity had already drawn traditional villages into today's intravillage household clusters. The relevance of these suggestions is that the Trio's *sip sip man* (mild strong talk) of the *turakane* (ceremonial dialogue), spoken only between agglomerates of the same group, and their *nokato* (severe strong talk), spoken only with people who live "further away, in one of the other two groups" (Rivière 1971:304) of agglomerates, show similar patterns of operation to the Waiwai oho. Within Waiwai traditional villages, within today's Waiwai household clusters, and within Trio traditional villages, no ceremonial dialogue would have been brought into action. In both ethnographic cases the so-called function and meaning of ceremonial dialogue—that is, "mediation in situations that are likely to give rise to conflict" (Rivière 1971:306) would, I argue, be the same.

8. I should add, however, that in my own interpretations of Foucault's presentations on power, I do not understand him to be following the classic Marxist definition, whereby access to and the amount of power possessed are criteria for defining power. In fact with regard to the "microphysics of power" he goes out of his way to say, "in short this power is exercised rather than possessed; it is not the 'privilege,' acquired or preserved, of the dominant class, but the overall effect of its strategic

positions—an effect that is manifested and sometimes extended by the position of those who are dominated" (Foucault 1979:26–27).

9. One of Clastres's more daring and penetrating attempts at illustrating what it takes for Amerindian societies to defeat the state can be seen in "What Makes Indians Laugh" (1989:129–50). Here we see that after the distribution of supernatural power to its shamanic location, the Amerindian "kills"—in the comedic genre of myth and with the equally powerful but human effects of laughter—the danger of this potential power lurking in the "distant" and "external" spaces.

10. In this regard the dark shaman is the "sensual code" into which the "floating signifier" of spiritual power becomes thought about and objectified (Gil 1998:93–105).

11. Here as the means of spiritual violence, the dark shaman is irreducible; shamanic power cannot be reduced to any kind of rigid apparatus of power like that pertaining to the state. In this sense it is "deterritorialized" beyond the zones of enclosed politics (Deleuze and Guattari 1987:351–56).

12. This is the clear message I receive from the purposefully horrific opening scenes of *Discipline and Punish*. In understanding my society and myself as just, lenient, and moral, I perform the modern act of identifying as the "true" criminal not Damiens, the regicide, but his torturers and executioner. We are no longer this barbaric, this uncivilized. We have "progressed" to a more lenient and humane form of punishment. We now offer the body of the condemned more democratic and rational forms of punishment—ones that reduce pain, yet nevertheless clearly manifest their external power over the modern soul (Foucault 1979).

The Archer and His Bow

1. This much I had learned from the austere disciples of Malinowski.

2. I did, however, hear the rumor that at the larger Mapuera village in Brazil women are now allowed to take part in the contest.

3. The average length of a bow, ideally made from "letter wood" or "leopard wood" (*Brosimum aubletii*), is around 2.6 meters, but many men have bows reaching 2.29 meters. Bowstrings are made from a plant

called *krewetu*, specially grown in farms and manufactured into strong rope by shredding its leaves into fiber and twisting them together.

4. Arrows are made from a light, straight arrow reed often grown in a single patch among a householder's regular farm crops. The minimum length of Waiwai arrows is 1.91 meters, the maximum length 2.03 meters, and the average length 1.97 meters (as recorded by Heath and Chiara 1977:143).

5. They cut a single feather in half along its quill and trim each half in the shape of a parallelogram. The halves of the feather are placed in a radial position along the length of the arrow shaft. They are attached using a variety of binding techniques, for example, a "continuous open bind," an "interval bind," a "continuous close bind" or a combination of one or the other of these (following Heath and Chiara 1977:159–60).

6. In Waiwai belief, as I have stated, the final resting place for all human "ekatï of the eye" is among the Guan-people—to be more precise, the eye ekatï of the human dead actually take up residence in the narrow void between the strata of the earth and Maratu-yena, but to all intents and purposes this void is thought to be part of Maratu-yena.

7. One has merely to enter at any page of *Beyond a Boundary* by C. L. R. James (1993) to find an eminently prepared eloquence on these topics.

8. We are all, for example, supposed to recognize the wrongdoing and certainly to disapprove of the boxer who bites off a piece of his opponent's ear in an internationally televised championship fight. We are all, in addition, supposed to recognize and condone the right of boxing's governing body to fine and suspend the boxer for his action, which, after all, was not just against the rules and hence outlawed but was also immoral, bringing deplorable "shame" and "dishonor" to the sport of boxing. In collectively responding with similar abhorrence to the outlawed immoral actions of the boxer, we make claims to ourselves and to others that we recognize, know, and abide by similar standards of social life—the very same standards that allow us to imagine we live and belong to a national community of people who share the same values. One could note, incidentally, how support for the governing body of sport can also be translated into support for the governing body of the state.

9. One might think here of the tightening in the chest and the welling up of tears at the sight of the flag and sound of the anthem as our athlete stands on the winner's podium.

10. For surely the game could not and would not support an unjust and immoral nation? One might think, for example, of the ways in which Jesse Owens's heroic but unpredictable successes at the "Nazi" Olympics has been interpreted as if they were an independent vindication for the injustices and evils of racism—a remarkably strange contradiction when one considers how the concepts of race themselves rely heavily on the independent variable of nature.

When the Cicadas First Sing

1. The explanation for the life cycle of the American southern periodical cicada has the nymphs living a subterranean life, sucking on tree and shrub roots, for as long as thirteen years. The annual creeping from the ground to the trees by a batch of mature cicada during the summer months in order to mate and produce their young is accompanied by the "song" of the vibrating membranes of the males.

2. Yde (1965:23–24) has the term *sarapo* meaning cultivated field and *marara* meaning a newly burned field. As I understand it from the Waiwai, the term *sarapo* refers to the woody stem of yuca, while the term *marara* could be a derivative of *mararï*.

3. Some authors (Descola 1992, 1996a; Århem 1996) have recently used the term *nature* as if it was in opposition to and/or outside of culture rather than being the very product of culture itself. Even more problematic—certainly for comparative analysis—it appears as if they have either assumed (1) that the term carries such deep-seated meanings and histories from our own Western-influenced culture that it no longer needs to be explained, or (2) that it is a specific term used by us merely to refer to a universal category. In the latter instance the assumption seems to be that the world exists out there and that the word we have for this world, while being specific to us, nevertheless refers to a category all cultures in history and society recognize. While I have no problem with any attempt to describe and interpret the different contents of the various representations of this category, I do take issue with the

unchallenged view that the term *nature* exists outside of any specific history and beyond any confines of culture.

4. I recorded only one exceptionally large field in the upper Essequibo (field no. 15 in fig. 6). This field originally had thirteen farm plots in it before finally being reallocated to six plots after it was prematurely abandoned by its first occupants.

5. While I cannot draw the conclusive correlation for the Waiwai between the making of baskets and the development of their domestic cycle or shamanic contact with the spiritual world, as others have done for neighboring groups (Wilbert 1975; Guss 1990), I would nonetheless acknowledge their similar concerns with such relations. I have to say, however, that in the many other settings outside basketmaking, the key concern for "penetrating" visible realities—or, indeed, for contacting invisible realities by penetrating the visible ones—does not appear to be driven by an understanding that the invisible controls the visible or that the visible controls the invisible. In Waiwai ideas the relation is self-evident but not determined by control.

6. Often, if a people do not succumb to the paradigm of Being that has been prescribed for them by dominant Western criteria, this puts them in the position of being considered either to lack all humanity or not to exist at all. One might consider the view from the World Development Report 2000/2001 by the World Bank: "Of the world's 6 billion people, 2.8 billion—almost half—live on less than $2 a day, and 1.2 billion—a fifth—live on less than $1 a day." Citing "poverty amid plenty" as "the world's greatest challenge," the evaluators of wealth write with righteous indignation about our global economic struggle. Yet what does it mean to suggest a life within the singular currency of the dollar? What does it actually mean to suggest a life lived on less than a dollar a day? Could it in actuality mean that there is no place, no time, and no being outside a monetary criterion? Within this context and this definition of a global monetary system, any such existence would not be a people of this world.

7. The assumption is that in the more complex economies, the material base plays such an important role that those possessing control over its

crucial parts also have "the most efficient means of exercising control over the producers" (Meillassoux 1980:136).

The Plaited Design of Human Life

1. This is not necessarily the place to delve into such matters, nor indeed to introduce the thorny topic of "absence" or of "missing" an experience of the world. Nonetheless, I am struck by the contrast between our modern world of specialized individualism and a world such as the Waiwais', where a sustained intimacy exists between the skins of humans, animals, and plants or between the products of human labor and labor itself. I think that when that which we produce and with whom we produce it gets separated from us in the modern West, we lose a great deal of humanity's potential for filling all the senses and the mind.

2. I am here speaking (perhaps with some jealousy of the lowland specialist) about the volume of highly read literature on Aztec and Inca architecture.

3. Roof plaiting must once have been considered important enough to claim a major ceremonial festival (see Fock 1963:169 and Yde 1965:153).

4. I can say that this notion of culture as "limit" does not conceive of limit in any kind of negative capacity. I do not, for example, consider the limit of culture to be an infringement on something that might be called the "natural liberty" of the individual. Even if there were some additional space or time that could be considered beyond the limit of culture, the human ability to know and experience it would be an addition of another cultural limit. The trick, it seems to me—if it could be called a trick—is not to think of limit and culture as negatively influencing human experience, especially if the reasons for so thinking imagined some authentic or original point at which cultural limit could be denied.

5. Let me add (if it is not already very obvious) that—even with our own "modern" desires for it to be otherwise—Waiwai women openly invest in the privileging of masculinity. It is perhaps here more than at any other place that I have sought to take seriously the advice mentioned earlier that "we must cease once and for all to describe the effects of power in negative terms: it 'excludes', it 'represses', it 'censors', it 'abstracts', it 'masks', it 'conceals'. In fact, power produces; it produces

reality; it produces domains of objects and rituals of truth" (Foucault 1979:194).

6. This may even be the case of a "moral concentration . . . upon obligations" or a "rights-centred . . . moral system" (Overing and Passes 2000:4), which arrives at a masculine determined conviviality, but only after being transformed into such by the more feminine virtue-centered system at the erotic base of society.

7. I think it is worth noting how this Waiwai concern for excess appears very similar to that mentioned for other lowland Amerindian societies. For instance from what I can gather about the Guayaki examples of supplementarity, which occurs most definitively for them at the moments of human birth (Clastres 1998:16), the imbalance caused by the individual human addition—who threatens the life of the father and the community—can only be transformed by the organizing force of ritual. In the case of the Huaorani, "the asocial nature of excessive sexual desire" (Rival 1998a:622) must be confined by the institution of marriage and the roles of parenthood. The difference I see in the Waiwai example, however, is in the kind of balance sought when excess occurs. In the Waiwai case balance does not necessarily result in the restoration of order and the eradication of inequalities, but in the accommodation and equilibrium of complementary opposition.

8. In at least one example of the anthropological literature, we can find a case of this "collective appropriation," whose moral function is "social reproduction" (Terence Turner 1980:119). Here symbolic logic apparently permits society to identify with the reproductive powers of nature and, hence, seek to transform nature into a "collective social form" or "order" (Terence Turner 1980:119).

The Wayamnu Sentiment

1. To be wayamnu is to be a "tortoise" to another person—that is, to be in an opposite-sex category either to someone unrelated to you or to a cross-cousin, and, of course, to be sexually attracted to that person. In either case its specific reference always carries the explicit meaning of sexual partner. As such, it can be understood to give authority to the erotic desire and joy found in sexual relations. It even seems to

be able to bring about the attraction and the emotion. Perhaps the sanctioned strangeness or unfamiliarity imbued to individuals by the category provides the stimulus for the attraction. The danger often assumed in the feature of strangeness seems to add to the desire for the individual in the wayamnu category. It does so in ways that suggest it is in the removing of the danger with the intimacy of erotic affection that the thrill of the wayamnu sentiment resides.

References

Aldington, Richard. 1949. *The Strange Life of Charles Waterton, 1782–1865*. New York: Duel, Sloan and Pearce.

Althusser, Louis. 1983. "From *Capital* to Marx's Philosophy." In *Reading Capital*, by Louis Althusser and Etienne Balibar, 13–69. London: Verso.

Amerindian Lands Commission. 1969. *Report by the Amerindian Lands Commission*. Georgetown: Government of Guyana.

Anderson, Benedict. 1992. *Imagined Communities: Reflections on the Origin and Spread of Nationalism*. London: Verso.

Anzieu, D. 1989. *The Skin Ego*. New Haven: Yale University Press.

Århem, Kaj. 1996. "The Cosmic Food Web: Human-Nature Relatedness in the Northwest Amazon." In *Nature and Society: Anthropological Perspectives*, ed. Philippe Descola and Gísli Pálsson, 186–204. London: Routledge.

Armstrong, Gary. 1998. *Football Hooligans: Knowing the Score*. Oxford: Berg.

Bailey, Fredrick G. 1969. *Stratagems and Spoils: A Social Anthropology of Politics*. Oxford: Basil Blackwell.

Bale, John. 1994. *Landscapes of Modern Sport*. Leicester: Leicester University Press.

Balée, William. 1994. *Footprints of the Forest: Ka'apor Ethnobotany: The Historical Ecology of Plant Utilization by an Amazonian People*. New York: Columbia University Press.

Balsamo, Anne. 1997. *Technologies of the Gendered Body: Reading Cyborg Women*. Durham: Duke University Press.

Barrington Brown, C. 1876. *Canoe and Camp Life in British Guiana*. London: Edward Stanford.

Barthes, Roland. 1975 [1961]. "Toward a Psychosociology of Contemporary Food Consumption." In *European Diet from Preindustrial to Modern Times*, ed. M. Elborg and Robert Forster, 47–59. New York: Harper and Row.

———. 1981. *Mythologies*. New York: Hill and Wang.

———. 1988. *Writing Degree Zero*. New York: The Noonday Press.

Basso, Ellen. 1992. "The Implications of a Progressive Theory of Dreaming." In *Dreaming: Anthropological and Psychological Interpretations*, ed. Barbara Tedlock, 86–104. Santa Fe: School of American Research Press.

Berg, C. 1951. *The Unconscious Significance of Hair*. London: Allen and Unwin.

Bloch, Maurice. 1998. "Why Trees, Too, Are Good to Think With: Towards an Anthropology of the Meaning of Life." In *The Social Life of Trees: Anthropological Perspectives on Tree Symbolism*, ed. Laura Rival. Oxford: Berg.

Bos, G. 1985. "Atorai, Trio, Tunayana, and Waiwai in Early Eighteenth Century Records." *FOLK* 27:5–15.

Bourdieu, Pierre. 1990. *In Other Words: Essays Towards a Reflexive Sociology*. Stanford: Stanford University Press.

Brydon, Anne. 1998. "Sensible Shoes." In *Consuming Fashion: Adorning the Transnational Body*, ed. A. Brydon and S. Niessen, 1–22. Oxford: Berg.

Butt Colson, Audrey. 1973. "Inter-Tribal Trade in the Guiana Highlands." *Antropológica* 28:25–58.

Butt Colson, Audrey, and Cesareo de Armellada. 1983. "An Amerindian Derivation for Latin American Creole Illnesses and Their Treatment." *Social Science and Medicine* 17:1229–48.

Butt Colson, Audrey, and John Morton. 1982. "Early Missionary Work among the Taruma and Waiwai of Southern Guiana: The Visits of Fr. Cuthbert Cary-Elwes, S.J., in 1919, 1922, and 1923." *FOLK* 24:203–61.

Caixeta de Queiroz, Ruben. 1996. "A Saga de Ewká: Epidemias e Evangelização Entre os Waiwai." In *Transformando os Deuses: Os Múltiplos Sentidos da Conversão entr os Povos Indígenas no Brasil*, ed. Robin M. Wright, 255–84. Campinas, Brazil: Editora da Unicamp.

Carsten, Janet, and Stephen Hugh-Jones, eds. 1995. *About the House: Lévi-Strauss and Beyond*. Cambridge: Cambridge University Press.

Cavallaro, Dani, and Alexandra Warwick. 1998. *Fashioning the Frame: Boundaries, Dress, and Body*. Oxford: Berg.

Chagnon, Napoleon. 1968. *Yanomamö: The Fierce People*. New York: Holt, Rinehart, and Winston.

Clark, Kenneth. 1964 [1956]. *The Nude: A Study in Ideal Form*. Harmondsworth, England: Penguin Books.

Clastres, Pierre. 1989. *Society Against the State: Essays in Political Anthropology*. New York: Zone Books.

———. 1994. *Archeology of Violence*. New York: Semiotext(e).

———. 1997. "The Life and Death of a Homosexual." *Granta* 60. *Unbelievable*: 204–21.

———. 1998. *Chronicle of the Guayaki Indians*. New York: Zone Books.

Clendinnen, Inga. 1989. *Ambivalent Conquests: Maya and Spaniard in Yucatan, 1517–1570*. Cambridge: Cambridge University Press.

Crocker, Jon Christopher. 1977. "My Brother the Parrot." In *The Social Use of Metaphor*, ed. J. D. Sapir and J. C. Crocker, 164–92. Philadelphia: University of Pennsylvania Press.

———. 1985. *Vital Souls: Bororo Cosmology, Natural Symbolism, and Shamanism*. Tucson: University of Arizona Press.

Dagon, R. 1967. "Current Agricultural Practices among the Waiwai: A Preliminary Report with Other Miscellaneous Observations." In *McGill University Savanna Research Project*, Research Series No. 8.

DeFreitas, Caesar P. 1944. "On the Frontier of British Guiana and Brazil." *Timehri* 26 (Nov.): 124–45.

———. 1993. *On the Frontier of British Guiana and Brazil*. Georgetown: Guyana National Printers.

De Goeje, C. H. 1943. *Neolithische Indianen in Suriname*. Tijdschrift v.h. Nederlandsch Aardrijkskundig Genootschap, Tweede serie, deel 9.

Deleuze, Gilles, and Félix Guattari. 1987. *A Thousand Plateaus: Capitalism and Schizophrenia*. Minneapolis: University of Minnesota Press.

Derrida, Jacques. 1991. *A Derrida Reader: Between the Blinds*. Peggy Kamuf, ed. New York: Columbia University Press.

———. 1992. *Given Time: 1. Counterfeit Money*. Chicago: University of Chicago Press.

Descola, Philippe. 1992. "Societies of Nature and the Nature of Society." In *Conceptualizing Society*, ed. Adam Kuper, 107–26. London: Routledge.

———. 1996a. "Constructing Natures: Symbolic Ecology and Social Practice." In *Nature and Society: Anthropological Perspectives*, ed. Philippe Descola and Gísli Pálsson, 82–102. London: Routledge.

———. 1996b. *The Spears of Twilight: Life and Death in the Amazon Jungle*. New York: New Press.

Douglas, Mary, ed. 1970. *Witchcraft Confessions and Accusations*. London: Tavistock Publications.

———. 1971. "Do Dogs Laugh? A Cross-Cultural Approach to Body Symbolism." *Journal of Psychosomatic Research* 15:387–90.

———. 1996. *Natural Symbols: Exploration in Cosmology*. London: Routledge.

Dowdy, Homer. 1964. *Christ's Witchdoctor: From Savage Sorcerer to Jungle Missionary*. London: Hodder and Stoughton.

Drummond, Lee. 1980. "The Cultural Continuum: A Theory of Intersystems." *MAN* (NS) 15:352–74.

Dumont, Jean-Paul. 1978. *The Headman and I: Ambiguity and Ambivalence in the Fieldworking Experience*. Austin: University of Texas Press.

Dundes, Alan. 1962. "Earth-Diver: Creation of the Mythopoeic Male." *American Anthropologist* 64:1032–51.

Durbin, Marshall. 1977. "A Survey of the Carib Language Family." In *Carib-Speaking Indians: Culture, Society and Language*, ed. Ellen B. Basso, 23–28. Tucson: University of Arizona Press.

Dutton, Kenneth R. 1995. *The Perfectible Body: The Western Ideal of Male Physical Development*. New York: Continuum.

Eisler, Michael Joseph. 1921. "A Man's Unconscious Phantasy of Pregnancy in the Guise of Traumatic Hysteria: A Clinical Contribution to Anal Erotism." *International Journal of Psycho-Analysis* 2:255–86.

Eliade, Mircea. 1989. *Shamanism: Archaic Techniques of Ecstasy*. London: Arkana, Penguin Books.

Evans, Clifford, and Betty Meggers. 1955. "Life among the Waiwai Indian." *National Geographical Magazine* 107(3): 329–46.

———. 1960. *Archeological Investigations in British Guiana*. Smithsonian Institution Bureau of American Ethnology Bulletin 177. Washington DC: U.S. Government Printing Office.

———. 1964. "Genealogical and Demographic Information on the Waiwai of British Guiana." *Volkerkundliche Abhandlungen. Band 1. Beitrage zur Volkerkunde Sudamerikas*, 199–208.

Evans-Pritchard, E. E. 1974 [1940]. *The Nuer: A Description of the Modes of Livelihood and Political Institutions of a Nilotic People*. New York: Oxford University Press.

Farabee, William. 1967 [1924]. *The Central Caribs*. Oosterhout N. B., Netherlands: Anthropological Publications.

Faure, Jean-Michel. 1996. "Forging a French Fighting Spirit: The Nation, Sport, Violence and War." In *Tribal Identities: Nationalism, Europe, Sport*, ed. J. A. Mangan, 75–93. London: Frank Cass.

Fock, Niels. 1963. *Waiwai: Religion and Society of an Amazonian Tribe*. Copenhagen: National Museum.

Fortes, Meyer. 1973. "On the Concept of the Person among the Tallensi." In *La Notion de la Personne en Afrique Noire*, ed. G. Dieterlen, 283–319. Paris: Editions du Centre National de la Recherche Scientifique.

Foucault, Michel. 1972. *The Archaeology of Knowledge and the Discourse on Language*. New York: Pantheon Books.

———. 1979. *Discipline and Punish: The Birth of the Prison*. New York: Vintage Books.

———. 1993. "What Is an Author?" In *Language, Counter-Memory, Practice: Selected Essays and Interviews by Michel Foucault*, ed. D. F. Bouchard, 113–38. Ithaca: Cornell University Press.

Fox, Robin. 1967. *Kinship and Marriage: An Anthropological Perspective*. Harmondsworth, England: Penguin Books.

Furst, Peter, ed. 1972. *Flesh of the Gods: The Ritual Use of Hallucinogens*. London: George Allen and Unwin.

Gadow, Sally. 1980. "Body and Self: A Dialectic." *Journal of Medicine and Philosophy* 5:172–85.

Geertz, Clifford. 1993. *The Interpretations of Cultures: Selected Essays*. New York: Basic Books.

Gell, Alfred. 1996. *Wrapping in Images: Tattooing in Polynesia*. Oxford: Clarendon Press.

Gil, José. 1998. *Metamorphoses of the Body*. Minneapolis: University of Minnesota Press.

Guppy, Nicholas. 1958. *Wai-Wai: Through the Forests North of the Amazon*. London: John Murray.

———. 1963. "The World's Greatest Dog-Lovers." *Animals* 1 (16): 8–11.

Guss, David. 1990. *To Weave and Sing: Art, Symbol, and Narrative in the South American Rain Forest*. Berkeley: University of California Press.

Guyana Government. 1969. *Report by the Amerindian Lands Commission*. Georgetown: Government of Guyana.

Habermas, Jürgen. 1987. *The Philosophical Discourse of Modernity*. Frederick Lawrence, trans. Cambridge: MIT Press.

Hargreaves, John. 1986. *Sport, Power, and Culture: A Social and Historical Analysis of Popular Sports in Britain*. Cambridge: Polity Press.

Harner, Michael. 1973. "The Sound of Rushing Water." In *Hallucinogens and Shamanism*, ed. M. Harner, 15–27. London: Oxford University Press.

Harris, Grace G. 1989. "Concepts of Individual, Self, and Person in Description and Analysis." *American Anthropologist* 91:599–612.

Harrison, Robert Pogue. 1992. *Forests and Forestry in Literature*. Chicago: University of Chicago Press.

Hawkins, Robert. 1962. *A Morfologia do Substantivo na Língua UaiUai*. Publicações Avulsas 21, Museu Nacional. Rio de Janeiro: Universidade do Brasil.

———. 1998. "Wai Wai." In *Handbook of Amazonian Languages, Volume 4*, ed. D. Derbyshire and G. Pullum, 25–224. Berlin: Mouton de Gruyter.

Hawkins, W. Neill, and Robert E. Hawkins. 1953. "Verb Inflections in Waiwai (Carib)." *International Journal of American Linguistics* 19:201–21.

Heath, E. G., and Vilma Chiara. 1977. *Brazilian Indian Archery: A Preliminary Ethno-Toxological Study of the Archery of the Brazilian Indians*. Manchester: Simon Archery Foundation.

Heidegger, Martin. 1972. *On Time and Being*. New York: Harper Torchbooks.

Hertz, Robert. 1960. *Death and the Right Hand*, trans. R. Needham and C. Needham. Aberdeen: Cohen and West.

Hill, Jonathan D., ed. 1988. *Rethinking History and Myth: Indigenous South American Perspectives on the Past*. Urbana: University of Illinois Press.

Hills, Theo L. 1968. "Amerindian Agriculture." In *Ethnographic Notes on Amerindian Agriculture*, ed. R. F. Salisbury, M. J. Dummett, T. L. Hills, and D. Cook, 31–71. McGill University Savanna Research Project 9.

Hindess, Paul, and Paul Q. Hirst. 1979. *Pre-Capitalist Modes of Production*. London: Routledge and Kegan Paul.

Howard, Catherine. 1991. "Fragments of the Heavens: Feathers as Ornaments among the Waiwai." In *The Gift of Birds: Featherwork of Native South American Peoples*, ed. R. Reina and K. Kensinger, 50–69. Philadelphia: University Museum of Archaeology and Anthropology, University of Pennsylvania.

Hugh-Jones, Christine. 1988. *From the Milk River: Spatial and Temporal Processes in Northwest Amazonia*. Cambridge: Cambridge University Press.

Hugh-Jones, Stephen. 1979. *The Palm and the Pleiades: Initiation and Cosmology in Northwest Amazonia*. Cambridge: University of Cambridge Press.

———. 1996. "Bonnes Raisons ou Mauvaise Conscience? De l'Ambivalence de Certains Amazoniens Envers la Consommation de Viande." *Terrain* 26:123–48.

Ijzerman, J. W. 1911. "Twee reizen van Paramaribo, een naar de Parima in 1781 en een naar de Boven-Corantijn in 1720." *Tijdschrift van het Koninklijk Nederlandsch Aardrijkskundig Genootschap* 28:648–61.

Im Thurn, Everard. 1967 [1883]. *Among the Indians of Guiana: Being Sketches Chiefly Anthropologic from the Interior of British Guiana*. New York: Dover Publications.

James, C. L. R. 1993. *Beyond a Boundary*. Durham, Duke University Press.

Kensinger, Kenneth M., ed. 1984. *Marriage Practices in Lowland South America*. Urbana: University of Illinois Press.

Kidd, Stephen W. 2000. "Knowledge and the Practice of Love and Hate among the Enxet of Paraguay." In *The Anthropology of Love and Anger: The Aesthetics of Conviviality in Native Amazonia*, ed. Joanna Overing and Alan Passes, 114–32.

Koch-Grünberg, Theodor. 1916–28. *Vom Roroima zum Orinoco 1–4*. Stuttgart.

Kracke, Waud H. 1978. *Force and Persuasion: Leadership in an Amazonian Society*. Chicago: University of Chicago Press.

———. 1992. "Myths in Dreams, Thought in Images: An Amazonian Contribution to the Psychoanalytic Theory of Primary Process." In *Dreaming: Anthropological and Psychological Interpretations*, ed. Barbara Tedlock, 31–54. Santa Fe: School of American Research Press.

Lacan, Jacques. 1977. *The Four Fundamental Concepts of Psychoanalysis*, ed. Jacques-Alain Miller, trans. A. Sheridan. Harmondsworth, England: Penguin Books.

La Fontaine, Jean S. 1989. "Person and Individual: Some Anthropological Reflections." In *The Category of the Person: Anthropology, Philosophy, History*, ed. M. Carrithers, S. Collins, and S. Lukes, 123–40. Cambridge: Cambridge University Press.

Lave, Jean Carter. 1966. "A Formal Analysis of Preferential Marriage with the Sister's Daughter." MAN (NS) 1:185–200.

Lea, Vanessa. 1992. "M?benbokre (Kayapó) Onomastics: A Facet of Houses as Total Social Facts in Central Brazil." MAN (NS) 27:129–53.

Leach, Edmund. 1958. "Magical Hair." *Journal of the Royal Anthropological Institute* 88:147–64.

———. 1970. "The Epistemological Background to Malinowski's Empiricism." In *Man and Culture: An Evaluation of the Work of Bronislaw Malinowski*, ed. Raymond Firth, 119–37. London: Routledge and Kegan Paul.

———. 1976. *Culture and Communication: The Logic by Which Symbols Are Connected*. Cambridge: Cambridge University Press.

———. 1977. *Custom, Law, and Terrorist Violence*. Edinburgh: Edinburgh University Press.

Lévi-Strauss, Claude. 1969 [1949]. *The Elementary Structures of Kinship*. Boston: Beacon Press.

———. 1970. *The Raw and the Cooked: Introduction to a Science of Mythology: 1*. London: Jonathan Cape.

———. 1972. *Structural Anthropology*. Harmondsworth, England: Penguin Books.

————. 1973. *Totemism*. Harmondsworth, England: Penguin Books.

————. 1974. *The Savage Mind (La Pensée Sauvage)*. London: Weidenfeld and Nicolson.

————. 1982. *The Way of the Masks*. Seattle: University of Washington Press.

————. 1988. *The Jealous Potter*. Chicago: University of Chicago Press.

Little, W., H. Fowler, and J. Coulson. 1980. *The Shorter Oxford English Dictionary: On Historical Principles*, rev. and ed. C. T. Onions. 3rd ed., reset with rev. etymologies by G. W. S. Friedrichsen. Oxford: Clarendon Press.

Lizot, Jacques. 1985. *Tales of the Yanomami: Daily Life in the Venezuelan Forest*. Cambridge: Cambridge University Press.

Malinowski, Bronislaw. 1984 [1922]. *Argonauts of the Western Pacific: An Account of Native Enterprise and Adventure in the Archipelagoes of Melanesian New Guinea*. Prospect Heights: Waveland Press.

Maranda, Pierre. 1972. "Introduction." In *Mythology: Selected Readings*, ed. Pierre Maranda, 7–20. Harmondsworth, England: Penguin Books.

Marx, Karl. 1976a. *Capital: Critique of Political Economy*, vol. 1. New York: Vintage Books.

————. 1976b [1859]. *Preface and Introduction to a Contribution to the Critique of Political Economy*. Peking: Foreign Languages Press.

Mauss, Marcel. 1990 [1950]. *The Gift: The Form and Reason for Exchange in Archaic Societies*. New York: W. W. Norton.

Mauss, Marcel. 1973 [1935]. "Techniques of the Body." *Economy and Society* 2 (1): 70–88.

Meggers, Betty. 1973 [1971]. *Amazonia: Man and Culture in a Counterfeit Paradise*. Chicago: Aldine Publishing.

Meillassoux, Claude. 1980. " 'The Economy' in Agricultural Self-Sustaining Societies: A Preliminary Analysis." In *Relations of Production: Marxist Approaches to Economic Anthropology*, ed. David Seddon, 127–57. London: Frank Cass.

Menget, Patrick. 1979. "Temps de Naîtr, Temps d'Être: La Couvade." In *La Fonction Symbolique: Essais d'Anthropologie*, ed. M. Izard and P. Smith. Paris: Gallimard.

Merleau-Ponty, Maurice. 1992. *Phenomenology of Perception*. London: Routledge.

Migliazza, Ernest C. 1980. "Languages of the Orinoco-Amazon Basin: Current Status." *Antropológica* 53:95–162.

Mintz, Sidney. 1986. *Sweetness and Power: The Place of Sugar in Modern History*. Harmondsworth, England: Penguin Books.

Morgan, Lewis H. 1870. *Systems of Consanguinity and Affinity of the Human Family*. Smithsonian Institution Bureau of American Ethnology Bulletin 218. Washington DC U.S. Government Printing Office.

Morton, John. 1979. "Conceptions of Fertility and Mortality among the Waiwai Indians of Southern Guiana." M.Litt. thesis, University of Oxford.

———. 1983–84. "Women as Values, Sign, and Power: Aspects of the Politics of Ritual among the Waiwai." *Antropologica* 59–62:223–61.

Nestle, Marion. 2001. "Rumblings from the World of Food." *Gastronomica: The Journal of Food and Culture* 1(1): 3–4.

Niebuhr, H. Richard. 1999. *The Responsible Self: An Essay in Christian Moral Philosophy*. Louisville: Westminster John Knox Press.

Noll, Richard. 1985. "Mental Imagery Cultivation as a Cultural Phenomenon: The Role of Visions in Shamanism." *Current Anthropology* 26(4): 443–61.

Nuffield Biology. 1966. *The Maintenance of Life, Text III*. London: Longmans, Penguin Books.

Overing, Joanna. 1981. "Review Article: Amazonian Anthropology." *Journal of Latin American Studies* 13(1): 151–64.

———. 1983–84. "Elementary Structures of Reciprocity: A Comparative Note on Guianese, Central Brazilian, and North-West Amazon Socio-Political Thought." *Antropologica* 59–62:331–48.

———. 1986. "Images of Cannibalism, Violence and Domination in a 'Non-Violent' Society." In *The Anthropology of Violence*, ed. D. Riches, 86–102. Oxford: Basil Blackwell.

———. 1996. "Aesthetics Is a Cross-Cultural Category: Against the Motion." In *Key Debates in Anthropological Theory*, ed. Tim Ingold, 260–66, 276–93. London: Routledge.

———. 2000. "The Efficacy of Laughter: The Ludic Side of Magic within

Amazonian Sociality." In *The Anthropology of Love and Anger: The Aesthetics of Conviviality in Native Amazonia*, ed. Joanna Overing and Alan Passes, 64–81. London: Routledge.

Overing, Joanna, and Alan Passes, eds. 2000. *The Anthropology of Love and Anger: The Aesthetics of Conviviality in Native Amazonia*. London: Routledge.

Overing Kaplan, Joanna. 1984. "Dualism as an Expression of Differences and Danger: Marriage Exchange and Reciprocity among the Piaroa of Venezuela." In *Marriage Practices in Lowland South America*, ed. Kenneth M. Kensinger, 127–55. Urbana: University of Illinois Press.

Radcliffe-Brown, A. R. 1971 [1952]. *Structure and Function in Primitive Society*. London: Cohen and West.

Radcliffe-Brown, A. R., and Daryll Forde, eds. 1975 [1950]. *African Systems of Kinship and Marriage*. London: Oxford University Press.

Ramos, Alcida Rita. 1998. *Indigenism: Ethnic Politics in Brazil*. Madison: University of Wisconsin Press.

Reichel-Dolmatoff, Gerardo. 1971. *Amazonian Cosmos: The Sexual and Religious Symbolism of the Tukano Indians*. Chicago: University of Chicago Press.

———. 1997. *Rainforest Shamans: Essays on the Tukano Indians of the Northwest Amazon*. Devon: Themis Books.

Ricardo, Carlos Alberto, comp. 1983. *Povos Indígenas no Brasil: 3 Amapá / Norte Do Pará*. São Paulo: Centro Ecumênico de Documentação e Informação.

Riches, David. 1986. *The Anthropology of Violence*. Oxford: Basil Blackwell.

Rival, Laura. 1998a. "Androgynous Parents and Guest Children: The Huaorani Couvade." *Journal of the Royal Anthropological Institute* (NS) 4:619–42.

———, ed. 1998b. *The Social Life of Trees: Anthropological Perspectives on Tree Symbolism*. Oxford: Berg.

Rivière, Peter G. 1963. "An Ethnographic Survey of the Indians of the Divide of the Guianese and Amazonian River Systems." B.Litt. thesis, University of Oxford.

———. 1966a. "A Note on Marriage with the Sister's Daughter." *MAN* (NS) 1(4): 550–56.

———. 1966b. "Oblique Discontinuous Exchange: A New Formal Type of Prescriptive Alliance." *American Anthropologist* 68(3): 738–40.

———. 1966–67. "Some Ethnographic Problems of Southern Guyana." FOLK 8–9:301–12.

———. 1969a. *Marriage among the Trio: A Principle of Social Organisation.* Oxford: Clarendon Press.

———. 1969b. "Myth and Material Culture: Some Symbolic Interrelations." In *Forms of Symbolic Action: Proceedings of the 1969 Annual Spring Meeting of the American Ethnological Society*, ed. Robert Spencer, 151–66. Seattle: University of Washington Press.

———. 1970. "Factions and Exclusions in Two South American Village Systems." In *Witchcraft Confessions and Accusations*, ed. M. Douglas, 245–55. London: Tavistock Publications.

———. 1971. "The Political Structure of the Trio Indians as Manifested in a System of Ceremonial Dialogue." In *The Translation of Culture*, ed. T. O. Beidelman, 293–311. London: Tavistock Publications.

———. 1974. "The Couvade: A Problem Reborn." MAN (NS) 9:423–35.

———. 1977. "Some Problems in the Comparative Study of Carib Societies." In *Carib-Speaking Indians: Culture, Society, and Language*, ed. Ellen Basso, 39–41. Tucson: University of Arizona Press.

———. 1983–84. "Aspects of Carib Political Economy." *Antropologica* 59–62:349–58.

———. 1984. *Individual and Society in Guiana: A Comparative Study of Amerindian Social Organization.* Cambridge: Cambridge University Press.

———. 1995. "Houses, Places, and People: Community and Continuity in Guiana." In *About the House: Lévi-Strauss and Beyond*, ed. J. Carsten and S. Hugh-Jones, 472–81. Cambridge: Cambridge University Press.

Roe, Peter. 1982. *The Cosmic Zygote: Cosmology in the Amazon Basin.* New Brunswick: Rutgers University Press.

Rorty, Richard. 1989. *Contingency, Irony, and Solidarity.* Cambridge: Cambridge University Press.

Roth, Walter E. 1929. *Additional Studies of the Arts, Crafts, and Customs of the Guiana Indians: With Special Reference to Those of Southern British*

Guiana. Smithsonian Institution Bureau of American Ethnology Bulletin 91. Washington DC: U.S. Government Printing Office.

Rouget, Gilbert. 1985. *Music and Trance: A Theory of the Relations between Music and Possession*. Chicago: University of Chicago Press.

Royal Anthropological Institute. 1951 [1874]. *Notes and Queries on Anthropology*. London: Routledge and Keegan Paul.

Sahlins, Marshall. 1974. *Stone Age Economics*. London: Tavistock Publications.

Sanders, Andrew. 1987. *The Powerless People: An Analysis of the Amerindians of the Corentyne River*. London: Macmillan.

Santos-Granero, Fernando. 1991. *The Power of Love: The Moral Use of Knowledge amongst the Amuesha of Central Peru*. London: Athlone Press.

———. 1993. "Power, Ideology and the Ritual of Production in Lowland South America." *MAN* (NS) 21:657–79.

Sapir, David, and Jon Christopher Crocker, eds. 1977. *The Social Use of Metaphor: Essays on the Anthropology of Rhetoric*. Philadelphia: University of Pennsylvania Press.

Scarry, Elaine. 1985. *The Body in Pain: The Making and Unmaking of the World*. New York: Oxford University Press.

Scheper-Hughes, Nancy. 1991. "The Subversive Body: Illness and the Micropolitics of Resistance." Public lecture presented by the Department of Psychiatry, University of California, Los Angeles, April 23.

Schomburgk, Richard. 1922 [1848]. *Travels in British Guiana, 1840–1844*. 2 vols. Georgetown: Daily Chronicle.

Schomburgk, Robert H. 1931 [1841]. *Travels in the Interior of British Guiana, 1835–1839*. Georgetown: Argosy.

Schwerin, Karl H. 1983–84. "The Kin-Integration System among Caribs." *Antropologica* 59–62:125–53.

Seeger, Anthony. 1975. "The Meaning of Body Ornaments." *Ethnology* 14(3): 211–24.

Shapiro, Judith R. 1984. "Marriage Rules, Marriage Exchange, and the Definition of Marriage in Lowland South American Societies." In *Marriage Practices in Lowland South America*, ed. Kenneth M. Kensinger, 1–30. Urbana: University of Illinois Press.

Smith, Raymond T. 1962. *British Guiana*. London: Oxford University Press.

———. 1971 [1956]. *The Negro Family in British Guiana: Family Structure and Social Status in the Villages* London: Routledge and Kegan Paul.

Sperber, Dan. 1985. *On Anthropological Knowledge*. Cambridge: Cambridge University Press.

Sullivan, Lawrence. 1988. *Icanchu's Drum: An Orientation to Meaning in South American Religions*. New York: Macmillan.

Taussig, Michael. 1993. *Mimesis and Alterity: A Particular History of the Senses*. New York: Routledge.

Taylor, Ann C. 1996. "The Soul's Body and Its States: An Amazonian Perspective on the Nature of Being Human." *Journal of the Royal Anthropological Institute* (NS) 2:201–15.

Thomas, David. 1982. *Order without Government: The Society of the Pemon Indians of Venezuela*. Urbana: University of Illinois Press.

Todorov, Tzvetan. 1987. *The Conquest of America: The Question of the Other*. New York: Harper Torchbooks.

Turner, Terence. 1979. "Kinship, Household, and Community Structure among the Kayapó." In *Dialectical Societies: The Gê and Bororo of Central Brazil*, ed. D. Maybury-Lewis, 179–214. Cambridge: Harvard University Press.

———. 1980. "The Social Skin." In *Not Work Alone: A Cross Cultural View of Activities Superfluous to Survival*, ed. T. Cherfas and R. Lewin, 112–40. Beverly Hills: Sage Publications.

Turner, Victor. 1974. *The Forest of Symbols: Aspects of Ndembu Ritual*. Ithaca: Cornell University Press.

———. 1988. *The Anthropology of Performance*. New York: PAJ Publications.

Urban, Greg. 1991. *A Discourse-Centered Approach to Culture: Native South American Myths and Rituals*. Austin: University of Texas Press.

———. 1996. *Metaphysical Community: The Interplay of the Senses and the Intellect*. Austin: University of Texas Press.

Viveiros de Castro, Eduardo. 1992. *From the Enemy's Point of View: Humanity and Divinity in an Amazonian Society*. Chicago: University of Chicago Press.

————. 1998. "Cosmological Deixis and Amerindian Perspectivism." *Journal of the Royal Anthropological Institute* (NS) 4:469–88.

Wagner, Roy. 1977. "Analogic Kinship: A Daribi Example." *American Ethnologist* 4:623–42.

————. 1981. *The Invention of Culture*. Chicago: University of Chicago Press.

Waterton, Charles. 1906 [1825]. *Wanderings in South America*. London: Hutchinson.

Whitehead, Neil L. 1990. "The Mazaruni Pectoral: A Golden Artifact Discovered in Guyana and the Historical Sources Concerning Native Metallurgy in the Caribbean, Orinoco, and Northern Amazonia." *Archaeology and Anthropology* 7:19–40.

Wilbert, Johannes. 1972. "Tobacco and Shamanistic Ecstasy among the Warao Indians of Venezuela." In *Flesh of the Gods: The Ritual Use of Hallucinogens*, ed. P. Furst, 56–83. London: George Allen and Unwin.

————. 1975. *Warao Basketry: Form and Function*. Occasional Papers of the Museum of Cultural History, no. 3. Berkeley: University of California Press.

Yde, Jens. 1959. "Resist-Dyed Bark Costumes of the Waiwai Indians." FOLK 1:59–66.

————. 1960. "Agriculture and Division of Work among the Waiwái." FOLK 2:83–97.

————. 1965. *Material Culture of the Waiwái*. Copenhagen: National Museum.

Illustration Credits

Index